遠藤 MINARI ENDOH 海成

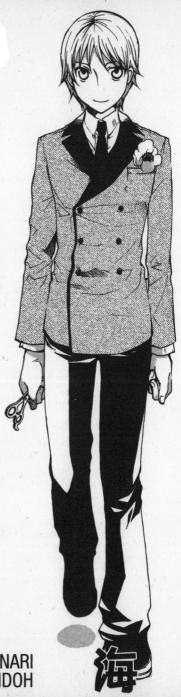

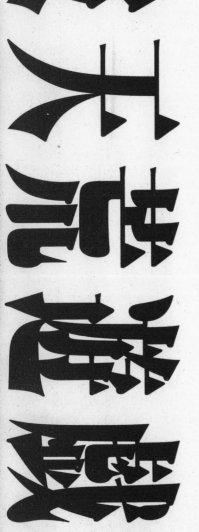

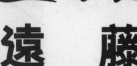

Dazzle Volume 9
Created by Minari Endoh

Translation - Yuko Fukami
English Adaptation - Karen S. Ahlstrom
Retouch and Lettering - Star Print Brokers
Production Artist - Michael Paolilli
Graphic Designer - Jose Macasocol, Jr.

Editor - Peter Ahlstrom
Digital Imaging Manager - Chris Buford
Pre-Production Supervisor - Vicente Rivera, Jr.
Production Specialist - Lucas Rivera
Managing Editor - Vy Nguyen
Art Director - Al-Insan Lashley
Editor-in-Chief - Rob Tokar
Publisher - Mike Kiley
President and C.O.O. - John Parker
C.E.O. and Chief Creative Officer - Stu Levy

A  Manga

TOKYOPOP and  are trademarks or registered trademarks of TOKYOPOP Inc.

TOKYOPOP Inc.
5900 Wilshire Blvd. Suite 2000
Los Angeles, CA 90036

E-mail: info@TOKYOPOP.com
Come visit us online at www.TOKYOPOP.com

ISBN: 978-1-4278-0169-2

First TOKYOPOP printing: September 2008
10 9 8 7 6 5 4 3 2 1
Printed in the USA

Contents

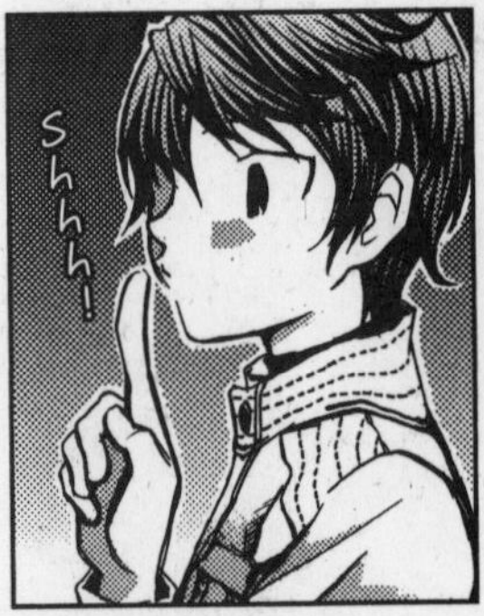
Shhh!

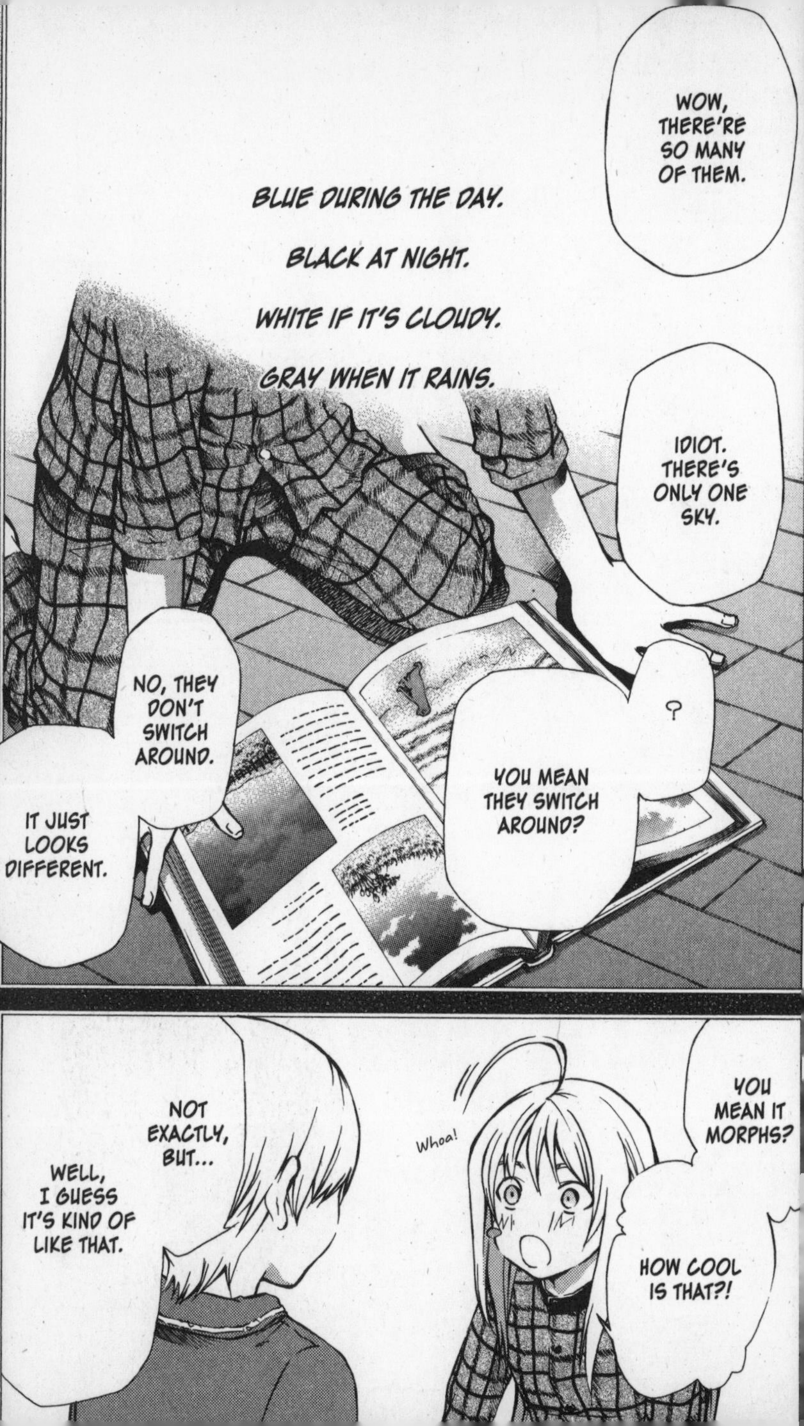
WOW, THERE'RE SO MANY OF THEM.
BLUE DURING THE DAY.
BLACK AT NIGHT.
WHITE IF IT'S CLOUDY.
GRAY WHEN IT RAINS.
IDIOT. THERE'S ONLY ONE SKY.
?
YOU MEAN THEY SWITCH AROUND?
NO, THEY DON'T SWITCH AROUND.
IT JUST LOOKS DIFFERENT.
YOU MEAN IT MORPHS?
HOW COOL IS THAT?!
Whoa!
NOT EXACTLY, BUT...
WELL, I GUESS IT'S KIND OF LIKE THAT.

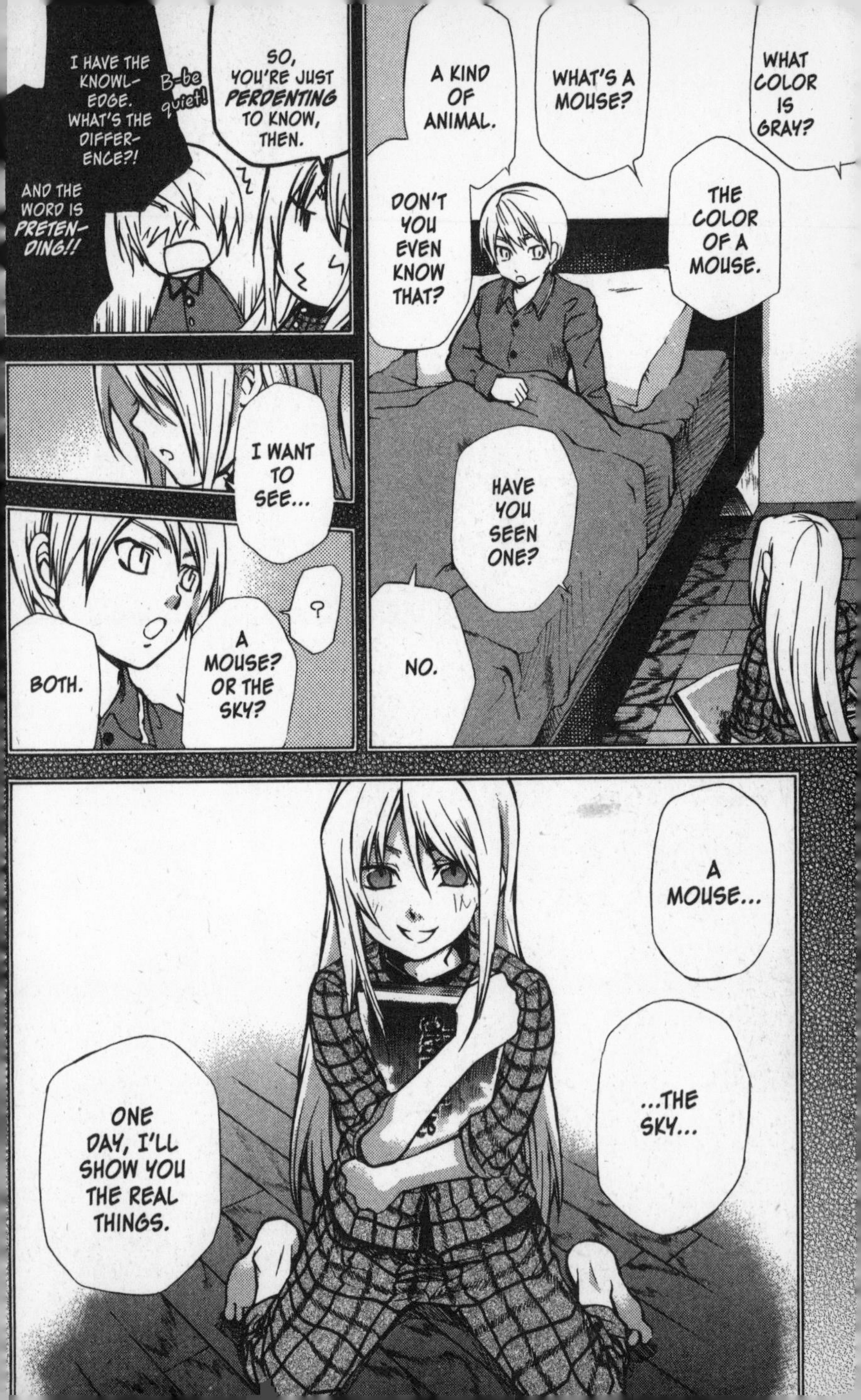
WHAT COLOR IS GRAY?
THE COLOR OF A MOUSE.
WHAT'S A MOUSE?
A KIND OF ANIMAL.
DON'T YOU EVEN KNOW THAT?
HAVE YOU SEEN ONE?
NO.
SO, YOU'RE JUST PERDENTING TO KNOW, THEN.
B-be quiet!
I HAVE THE KNOWL-EDGE. WHAT'S THE DIFFER-ENCE?!
AND THE WORD IS PRETEN-DING!!
I WANT TO SEE...
?
A MOUSE? OR THE SKY?
BOTH.
A MOUSE...
...THE SKY...
ONE DAY, I'LL SHOW YOU THE REAL THINGS.

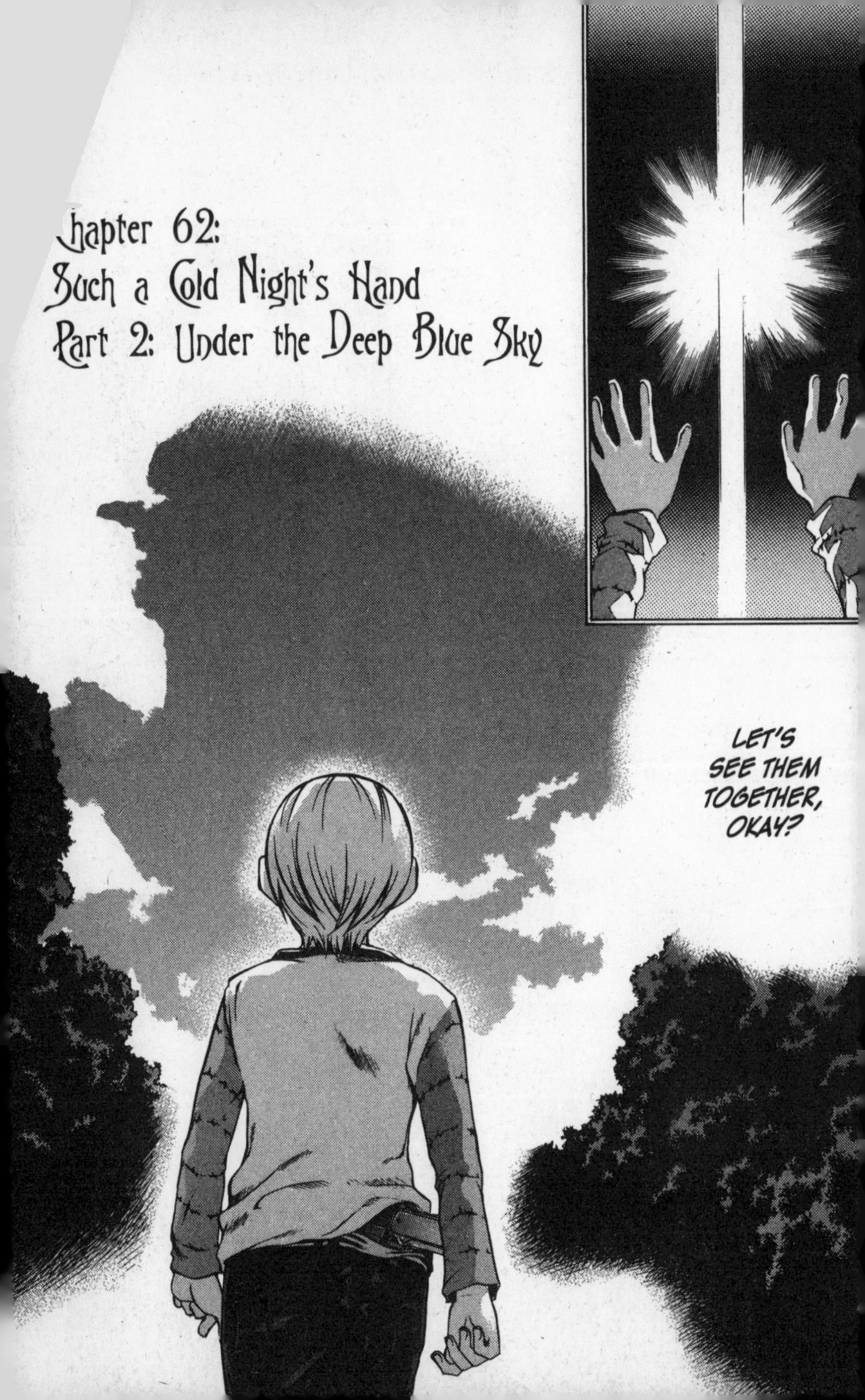
Chapter 62:
Such a Cold Night's Hand
Part 2: Under the Deep Blue Sky
LET'S SEE THEM TOGETHER, OKAY?

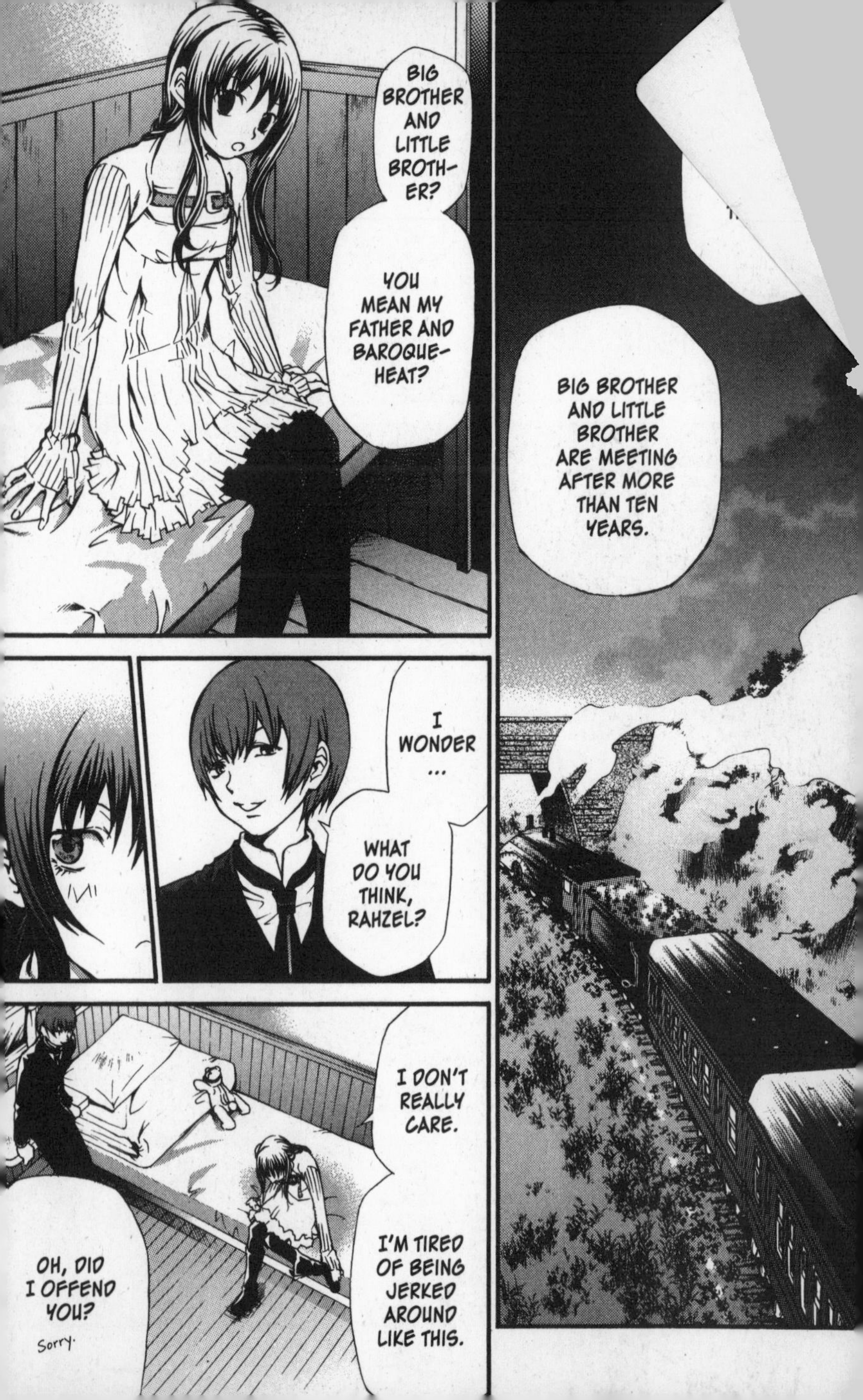

BIG BROTHER AND LITTLE BROTHER ARE MEETING AFTER MORE THAN TEN YEARS.
BIG BROTHER AND LITTLE BROTHER?
YOU MEAN MY FATHER AND BAROQUE-HEAT?
I WONDER ...
WHAT DO YOU THINK, RAHZEL?
I DON'T REALLY CARE.
I'M TIRED OF BEING JERKED AROUND LIKE THIS.
OH, DID I OFFEND YOU?
Sorry.

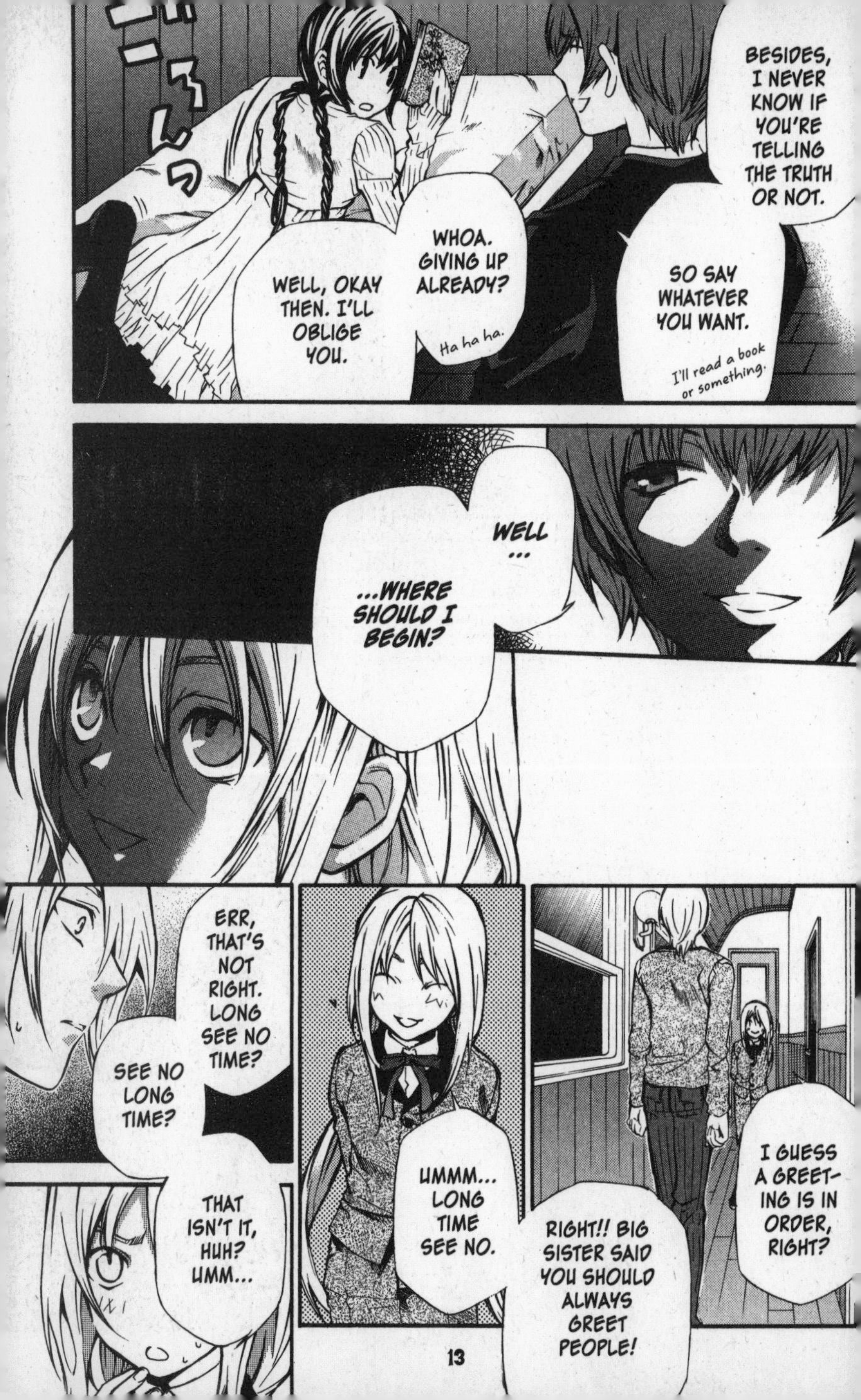
BESIDES, I NEVER KNOW IF YOU'RE TELLING THE TRUTH OR NOT.
SO SAY WHATEVER YOU WANT.
I'll read a book or something.
WHOA. GIVING UP ALREADY?
Ha ha ha.
WELL, OKAY THEN. I'LL OBLIGE YOU.
WELL ...
...WHERE SHOULD I BEGIN?
I GUESS A GREETING IS IN ORDER, RIGHT?
RIGHT!! BIG SISTER SAID YOU SHOULD ALWAYS GREET PEOPLE!
UMMM... LONG TIME SEE NO.
ERR, THAT'S NOT RIGHT. LONG SEE NO TIME?
SEE NO LONG TIME?
THAT ISN'T IT, HUH? UMM...

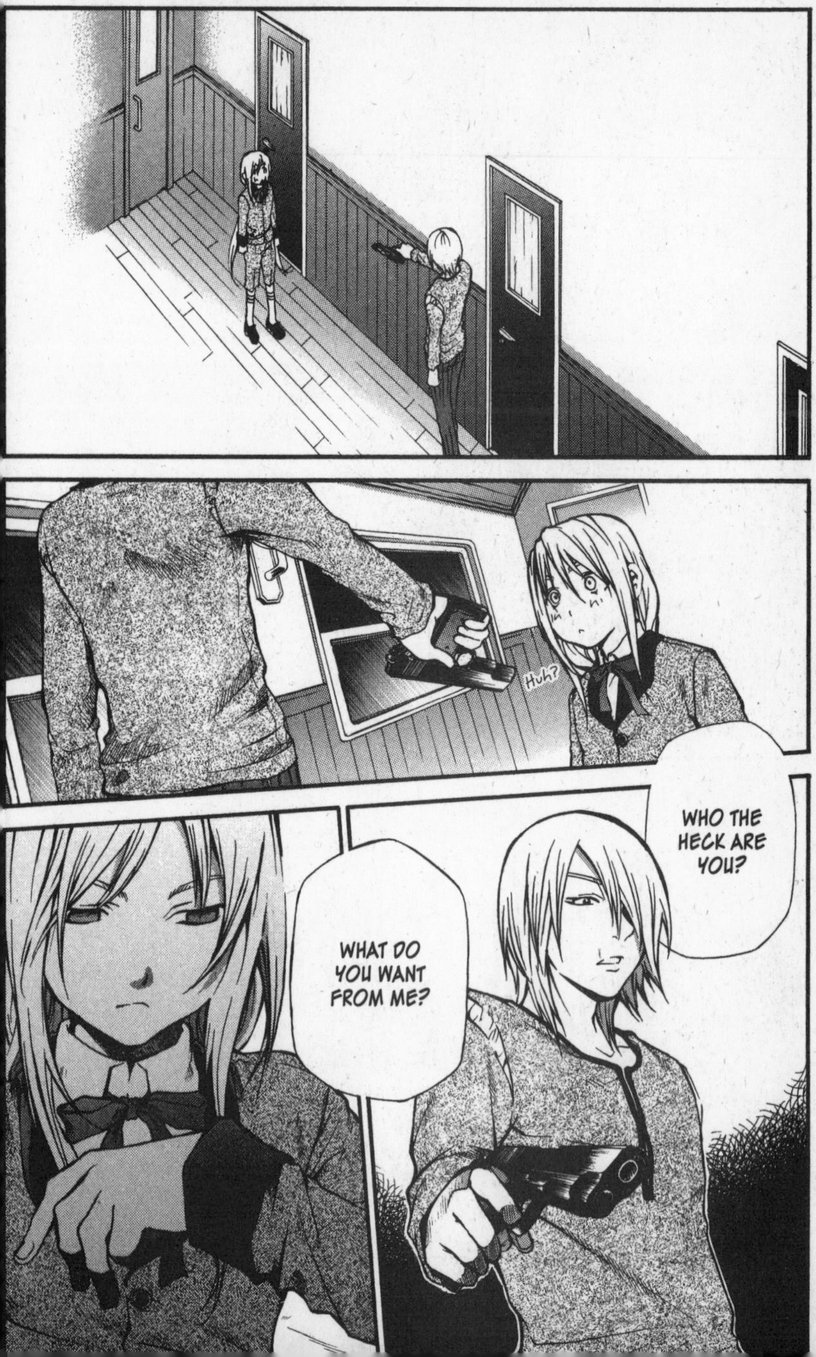
Huh?
WHO THE HECK ARE YOU?
WHAT DO YOU WANT FROM ME?

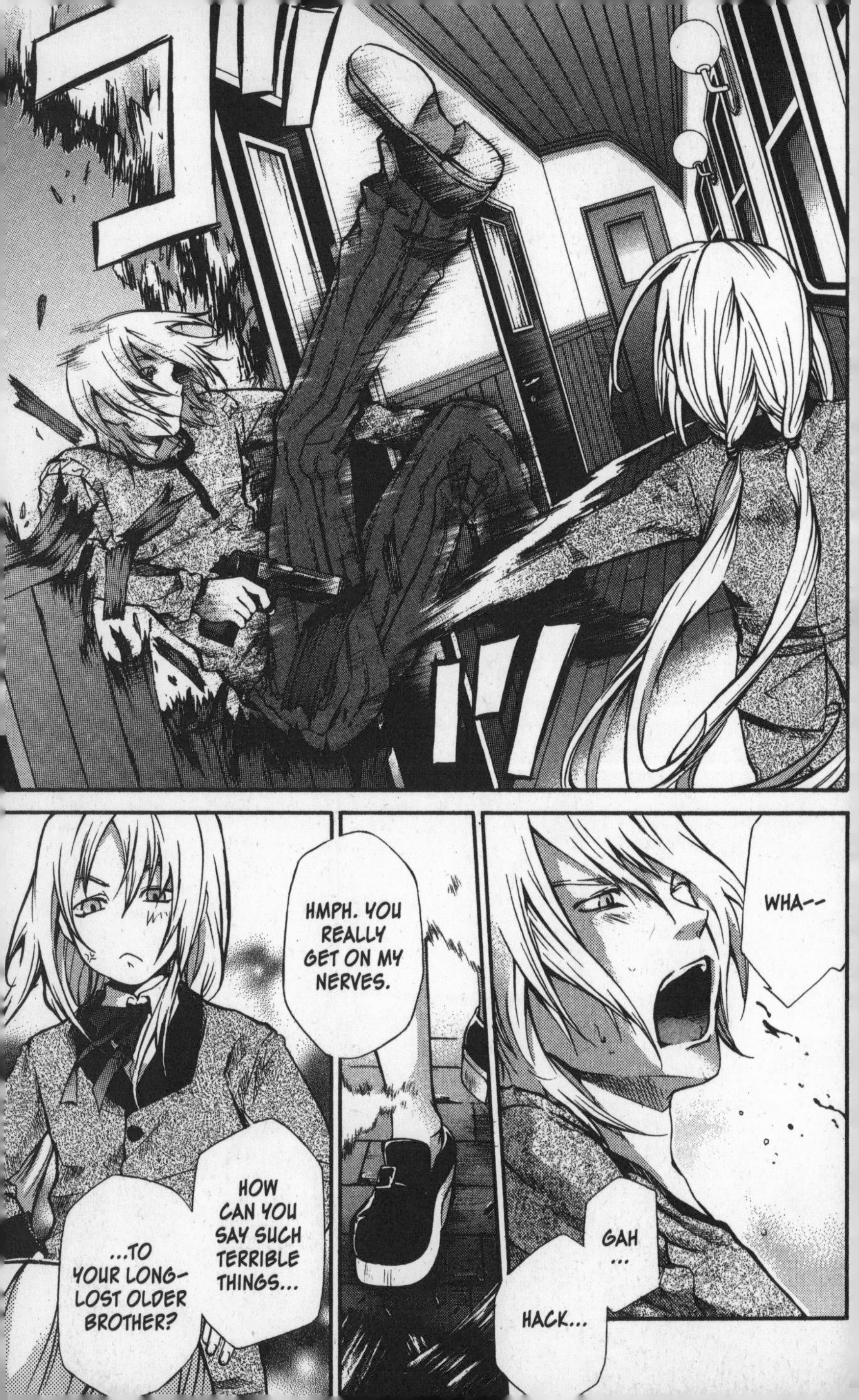
WHA--
GAH...
HACK...
HMPH. YOU REALLY GET ON MY NERVES.
HOW CAN YOU SAY SUCH TERRIBLE THINGS...
...TO YOUR LONG-LOST OLDER BROTHER?

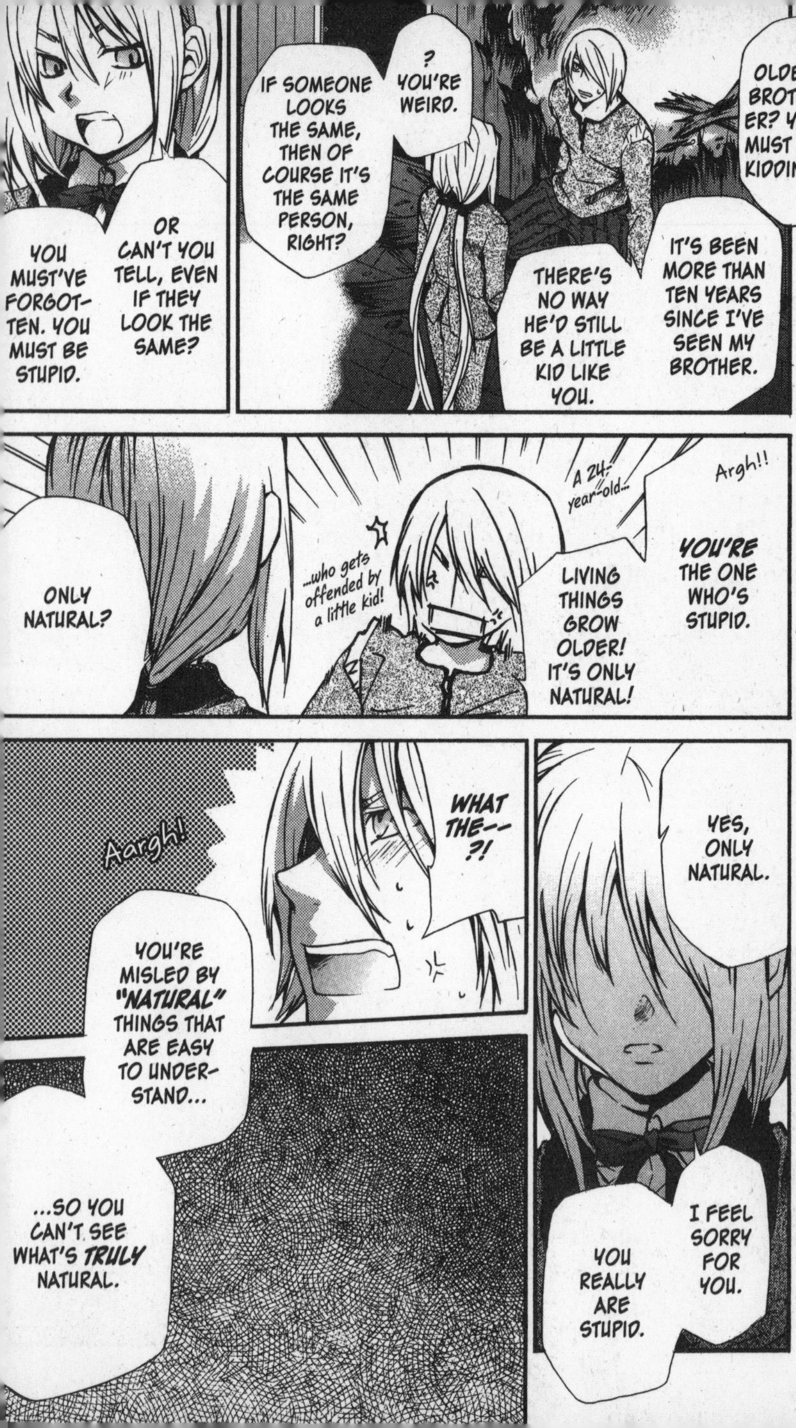
OLDER BROTHER? YOU MUST BE KIDDING.
IT'S BEEN MORE THAN TEN YEARS SINCE I'VE SEEN MY BROTHER.
THERE'S NO WAY HE'D STILL BE A LITTLE KID LIKE YOU.
? YOU'RE WEIRD.
IF SOMEONE LOOKS THE SAME, THEN OF COURSE IT'S THE SAME PERSON, RIGHT?
OR CAN'T YOU TELL, EVEN IF THEY LOOK THE SAME?
YOU MUST'VE FORGOTTEN. YOU MUST BE STUPID.
Argh!!
YOU'RE THE ONE WHO'S STUPID.
A 24-year-old...
LIVING THINGS GROW OLDER! IT'S ONLY NATURAL!
...who gets offended by a little kid!
ONLY NATURAL?
YES, ONLY NATURAL.
I FEEL SORRY FOR YOU.
YOU REALLY ARE STUPID.
WHAT THE--?!
Aargh!
YOU'RE MISLED BY *"NATURAL"* THINGS THAT ARE EASY TO UNDERSTAND...
...SO YOU CAN'T SEE WHAT'S *TRULY* NATURAL.

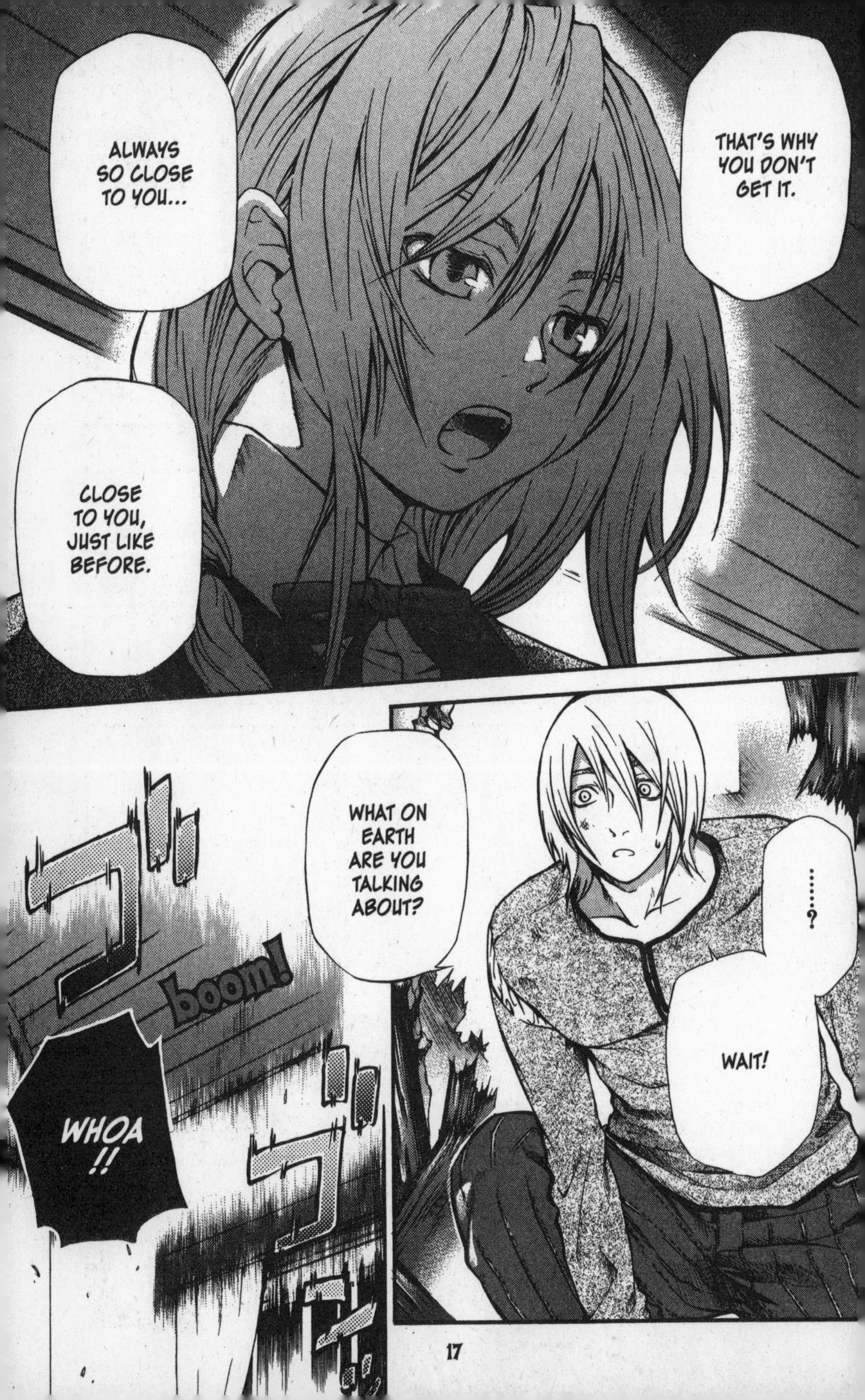
THAT'S WHY YOU DON'T GET IT.
ALWAYS SO CLOSE TO YOU...
CLOSE TO YOU, JUST LIKE BEFORE.
.....?
WHAT ON EARTH ARE YOU TALKING ABOUT?
WAIT!
boom!
WHOA !!

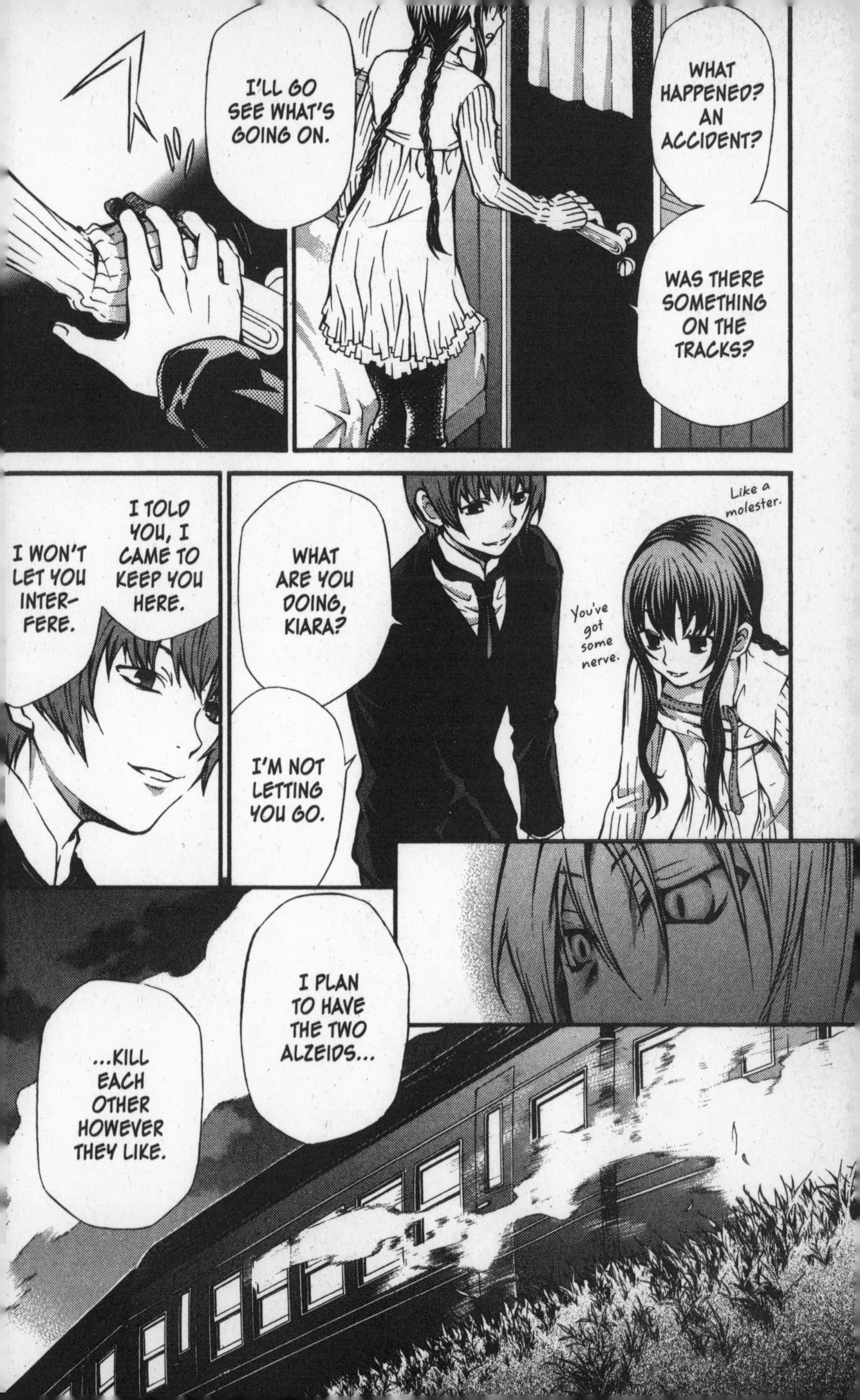
WHAT HAPPENED? AN ACCIDENT?
WAS THERE SOMETHING ON THE TRACKS?
I'LL GO SEE WHAT'S GOING ON.
Like a molester.
You've got some nerve.
WHAT ARE YOU DOING, KIARA?
I'M NOT LETTING YOU GO.
I TOLD YOU, I CAME TO KEEP YOU HERE.
I WON'T LET YOU INTER-FERE.
I PLAN TO HAVE THE TWO ALZEIDS...
...KILL EACH OTHER HOWEVER THEY LIKE.

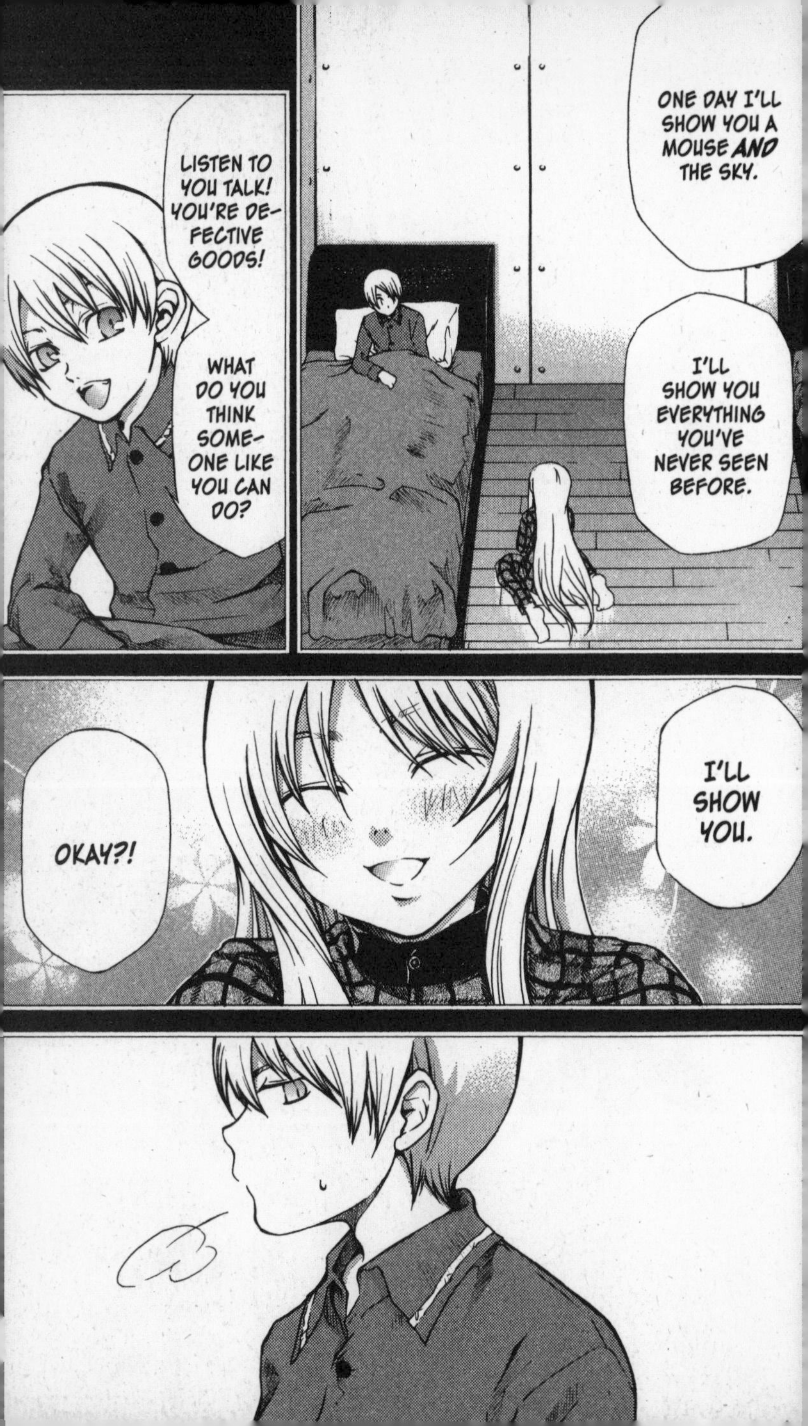
ONE DAY I'LL SHOW YOU A MOUSE AND THE SKY.
I'LL SHOW YOU EVERYTHING YOU'VE NEVER SEEN BEFORE.
LISTEN TO YOU TALK! YOU'RE DE-FECTIVE GOODS!
WHAT DO YOU THINK SOME-ONE LIKE YOU CAN DO?
I'LL SHOW YOU.
OKAY?!

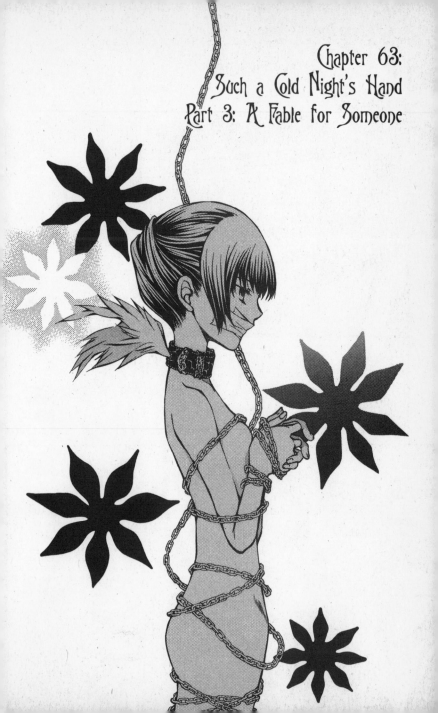

Chapter 63: Such a Cold Night's Hand Part 3: A Fable for Someone

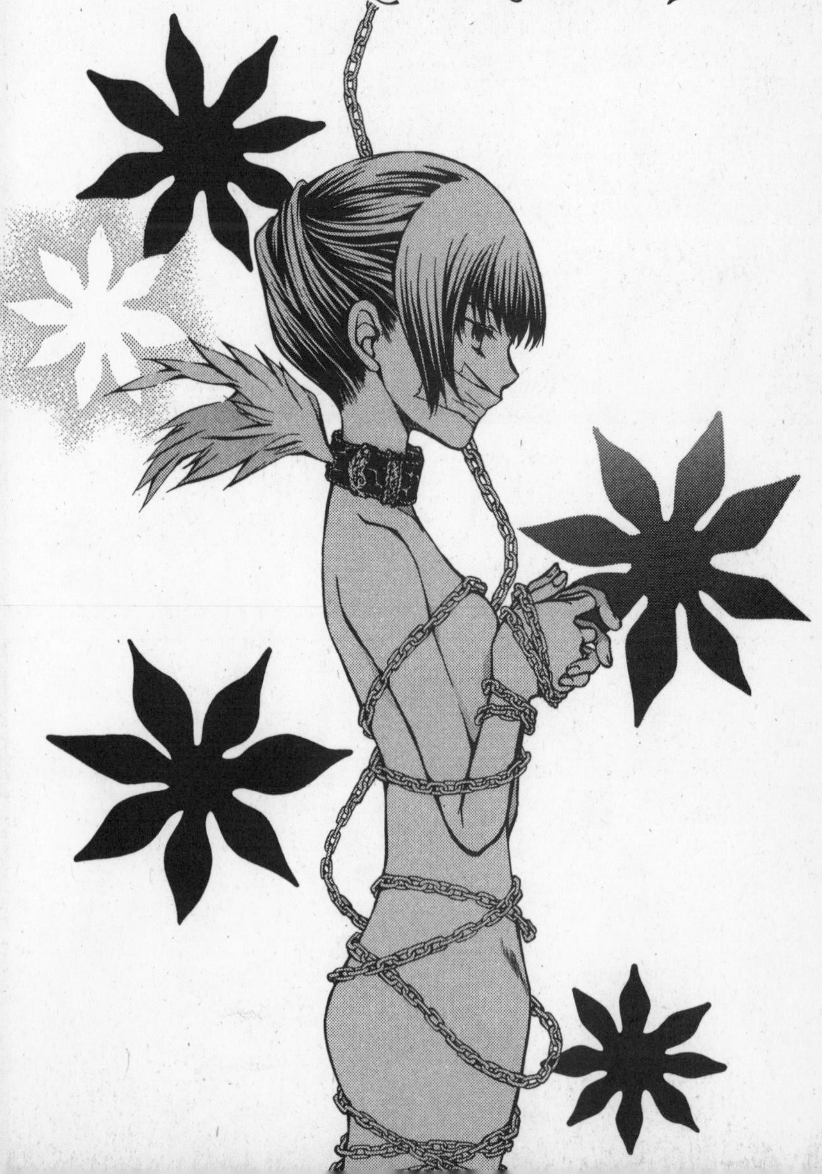

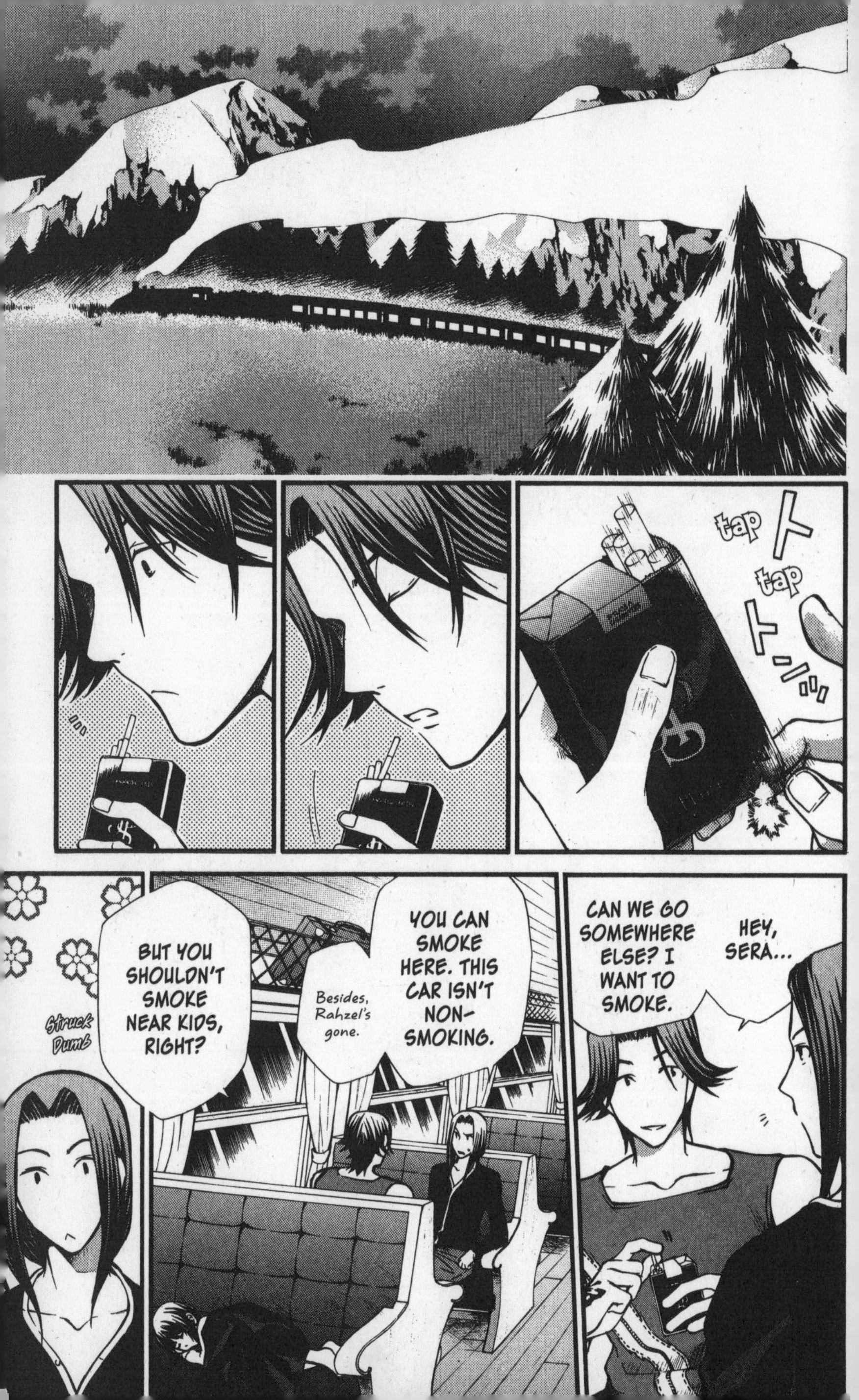
tap
tap
HEY, SERA...
CAN WE GO SOMEWHERE ELSE? I WANT TO SMOKE.
YOU CAN SMOKE HERE. THIS CAR ISN'T NON-SMOKING.
Besides, Rahzel's gone.
BUT YOU SHOULDN'T SMOKE NEAR KIDS, RIGHT?
Struck Dumb

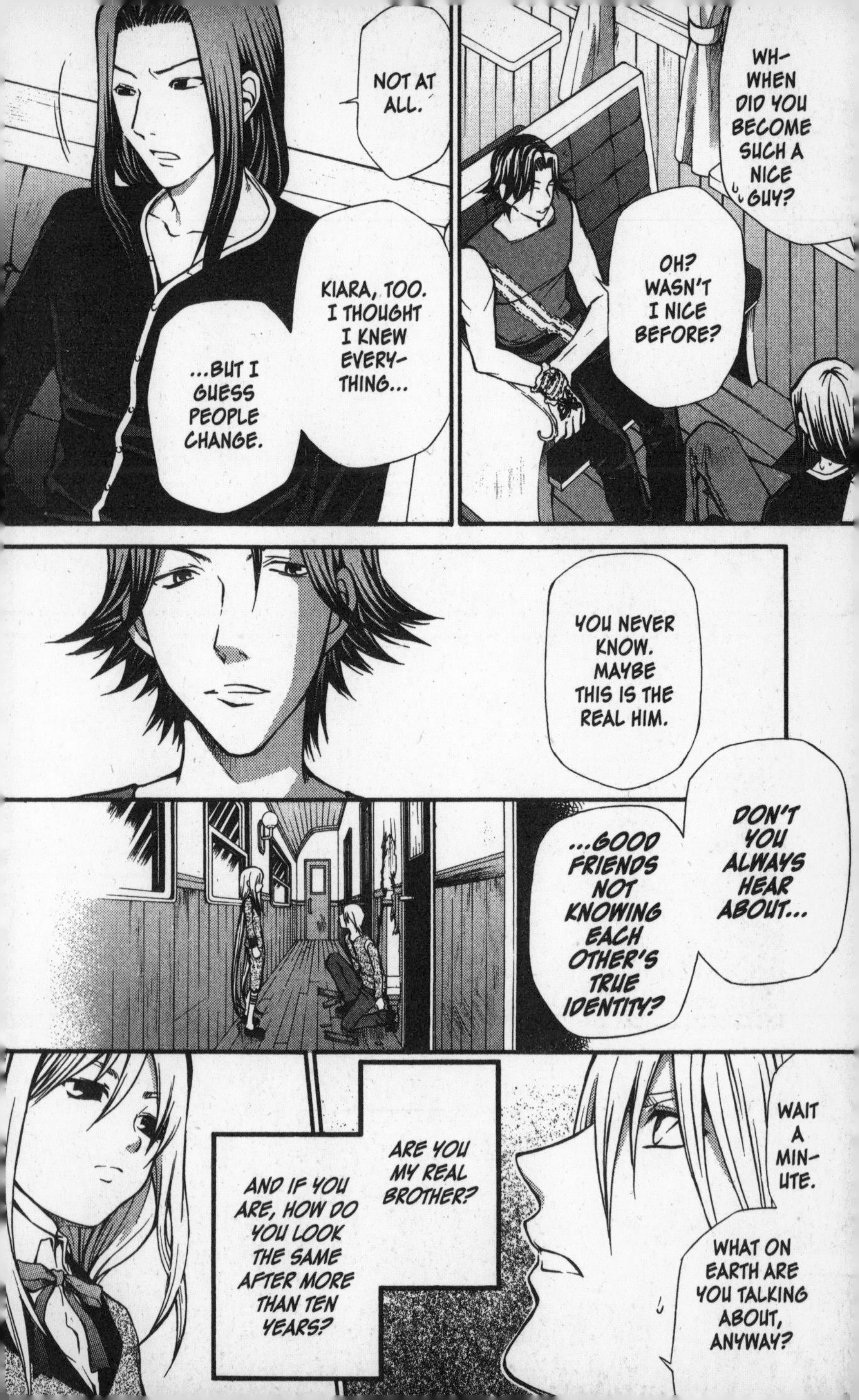
WH-WHEN DID YOU BECOME SUCH A NICE GUY?
OH? WASN'T I NICE BEFORE?
NOT AT ALL.
KIARA, TOO. I THOUGHT I KNEW EVERY-THING...
...BUT I GUESS PEOPLE CHANGE.
YOU NEVER KNOW. MAYBE THIS IS THE REAL HIM.
DON'T YOU ALWAYS HEAR ABOUT...
...GOOD FRIENDS NOT KNOWING EACH OTHER'S TRUE IDENTITY?
WAIT A MIN-UTE.
WHAT ON EARTH ARE YOU TALKING ABOUT, ANYWAY?
ARE YOU MY REAL BROTHER?
AND IF YOU ARE, HOW DO YOU LOOK THE SAME AFTER MORE THAN TEN YEARS?

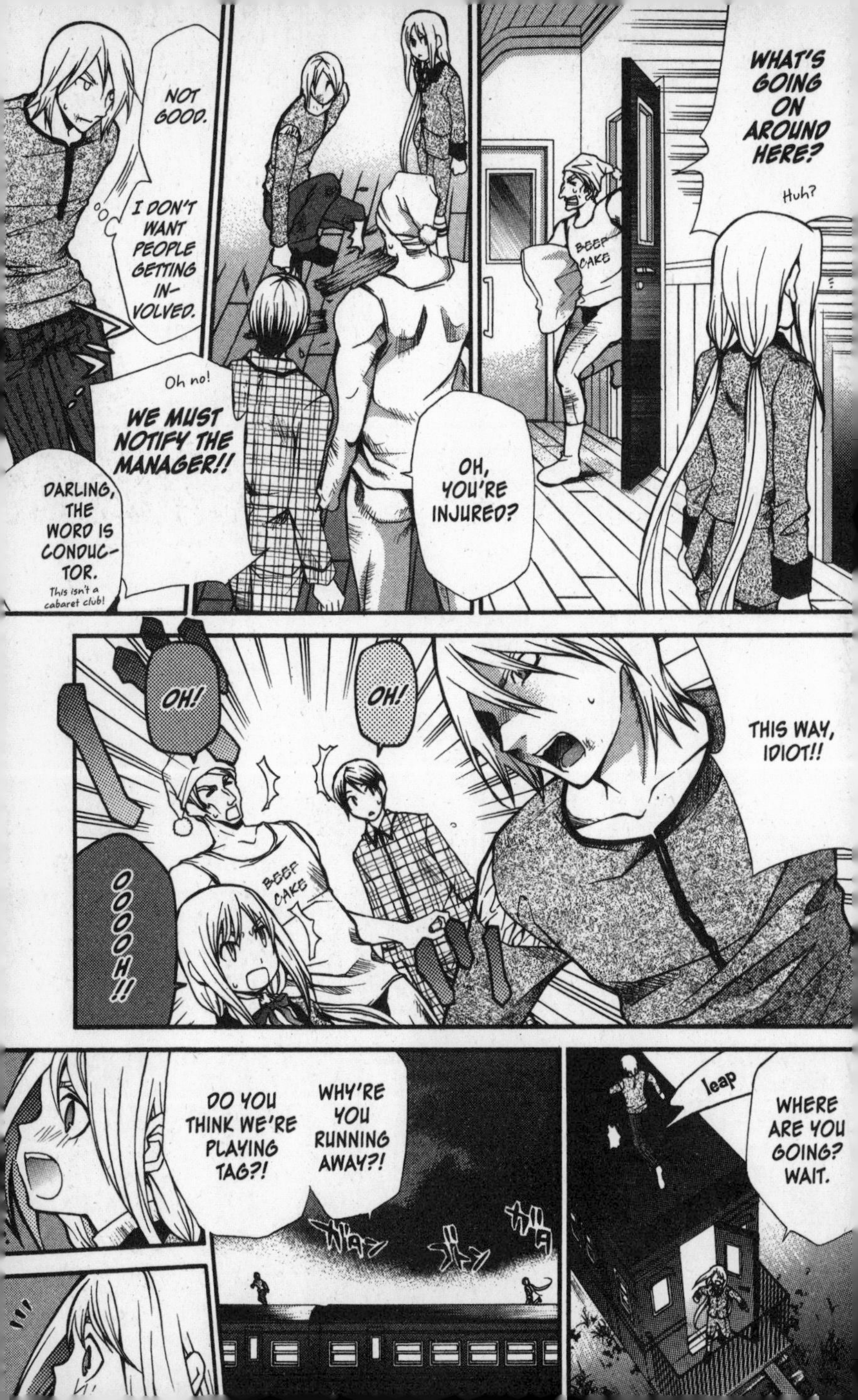
WHAT'S GOING ON AROUND HERE?
Huh?
OH, YOU'RE INJURED?
Oh no!
WE MUST NOTIFY THE MANAGER!!
DARLING, THE WORD IS CONDUC-TOR.
This isn't a cabaret club!
NOT GOOD.
I DON'T WANT PEOPLE GETTING IN-VOLVED.
BEEF CAKE
THIS WAY, IDIOT!!
OH!
OH!
OOOOOH!!
BEEF CAKE
leap
WHERE ARE YOU GOING? WAIT.
WHY'RE YOU RUNNING AWAY?!
DO YOU THINK WE'RE PLAYING TAG?!

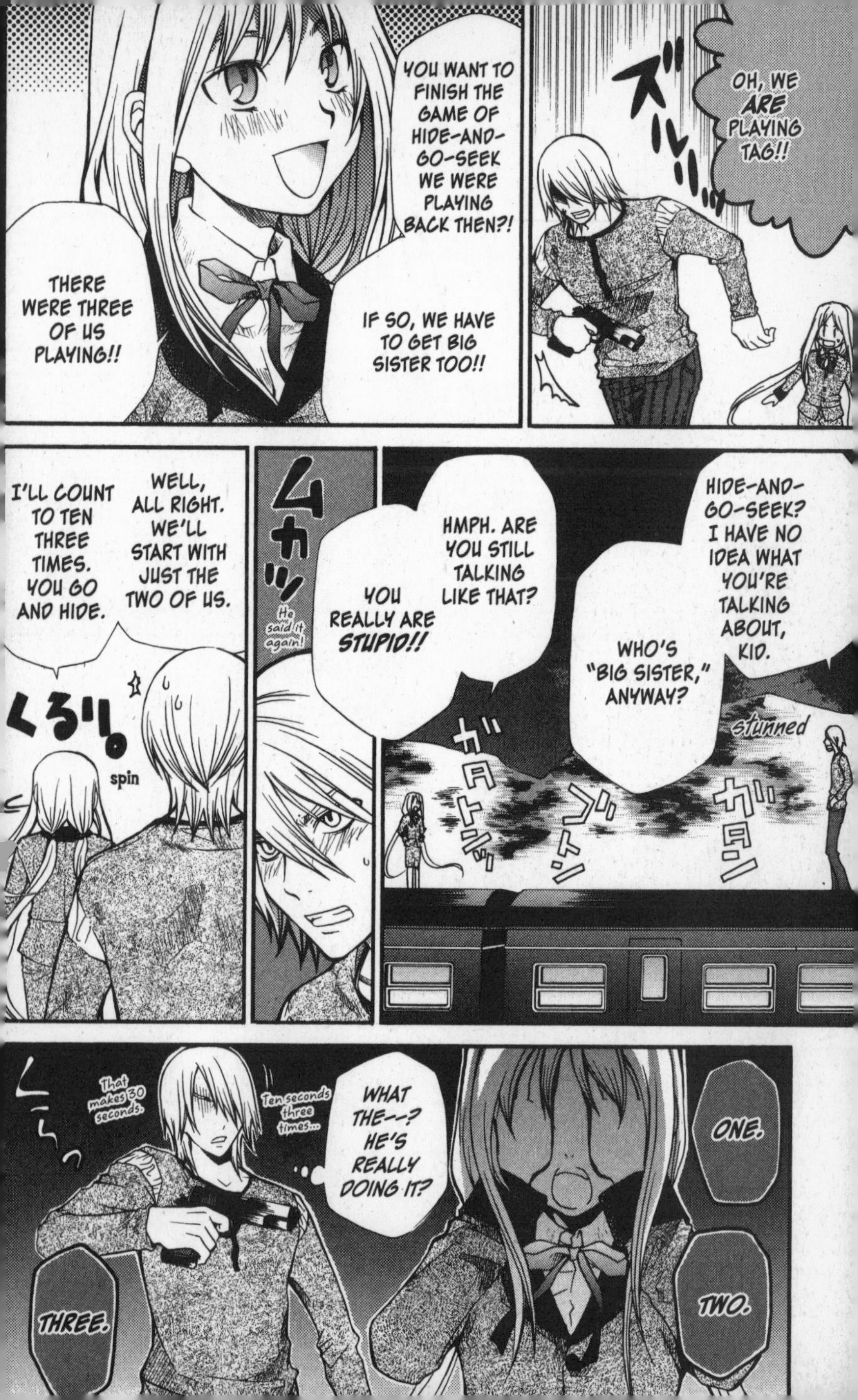
OH, WE ARE PLAYING TAG!!
YOU WANT TO FINISH THE GAME OF HIDE-AND-GO-SEEK WE WERE PLAYING BACK THEN?!
IF SO, WE HAVE TO GET BIG SISTER TOO!!
THERE WERE THREE OF US PLAYING!!
HIDE-AND-GO-SEEK? I HAVE NO IDEA WHAT YOU'RE TALKING ABOUT, KID.
WHO'S "BIG SISTER," ANYWAY?
stunned
HMPH. ARE YOU STILL TALKING LIKE THAT?
YOU REALLY ARE STUPID!!
He said it again!
WELL, ALL RIGHT. WE'LL START WITH JUST THE TWO OF US.
I'LL COUNT TO TEN THREE TIMES. YOU GO AND HIDE.
spin
ONE.
TWO.
WHAT THE--? HE'S REALLY DOING IT?
Ten seconds three times...
That makes 30 seconds.
THREE.

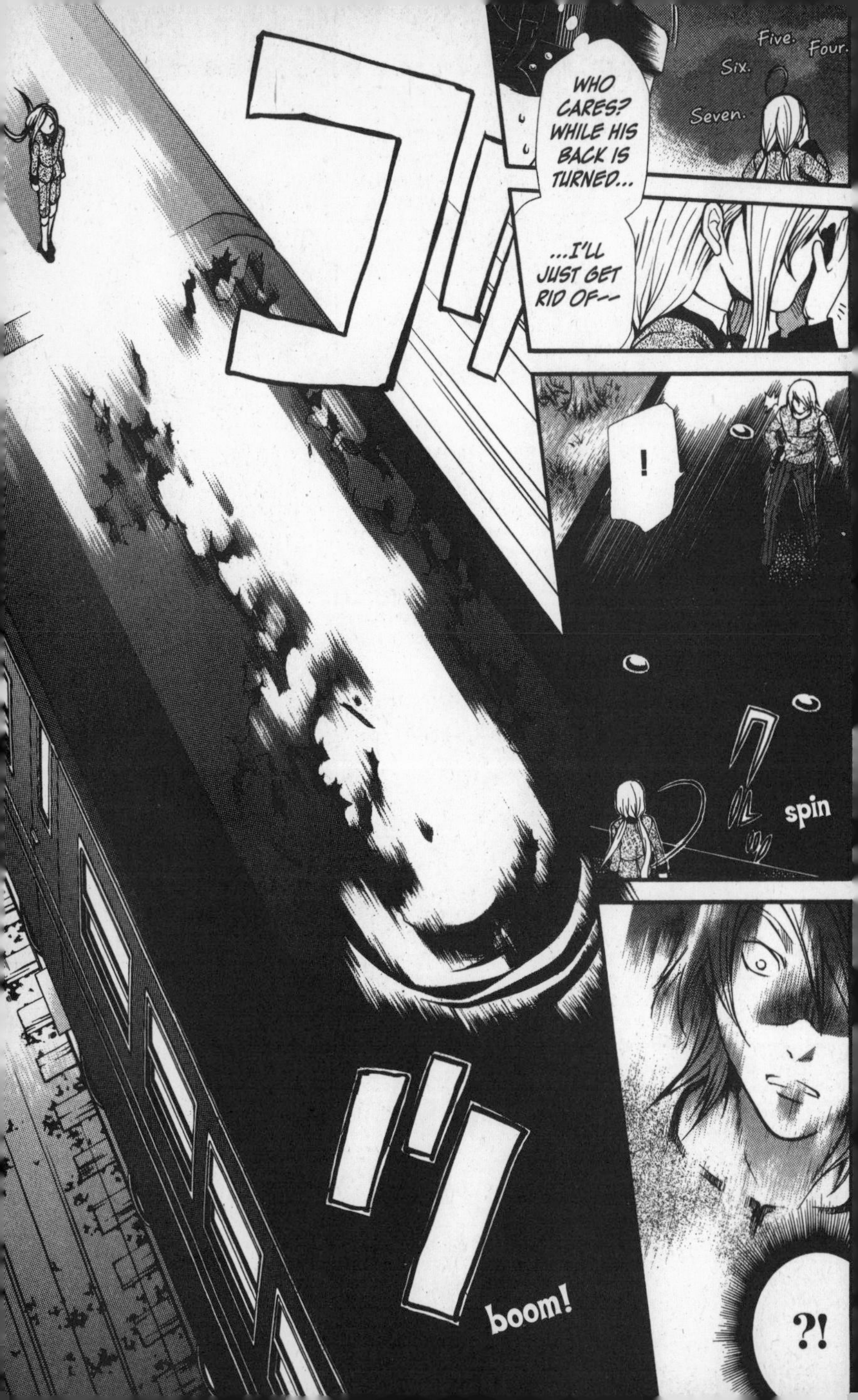
Seven.
Six.
Five.
Four.
WHO CARES? WHILE HIS BACK IS TURNED...
...I'LL JUST GET RID OF--
!
spin
?!
boom!

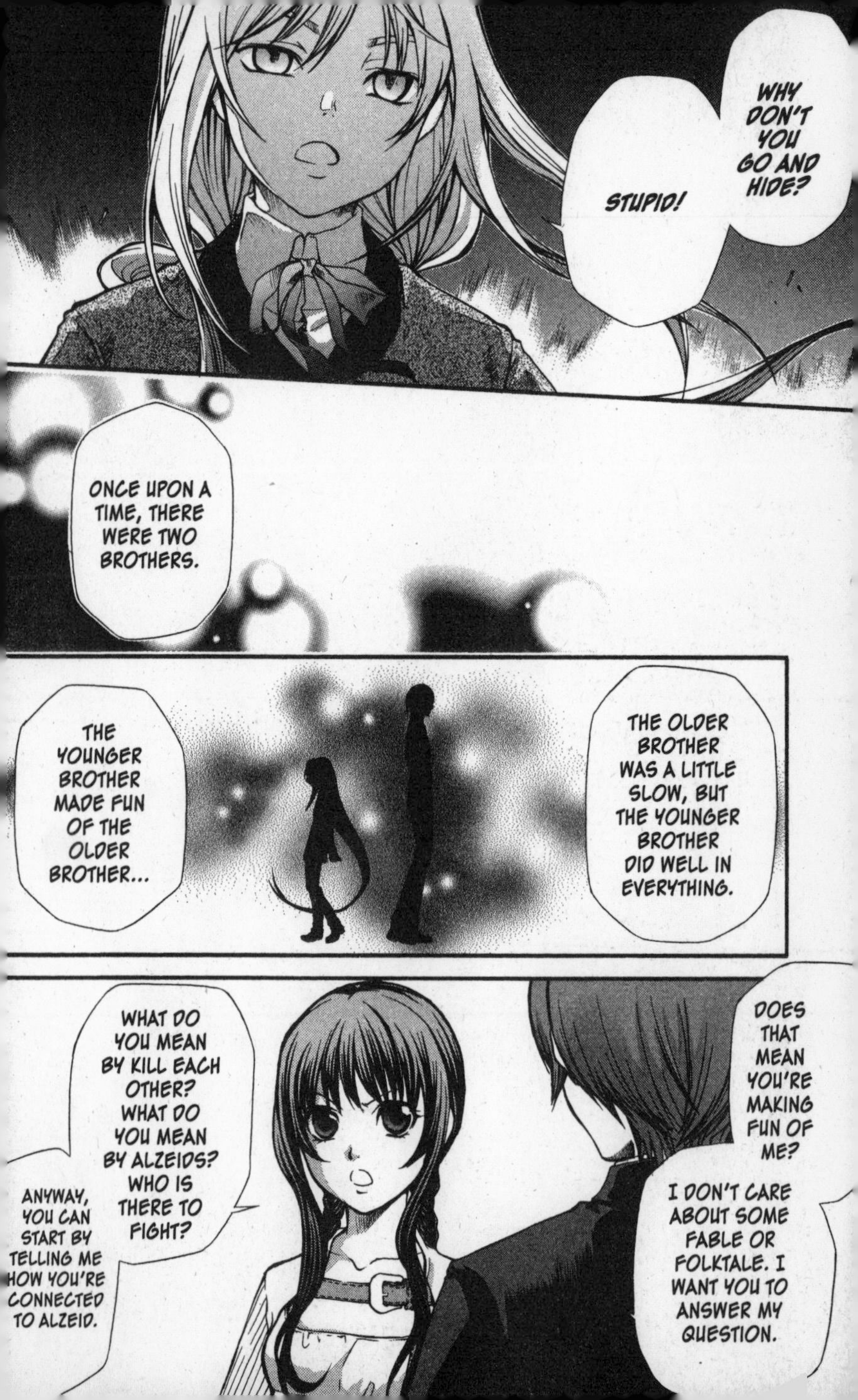
WHY DON'T YOU GO AND HIDE?
STUPID!
ONCE UPON A TIME, THERE WERE TWO BROTHERS.
THE OLDER BROTHER WAS A LITTLE SLOW, BUT THE YOUNGER BROTHER DID WELL IN EVERYTHING.
THE YOUNGER BROTHER MADE FUN OF THE OLDER BROTHER...
DOES THAT MEAN YOU'RE MAKING FUN OF ME?
I DON'T CARE ABOUT SOME FABLE OR FOLKTALE. I WANT YOU TO ANSWER MY QUESTION.
WHAT DO YOU MEAN BY KILL EACH OTHER? WHAT DO YOU MEAN BY ALZEIDS? WHO IS THERE TO FIGHT?
ANYWAY, YOU CAN START BY TELLING ME HOW YOU'RE CONNECTED TO ALZEID.

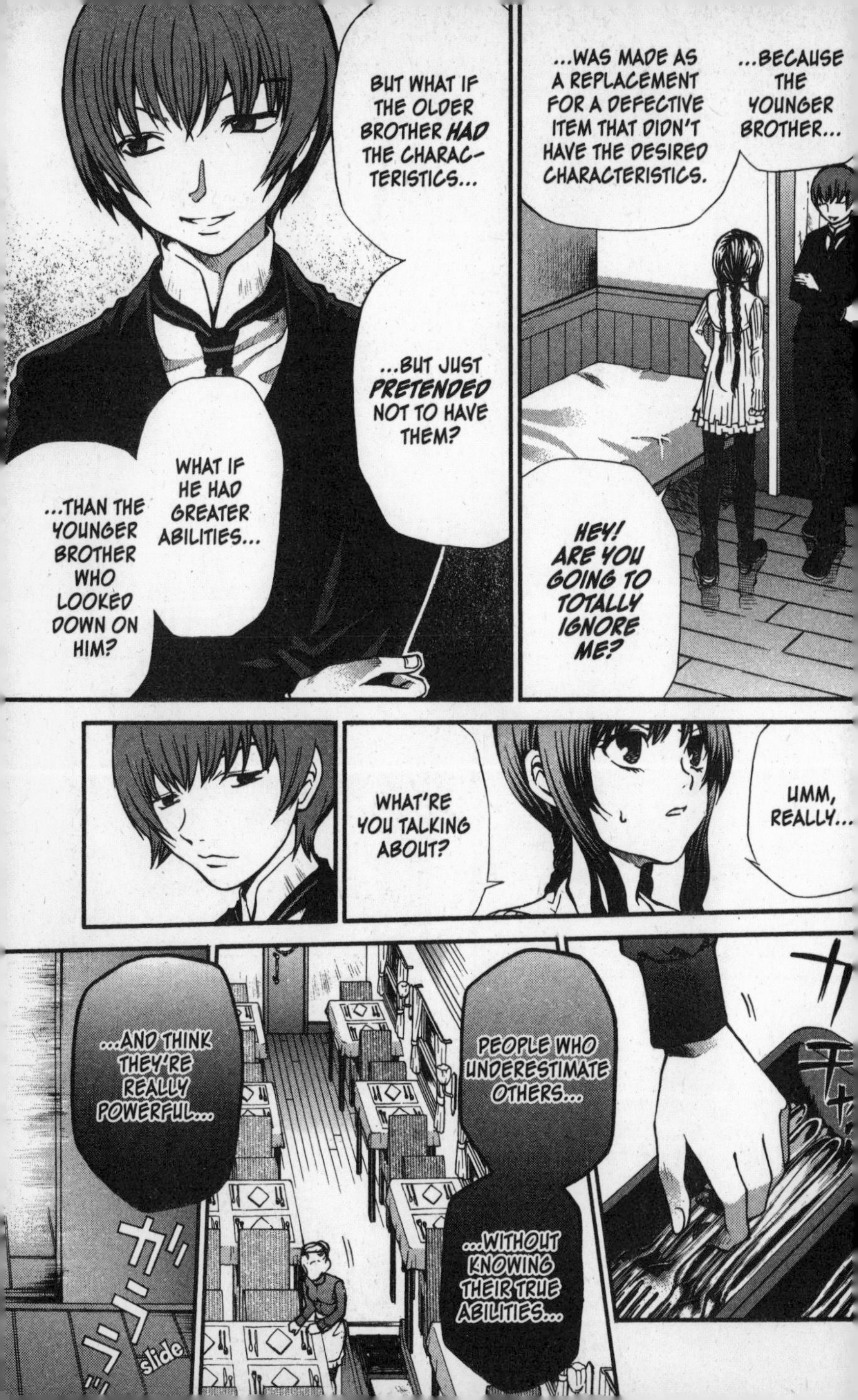
...BECAUSE THE YOUNGER BROTHER...
...WAS MADE AS A REPLACEMENT FOR A DEFECTIVE ITEM THAT DIDN'T HAVE THE DESIRED CHARACTERISTICS.
HEY! ARE YOU GOING TO TOTALLY IGNORE ME?
BUT WHAT IF THE OLDER BROTHER HAD THE CHARAC-TERISTICS...
...BUT JUST PRETENDED NOT TO HAVE THEM?
WHAT IF HE HAD GREATER ABILITIES...
...THAN THE YOUNGER BROTHER WHO LOOKED DOWN ON HIM?
UMM, REALLY...
WHAT'RE YOU TALKING ABOUT?
PEOPLE WHO UNDERESTIMATE OTHERS...
...WITHOUT KNOWING THEIR TRUE ABILITIES...
...AND THINK THEY'RE REALLY POWERFUL...
slide

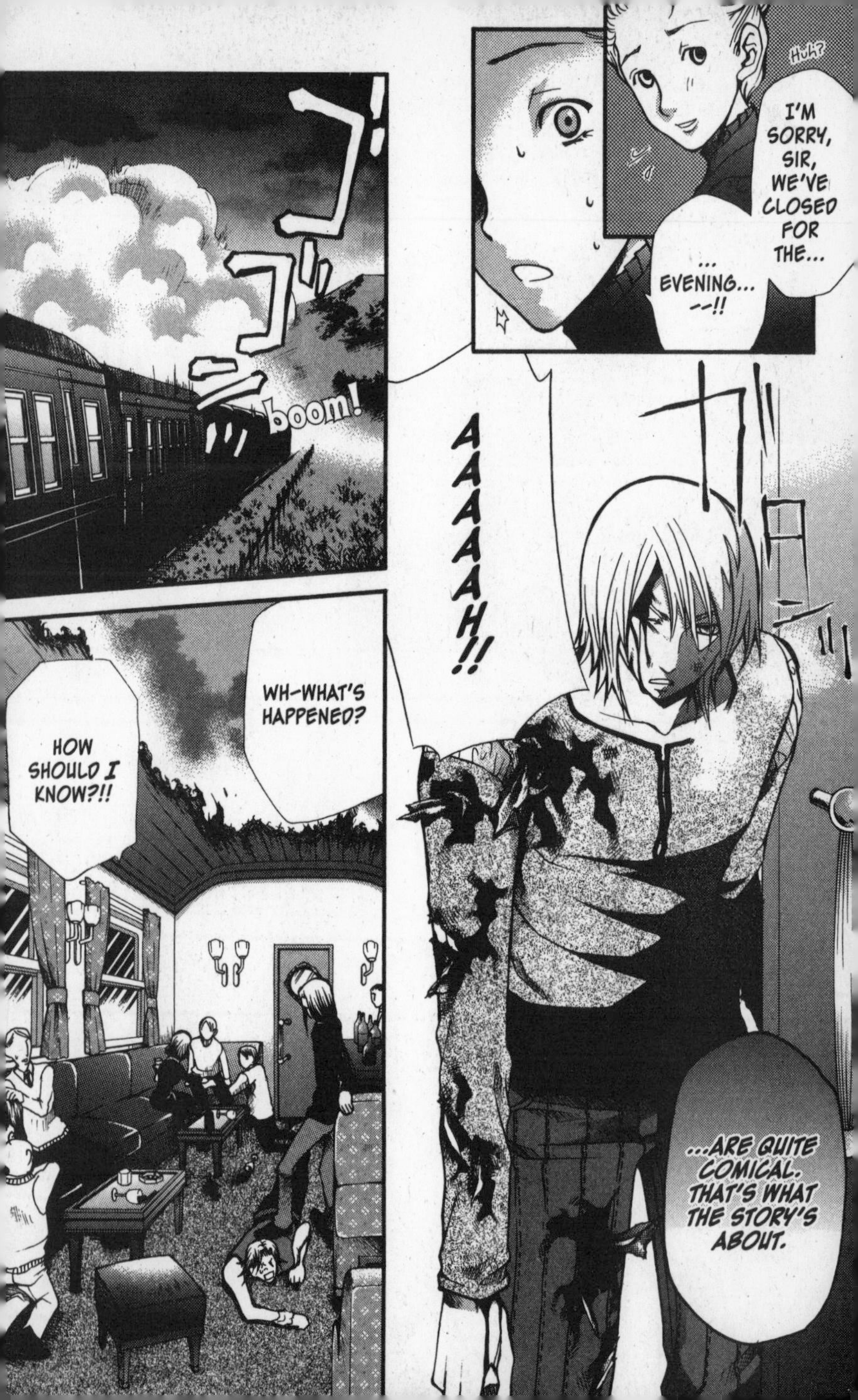

Huh?
I'M SORRY, SIR, WE'VE CLOSED FOR THE...
... EVENING... --!!
AAAAAAH!!
...ARE QUITE COMICAL. THAT'S WHAT THE STORY'S ABOUT.
boom!
WH-WHAT'S HAPPENED?
HOW SHOULD I KNOW?!!

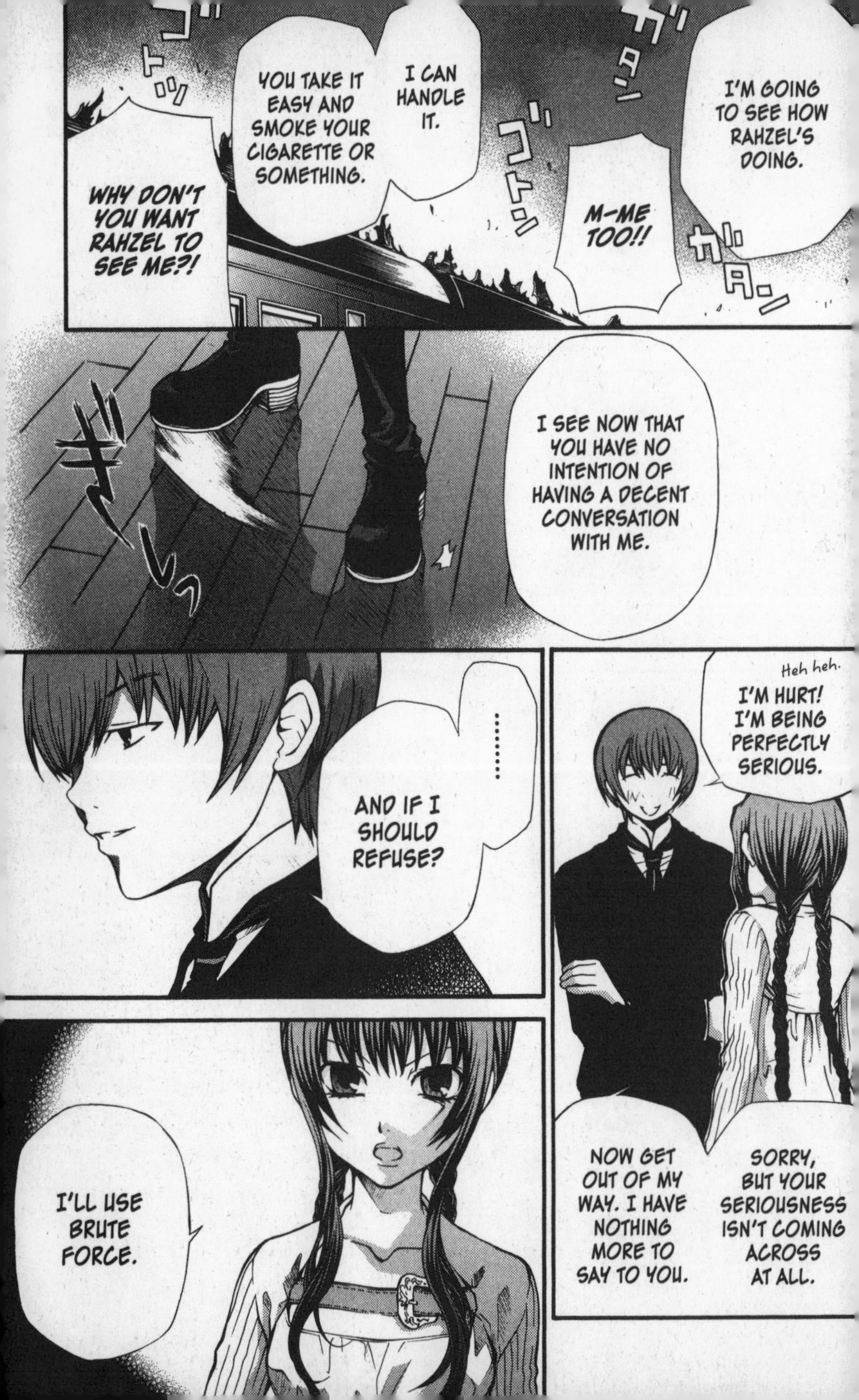
ガタン
I'M GOING TO SEE HOW RAHZEL'S DOING.
ゴトッ
M-ME TOO!!
ガタン
I CAN HANDLE IT.
YOU TAKE IT EASY AND SMOKE YOUR CIGARETTE OR SOMETHING.
ゴトッ
WHY DON'T YOU WANT RAHZEL TO SEE ME?!
I SEE NOW THAT YOU HAVE NO INTENTION OF HAVING A DECENT CONVERSATION WITH ME.
ギシッ
Heh heh.
I'M HURT! I'M BEING PERFECTLY SERIOUS.
SORRY, BUT YOUR SERIOUSNESS ISN'T COMING ACROSS AT ALL.
NOW GET OUT OF MY WAY. I HAVE NOTHING MORE TO SAY TO YOU.
......
AND IF I SHOULD REFUSE?
I'LL USE BRUTE FORCE.

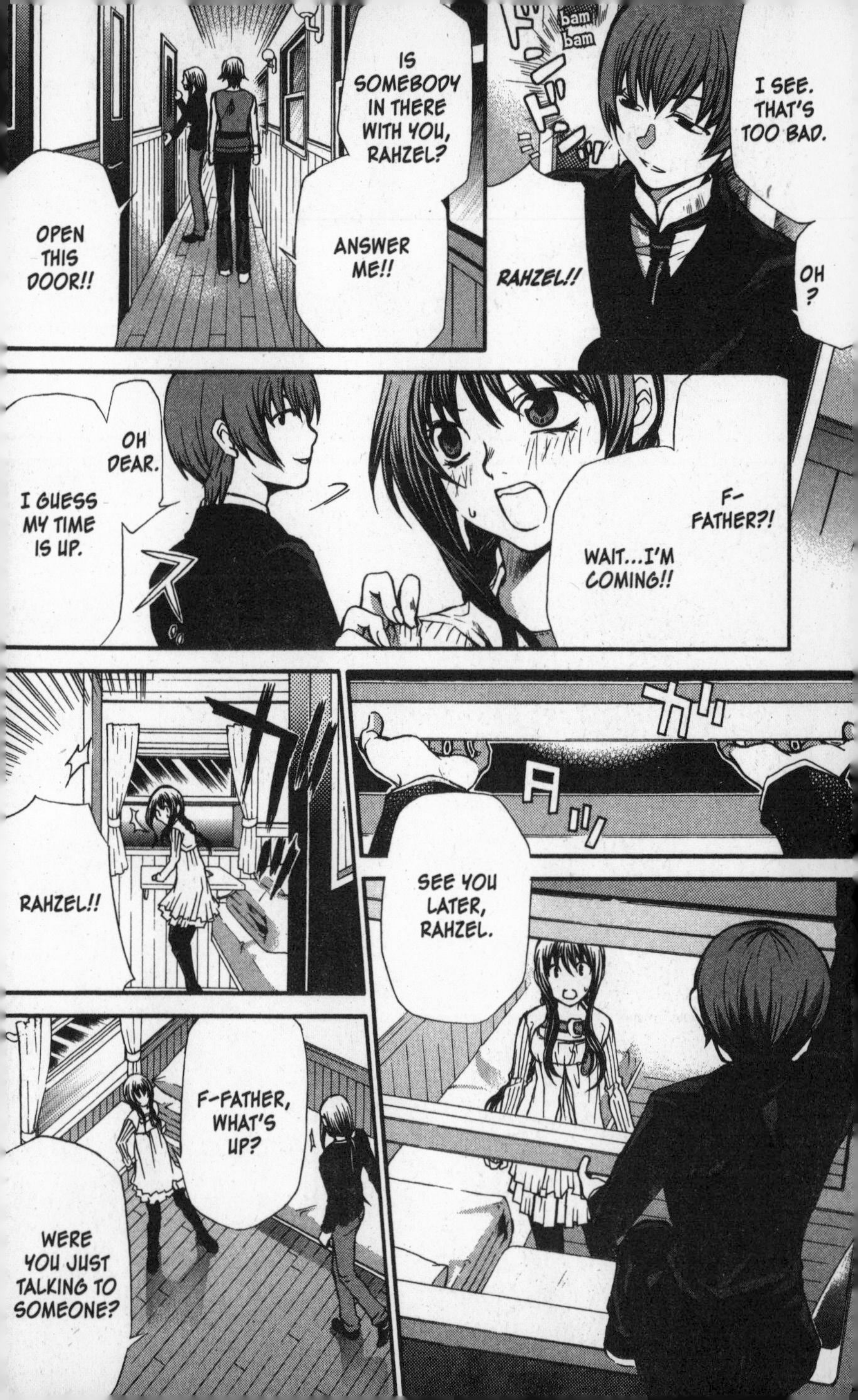
bam bam
I SEE. THAT'S TOO BAD.
OH ?
RAHZEL!!
IS SOMEBODY IN THERE WITH YOU, RAHZEL?
ANSWER ME!!
OPEN THIS DOOR!!
F-FATHER?!
WAIT...I'M COMING!!
OH DEAR.
I GUESS MY TIME IS UP.
SEE YOU LATER, RAHZEL.
RAHZEL!!
F-FATHER, WHAT'S UP?
WERE YOU JUST TALKING TO SOMEONE?

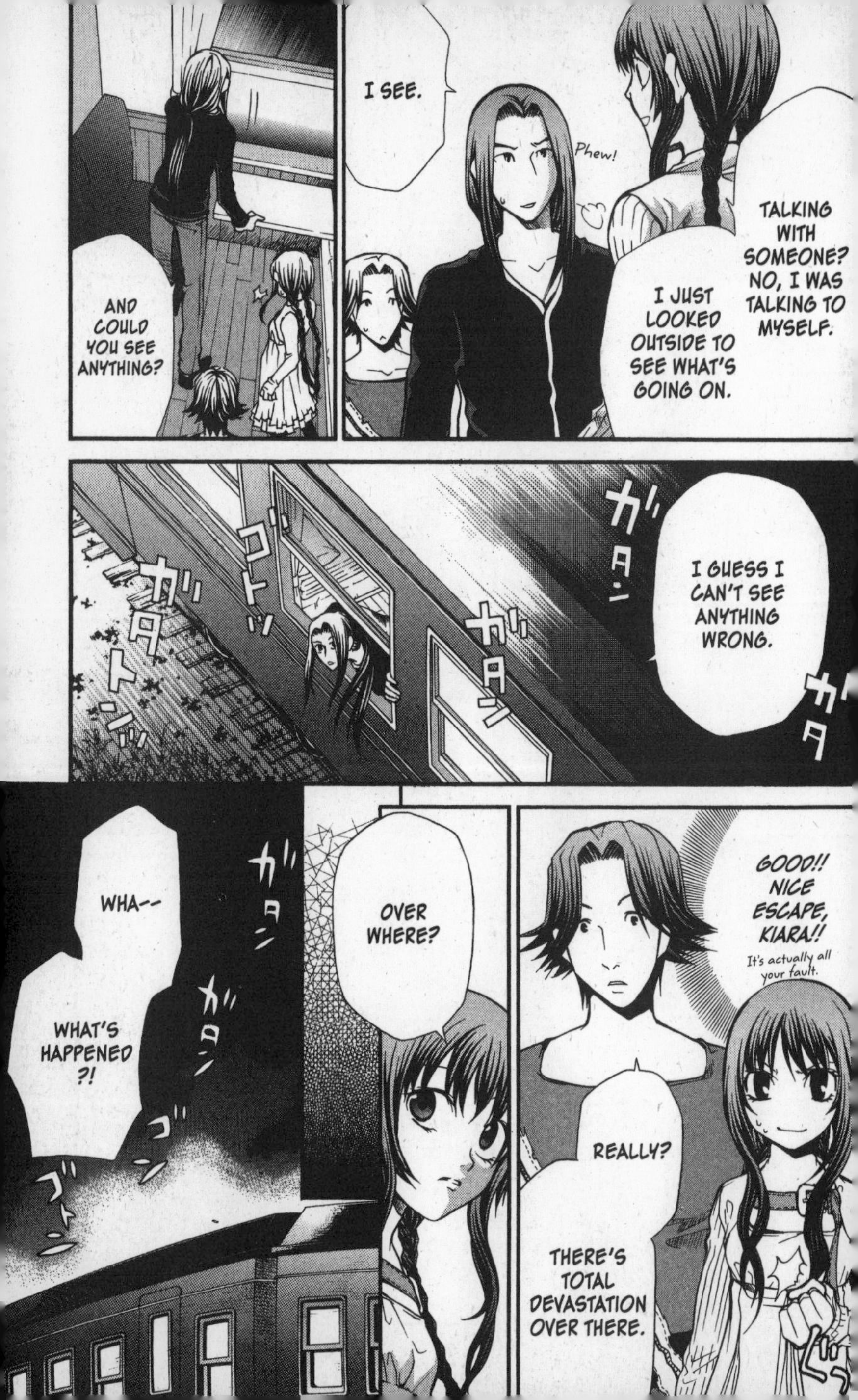
TALKING WITH SOMEONE? NO, I WAS TALKING TO MYSELF.
I JUST LOOKED OUTSIDE TO SEE WHAT'S GOING ON.
Phew!
I SEE.
AND COULD YOU SEE ANYTHING?
I GUESS I CAN'T SEE ANYTHING WRONG.
GOOD!! NICE ESCAPE, KIARA!!
It's actually all your fault.
REALLY?
THERE'S TOTAL DEVASTATION OVER THERE.
OVER WHERE?
WHA--
WHAT'S HAPPENED?!

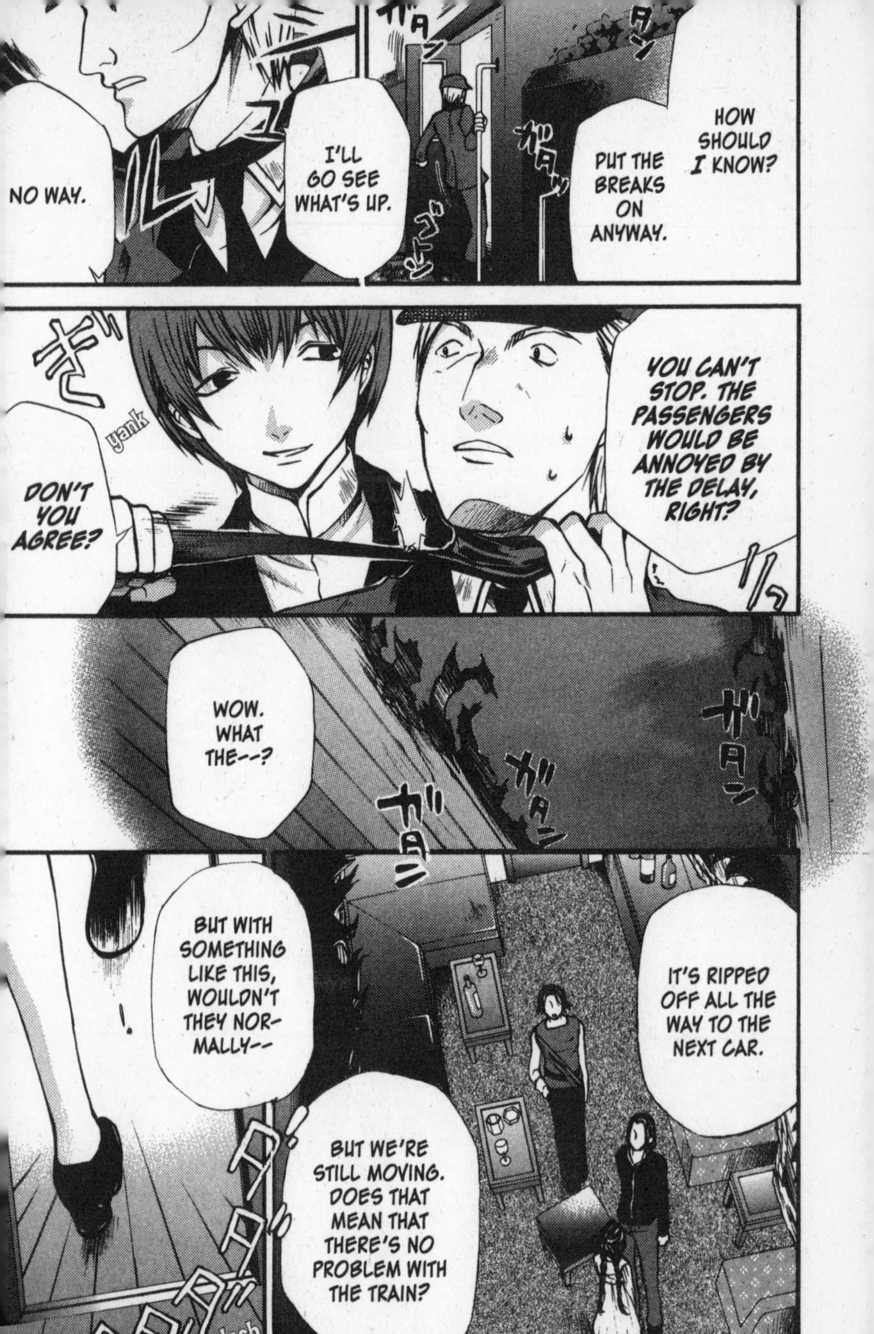
HOW SHOULD I KNOW?
PUT THE BREAKS ON ANYWAY.
I'LL GO SEE WHAT'S UP.
NO WAY.
YOU CAN'T STOP. THE PASSENGERS WOULD BE ANNOYED BY THE DELAY, RIGHT?
yank
DON'T YOU AGREE?
WOW. WHAT THE--?
IT'S RIPPED OFF ALL THE WAY TO THE NEXT CAR.
BUT WITH SOMETHING LIKE THIS, WOULDN'T THEY NOR-MALLY--
BUT WE'RE STILL MOVING. DOES THAT MEAN THAT THERE'S NO PROBLEM WITH THE TRAIN?
dash
dash

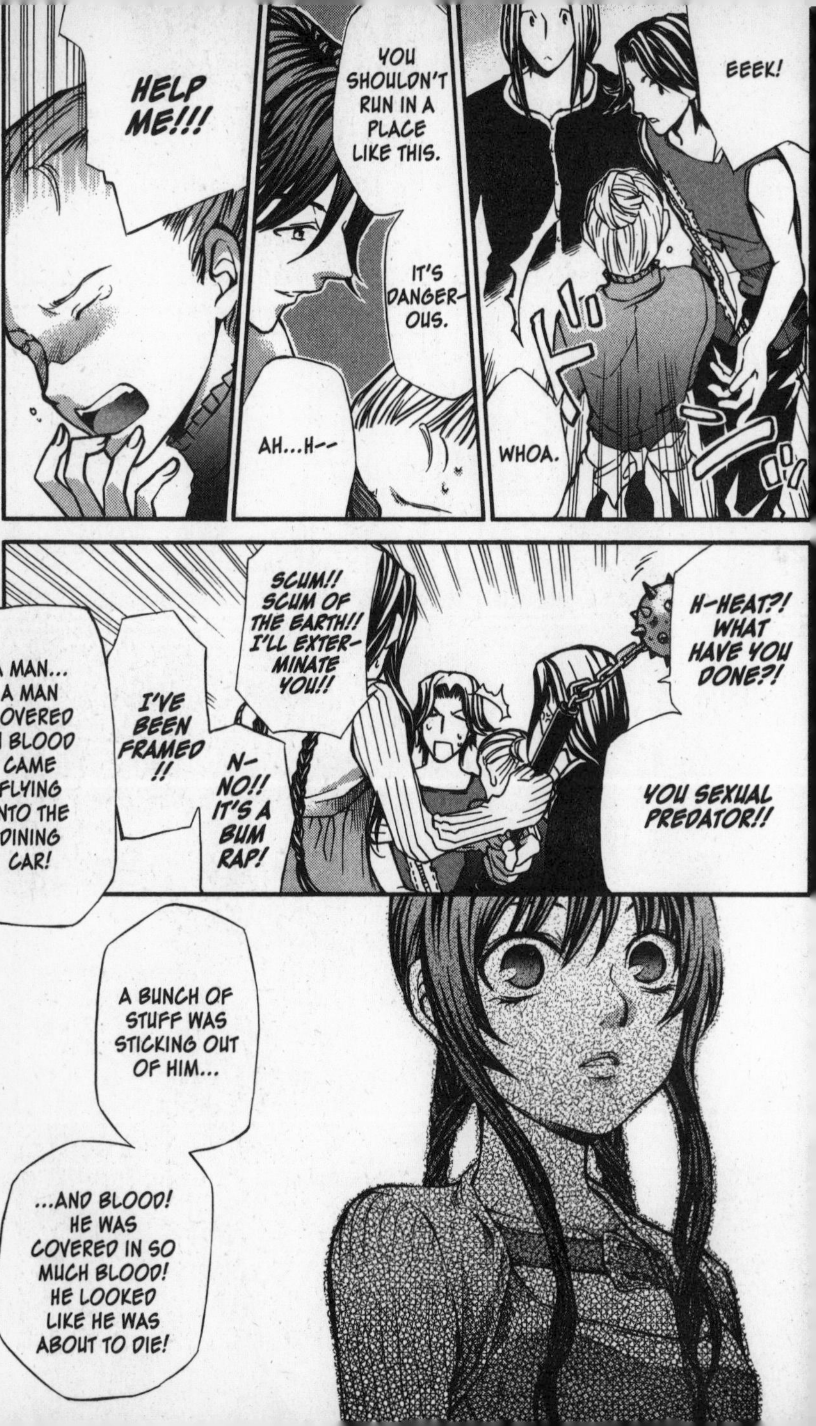
EEEK!
WHOA.
YOU SHOULDN'T RUN IN A PLACE LIKE THIS.
IT'S DANGER-OUS.
AH...H--
HELP ME!!!
H-HEAT?! WHAT HAVE YOU DONE?!
YOU SEXUAL PREDATOR!!
SCUM!! SCUM OF THE EARTH!! I'LL EXTER-MINATE YOU!!
N-NO!! IT'S A BUM RAP!
I'VE BEEN FRAMED!!
A MAN... A MAN COVERED IN BLOOD CAME FLYING INTO THE DINING CAR!
A BUNCH OF STUFF WAS STICKING OUT OF HIM...
...AND BLOOD! HE WAS COVERED IN SO MUCH BLOOD! HE LOOKED LIKE HE WAS ABOUT TO DIE!

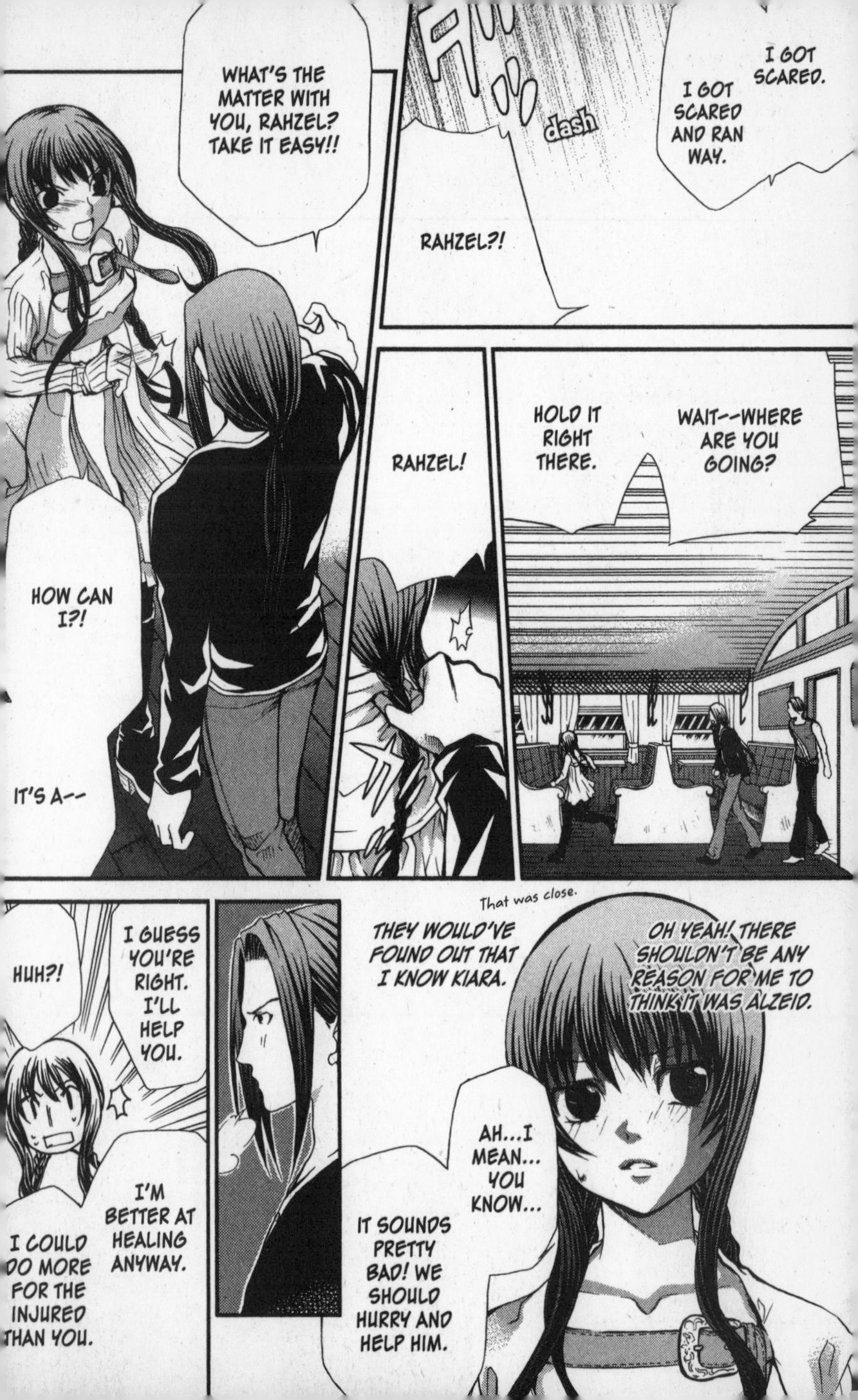

I GOT SCARED.
I GOT SCARED AND RAN WAY.
FU
dash
RAHZEL?!
WAIT--WHERE ARE YOU GOING?
HOLD IT RIGHT THERE.
RAHZEL!
WHAT'S THE MATTER WITH YOU, RAHZEL? TAKE IT EASY!!
HOW CAN I?!
IT'S A--
OH YEAH! THERE SHOULDN'T BE ANY REASON FOR ME TO THINK IT WAS ALZEID.
That was close.
THEY WOULD'VE FOUND OUT THAT I KNOW KIARA.
AH...I MEAN... YOU KNOW...
IT SOUNDS PRETTY BAD! WE SHOULD HURRY AND HELP HIM.
I GUESS YOU'RE RIGHT. I'LL HELP YOU.
HUH?!
I'M BETTER AT HEALING ANYWAY.
I COULD DO MORE FOR THE INJURED THAN YOU.

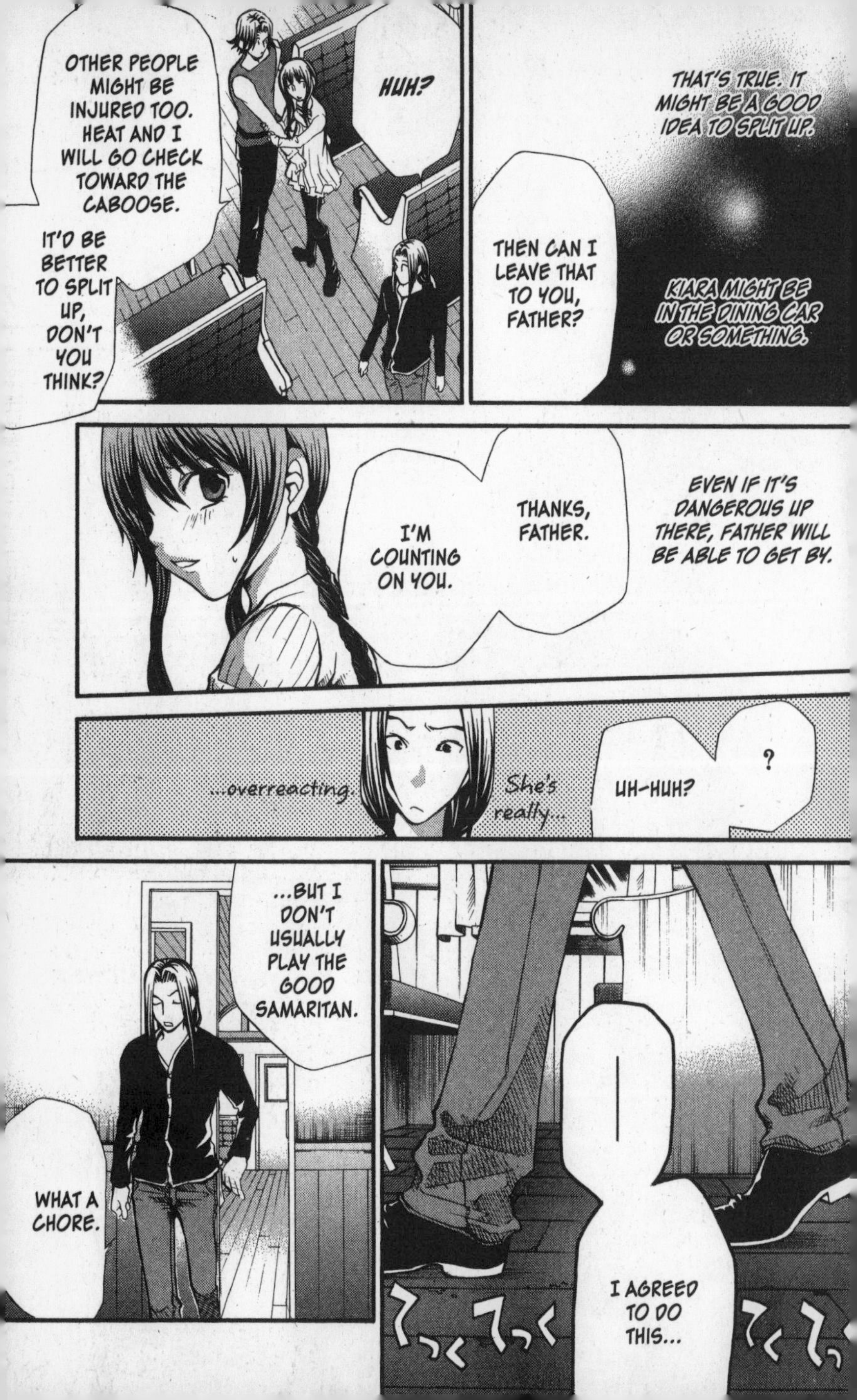
THAT'S TRUE. IT MIGHT BE A GOOD IDEA TO SPLIT UP.
KIARA MIGHT BE IN THE DINING CAR OR SOMETHING.
THEN CAN I LEAVE THAT TO YOU, FATHER?
HUH?
OTHER PEOPLE MIGHT BE INJURED TOO. HEAT AND I WILL GO CHECK TOWARD THE CABOOSE.
IT'D BE BETTER TO SPLIT UP, DON'T YOU THINK?
EVEN IF IT'S DANGEROUS UP THERE, FATHER WILL BE ABLE TO GET BY.
THANKS, FATHER.
I'M COUNTING ON YOU.
?
UH-HUH?
She's really...
...overreacting.
I AGREED TO DO THIS...
...BUT I DON'T USUALLY PLAY THE GOOD SAMARITAN.
WHAT A CHORE.

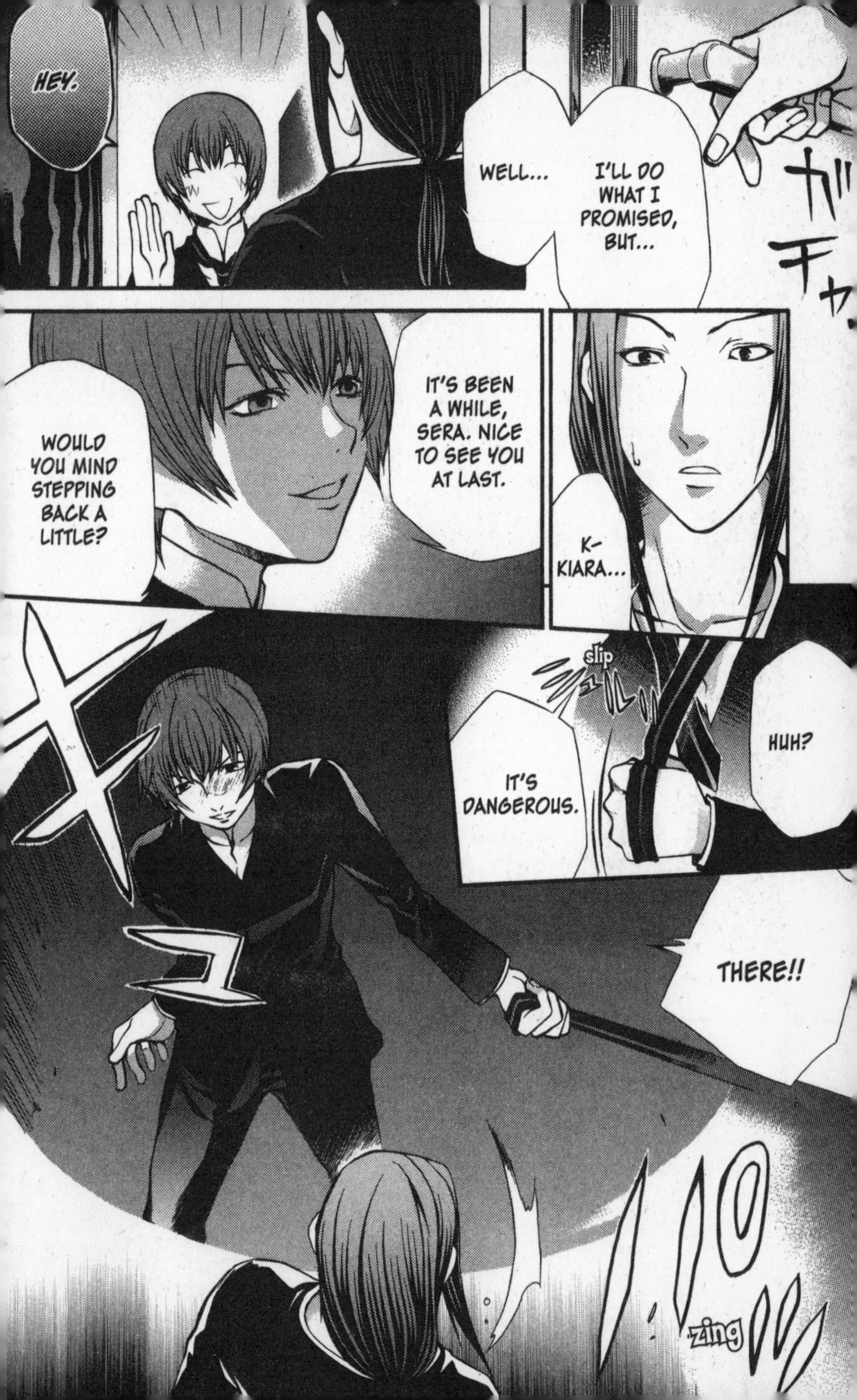

ガチャ
WELL... I'LL DO WHAT I PROMISED, BUT...
HEY.
K-KIARA...
IT'S BEEN A WHILE, SERA. NICE TO SEE YOU AT LAST.
WOULD YOU MIND STEPPING BACK A LITTLE?
HUH?
slip
IT'S DANGEROUS.
THERE!!
zing

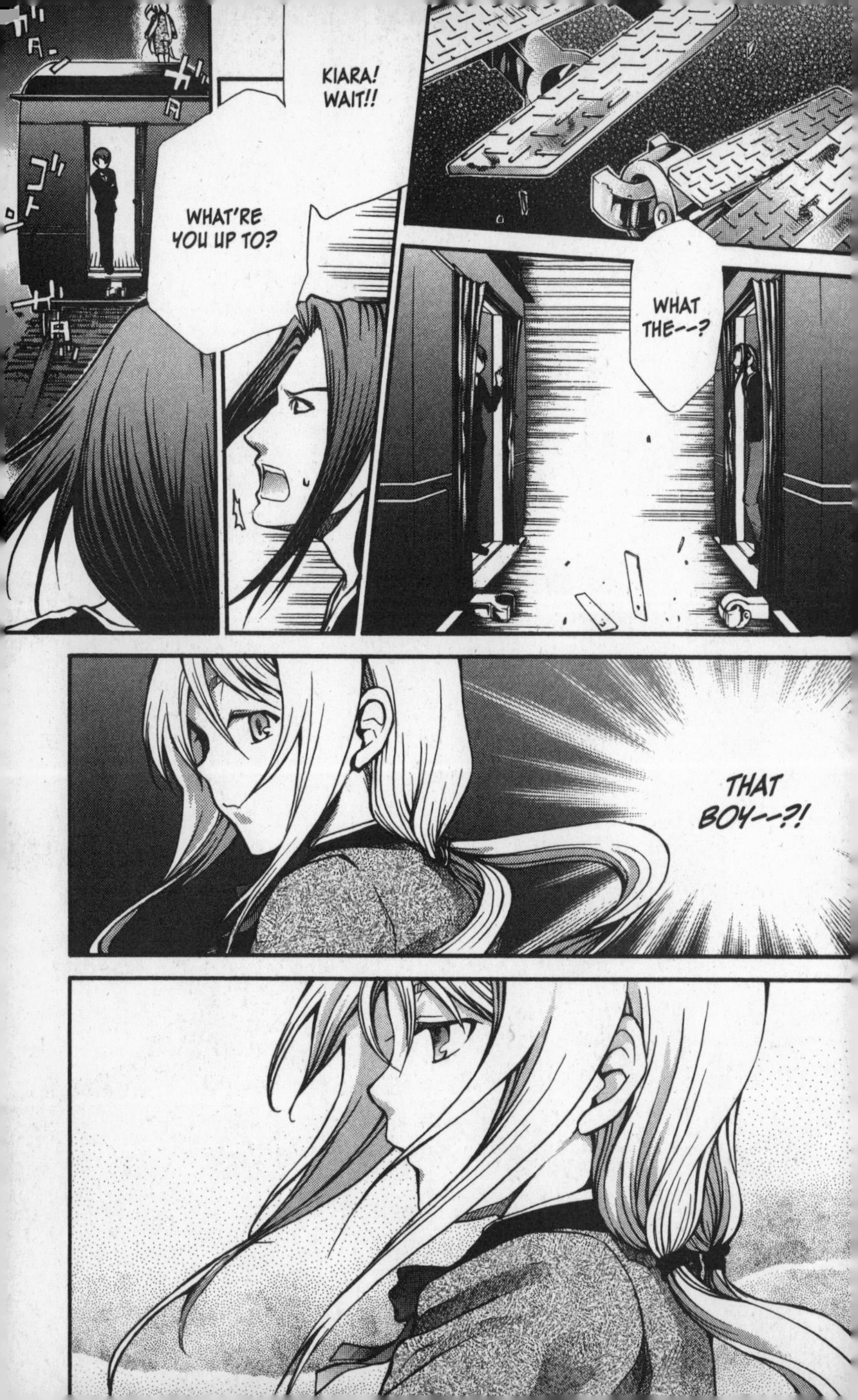
WHAT THE--?
KIARA! WAIT!!
WHAT'RE YOU UP TO?
THAT BOY--?!

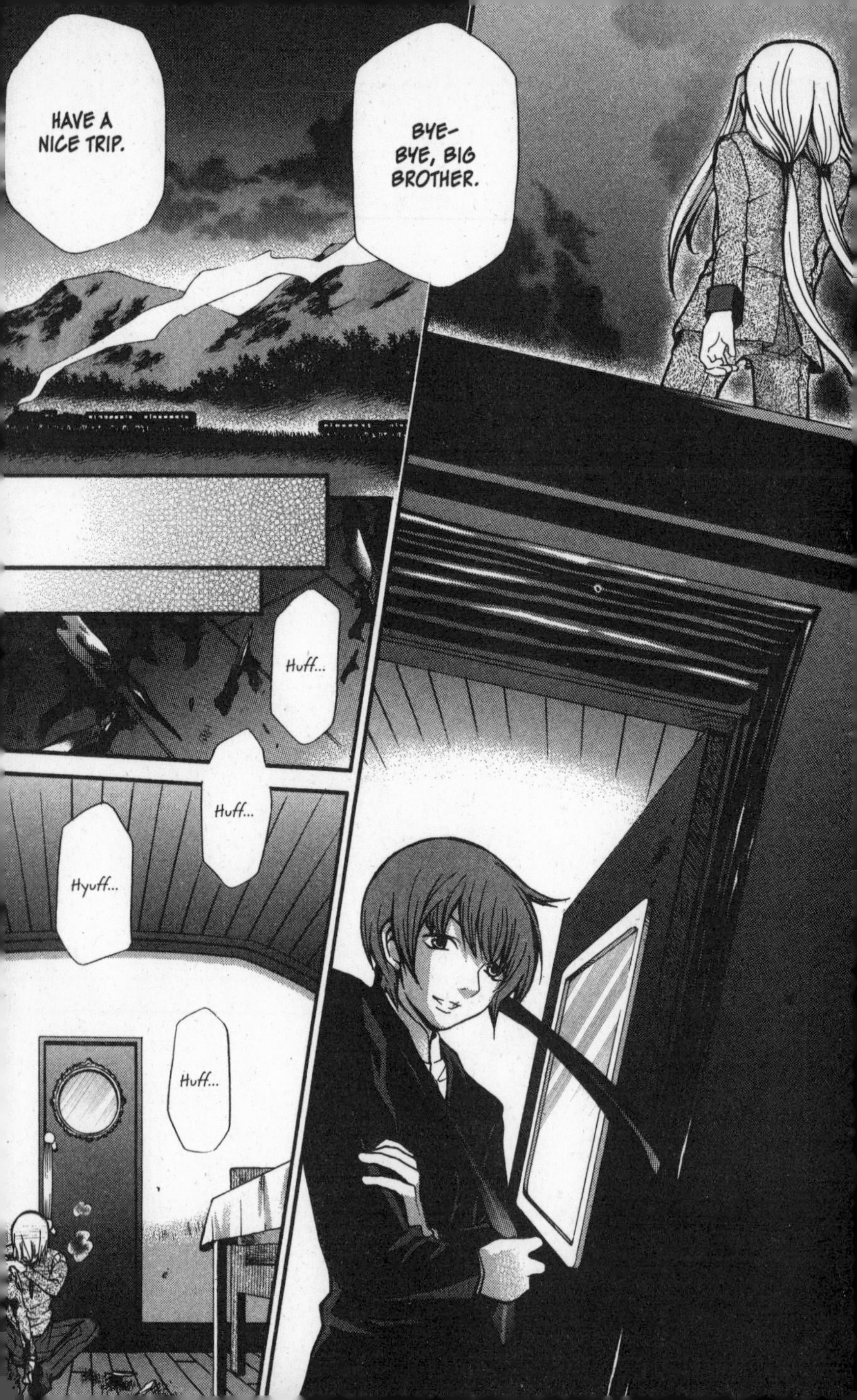
BYE-BYE, BIG BROTHER.
HAVE A NICE TRIP.
Huff...
Huff...
Hyuff...
Huff...

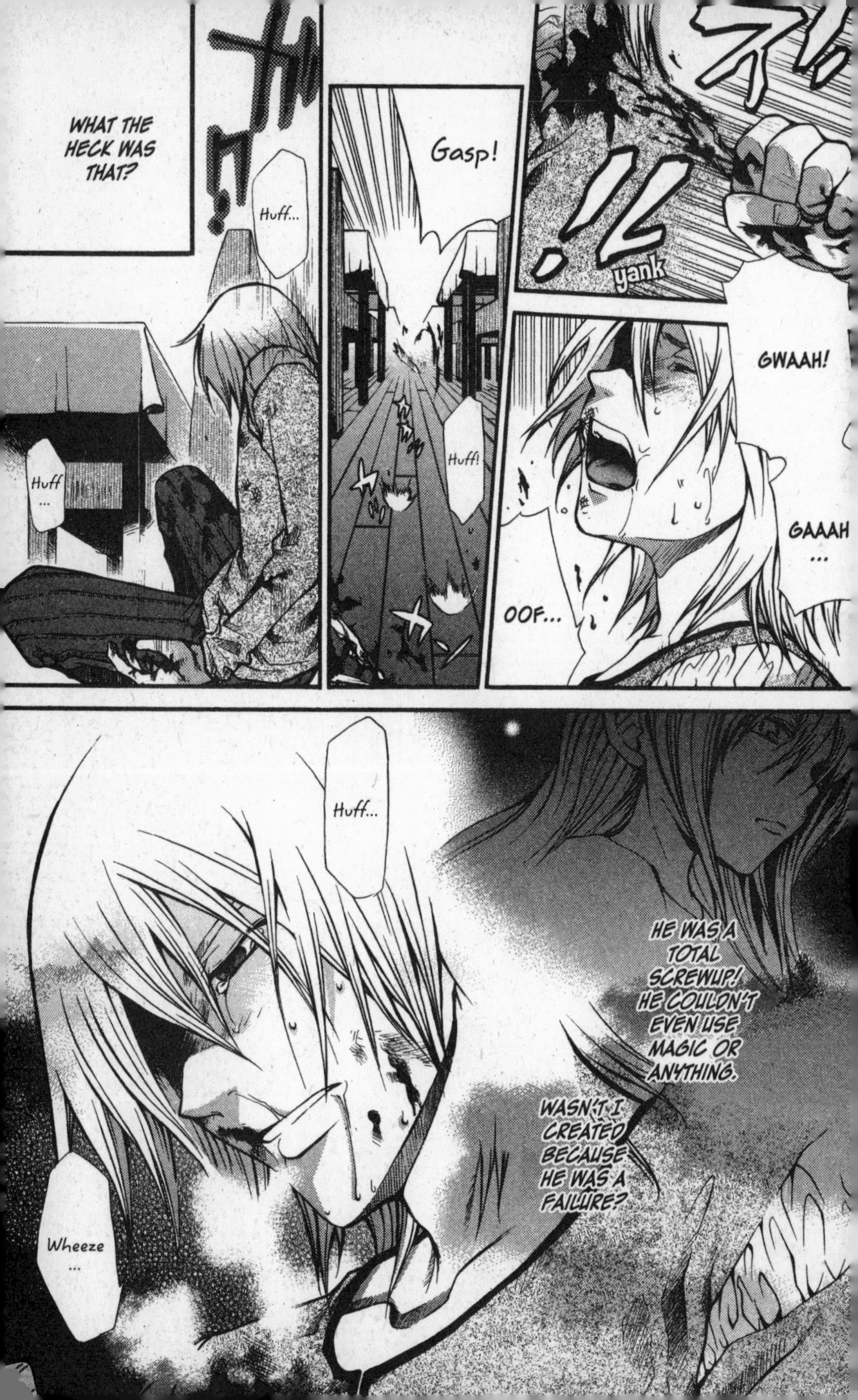
yank
GWAAH!
GAAAH...
OOF...
Gasp!
Huff!
WHAT THE HECK WAS THAT?
Huff...
Huff...
Huff...
HE WAS A TOTAL SCREWUP! HE COULDN'T EVEN USE MAGIC OR ANYTHING.
WASN'T I CREATED BECAUSE HE WAS A FAILURE?
Wheeze...

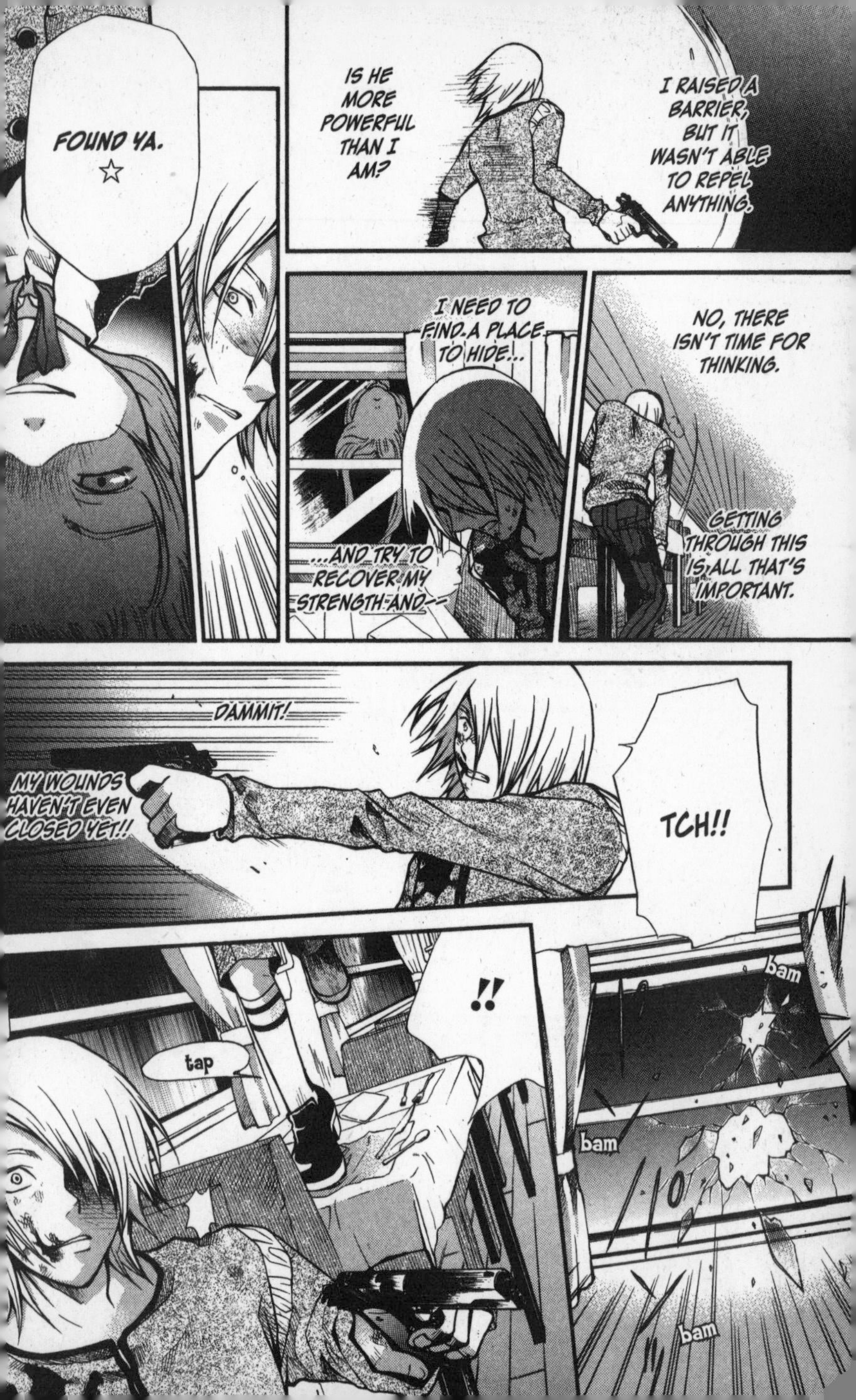
I RAISED A BARRIER, BUT IT WASN'T ABLE TO REPEL ANYTHING.
IS HE MORE POWERFUL THAN I AM?
NO, THERE ISN'T TIME FOR THINKING.
GETTING THROUGH THIS IS ALL THAT'S IMPORTANT.
I NEED TO FIND A PLACE TO HIDE...
...AND TRY TO RECOVER MY STRENGTH AND--
FOUND YA. ☆
TCH!!
DAMMIT!
MY WOUNDS HAVEN'T EVEN CLOSED YET!!
bam
!!
tap
bam
bam

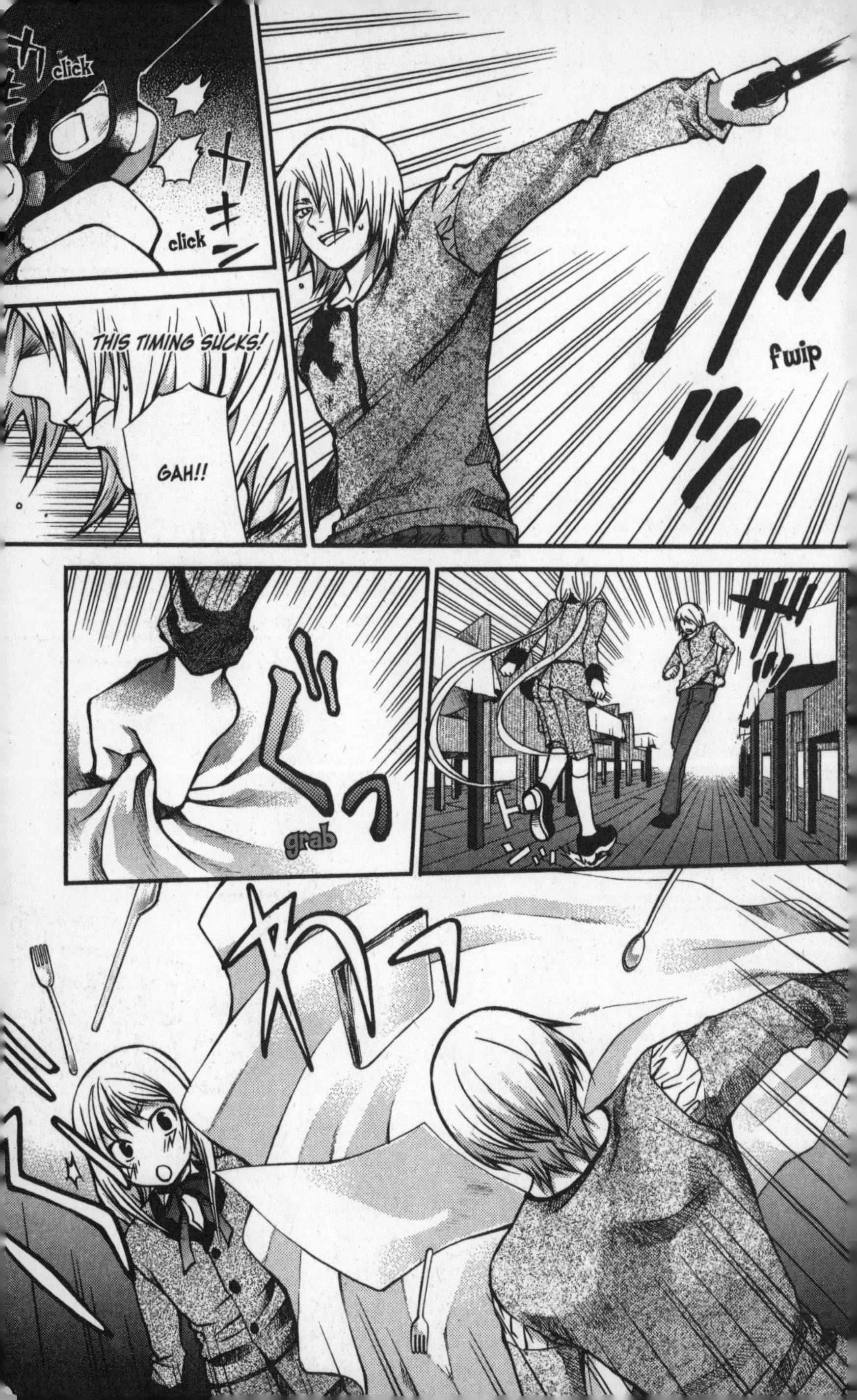
click
click
THIS TIMING SUCKS!
GAH!!
fwip
grab

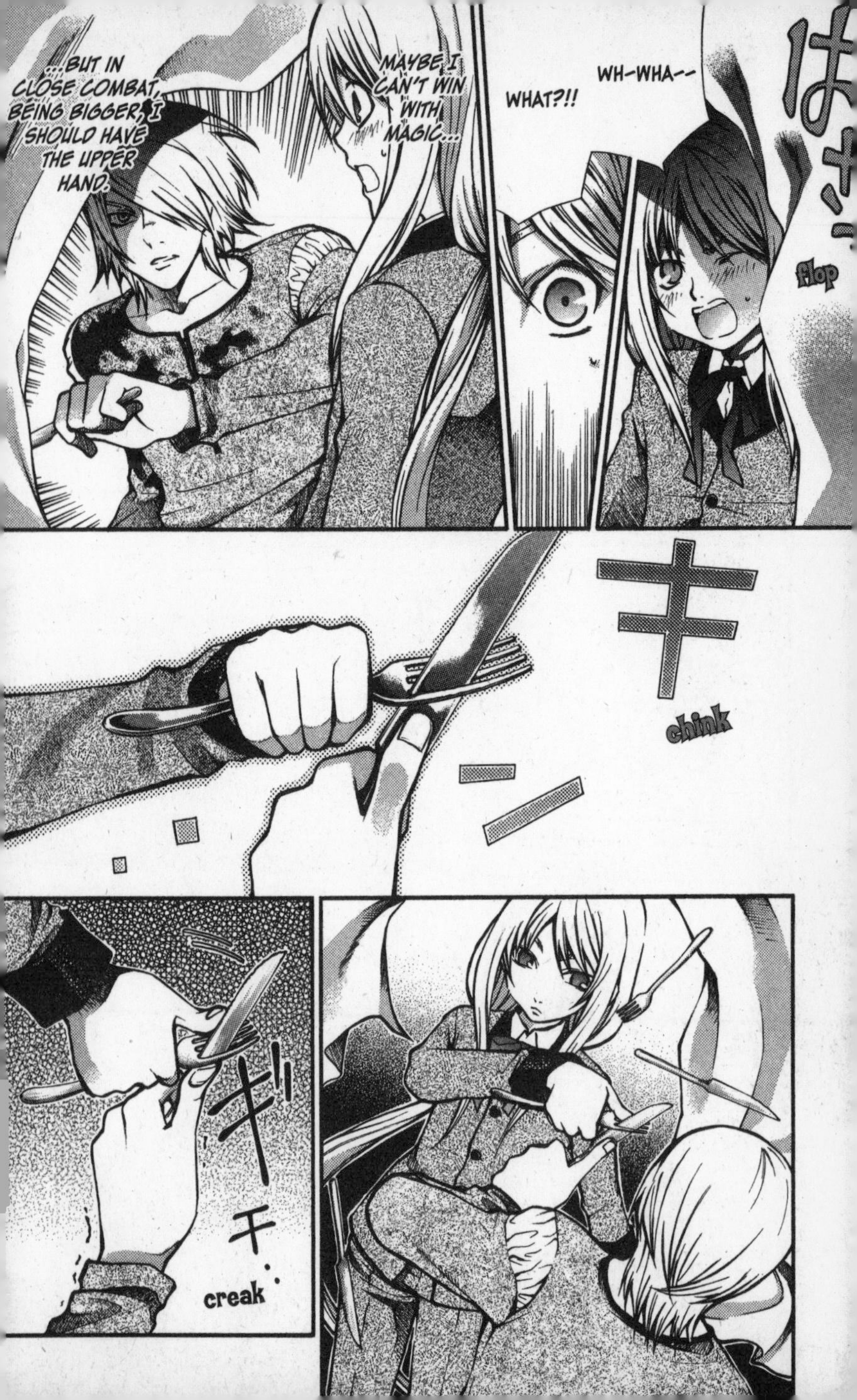
flop
WH-WHA--
WHAT?!!
MAYBE I CAN'T WIN WITH MAGIC...
...BUT IN CLOSE COMBAT, BEING BIGGER, I SHOULD HAVE THE UPPER HAND.
chink
creak

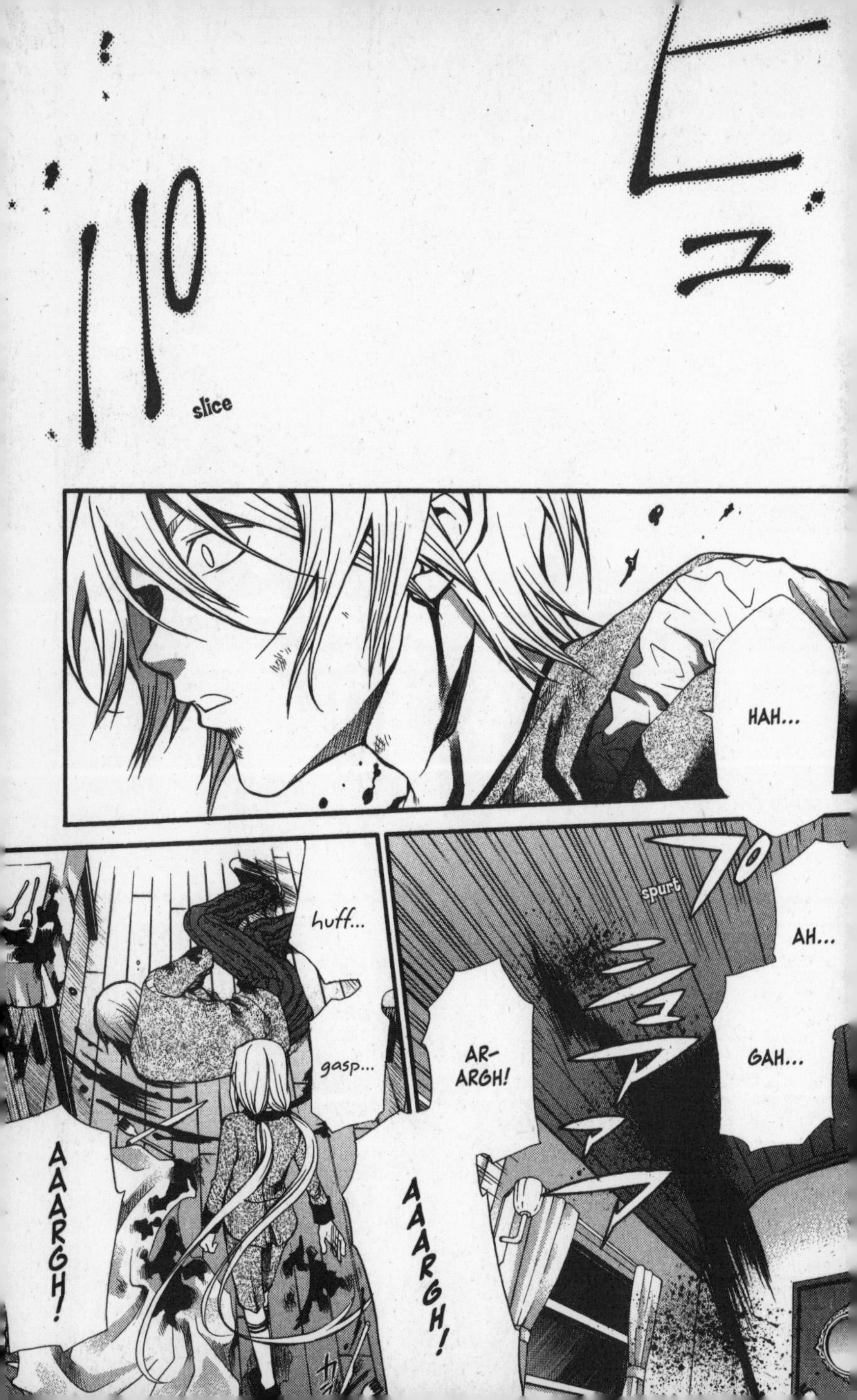
slice
HAH...
spurt
AH...
GAH...
AR-
ARGH!
AAARGH!
huff...
gasp...
AAARGH!

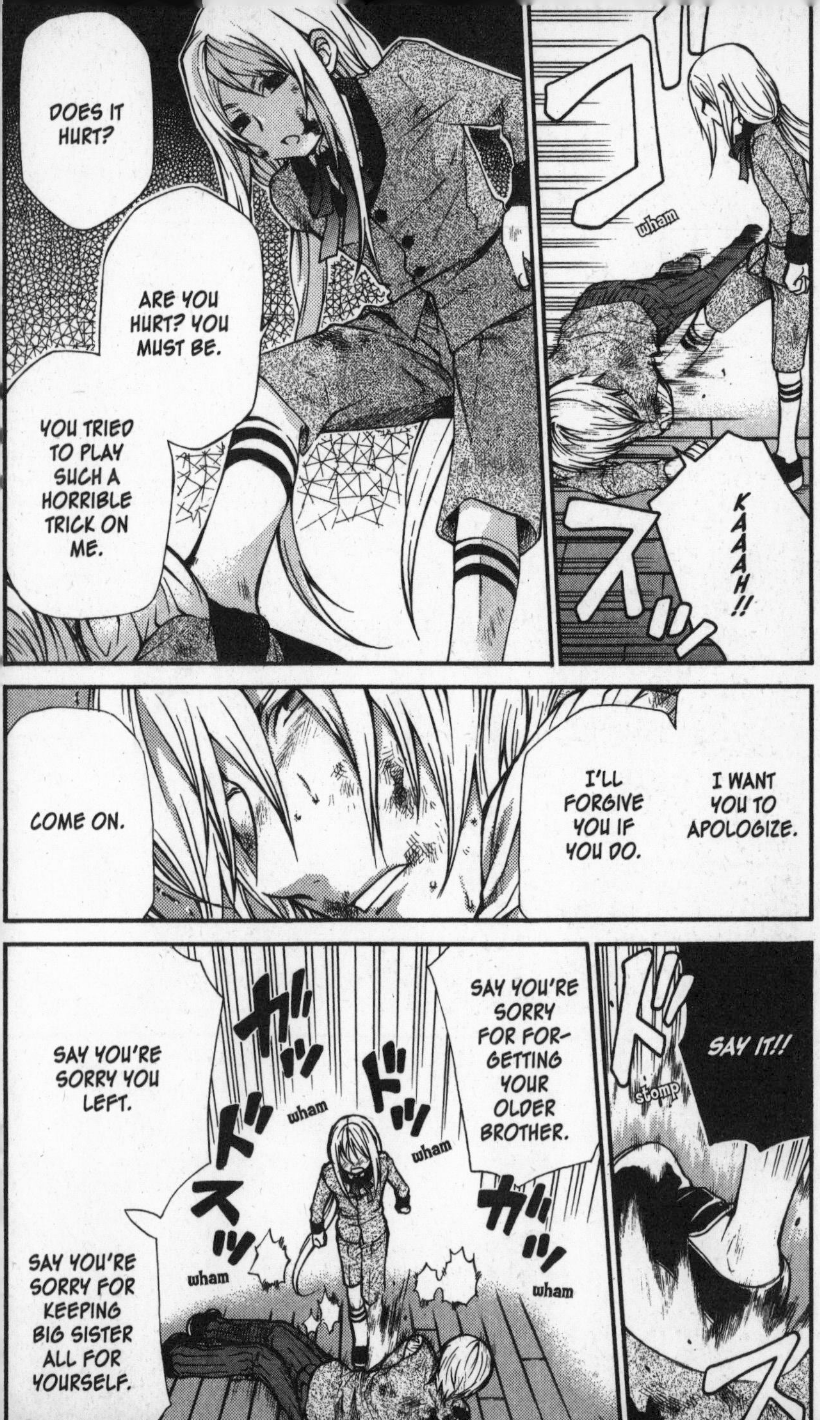
wham
KAAAH!!
DOES IT HURT?
ARE YOU HURT? YOU MUST BE.
YOU TRIED TO PLAY SUCH A HORRIBLE TRICK ON ME.
I WANT YOU TO APOLOGIZE.
I'LL FORGIVE YOU IF YOU DO.
COME ON.
SAY IT!!
stomp
SAY YOU'RE SORRY FOR FOR-GETTING YOUR OLDER BROTHER.
SAY YOU'RE SORRY YOU LEFT.
wham
wham
wham
wham
SAY YOU'RE SORRY FOR KEEPING BIG SISTER ALL FOR YOURSELF.

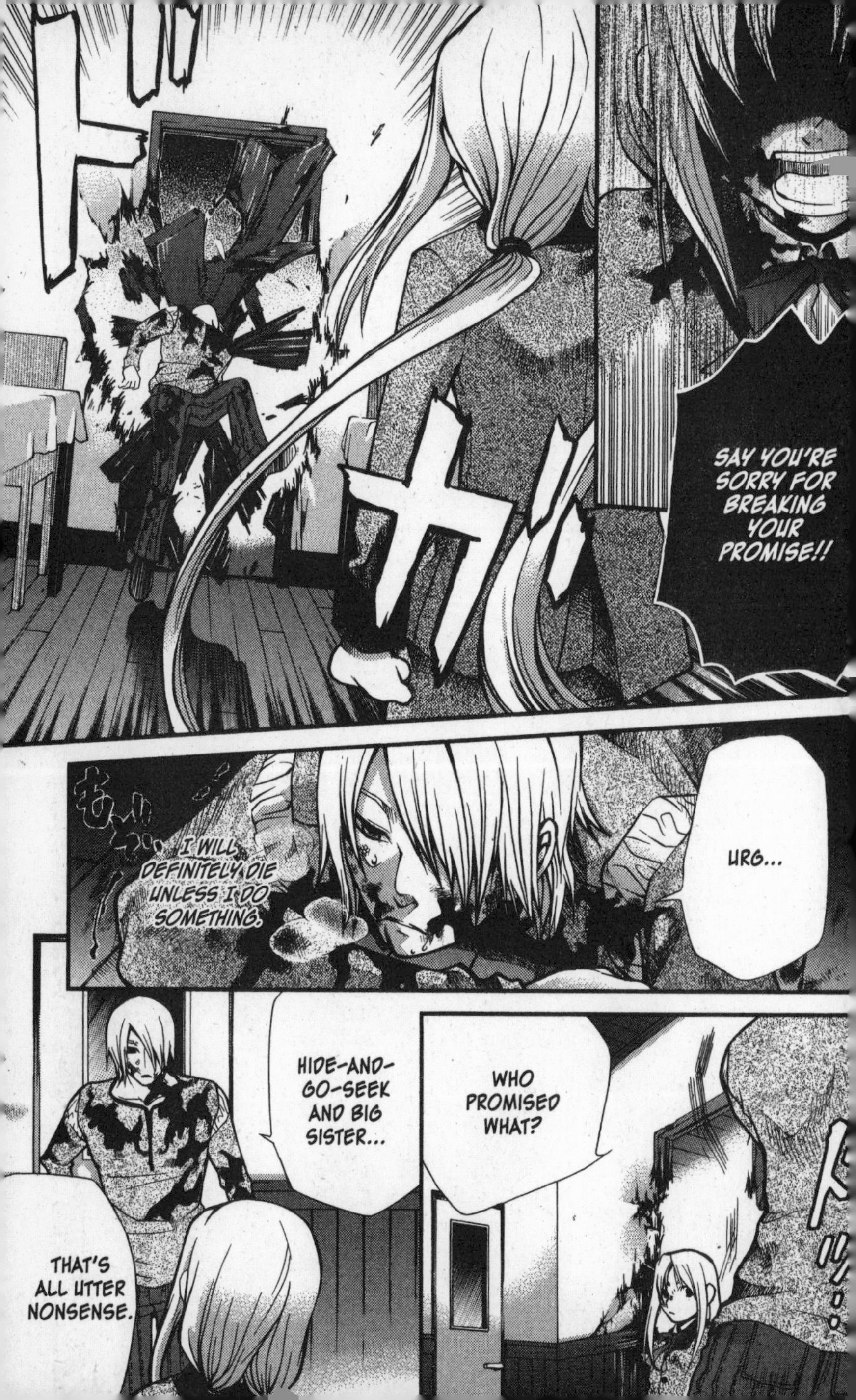
SAY YOU'RE SORRY FOR BREAKING YOUR PROMISE!!
URG...
I WILL DEFINITELY DIE UNLESS I DO SOMETHING.
WHO PROMISED WHAT?
HIDE-AND-GO-SEEK AND BIG SISTER...
THAT'S ALL UTTER NONSENSE.

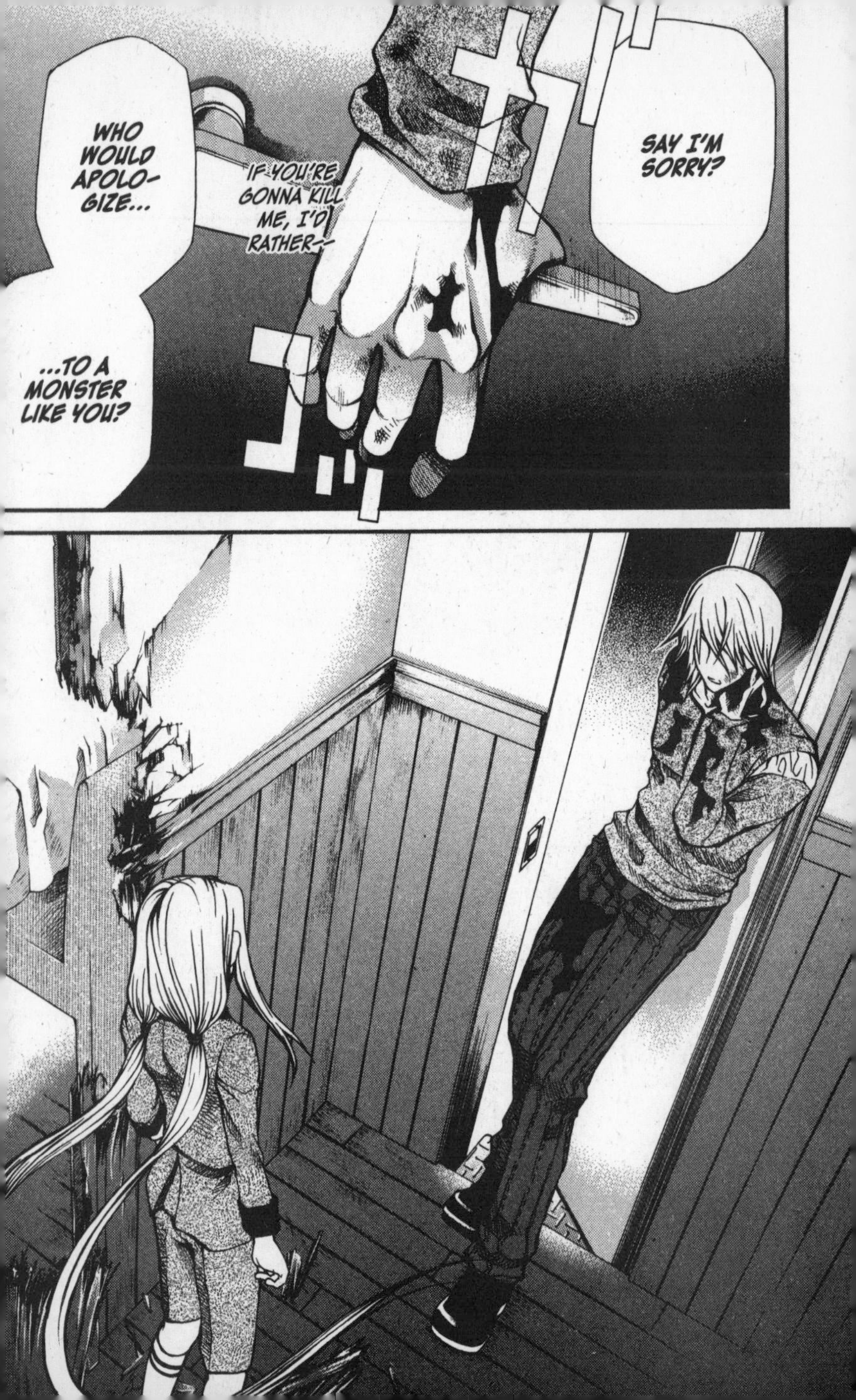
SAY I'M SORRY?
IF YOU'RE GONNA KILL ME, I'D RATHER--
WHO WOULD APOLOGIZE...
...TO A MONSTER LIKE YOU?

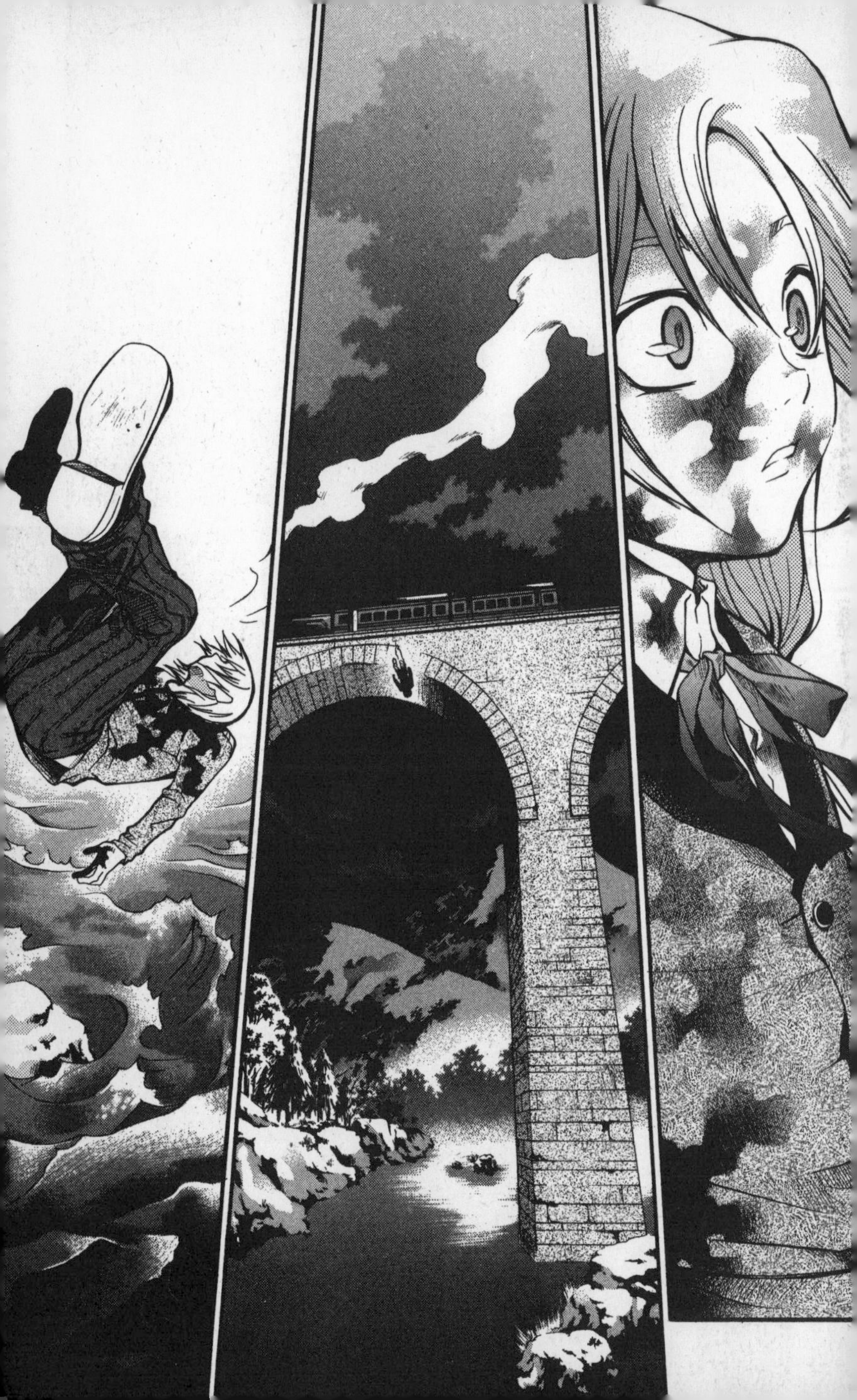

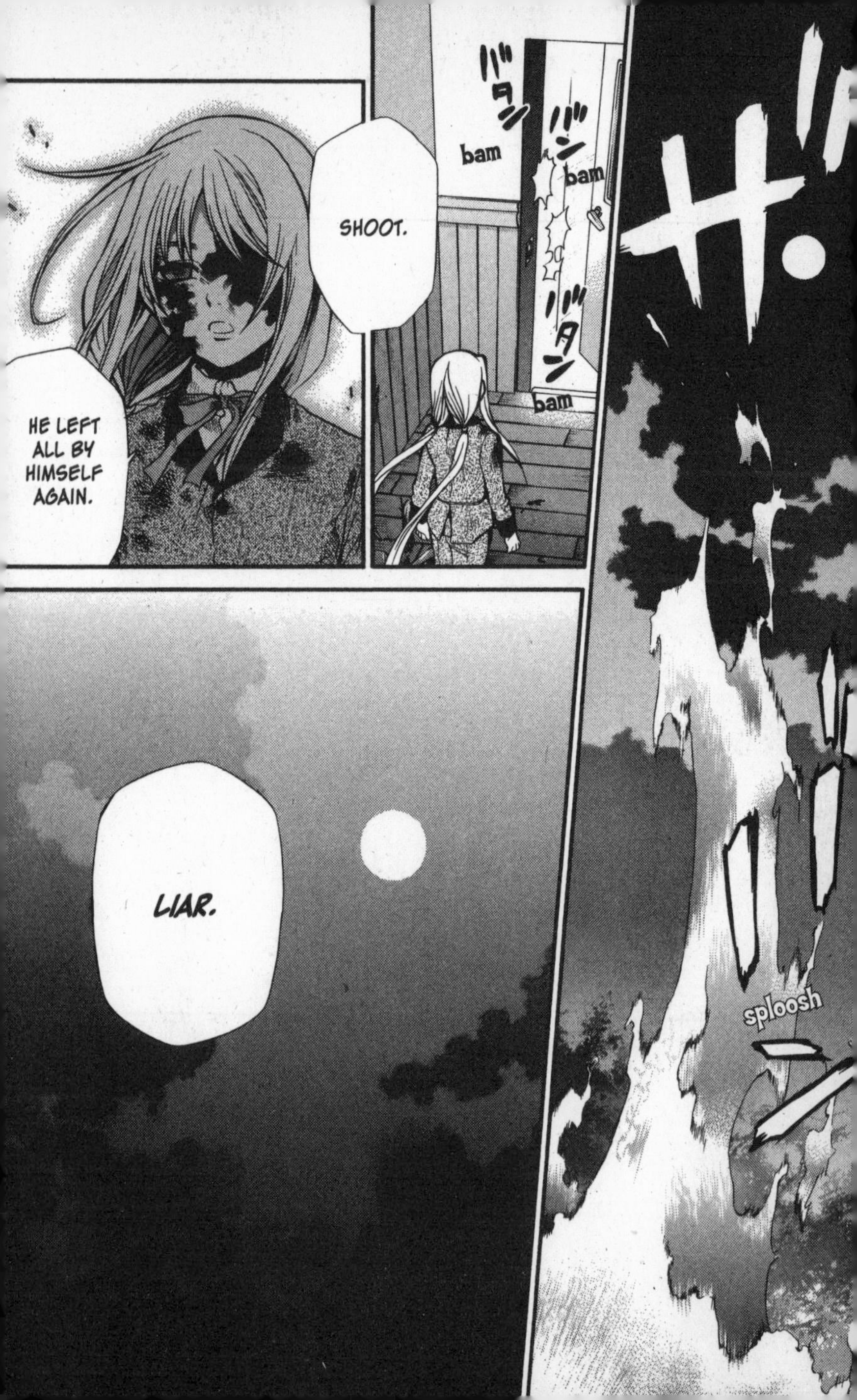

バタン
bam
バン
bam
バタン
bam
SHOOT.
HE LEFT ALL BY HIMSELF AGAIN.
LIAR.
ザッ
sploosh

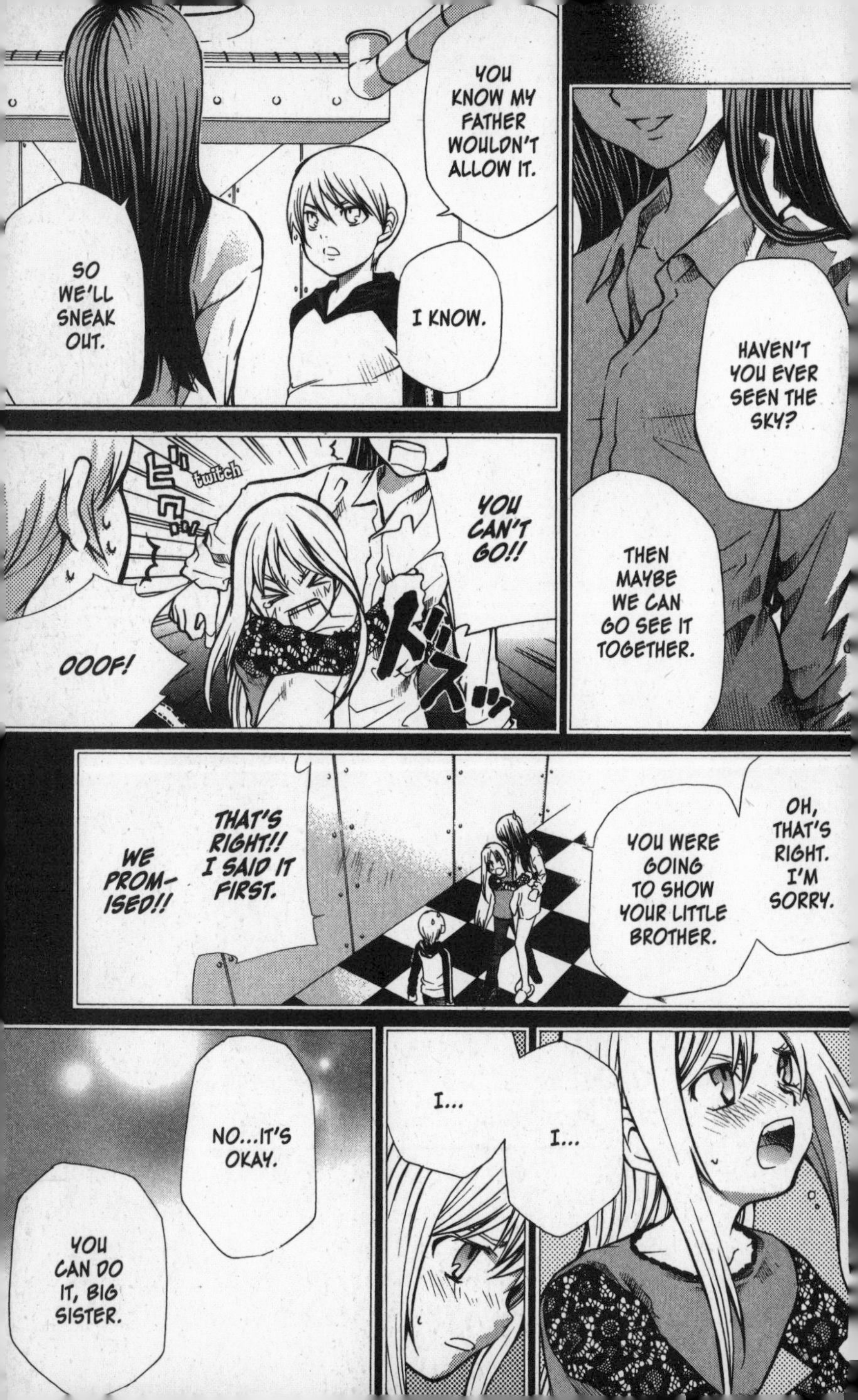
HAVEN'T YOU EVER SEEN THE SKY?
THEN MAYBE WE CAN GO SEE IT TOGETHER.
YOU KNOW MY FATHER WOULDN'T ALLOW IT.
I KNOW.
SO WE'LL SNEAK OUT.
twitch
YOU CAN'T GO!!
OOOF!
OH, THAT'S RIGHT. I'M SORRY.
YOU WERE GOING TO SHOW YOUR LITTLE BROTHER.
THAT'S RIGHT!! I SAID IT FIRST.
WE PROM-ISED!!
I...
I...
NO...IT'S OKAY.
YOU CAN DO IT, BIG SISTER.

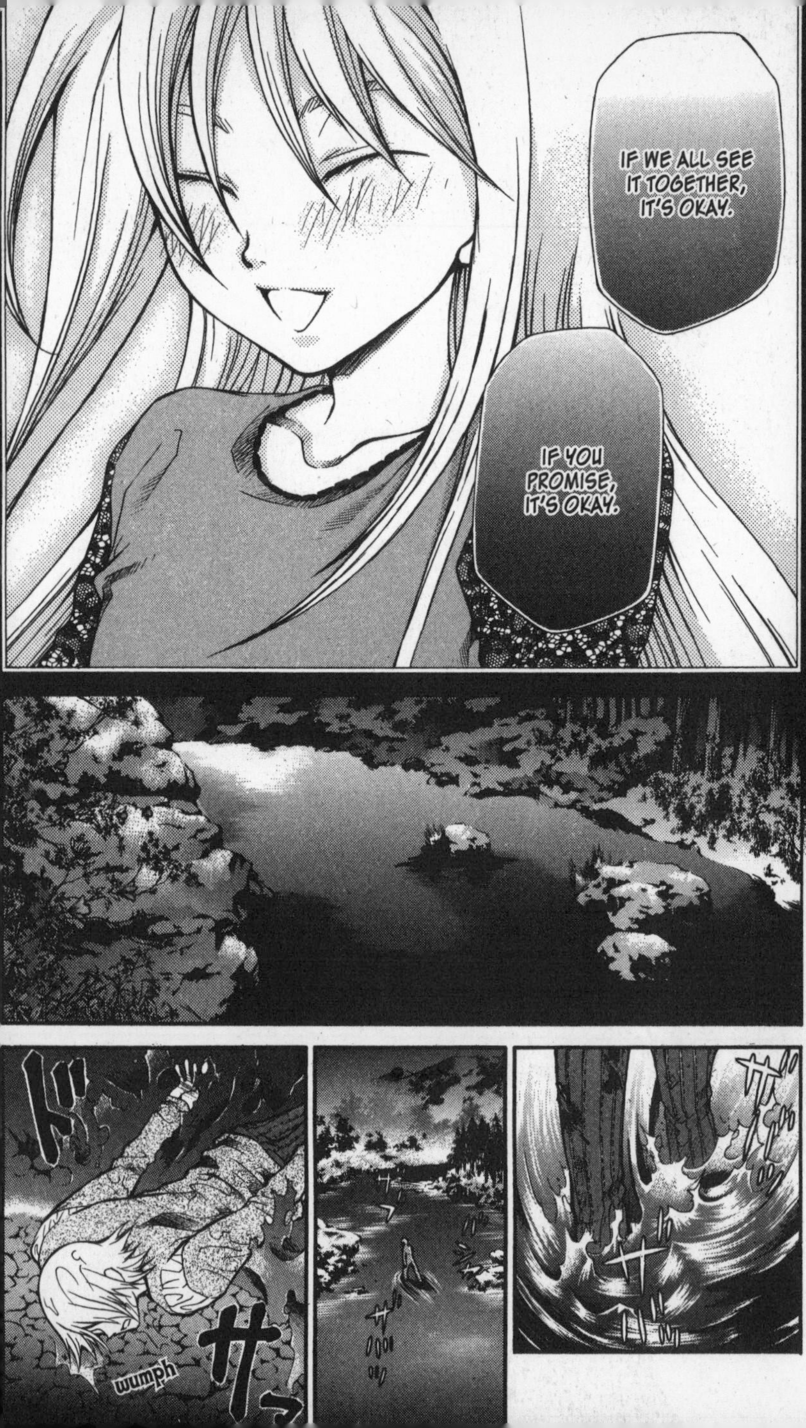
IF WE ALL SEE IT TOGETHER, IT'S OKAY.
IF YOU PROMISE, IT'S OKAY.
wumph

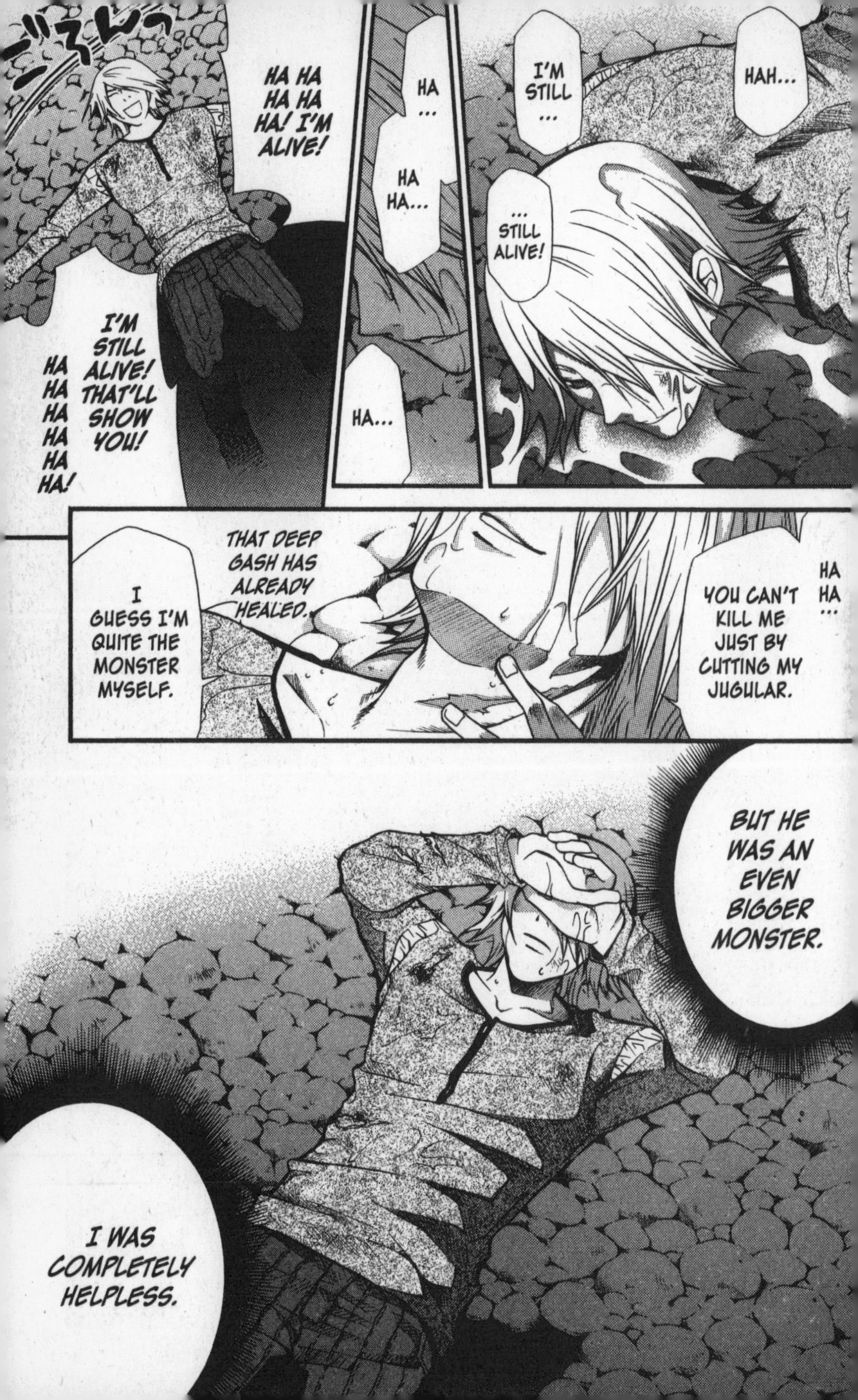
HAH...
I'M STILL ...
... STILL ALIVE!
HA ...
HA HA...
HA...
ゴろんっ
HA HA HA HA HA! I'M ALIVE!
I'M STILL ALIVE! THAT'LL SHOW YOU!
HA HA HA HA HA HA!
HA HA ...
YOU CAN'T KILL ME JUST BY CUTTING MY JUGULAR.
THAT DEEP GASH HAS ALREADY HEALED.
I GUESS I'M QUITE THE MONSTER MYSELF.
BUT HE WAS AN EVEN BIGGER MONSTER.
I WAS COMPLETELY HELPLESS.

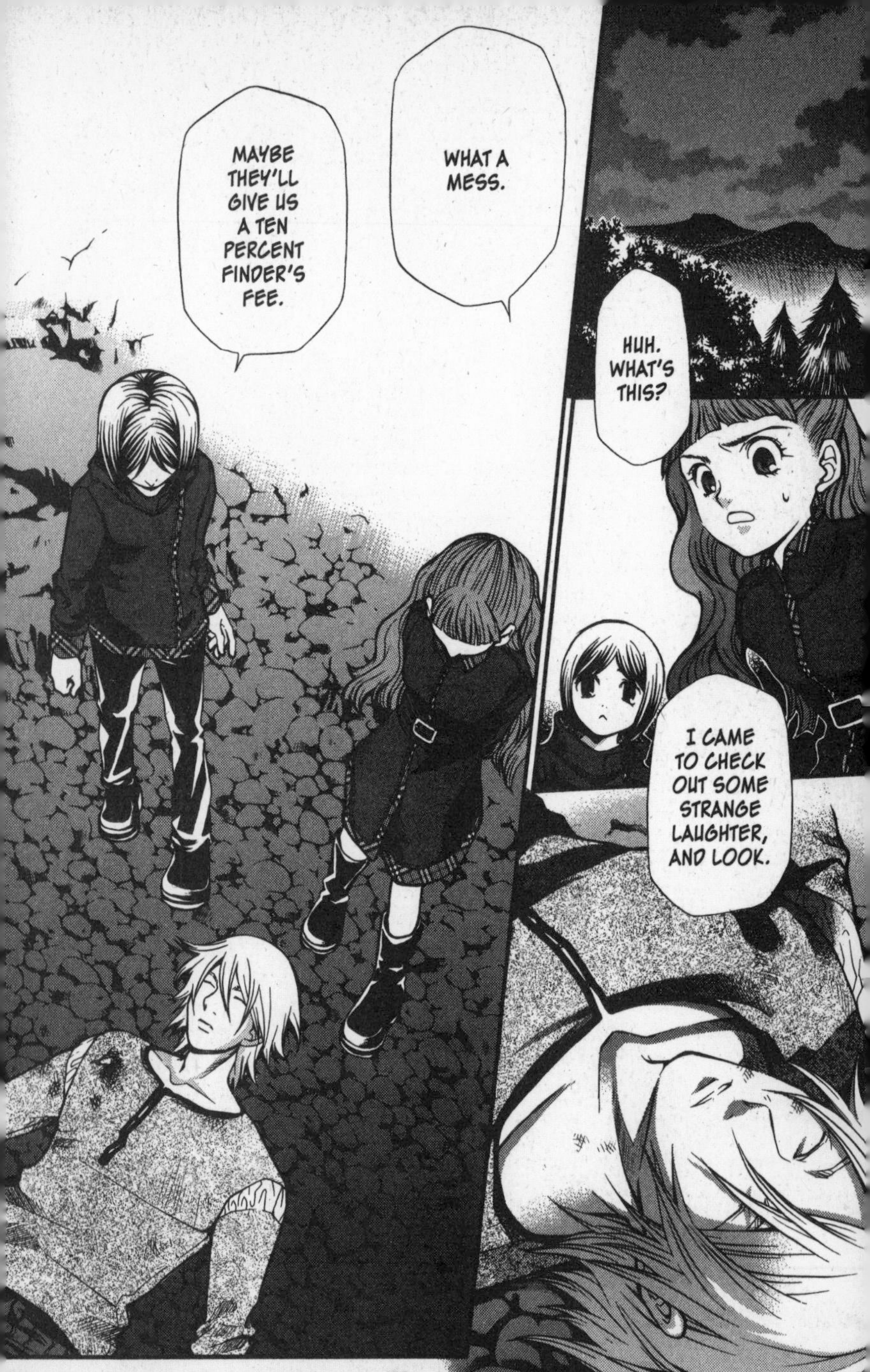
HUH. WHAT'S THIS?
I CAME TO CHECK OUT SOME STRANGE LAUGHTER, AND LOOK.
WHAT A MESS.
MAYBE THEY'LL GIVE US A TEN PERCENT FINDER'S FEE.

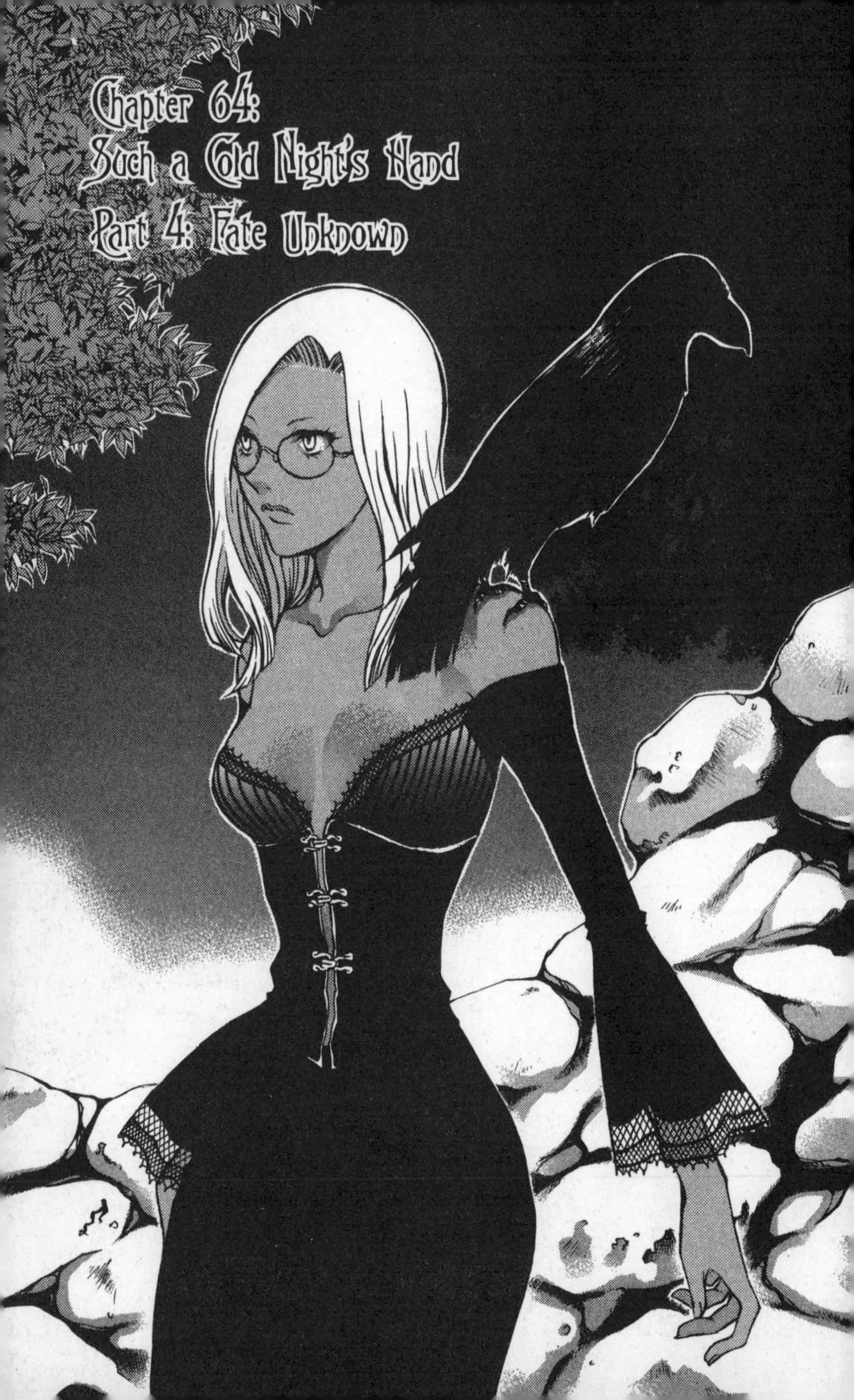
Chapter 64:
Such a Cold Night's Hand
Part 4: Fate Unknown

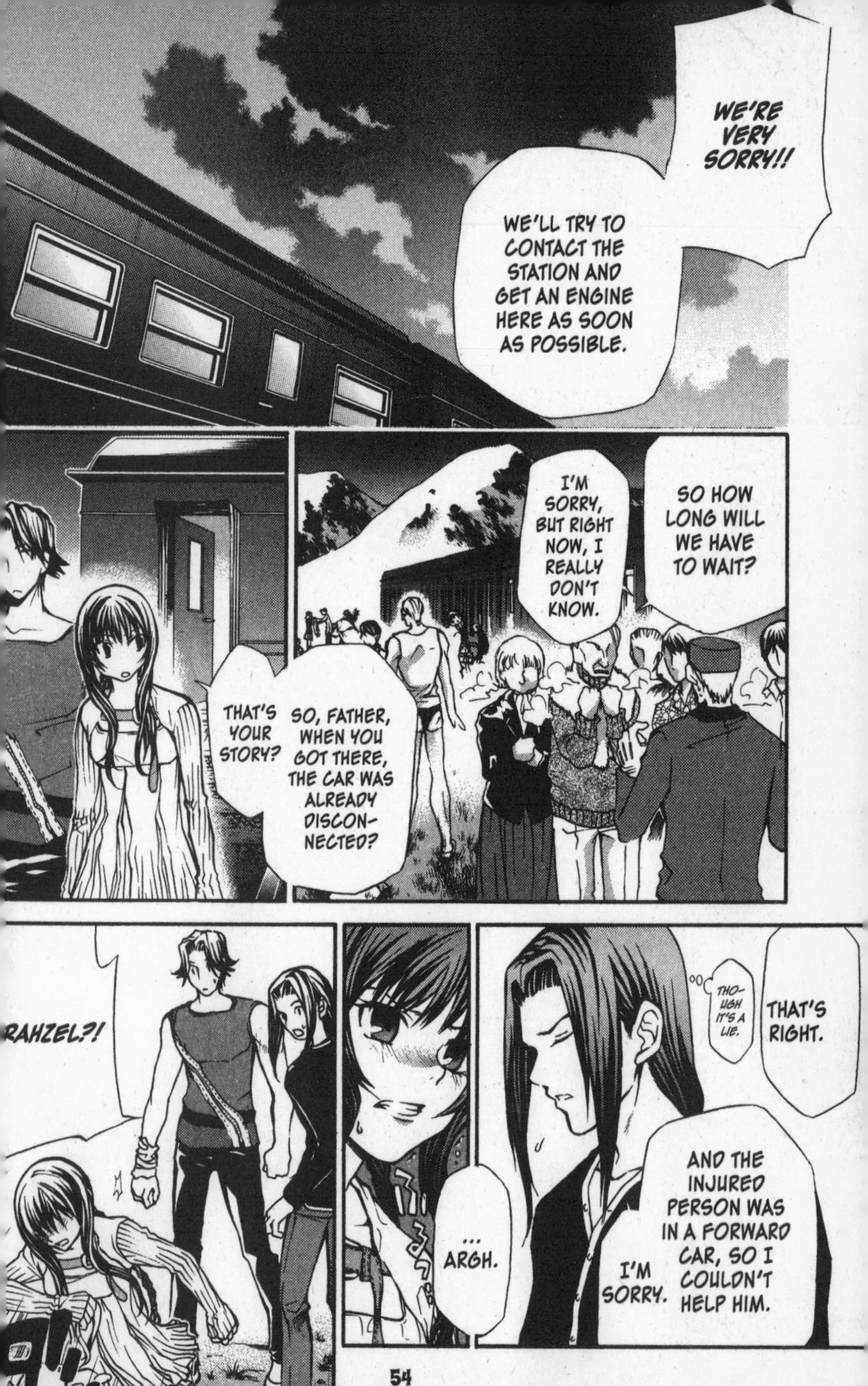
WE'RE VERY SORRY!!
WE'LL TRY TO CONTACT THE STATION AND GET AN ENGINE HERE AS SOON AS POSSIBLE.
SO HOW LONG WILL WE HAVE TO WAIT?
I'M SORRY, BUT RIGHT NOW, I REALLY DON'T KNOW.
SO, FATHER, WHEN YOU GOT THERE, THE CAR WAS ALREADY DISCON-NECTED?
THAT'S YOUR STORY?
THAT'S RIGHT.
THOUGH IT'S A LIE.
AND THE INJURED PERSON WAS IN A FORWARD CAR, SO I COULDN'T HELP HIM.
I'M SORRY.
... ARGH.
RAHZEL?!

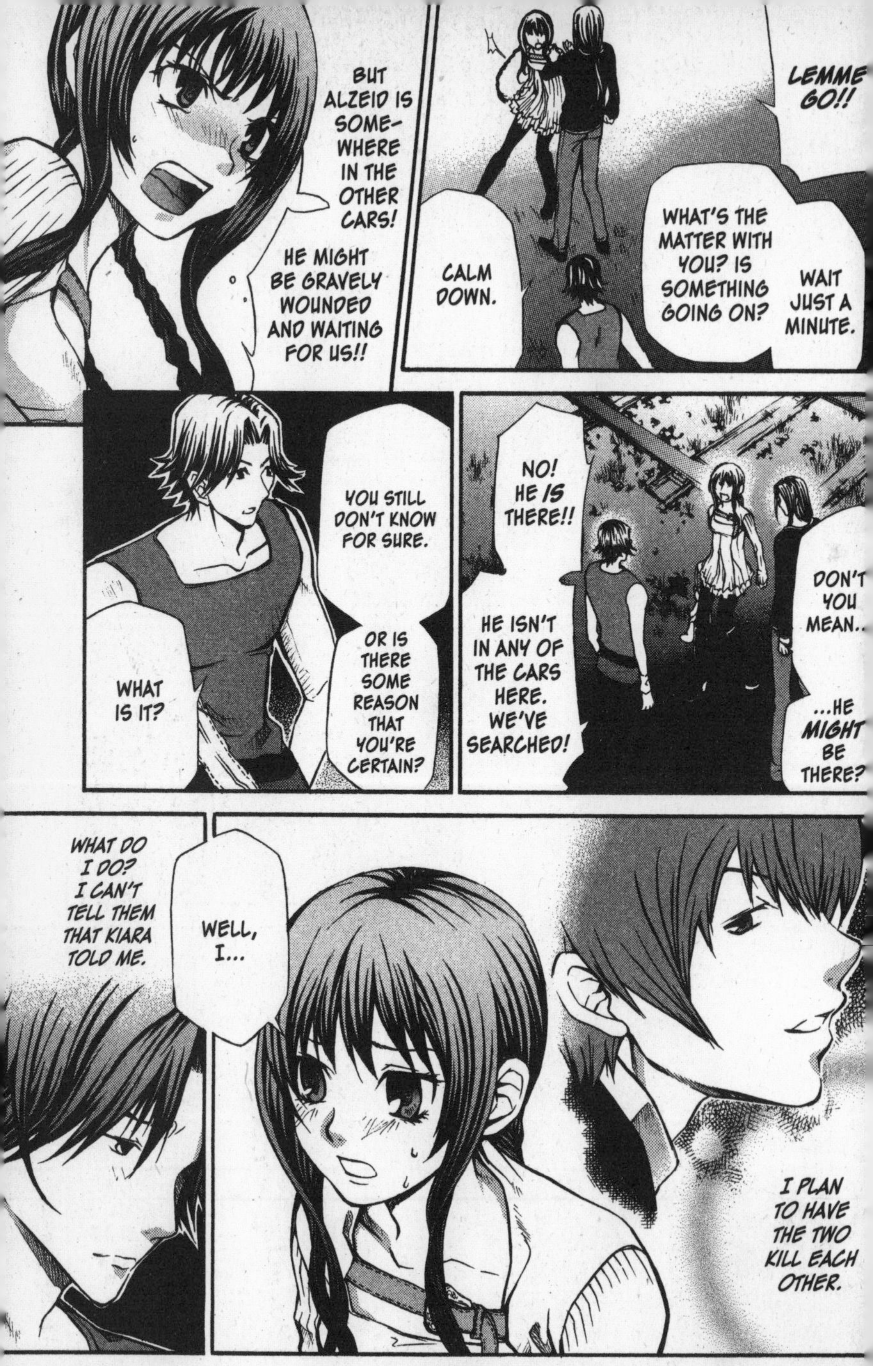
LEMME GO!!
WAIT JUST A MINUTE.
WHAT'S THE MATTER WITH YOU? IS SOMETHING GOING ON?
CALM DOWN.
BUT ALZEID IS SOME-WHERE IN THE OTHER CARS!
HE MIGHT BE GRAVELY WOUNDED AND WAITING FOR US!!
DON'T YOU MEAN...
...HE *MIGHT* BE THERE?
NO! HE *IS* THERE!!
HE ISN'T IN ANY OF THE CARS HERE. WE'VE SEARCHED!
YOU STILL DON'T KNOW FOR SURE.
OR IS THERE SOME REASON THAT YOU'RE CERTAIN?
WHAT IS IT?
I PLAN TO HAVE THE TWO KILL EACH OTHER.
WELL, I...
WHAT DO I DO? I CAN'T TELL THEM THAT KIARA TOLD ME.

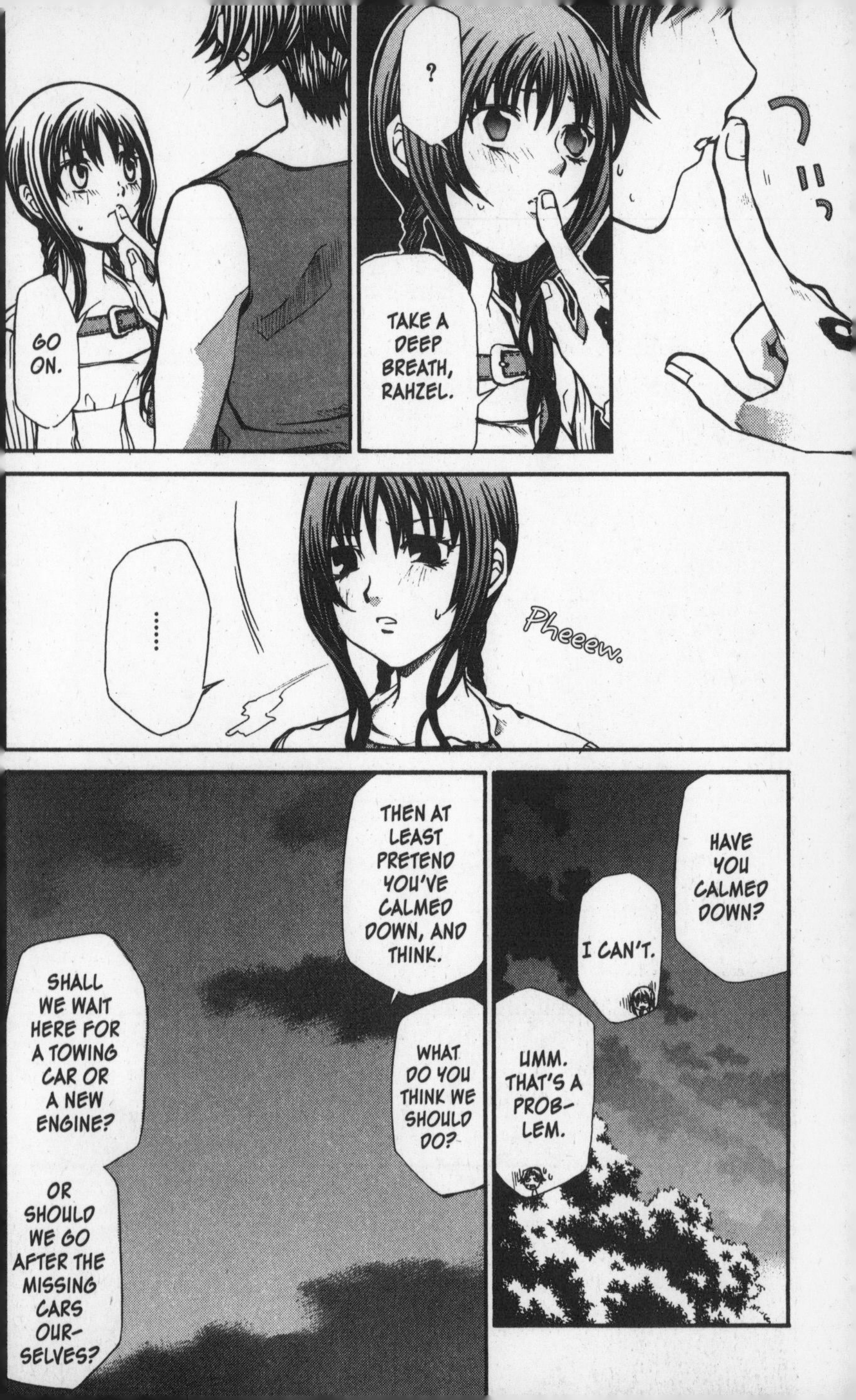
?
TAKE A DEEP BREATH, RAHZEL.
GO ON.
......
Pheeew.
HAVE YOU CALMED DOWN?
I CAN'T.
UMM. THAT'S A PROB-LEM.
THEN AT LEAST PRETEND YOU'VE CALMED DOWN, AND THINK.
WHAT DO YOU THINK WE SHOULD DO?
SHALL WE WAIT HERE FOR A TOWING CAR OR A NEW ENGINE?
OR SHOULD WE GO AFTER THE MISSING CARS OUR-SELVES?

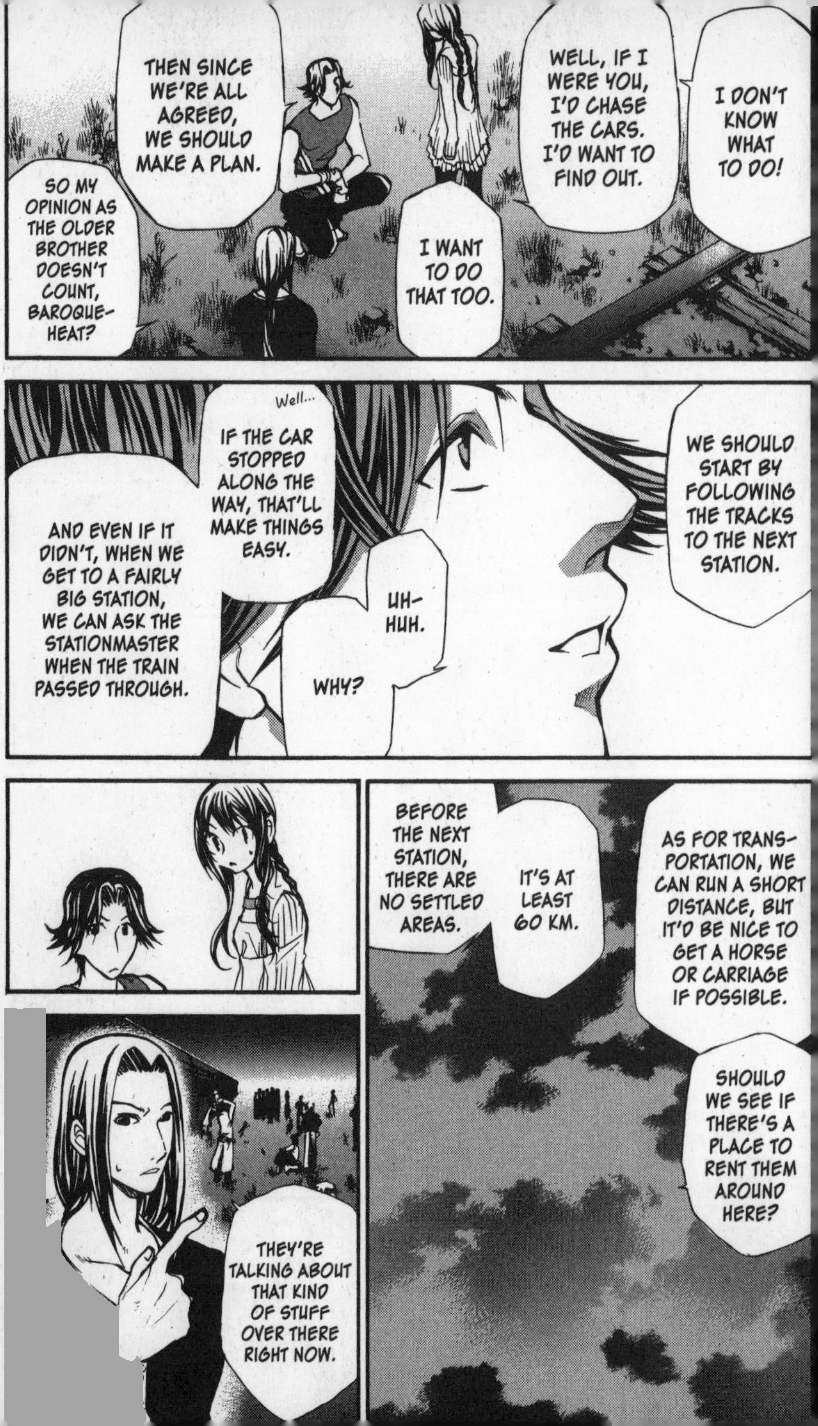
I DON'T KNOW WHAT TO DO!
WELL, IF I WERE YOU, I'D CHASE THE CARS. I'D WANT TO FIND OUT.
I WANT TO DO THAT TOO.
THEN SINCE WE'RE ALL AGREED, WE SHOULD MAKE A PLAN.
SO MY OPINION AS THE OLDER BROTHER DOESN'T COUNT, BAROQUE-HEAT?
WE SHOULD START BY FOLLOWING THE TRACKS TO THE NEXT STATION.
Well...
IF THE CAR STOPPED ALONG THE WAY, THAT'LL MAKE THINGS EASY.
UH-HUH.
WHY?
AND EVEN IF IT DIDN'T, WHEN WE GET TO A FAIRLY BIG STATION, WE CAN ASK THE STATIONMASTER WHEN THE TRAIN PASSED THROUGH.
AS FOR TRANSPORTATION, WE CAN RUN A SHORT DISTANCE, BUT IT'D BE NICE TO GET A HORSE OR CARRIAGE IF POSSIBLE.
IT'S AT LEAST 60 KM.
BEFORE THE NEXT STATION, THERE ARE NO SETTLED AREAS.
SHOULD WE SEE IF THERE'S A PLACE TO RENT THEM AROUND HERE?
THEY'RE TALKING ABOUT THAT KIND OF STUFF OVER THERE RIGHT NOW.

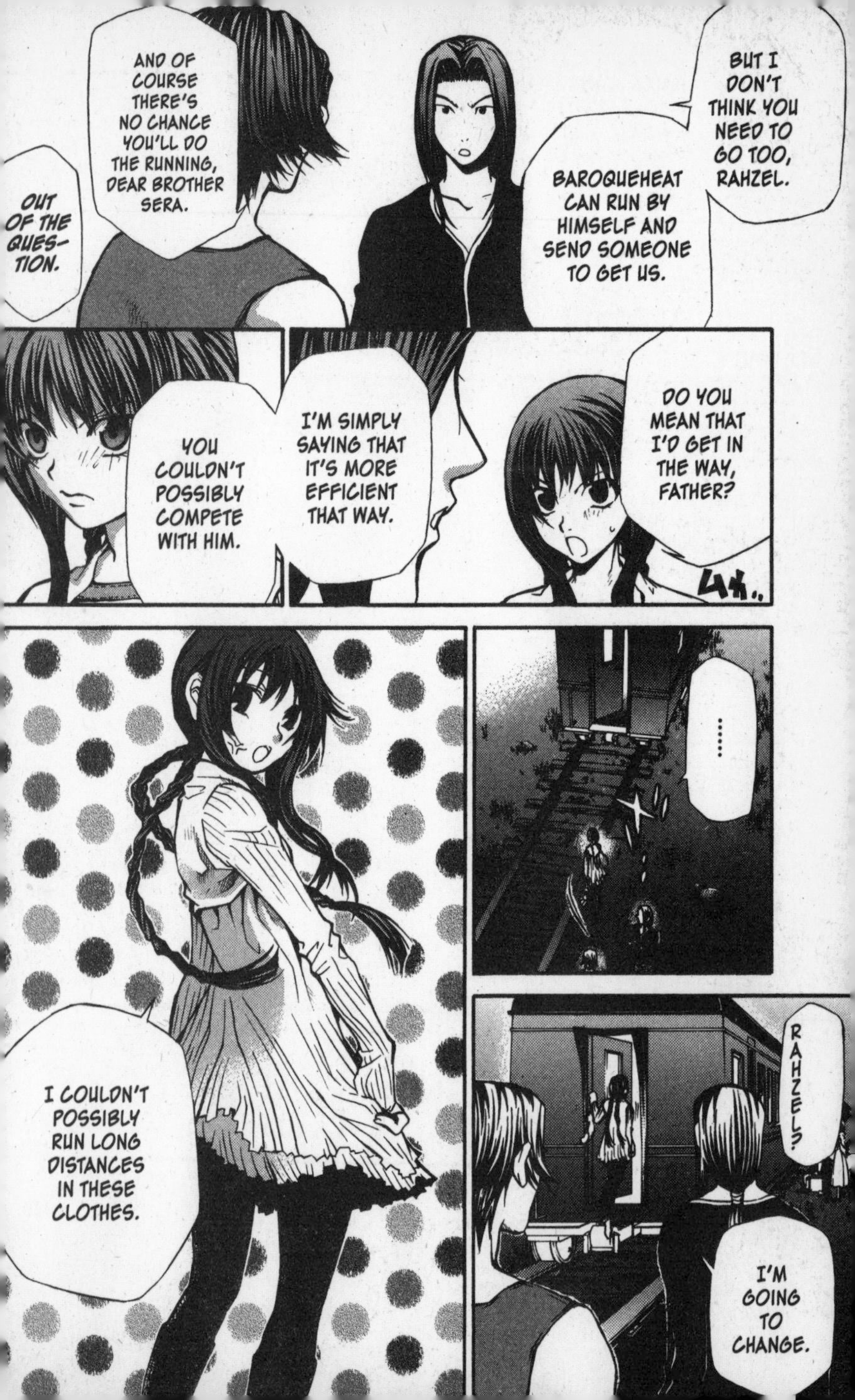
BUT I DON'T THINK YOU NEED TO GO TOO, RAHZEL.
BAROQUEHEAT CAN RUN BY HIMSELF AND SEND SOMEONE TO GET US.
AND OF COURSE THERE'S NO CHANCE YOU'LL DO THE RUNNING, DEAR BROTHER SERA.
OUT OF THE QUES-TION.
DO YOU MEAN THAT I'D GET IN THE WAY, FATHER?
ムッ..
I'M SIMPLY SAYING THAT IT'S MORE EFFICIENT THAT WAY.
YOU COULDN'T POSSIBLY COMPETE WITH HIM.
I COULDN'T POSSIBLY RUN LONG DISTANCES IN THESE CLOTHES.
......
RAHZEL?
I'M GOING TO CHANGE.

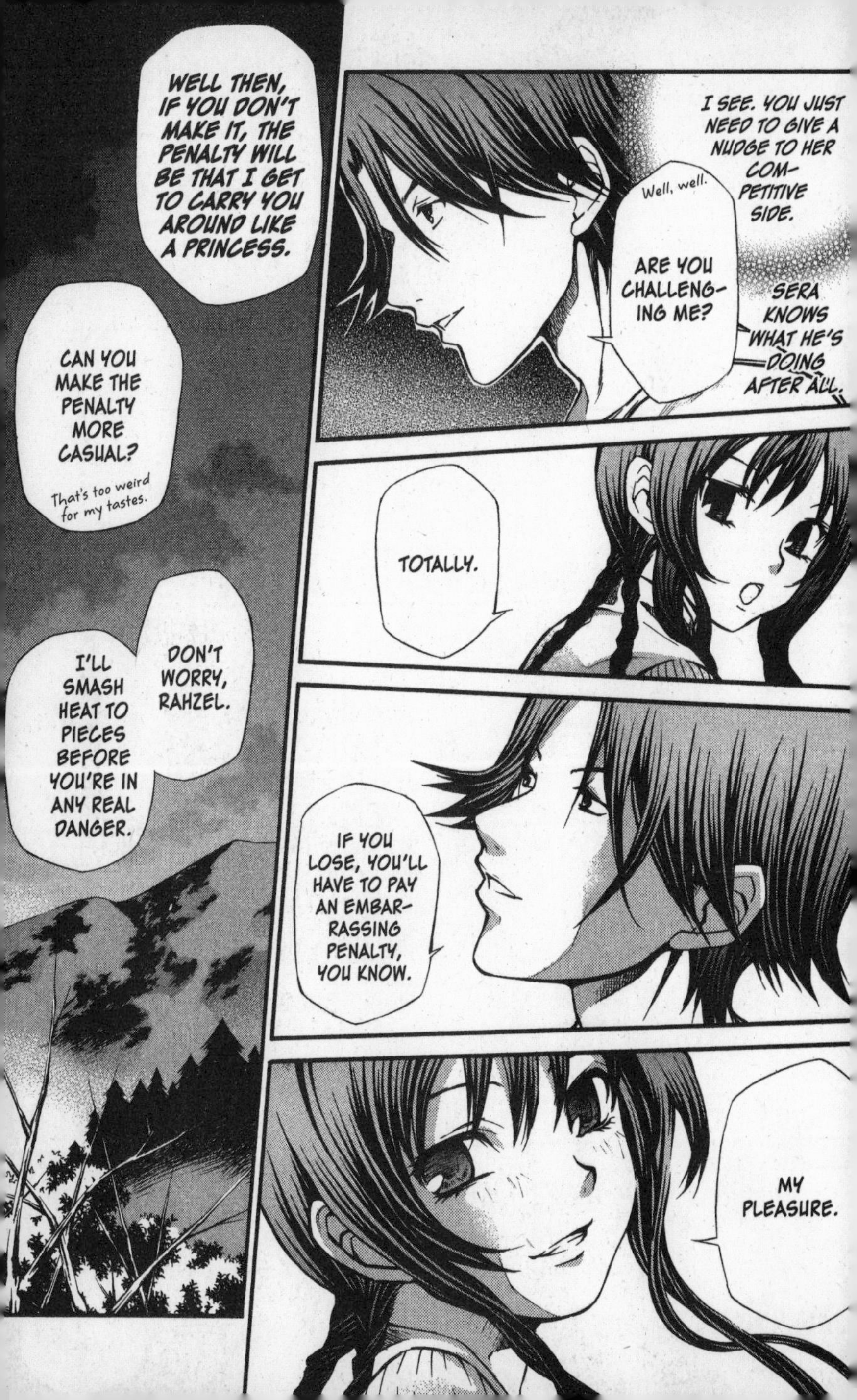
I SEE. YOU JUST NEED TO GIVE A NUDGE TO HER COMPETITIVE SIDE.
SERA KNOWS WHAT HE'S DOING AFTER ALL.
Well, well.
ARE YOU CHALLENGING ME?
TOTALLY.
IF YOU LOSE, YOU'LL HAVE TO PAY AN EMBARRASSING PENALTY, YOU KNOW.
MY PLEASURE.
WELL THEN, IF YOU DON'T MAKE IT, THE PENALTY WILL BE THAT I GET TO CARRY YOU AROUND LIKE A PRINCESS.
CAN YOU MAKE THE PENALTY MORE CASUAL?
That's too weird for my tastes.
DON'T WORRY, RAHZEL.
I'LL SMASH HEAT TO PIECES BEFORE YOU'RE IN ANY REAL DANGER.

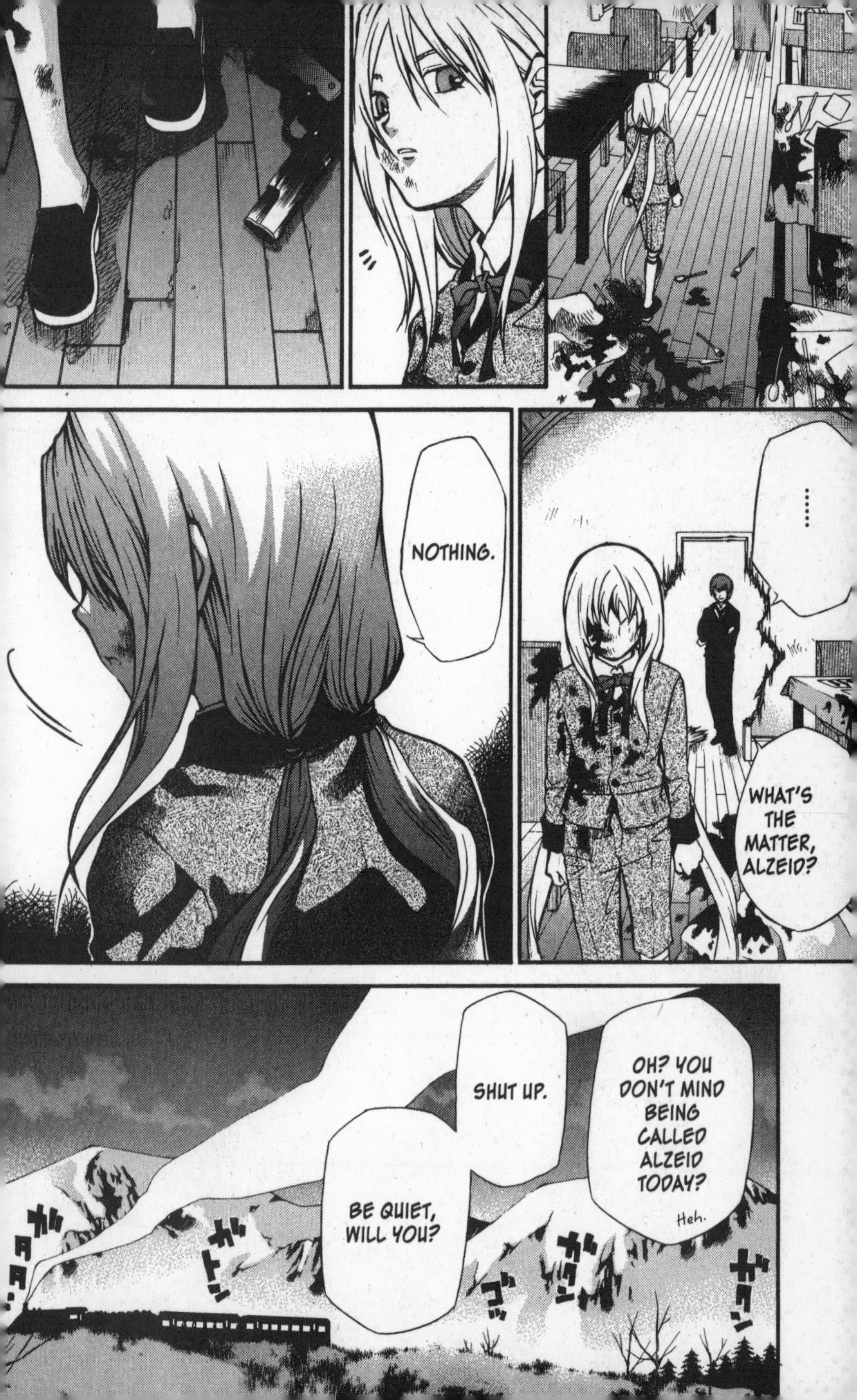
......
WHAT'S THE MATTER, ALZEID?
NOTHING.
OH? YOU DON'T MIND BEING CALLED ALZEID TODAY?
Heh.
SHUT UP.
BE QUIET, WILL YOU?

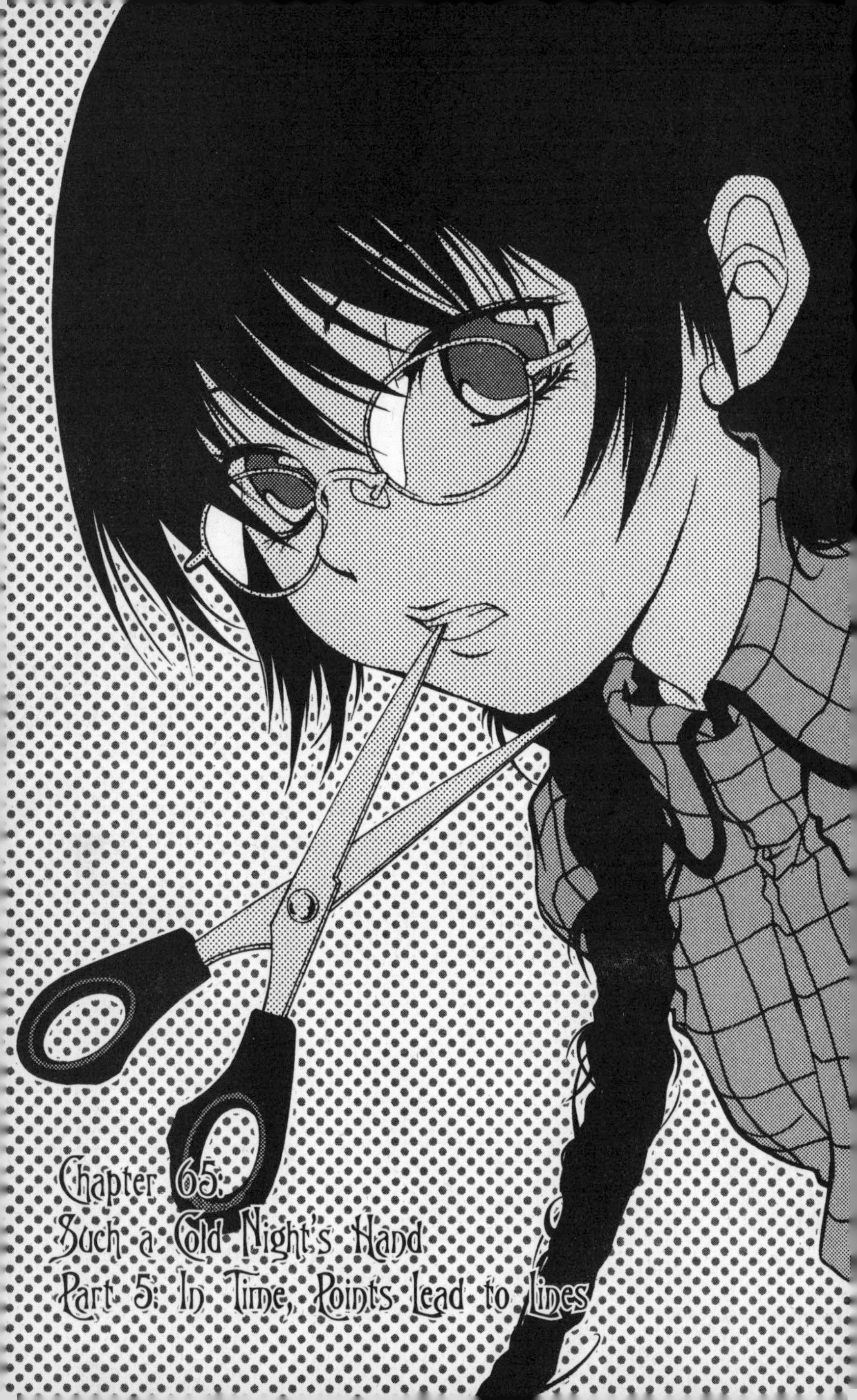
Chapter 65:
Such a Cold Night's Hand
Part 5: In Time, Points Lead to Lines

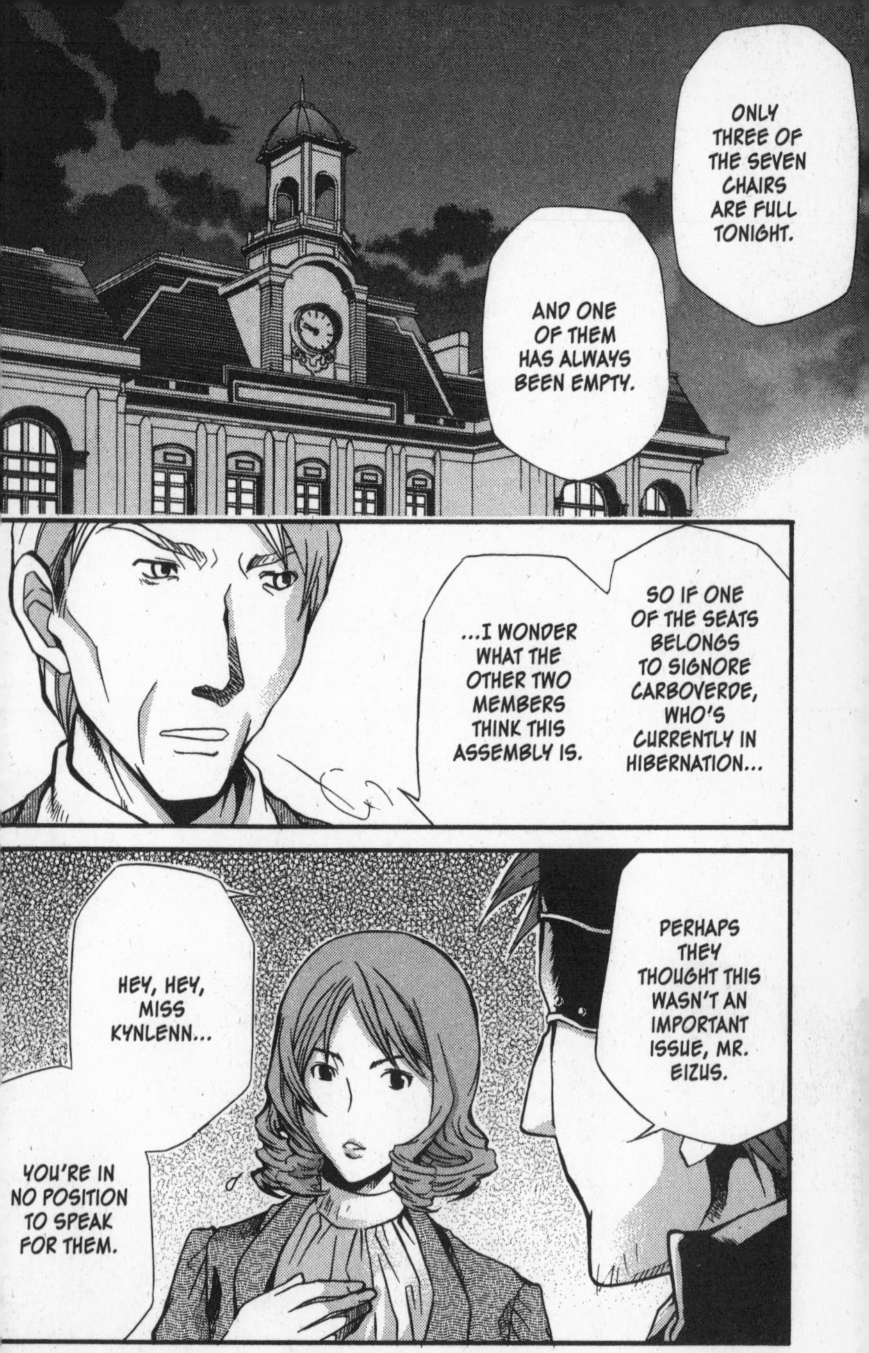
ONLY THREE OF THE SEVEN CHAIRS ARE FULL TONIGHT.
AND ONE OF THEM HAS ALWAYS BEEN EMPTY.
SO IF ONE OF THE SEATS BELONGS TO SIGNORE CARBOVERDE, WHO'S CURRENTLY IN HIBERNATION...
...I WONDER WHAT THE OTHER TWO MEMBERS THINK THIS ASSEMBLY IS.
PERHAPS THEY THOUGHT THIS WASN'T AN IMPORTANT ISSUE, MR. EIZUS.
HEY, HEY, MISS KYNLENN...
YOU'RE IN NO POSITION TO SPEAK FOR THEM.

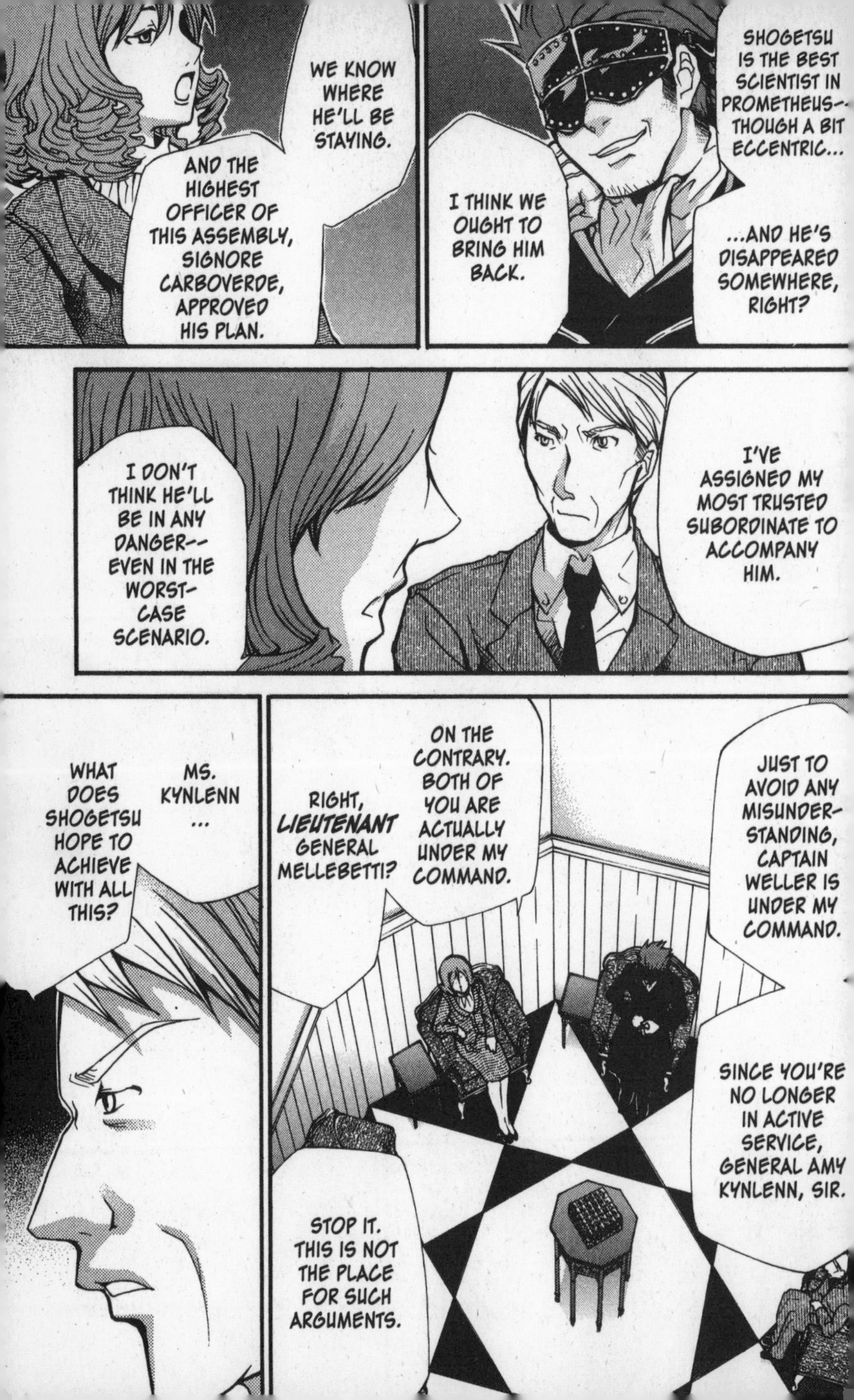

SHOGETSU IS THE BEST SCIENTIST IN PROMETHEUS--THOUGH A BIT ECCENTRIC...
...AND HE'S DISAPPEARED SOMEWHERE, RIGHT?
I THINK WE OUGHT TO BRING HIM BACK.
WE KNOW WHERE HE'LL BE STAYING.
AND THE HIGHEST OFFICER OF THIS ASSEMBLY, SIGNORE CARBOVERDE, APPROVED HIS PLAN.
I'VE ASSIGNED MY MOST TRUSTED SUBORDINATE TO ACCOMPANY HIM.
I DON'T THINK HE'LL BE IN ANY DANGER--EVEN IN THE WORST-CASE SCENARIO.
JUST TO AVOID ANY MISUNDERSTANDING, CAPTAIN WELLER IS UNDER MY COMMAND.
SINCE YOU'RE NO LONGER IN ACTIVE SERVICE, GENERAL AMY KYNLENN, SIR.
ON THE CONTRARY. BOTH OF YOU ARE ACTUALLY UNDER MY COMMAND.
RIGHT, *LIEUTENANT* GENERAL MELLEBETTI?
STOP IT. THIS IS NOT THE PLACE FOR SUCH ARGUMENTS.
MS. KYNLENN...
WHAT DOES SHOGETSU HOPE TO ACHIEVE WITH ALL THIS?

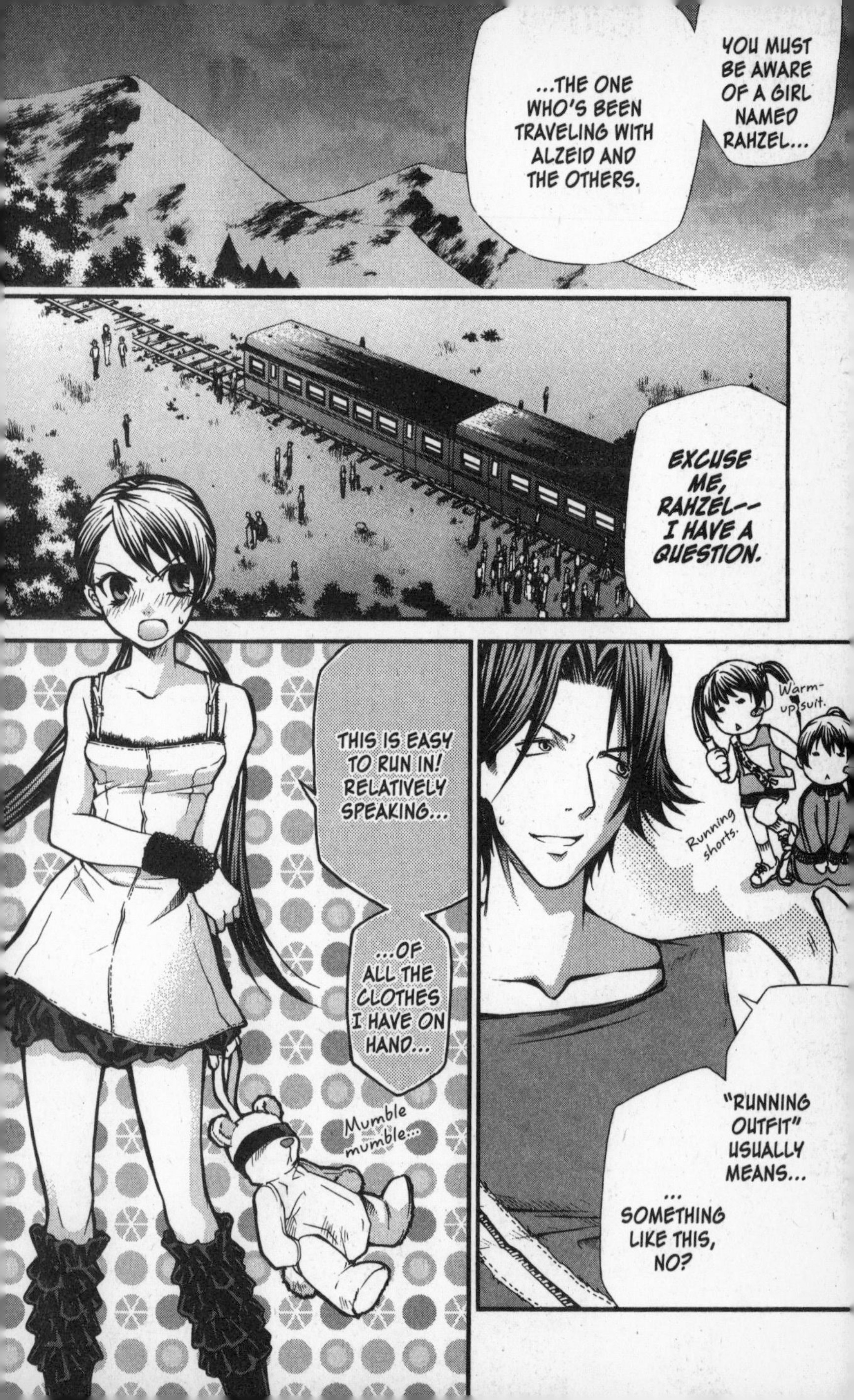
YOU MUST BE AWARE OF A GIRL NAMED RAHZEL...
...THE ONE WHO'S BEEN TRAVELING WITH ALZEID AND THE OTHERS.
EXCUSE ME, RAHZEL-- I HAVE A QUESTION.
"RUNNING OUTFIT" USUALLY MEANS...
... SOMETHING LIKE THIS, NO?
Warm-up suit.
Running shorts.
THIS IS EASY TO RUN IN! RELATIVELY SPEAKING...
...OF ALL THE CLOTHES I HAVE ON HAND...
Mumble mumble...

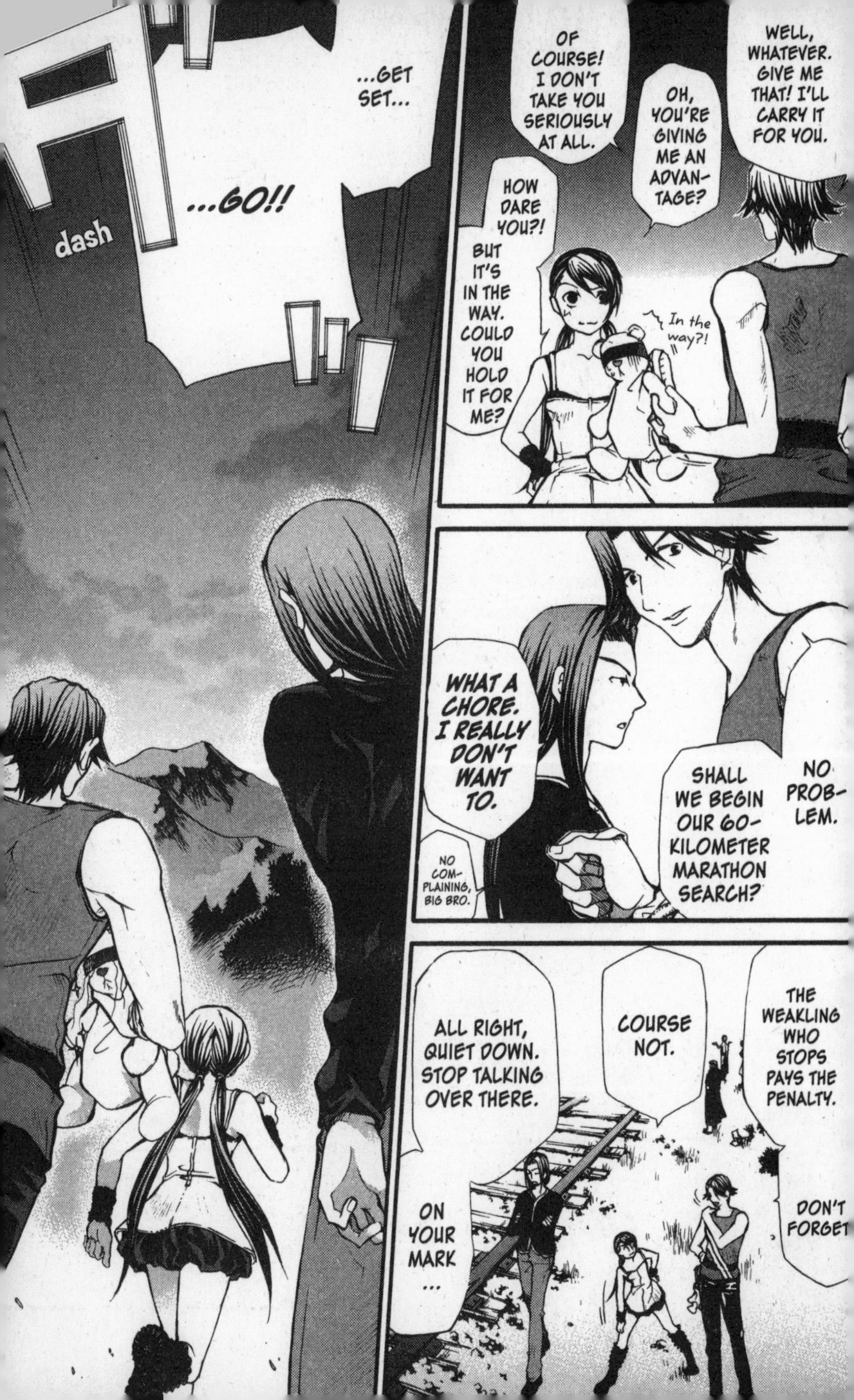
WELL, WHATEVER. GIVE ME THAT! I'LL CARRY IT FOR YOU.
OH, YOU'RE GIVING ME AN ADVANTAGE?
OF COURSE! I DON'T TAKE YOU SERIOUSLY AT ALL.
HOW DARE YOU?!
BUT IT'S IN THE WAY. COULD YOU HOLD IT FOR ME?
In the way?!
NO PROBLEM.
SHALL WE BEGIN OUR 60-KILOMETER MARATHON SEARCH?
WHAT A CHORE. I REALLY DON'T WANT TO.
NO COMPLAINING, BIG BRO.
THE WEAKLING WHO STOPS PAYS THE PENALTY.
DON'T FORGET
COURSE NOT.
ALL RIGHT, QUIET DOWN. STOP TALKING OVER THERE.
ON YOUR MARK ...
...GET SET...
...GO!!
dash

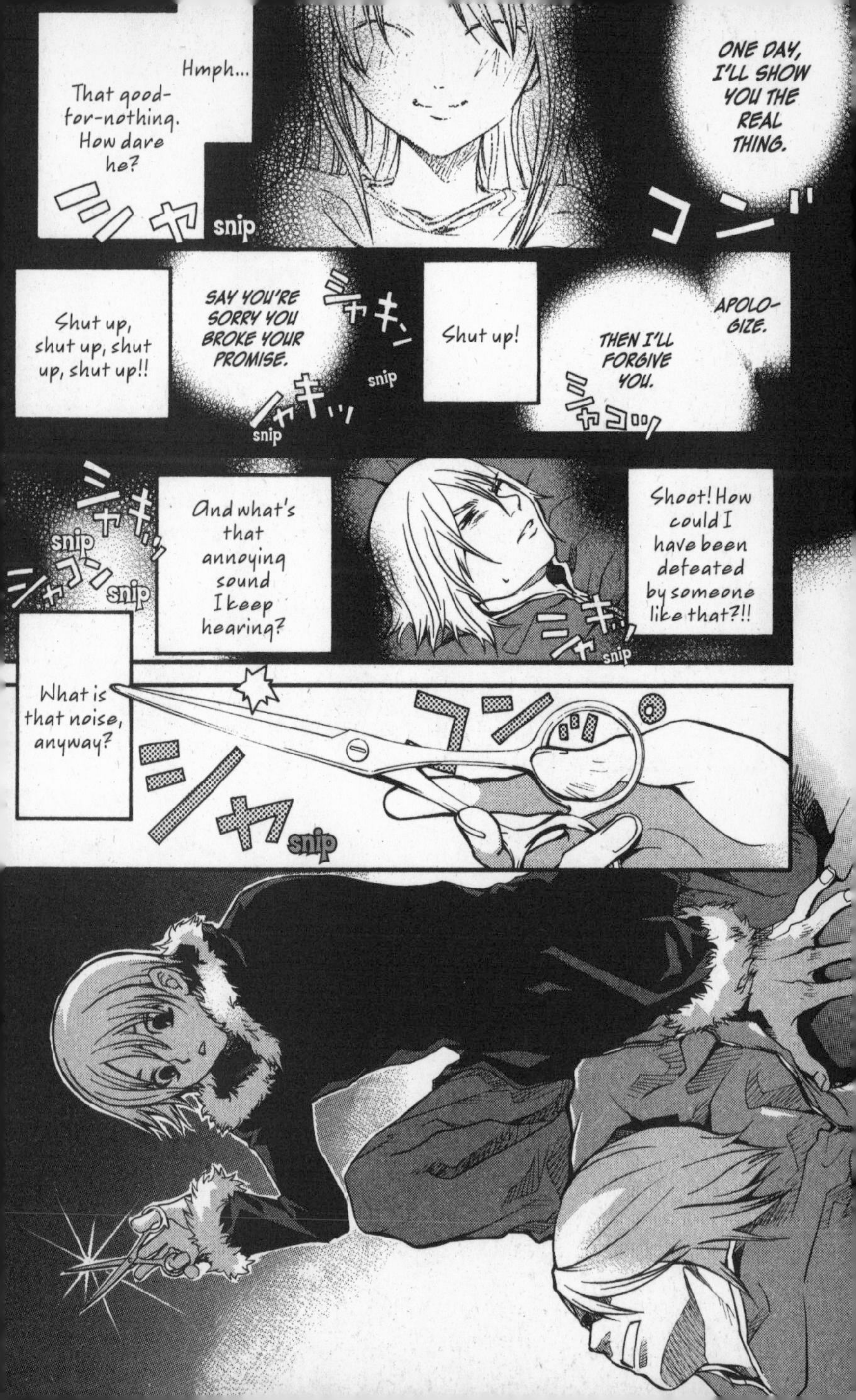

ONE DAY, I'LL SHOW YOU THE REAL THING.
Hmph... That good-for-nothing. How dare he?
snip
APOLOGIZE.
THEN I'LL FORGIVE YOU.
Shut up!
snip
SAY YOU'RE SORRY YOU BROKE YOUR PROMISE.
snip
Shut up, shut up, shut up, shut up!!
Shoot! How could I have been defeated by someone like that?!!
snip
And what's that annoying sound I keep hearing?
snip
snip
What is that noise, anyway?
snip

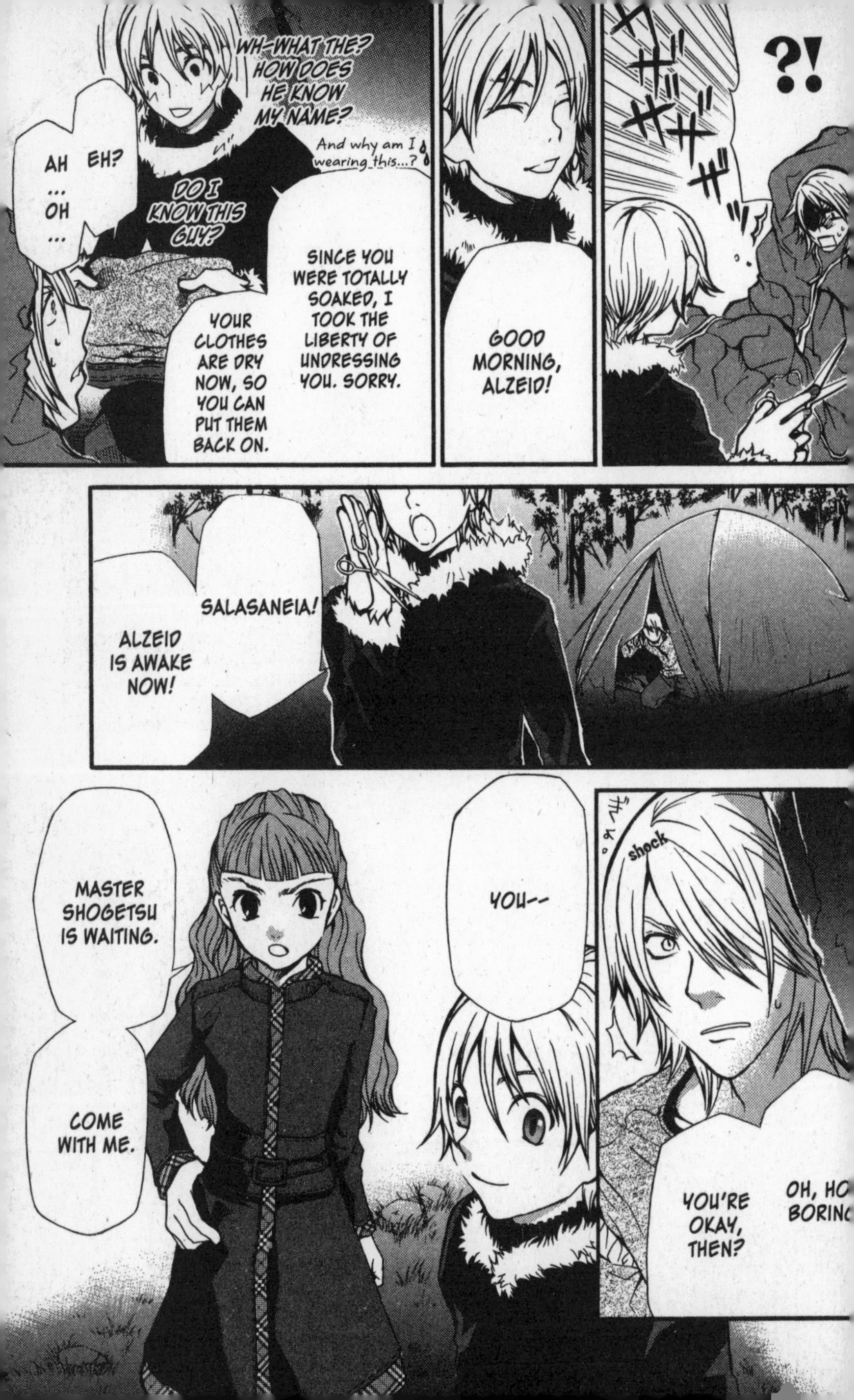
?!
GOOD MORNING, ALZEID!
SINCE YOU WERE TOTALLY SOAKED, I TOOK THE LIBERTY OF UNDRESSING YOU. SORRY.
YOUR CLOTHES ARE DRY NOW, SO YOU CAN PUT THEM BACK ON.
WH-WHAT THE? HOW DOES HE KNOW MY NAME?
And why am I wearing this...?
DO I KNOW THIS GUY?
AH ... OH ... EH?
SALASANEIA!
ALZEID IS AWAKE NOW!
shock
OH, HO BORING
YOU'RE OKAY, THEN?
YOU--
MASTER SHOGETSU IS WAITING.
COME WITH ME.

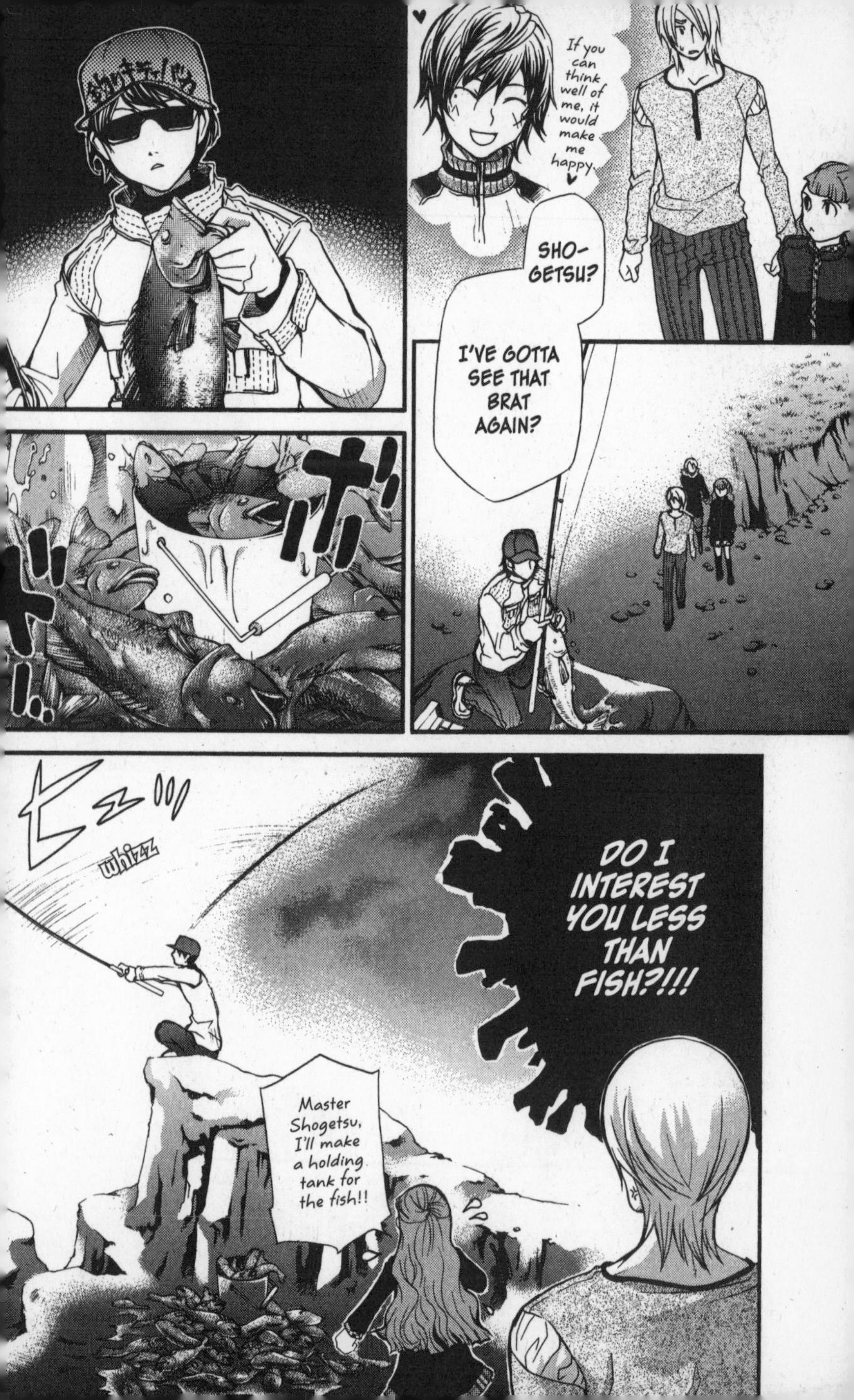
If you can think well of me, it would make me happy. ♥
SHO-GETSU?
I'VE GOTTA SEE THAT BRAT AGAIN?
whizzz
DO I INTEREST YOU LESS THAN FISH?!!!
Master Shogetsu, I'll make a holding tank for the fish!!

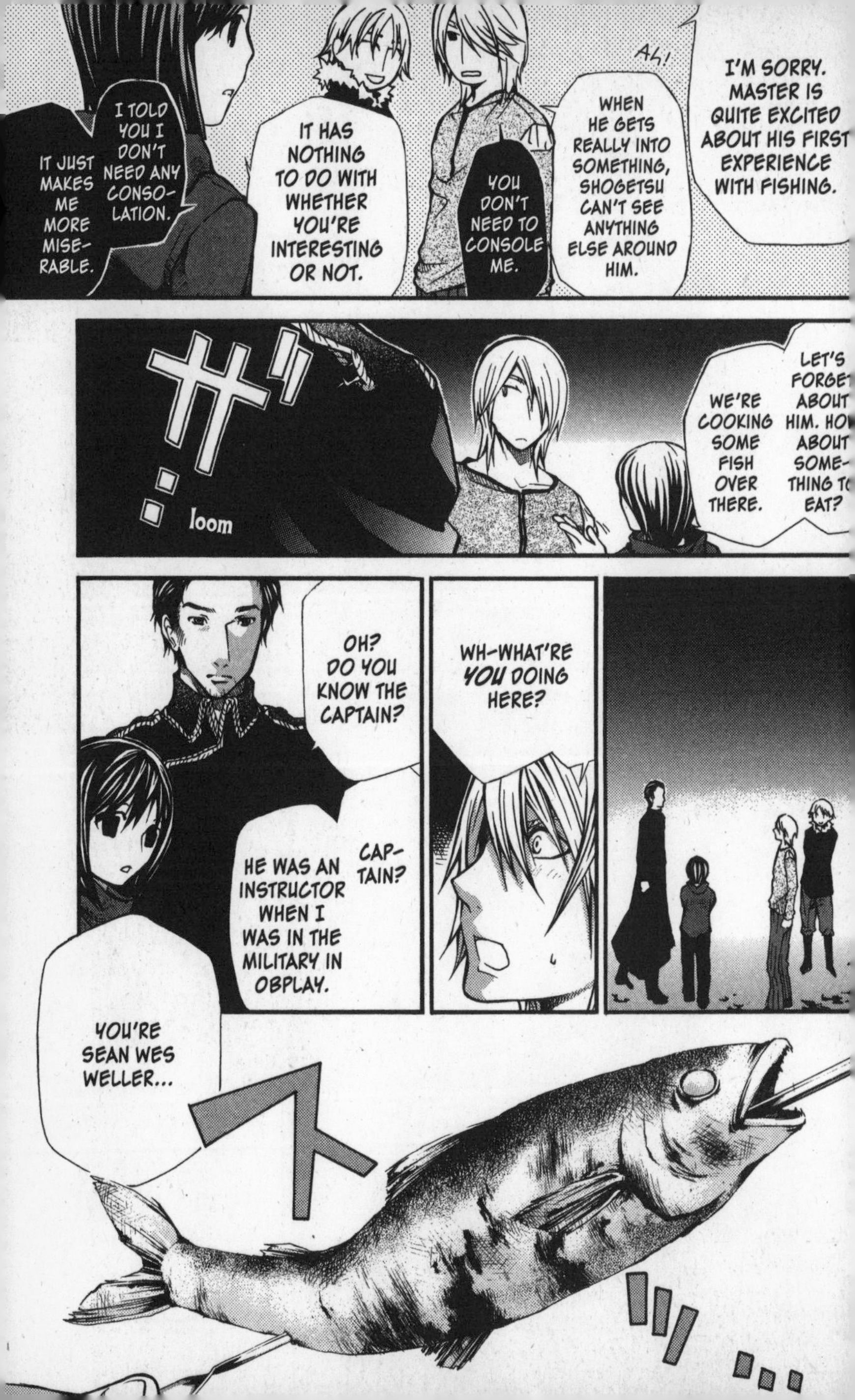
AH!
I'M SORRY. MASTER IS QUITE EXCITED ABOUT HIS FIRST EXPERIENCE WITH FISHING.
WHEN HE GETS REALLY INTO SOMETHING, SHOGETSU CAN'T SEE ANYTHING ELSE AROUND HIM.
YOU DON'T NEED TO CONSOLE ME.
IT HAS NOTHING TO DO WITH WHETHER YOU'RE INTERESTING OR NOT.
I TOLD YOU I DON'T NEED ANY CONSO-LATION.
IT JUST MAKES ME MORE MISE-RABLE.
LET'S FORGET ABOUT HIM. HOW ABOUT SOME-THING TO EAT?
WE'RE COOKING SOME FISH OVER THERE.
loom
WH-WHAT'RE *YOU* DOING HERE?
OH? DO YOU KNOW THE CAPTAIN?
CAP-TAIN?
HE WAS AN INSTRUCTOR WHEN I WAS IN THE MILITARY IN OBPLAY.
YOU'RE SEAN WES WELLER...

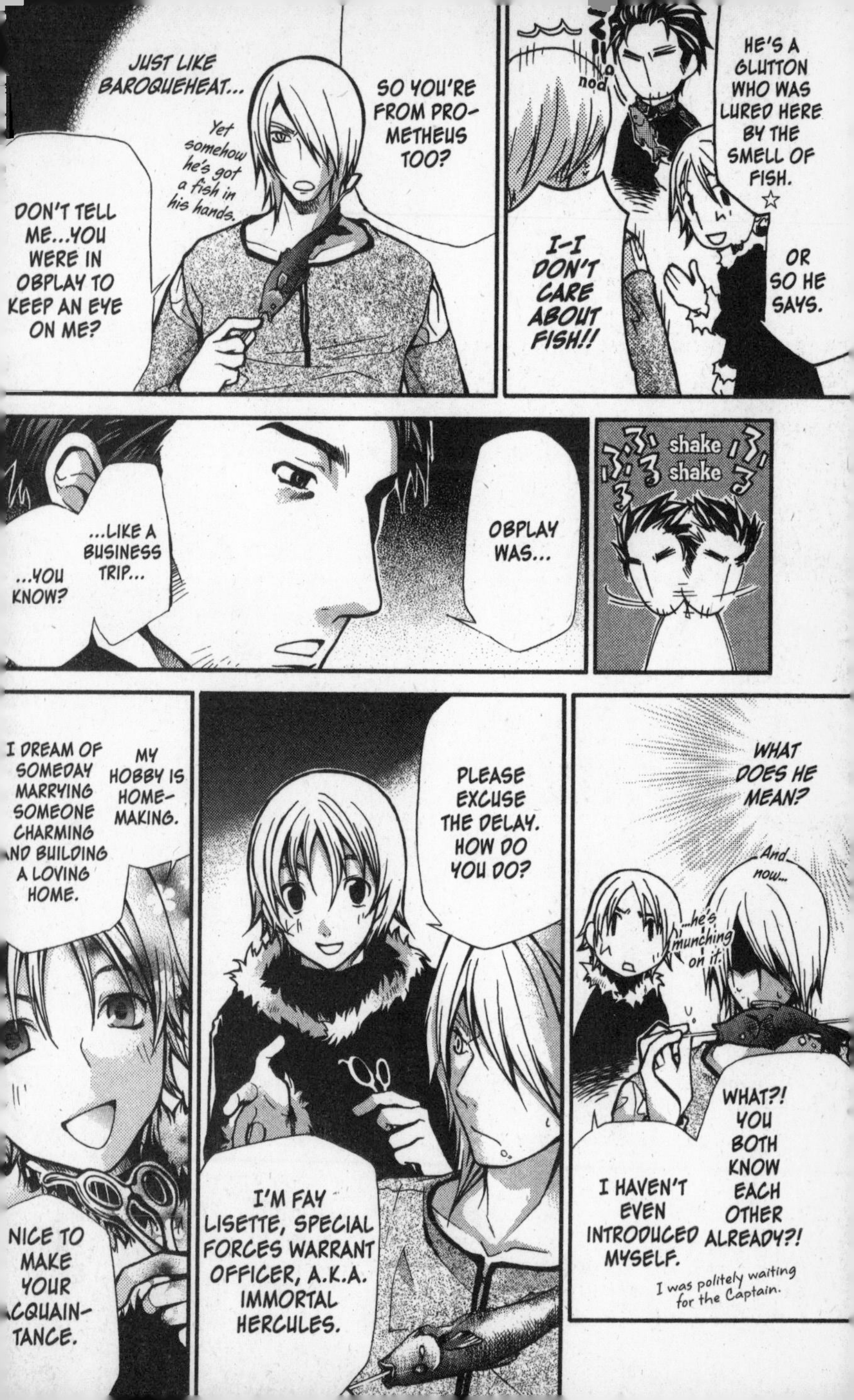

SO YOU'RE FROM PRO-METHEUS TOO?
JUST LIKE BAROQUEHEAT...
Yet somehow he's got a fish in his hands.
DON'T TELL ME...YOU WERE IN OBPLAY TO KEEP AN EYE ON ME?
nod
HE'S A GLUTTON WHO WAS LURED HERE BY THE SMELL OF FISH. ☆
OR SO HE SAYS.
I-I DON'T CARE ABOUT FISH!!
OBPLAY WAS...
...LIKE A BUSINESS TRIP...
...YOU KNOW?
shake shake
WHAT DOES HE MEAN?
And now...
...he's munching on it.
WHAT?! YOU BOTH KNOW EACH OTHER ALREADY?!
I HAVEN'T EVEN INTRODUCED MYSELF.
I was politely waiting for the Captain.
PLEASE EXCUSE THE DELAY. HOW DO YOU DO?
I'M FAY LISETTE, SPECIAL FORCES WARRANT OFFICER, A.K.A. IMMORTAL HERCULES.
MY HOBBY IS HOME-MAKING.
I DREAM OF SOMEDAY MARRYING SOMEONE CHARMING AND BUILDING A LOVING HOME.
NICE TO MAKE YOUR ACQUAIN-TANCE.

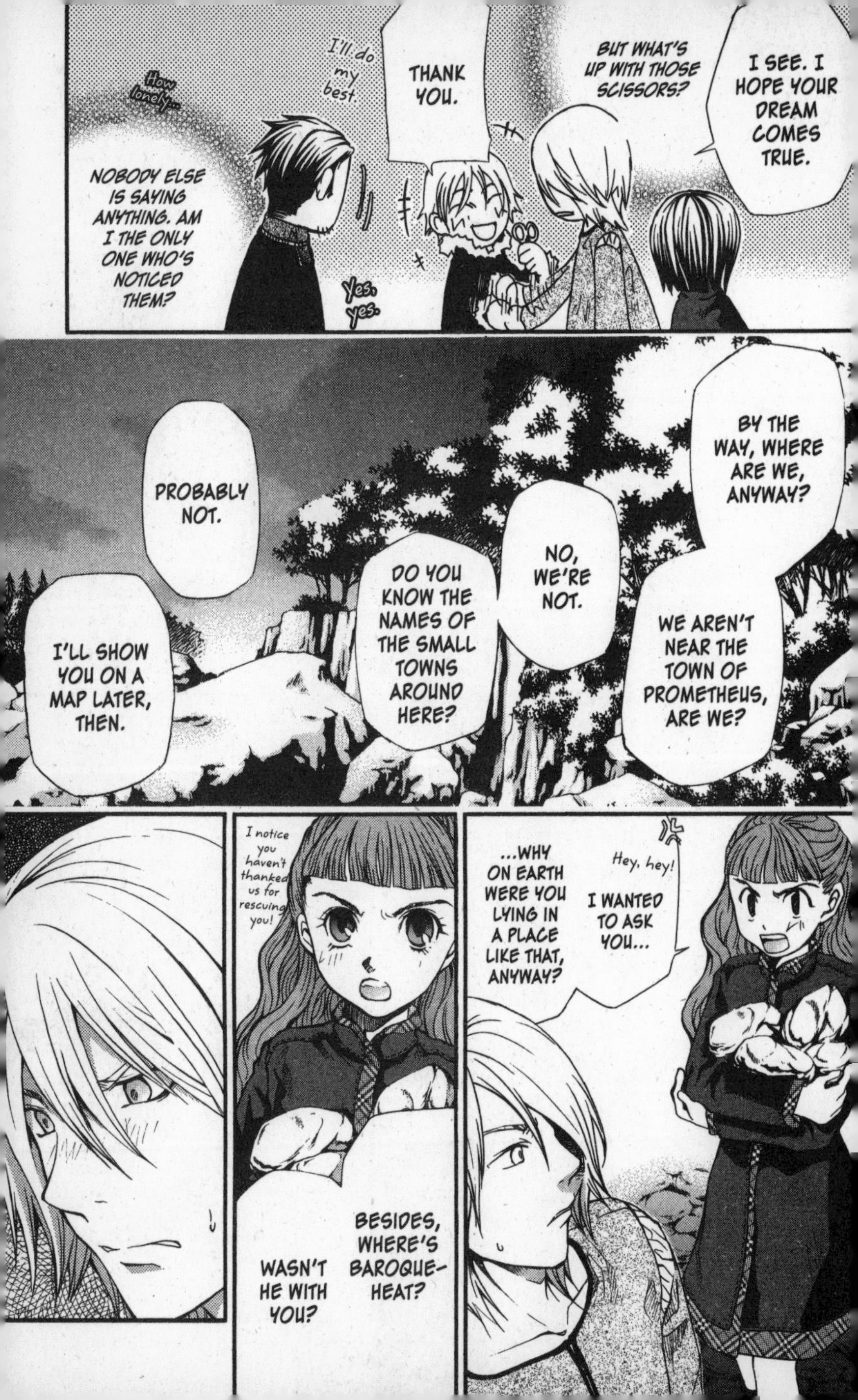

I SEE. I HOPE YOUR DREAM COMES TRUE.
BUT WHAT'S UP WITH THOSE SCISSORS?
THANK YOU.
I'll do my best.
How lonely...
NOBODY ELSE IS SAYING ANYTHING. AM I THE ONLY ONE WHO'S NOTICED THEM?
Yes, yes.
BY THE WAY, WHERE ARE WE, ANYWAY?
WE AREN'T NEAR THE TOWN OF PROMETHEUS, ARE WE?
NO, WE'RE NOT.
DO YOU KNOW THE NAMES OF THE SMALL TOWNS AROUND HERE?
PROBABLY NOT.
I'LL SHOW YOU ON A MAP LATER, THEN.
Hey, hey!
I WANTED TO ASK YOU...
...WHY ON EARTH WERE YOU LYING IN A PLACE LIKE THAT, ANYWAY?
BESIDES, WHERE'S BAROQUE-HEAT?
WASN'T HE WITH YOU?
I notice you haven't thanked us for rescuing you!

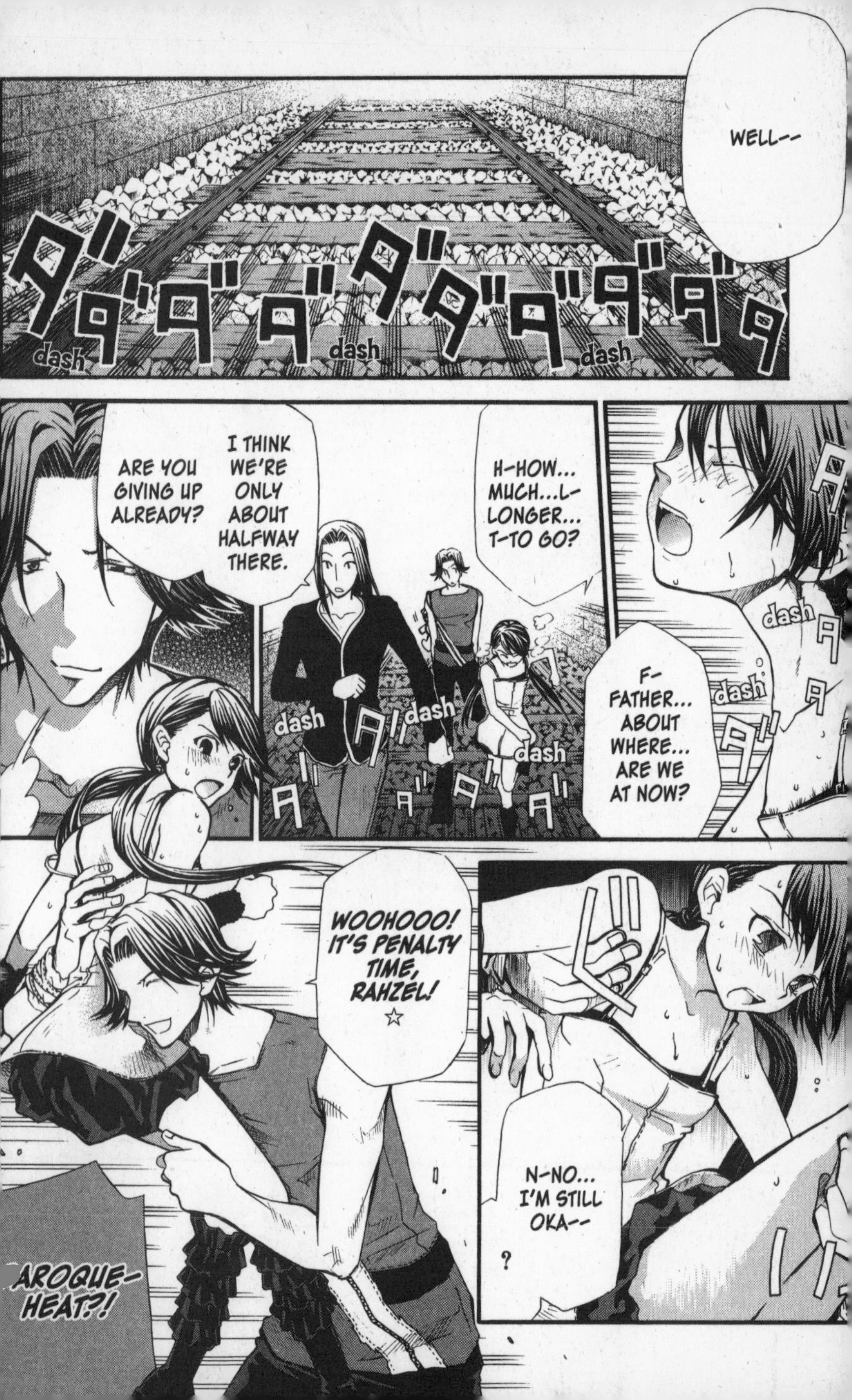
WELL--
dash
dash
dash
F-FATHER... ABOUT WHERE... ARE WE AT NOW?
dash
dash
H-HOW... MUCH...L-LONGER... T-TO GO?
I THINK WE'RE ONLY ABOUT HALFWAY THERE.
ARE YOU GIVING UP ALREADY?
dash
dash
dash
N-NO... I'M STILL OKA--
?
WOOHOOO! IT'S PENALTY TIME, RAHZEL! ☆
AROQUE-HEAT?!

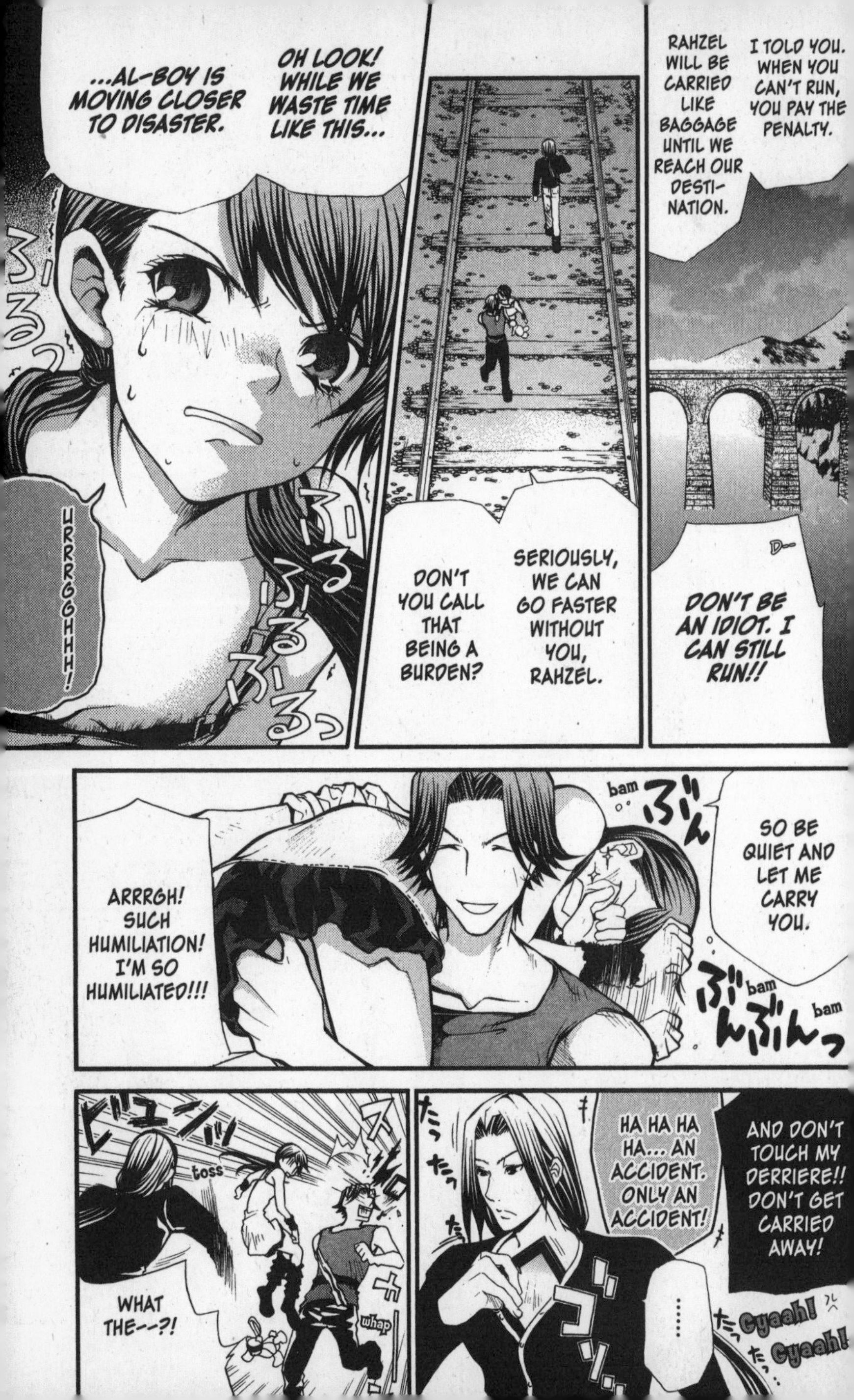
I TOLD YOU. WHEN YOU CAN'T RUN, YOU PAY THE PENALTY.
RAHZEL WILL BE CARRIED LIKE BAGGAGE UNTIL WE REACH OUR DESTI-NATION.
D--
DON'T BE AN IDIOT. I CAN STILL RUN!!
SERIOUSLY, WE CAN GO FASTER WITHOUT YOU, RAHZEL.
DON'T YOU CALL THAT BEING A BURDEN?
OH LOOK! WHILE WE WASTE TIME LIKE THIS...
...AL-BOY IS MOVING CLOSER TO DISASTER.
URRRGGHHH!
SO BE QUIET AND LET ME CARRY YOU.
bam
bam
bam
ARRRGH! SUCH HUMILIATION! I'M SO HUMILIATED!!!
AND DON'T TOUCH MY DERRIERE!! DON'T GET CARRIED AWAY!
HA HA HA HA... AN ACCIDENT. ONLY AN ACCIDENT!
......
Gyaah!
Gyaah!
toss
whap
WHAT THE--?!

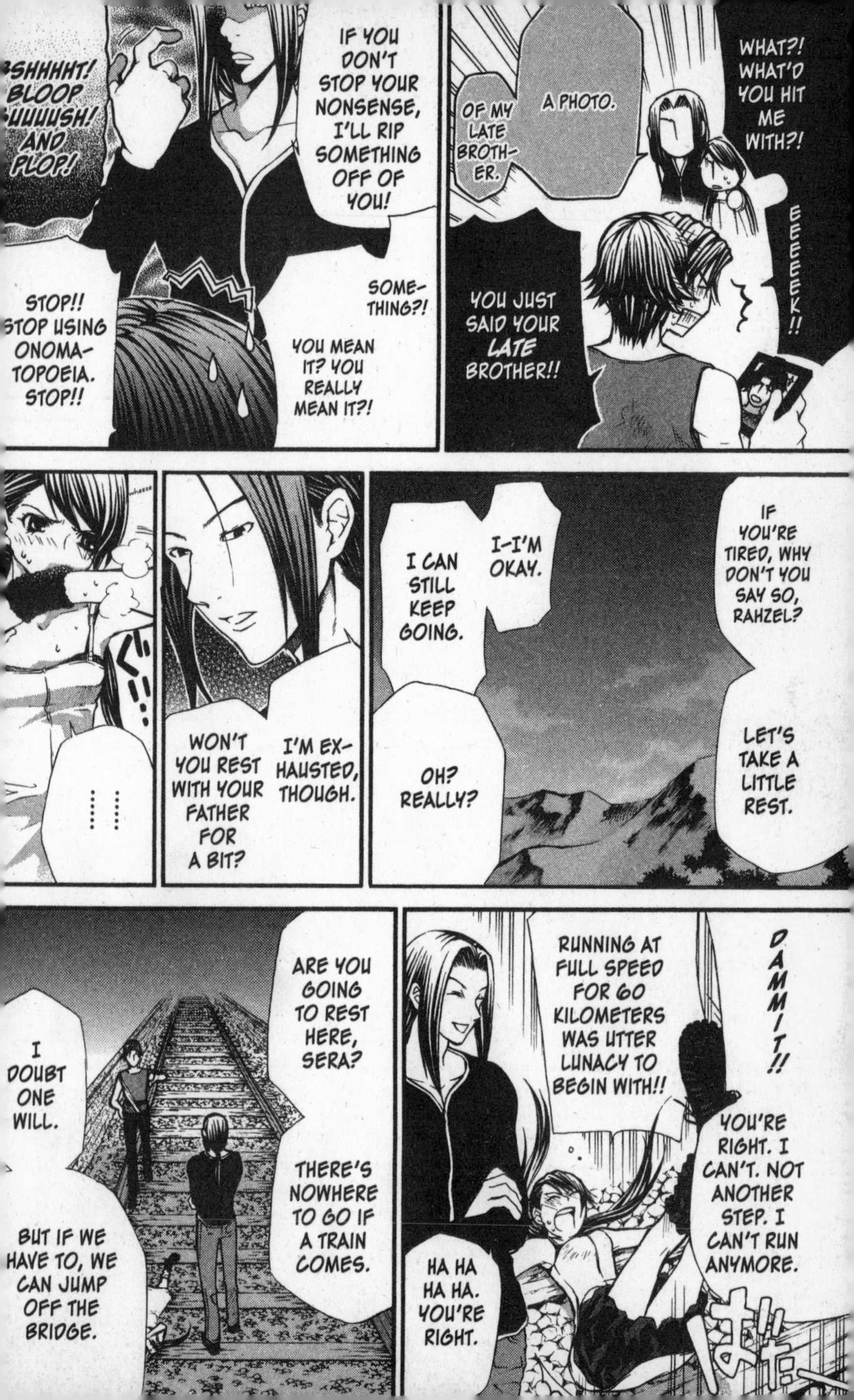
WHAT?! WHAT'D YOU HIT ME WITH?!
EEEEEK!!
A PHOTO.
OF MY LATE BROTHER.
YOU JUST SAID YOUR LATE BROTHER!!
IF YOU DON'T STOP YOUR NONSENSE, I'LL RIP SOMETHING OFF OF YOU!
SOME-THING?!
YOU MEAN IT? YOU REALLY MEAN IT?!
SHHHHT! BLOOP UUUUSH! AND PLOP!
STOP!! STOP USING ONOMATOPOEIA. STOP!!
IF YOU'RE TIRED, WHY DON'T YOU SAY SO, RAHZEL?
LET'S TAKE A LITTLE REST.
I-I'M OKAY.
I CAN STILL KEEP GOING.
OH? REALLY?
I'M EX-HAUSTED, THOUGH.
WON'T YOU REST WITH YOUR FATHER FOR A BIT?
wheeze
......
DAMMIT!!
RUNNING AT FULL SPEED FOR 60 KILOMETERS WAS UTTER LUNACY TO BEGIN WITH!!
YOU'RE RIGHT. I CAN'T. NOT ANOTHER STEP. I CAN'T RUN ANYMORE.
HA HA HA HA. YOU'RE RIGHT.
ARE YOU GOING TO REST HERE, SERA?
THERE'S NOWHERE TO GO IF A TRAIN COMES.
I DOUBT ONE WILL.
BUT IF WE HAVE TO, WE CAN JUMP OFF THE BRIDGE.

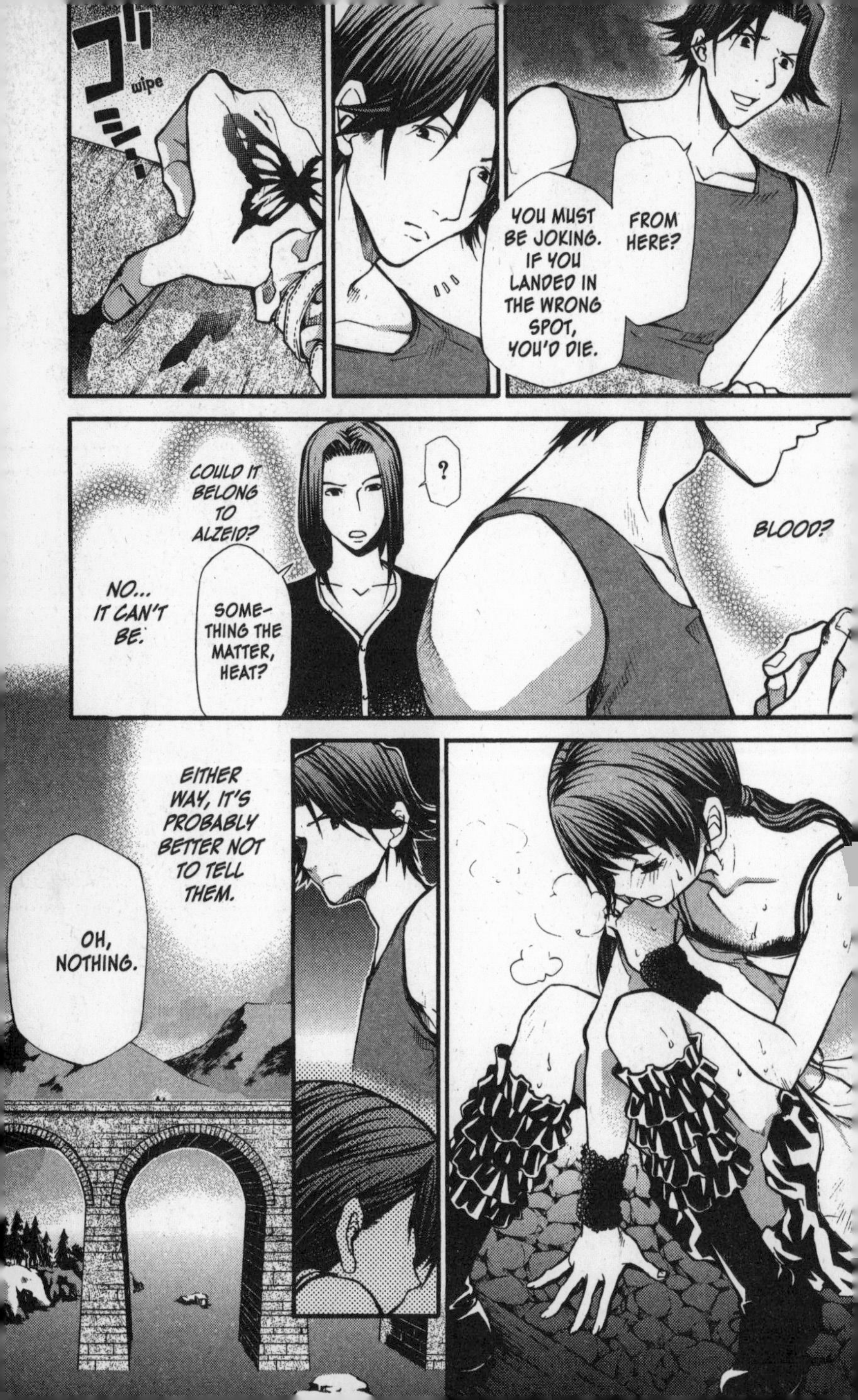
FROM HERE?
YOU MUST BE JOKING. IF YOU LANDED IN THE WRONG SPOT, YOU'D DIE.
wipe
BLOOD?
?
COULD IT BELONG TO ALZEID?
NO... IT CAN'T BE.
SOME-THING THE MATTER, HEAT?
EITHER WAY, IT'S PROBABLY BETTER NOT TO TELL THEM.
OH, NOTHING.

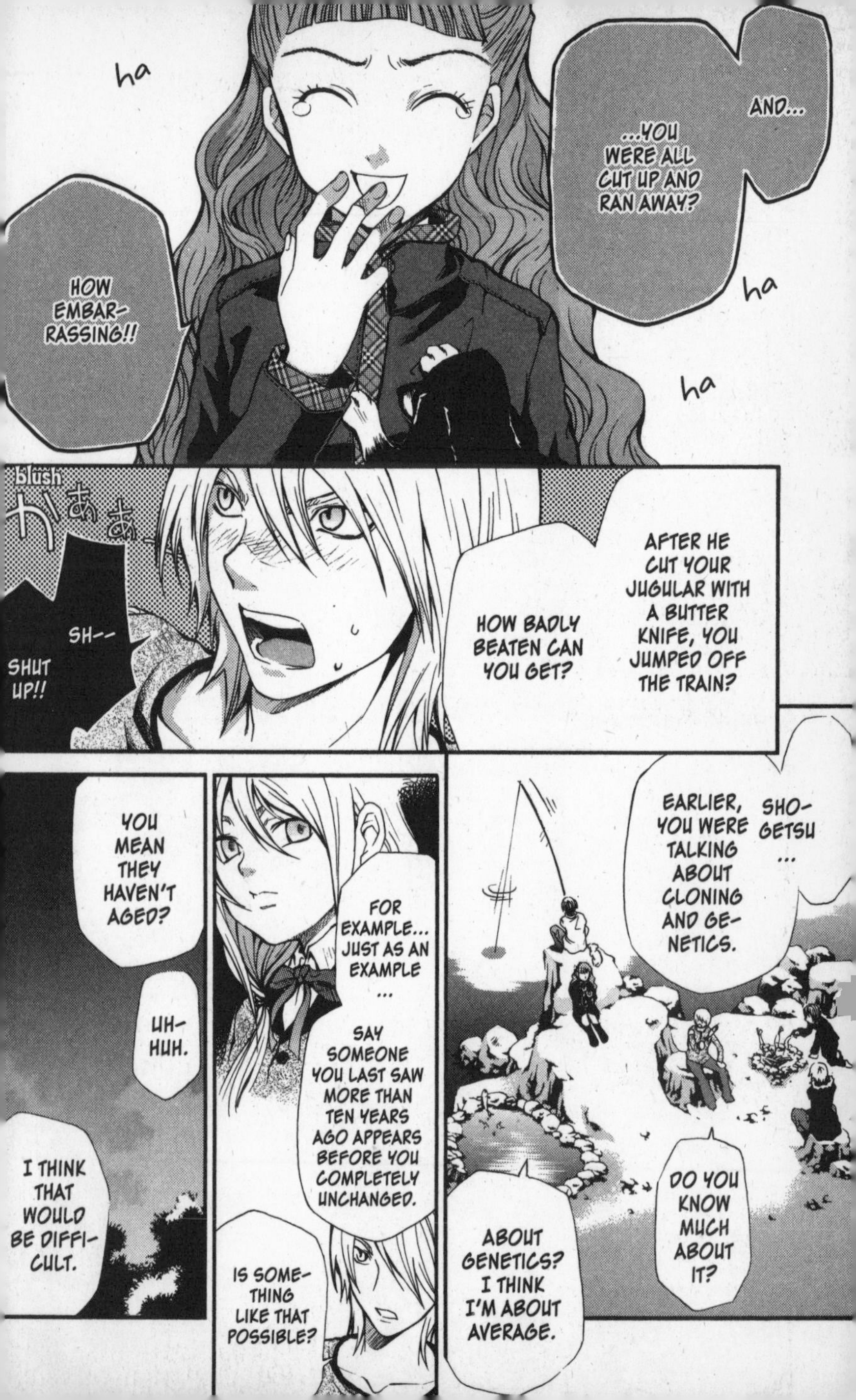
ha
AND...
...YOU WERE ALL CUT UP AND RAN AWAY?
ha
ha
HOW EMBARRASSING!!
AFTER HE CUT YOUR JUGULAR WITH A BUTTER KNIFE, YOU JUMPED OFF THE TRAIN?
HOW BADLY BEATEN CAN YOU GET?
blush
SH-- SHUT UP!!
SHO-GETSU ...
EARLIER, YOU WERE TALKING ABOUT CLONING AND GE-NETICS.
DO YOU KNOW MUCH ABOUT IT?
ABOUT GENETICS? I THINK I'M ABOUT AVERAGE.
FOR EXAMPLE... JUST AS AN EXAMPLE ...
SAY SOMEONE YOU LAST SAW MORE THAN TEN YEARS AGO APPEARS BEFORE YOU COMPLETELY UNCHANGED.
IS SOME-THING LIKE THAT POSSIBLE?
YOU MEAN THEY HAVEN'T AGED?
UH-HUH.
I THINK THAT WOULD BE DIFFI-CULT.

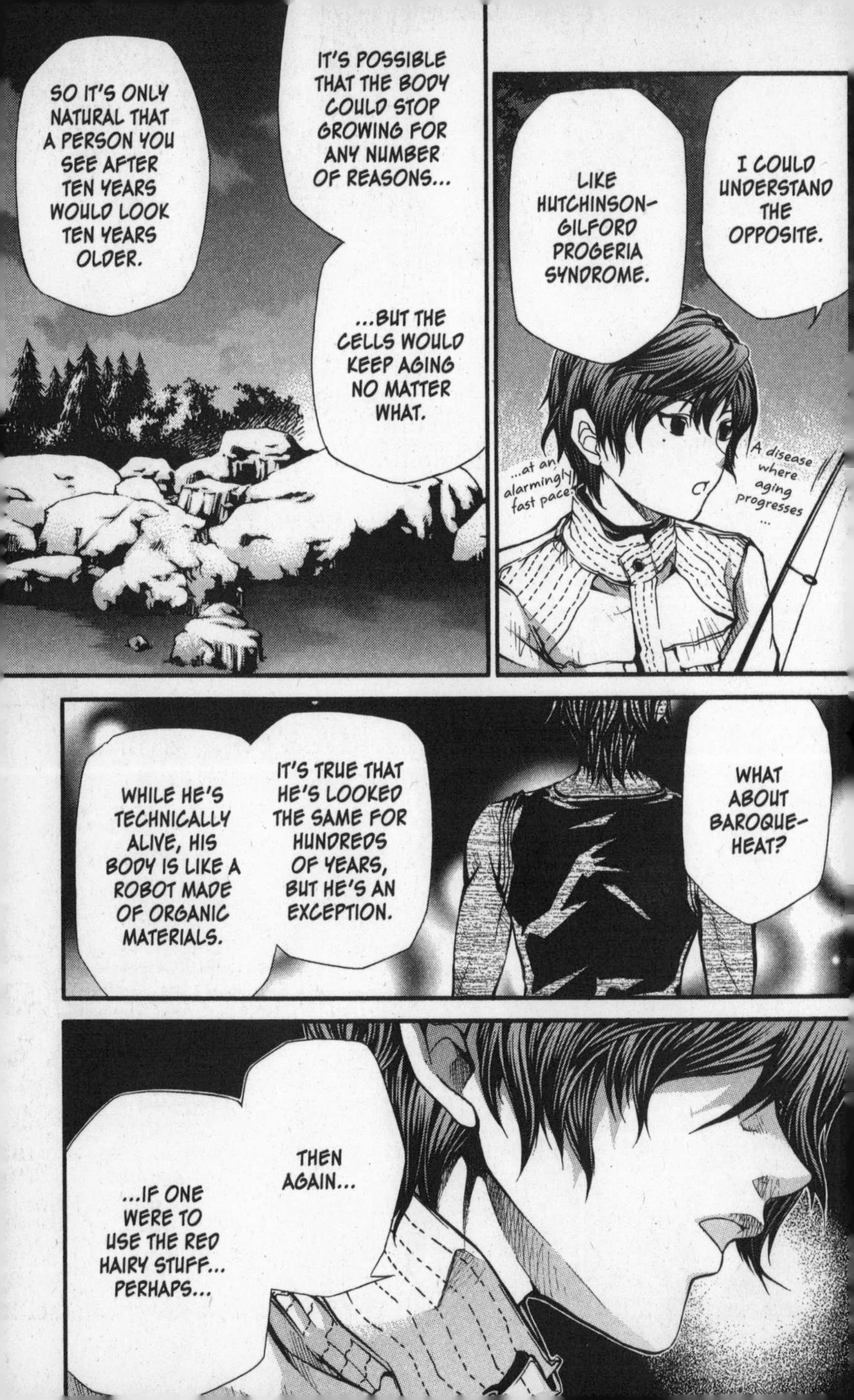

I COULD UNDERSTAND THE OPPOSITE.
LIKE HUTCHINSON-GILFORD PROGERIA SYNDROME.
A disease where aging progresses ...
...at an alarmingly fast pace.
IT'S POSSIBLE THAT THE BODY COULD STOP GROWING FOR ANY NUMBER OF REASONS...
...BUT THE CELLS WOULD KEEP AGING NO MATTER WHAT.
SO IT'S ONLY NATURAL THAT A PERSON YOU SEE AFTER TEN YEARS WOULD LOOK TEN YEARS OLDER.
WHAT ABOUT BAROQUE-HEAT?
IT'S TRUE THAT HE'S LOOKED THE SAME FOR HUNDREDS OF YEARS, BUT HE'S AN EXCEPTION.
WHILE HE'S TECHNICALLY ALIVE, HIS BODY IS LIKE A ROBOT MADE OF ORGANIC MATERIALS.
THEN AGAIN...
...IF ONE WERE TO USE THE RED HAIRY STUFF... PERHAPS...

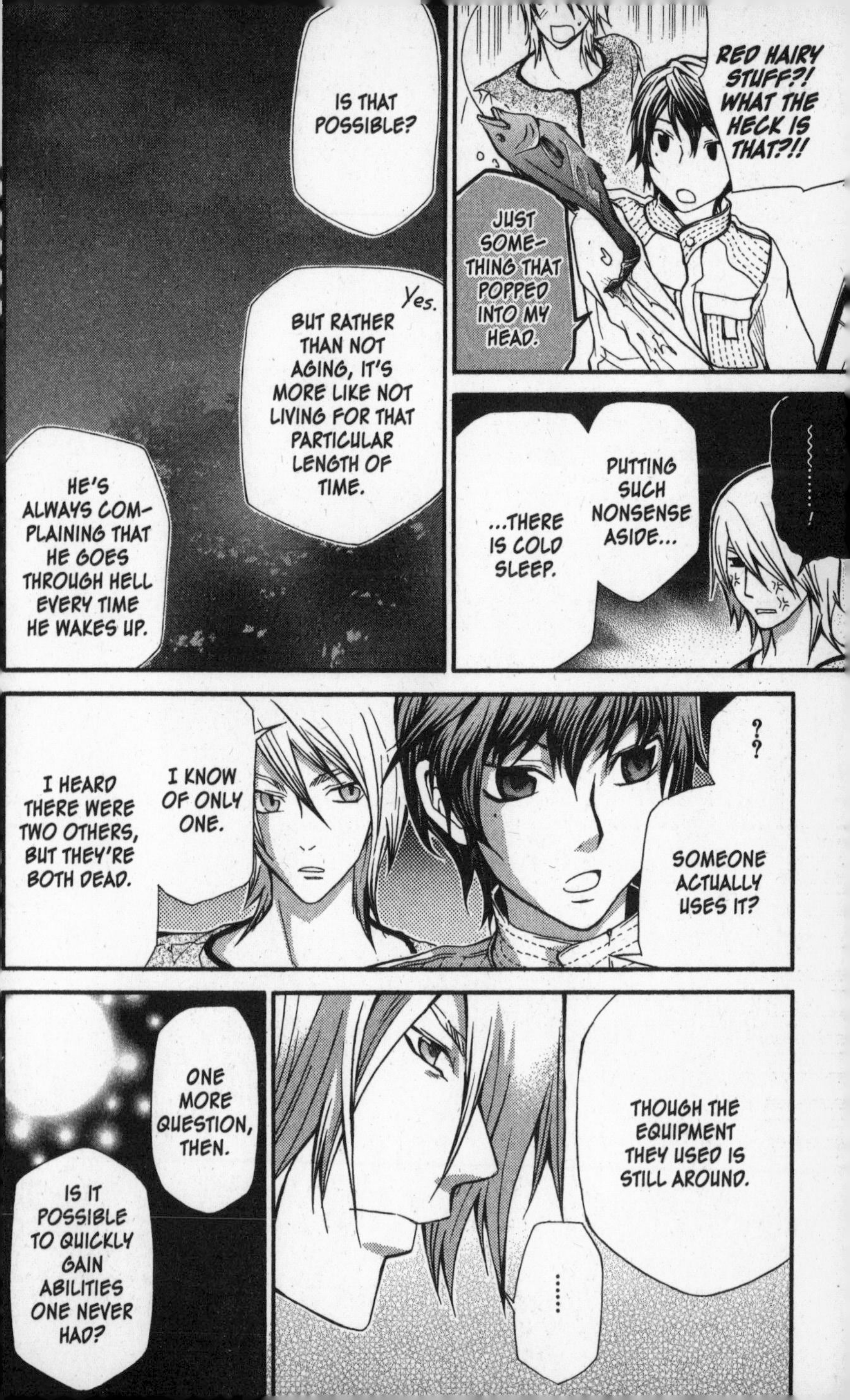
RED HAIRY STUFF?! WHAT THE HECK IS THAT?!!
JUST SOME-THING THAT POPPED INTO MY HEAD.
PUTTING SUCH NONSENSE ASIDE...
...THERE IS COLD SLEEP.
......!
IS THAT POSSIBLE?
Yes.
BUT RATHER THAN NOT AGING, IT'S MORE LIKE NOT LIVING FOR THAT PARTICULAR LENGTH OF TIME.
HE'S ALWAYS COM-PLAINING THAT HE GOES THROUGH HELL EVERY TIME HE WAKES UP.
??
SOMEONE ACTUALLY USES IT?
I KNOW OF ONLY ONE.
I HEARD THERE WERE TWO OTHERS, BUT THEY'RE BOTH DEAD.
THOUGH THE EQUIPMENT THEY USED IS STILL AROUND.
......
ONE MORE QUESTION, THEN.
IS IT POSSIBLE TO QUICKLY GAIN ABILITIES ONE NEVER HAD?

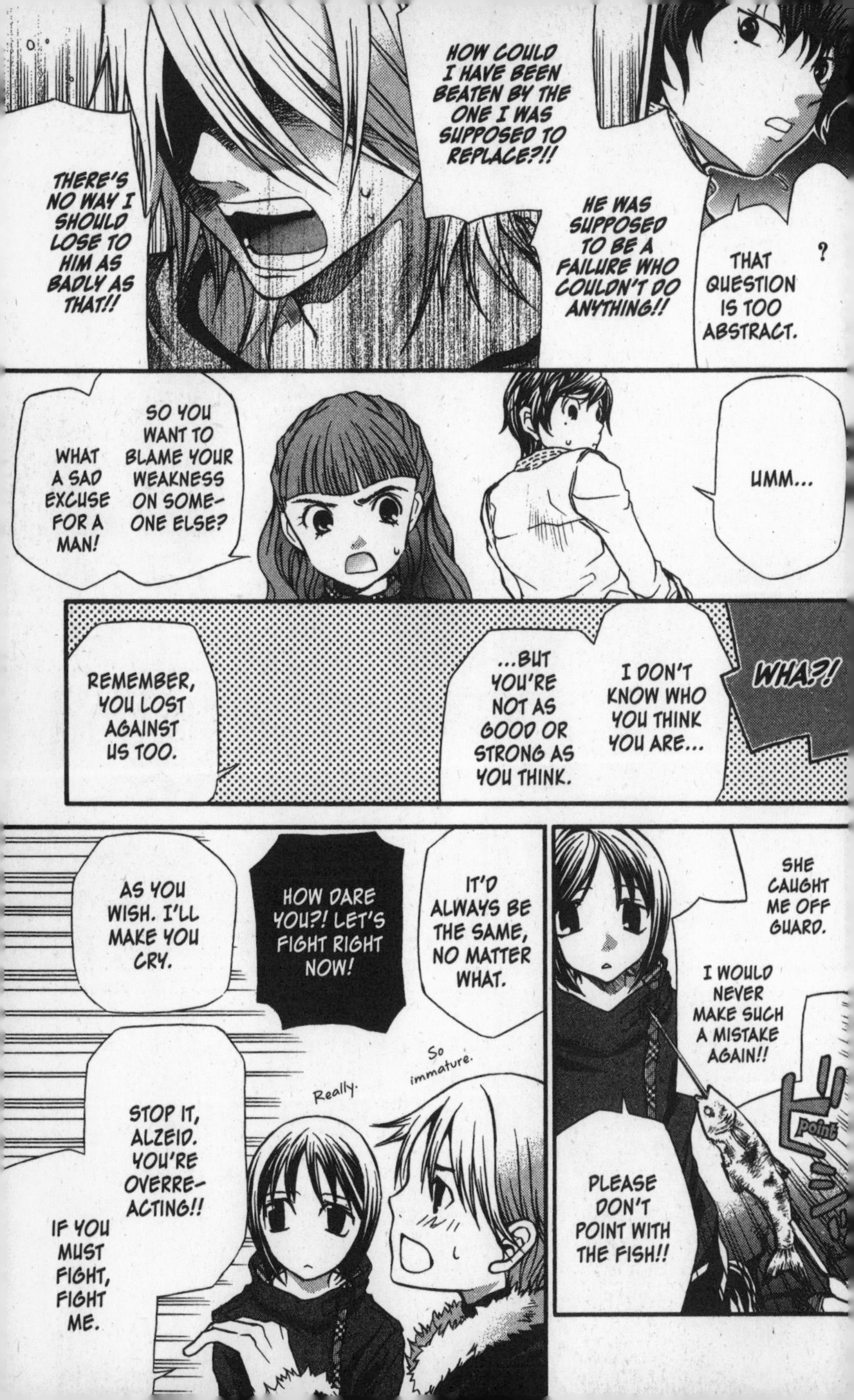
?
THAT QUESTION IS TOO ABSTRACT.
HE WAS SUPPOSED TO BE A FAILURE WHO COULDN'T DO ANYTHING!!
HOW COULD I HAVE BEEN BEATEN BY THE ONE I WAS SUPPOSED TO REPLACE?!!
THERE'S NO WAY I SHOULD LOSE TO HIM AS BADLY AS THAT!!
UMM...
SO YOU WANT TO BLAME YOUR WEAKNESS ON SOME-ONE ELSE?
WHAT A SAD EXCUSE FOR A MAN!
WHA?!
I DON'T KNOW WHO YOU THINK YOU ARE...
...BUT YOU'RE NOT AS GOOD OR STRONG AS YOU THINK.
REMEMBER, YOU LOST AGAINST US TOO.
SHE CAUGHT ME OFF GUARD.
I WOULD NEVER MAKE SUCH A MISTAKE AGAIN!!
point
PLEASE DON'T POINT WITH THE FISH!!
IT'D ALWAYS BE THE SAME, NO MATTER WHAT.
HOW DARE YOU?! LET'S FIGHT RIGHT NOW!
AS YOU WISH. I'LL MAKE YOU CRY.
So immature.
Really.
STOP IT, ALZEID. YOU'RE OVERRE-ACTING!!
IF YOU MUST FIGHT, FIGHT ME.

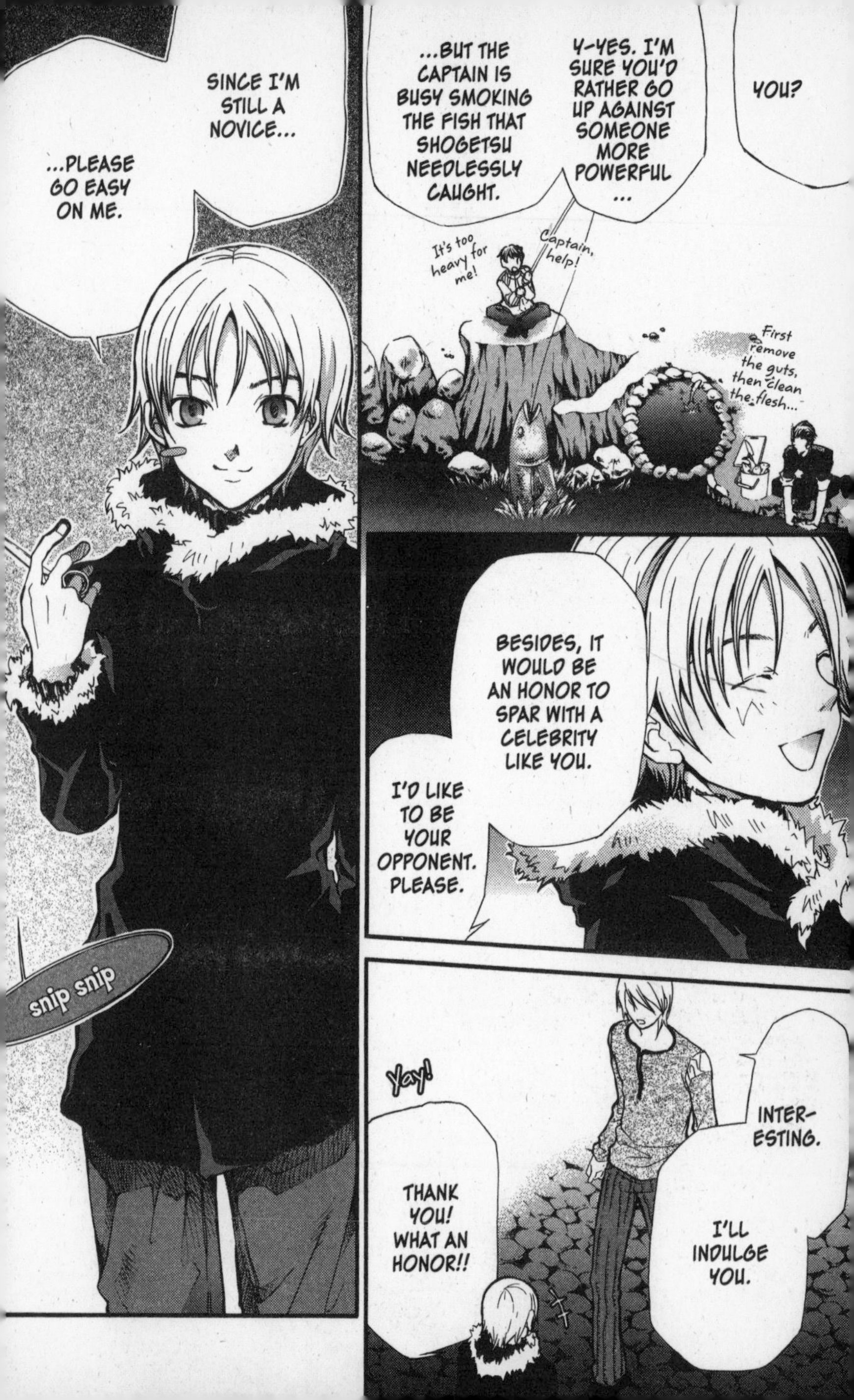
YOU?
Y-YES. I'M SURE YOU'D RATHER GO UP AGAINST SOMEONE MORE POWERFUL...
...BUT THE CAPTAIN IS BUSY SMOKING THE FISH THAT SHOGETSU NEEDLESSLY CAUGHT.
First remove the guts, then clean the flesh...
Captain, help!
It's too heavy for me!
SINCE I'M STILL A NOVICE...
...PLEASE GO EASY ON ME.
snip snip
BESIDES, IT WOULD BE AN HONOR TO SPAR WITH A CELEBRITY LIKE YOU.
I'D LIKE TO BE YOUR OPPONENT. PLEASE.
INTER-ESTING.
I'LL INDULGE YOU.
Yay!
THANK YOU! WHAT AN HONOR!!

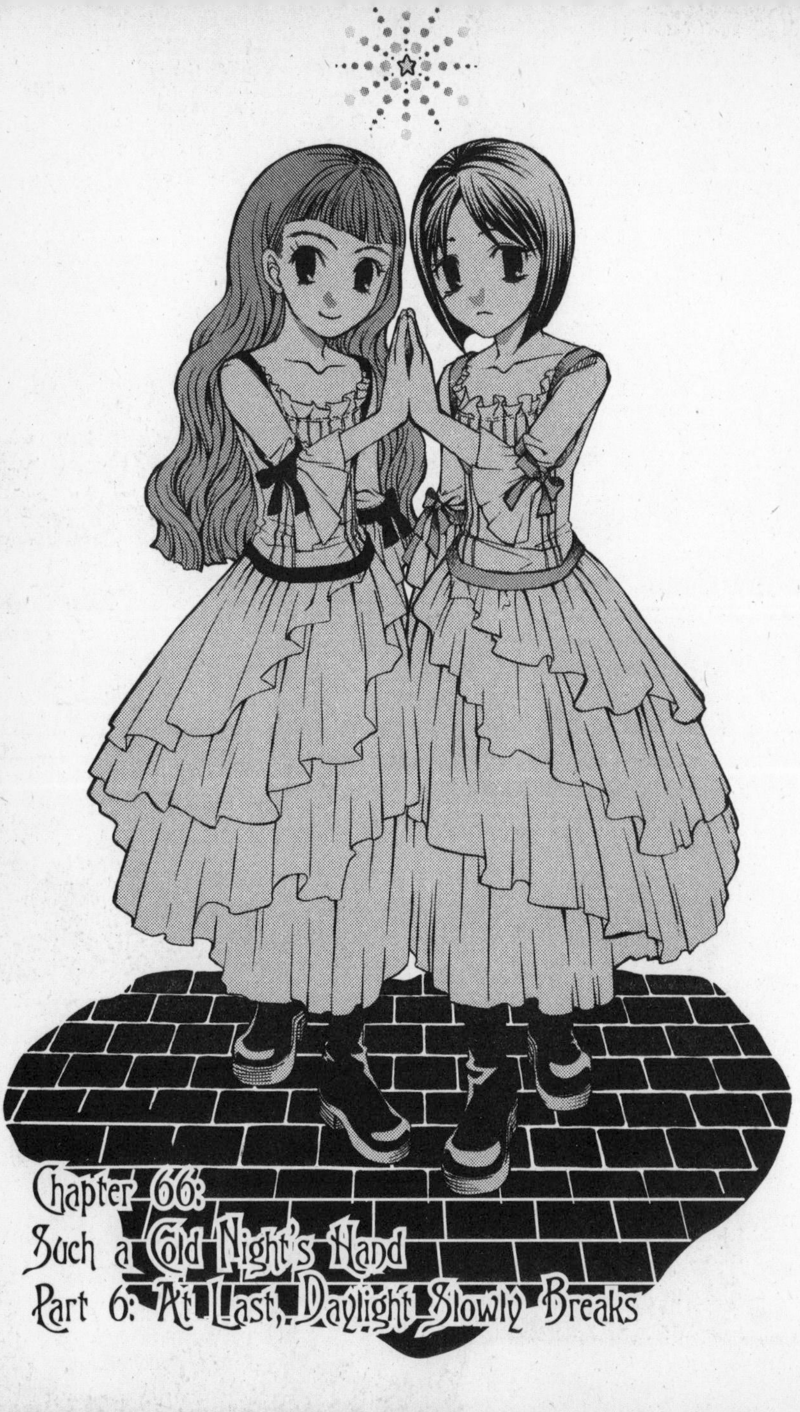
Chapter 66:
Such a Cold Night's Hand
Part 6: At Last, Daylight Slowly Breaks

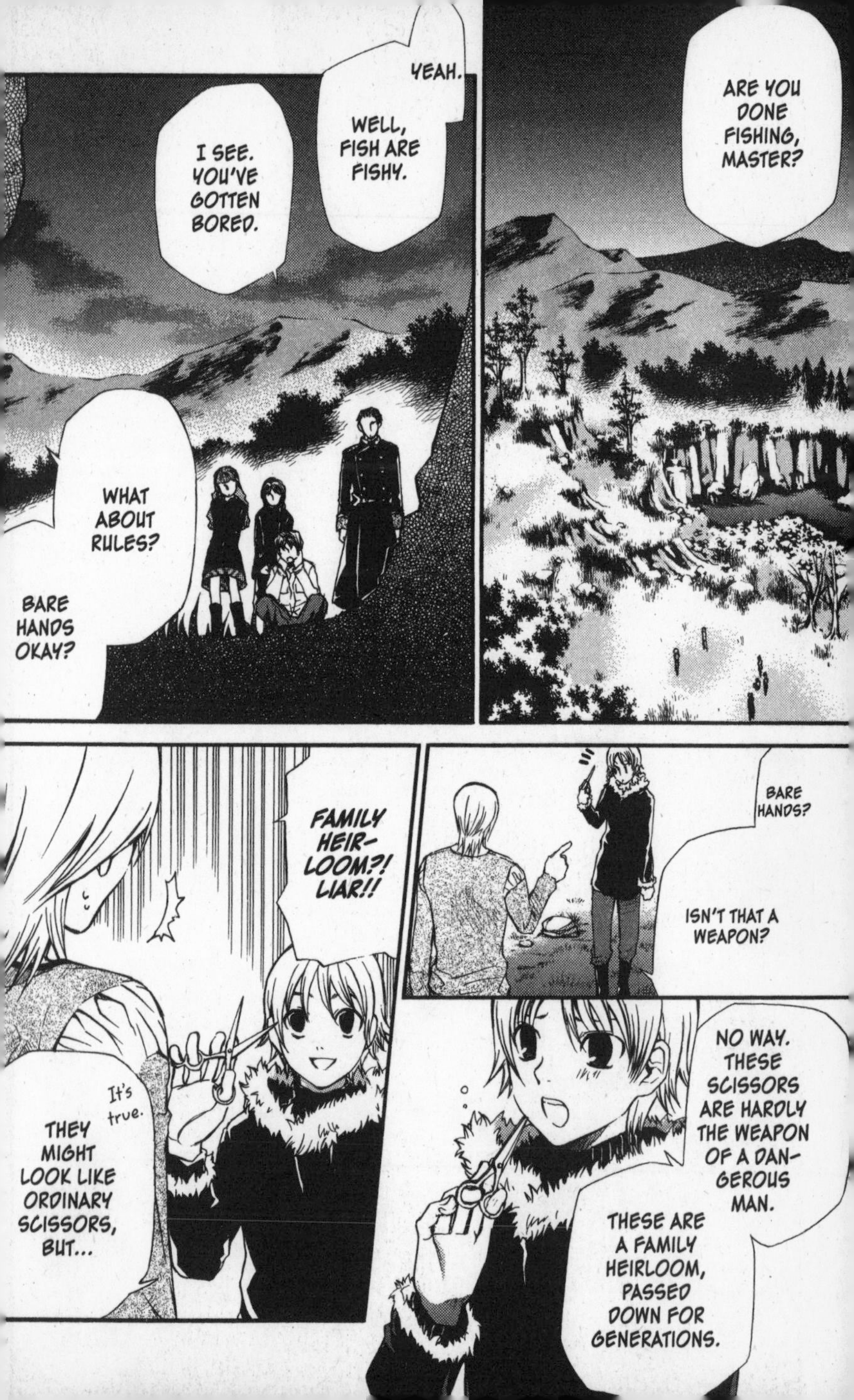

ARE YOU DONE FISHING, MASTER?
YEAH.
WELL, FISH ARE FISHY.
I SEE. YOU'VE GOTTEN BORED.
WHAT ABOUT RULES?
BARE HANDS OKAY?
BARE HANDS?
ISN'T THAT A WEAPON?
NO WAY. THESE SCISSORS ARE HARDLY THE WEAPON OF A DAN-GEROUS MAN.
THESE ARE A FAMILY HEIRLOOM, PASSED DOWN FOR GENERATIONS.
FAMILY HEIR-LOOM?! LIAR!!
It's true.
THEY MIGHT LOOK LIKE ORDINARY SCISSORS, BUT...

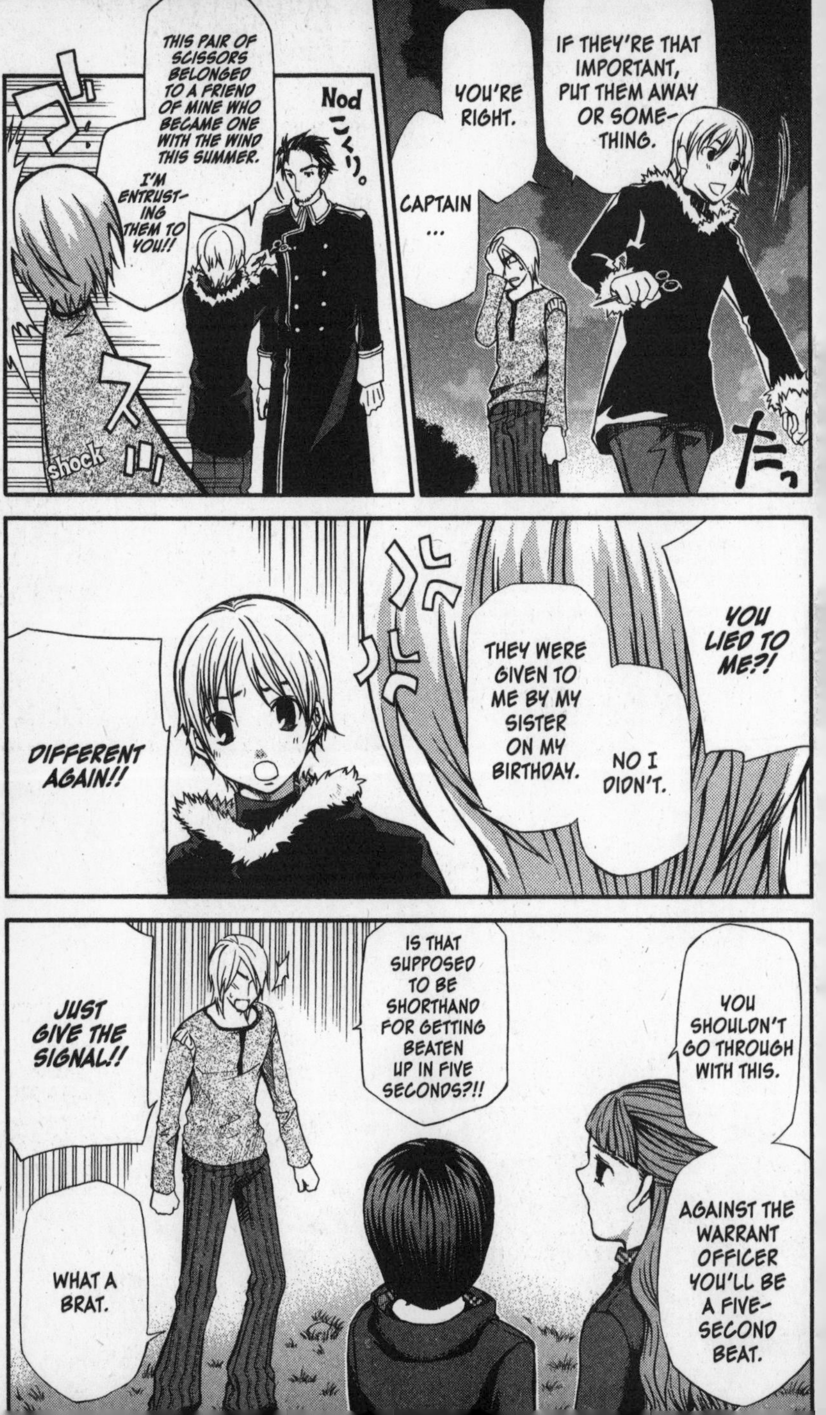
IF THEY'RE THAT IMPORTANT, PUT THEM AWAY OR SOME-THING.
YOU'RE RIGHT.
CAPTAIN ...
たっ
THIS PAIR OF SCISSORS BELONGED TO A FRIEND OF MINE WHO BECAME ONE WITH THE WIND THIS SUMMER.
Nod こくり。
I'M ENTRUST-ING THEM TO YOU!!
shock
YOU LIED TO ME?!
NO I DIDN'T.
THEY WERE GIVEN TO ME BY MY SISTER ON MY BIRTHDAY.
DIFFERENT AGAIN!!
YOU SHOULDN'T GO THROUGH WITH THIS.
AGAINST THE WARRANT OFFICER YOU'LL BE A FIVE-SECOND BEAT.
IS THAT SUPPOSED TO BE SHORTHAND FOR GETTING BEATEN UP IN FIVE SECONDS?!!
JUST GIVE THE SIGNAL!!
WHAT A BRAT.

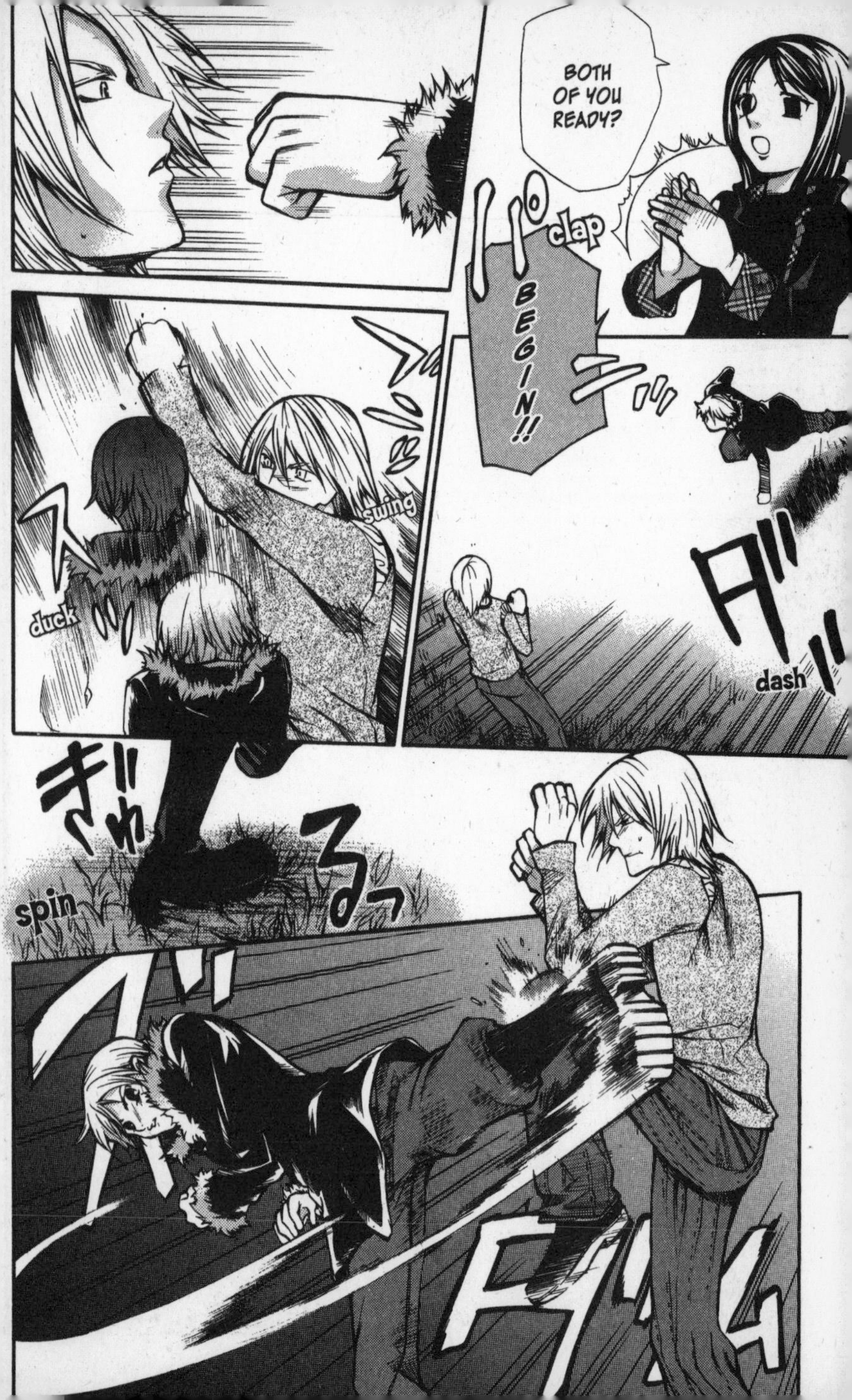
BOTH OF YOU READY?
clap
BEGIN!!
swing
duck
dash
spin

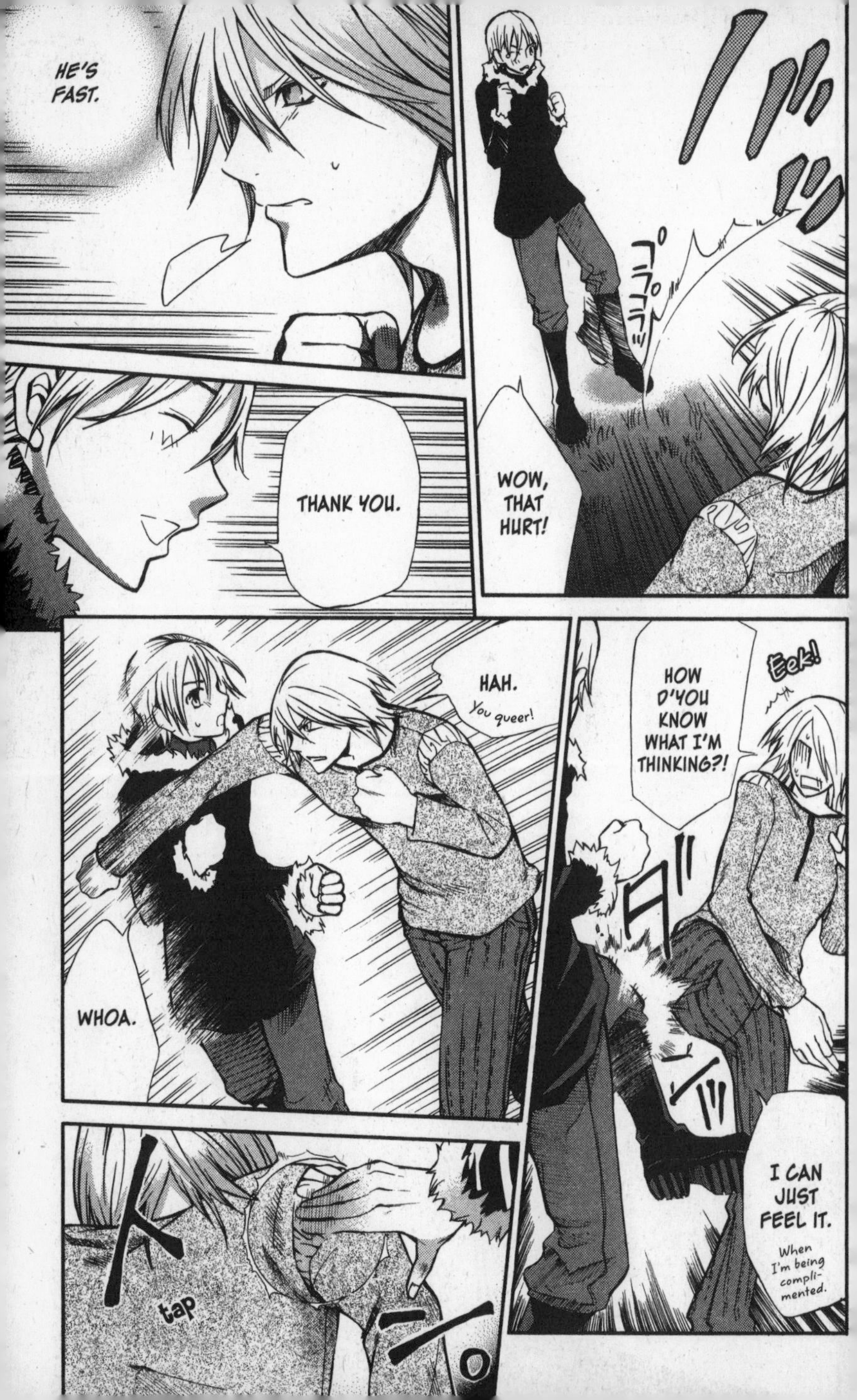
WOW, THAT HURT!
HE'S FAST.
THANK YOU.
HOW D'YOU KNOW WHAT I'M THINKING?!
Eek!
I CAN JUST FEEL IT.
When I'm being compli-mented.
HAH.
You queer!
WHOA.
tap

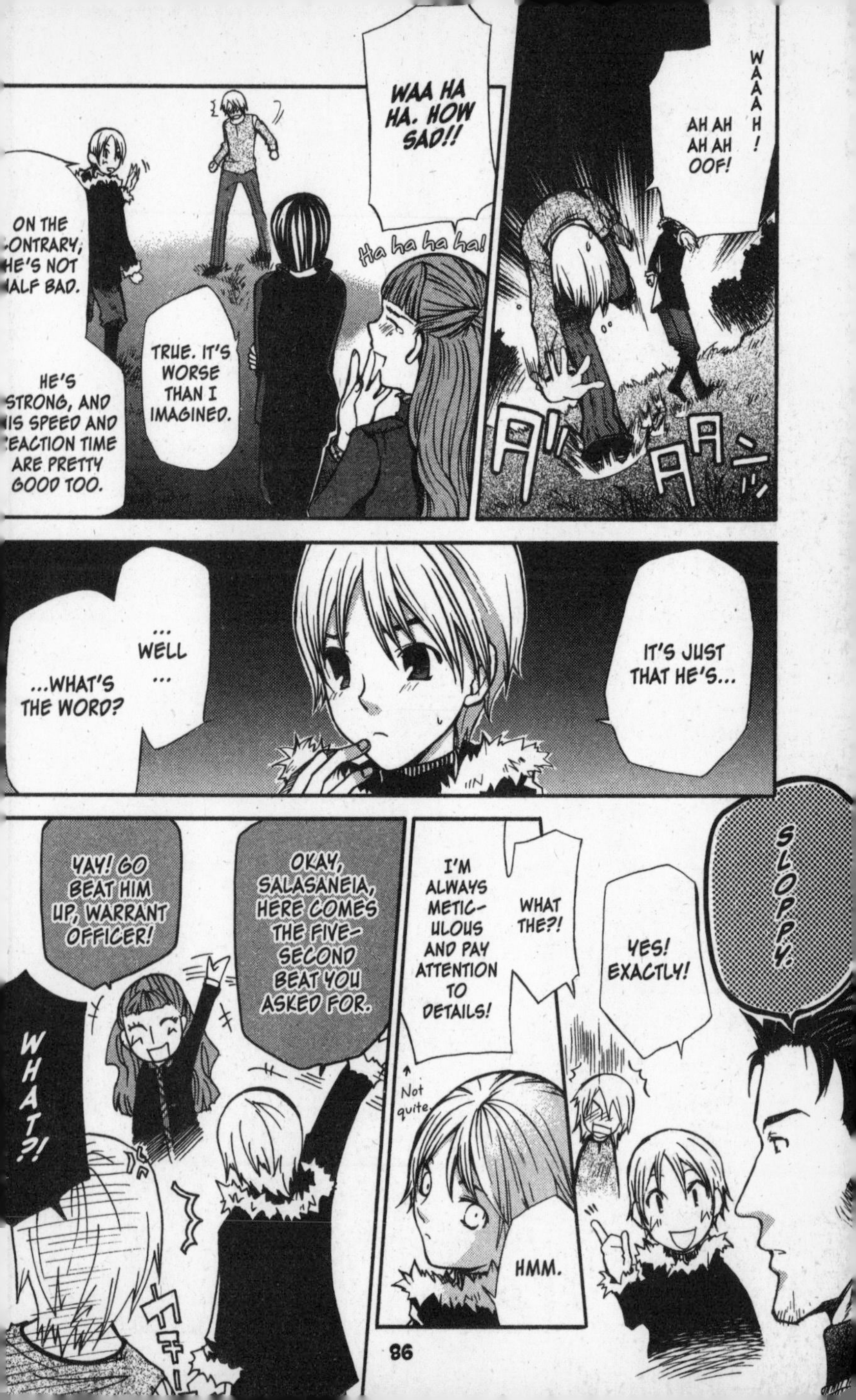
WAAAAH!
AH AH AH AH OOF!
WAA HA HA. HOW SAD!!
Ha ha ha ha!
TRUE. IT'S WORSE THAN I IMAGINED.
ON THE ONTRARY, HE'S NOT ALF BAD.
HE'S STRONG, AND IS SPEED AND EACTION TIME ARE PRETTY GOOD TOO.
IT'S JUST THAT HE'S...
... WELL ...
...WHAT'S THE WORD?
SLOPPY.
YES! EXACTLY!
WHAT THE?!
I'M ALWAYS METIC-ULOUS AND PAY ATTENTION TO DETAILS!
Not quite.
HMM.
OKAY, SALASANEIA, HERE COMES THE FIVE-SECOND BEAT YOU ASKED FOR.
YAY! GO BEAT HIM UP, WARRANT OFFICER!
WHAT?!

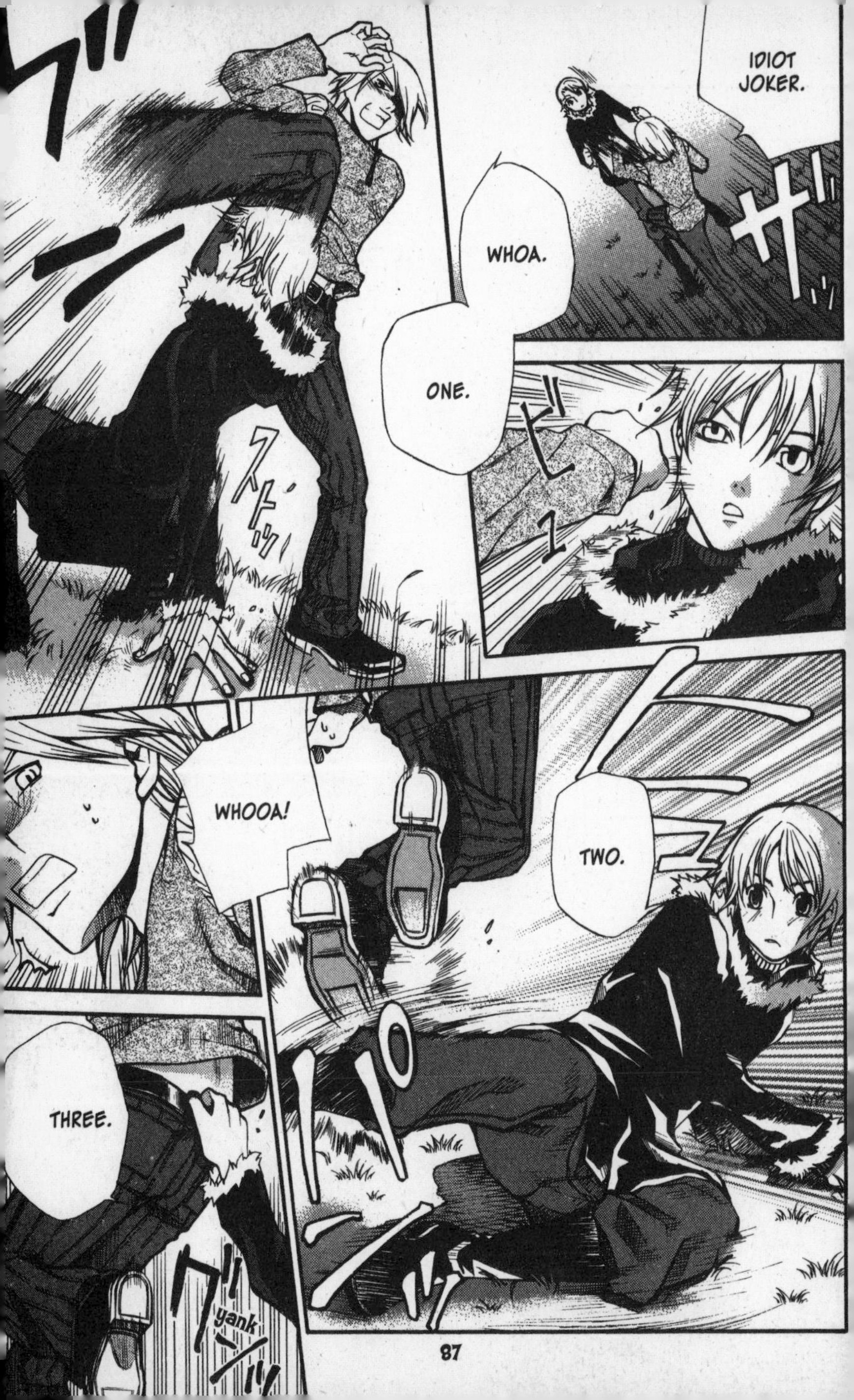
IDIOT JOKER.
WHOA.
ONE.
TWO.
WHOOA!
THREE.
yank

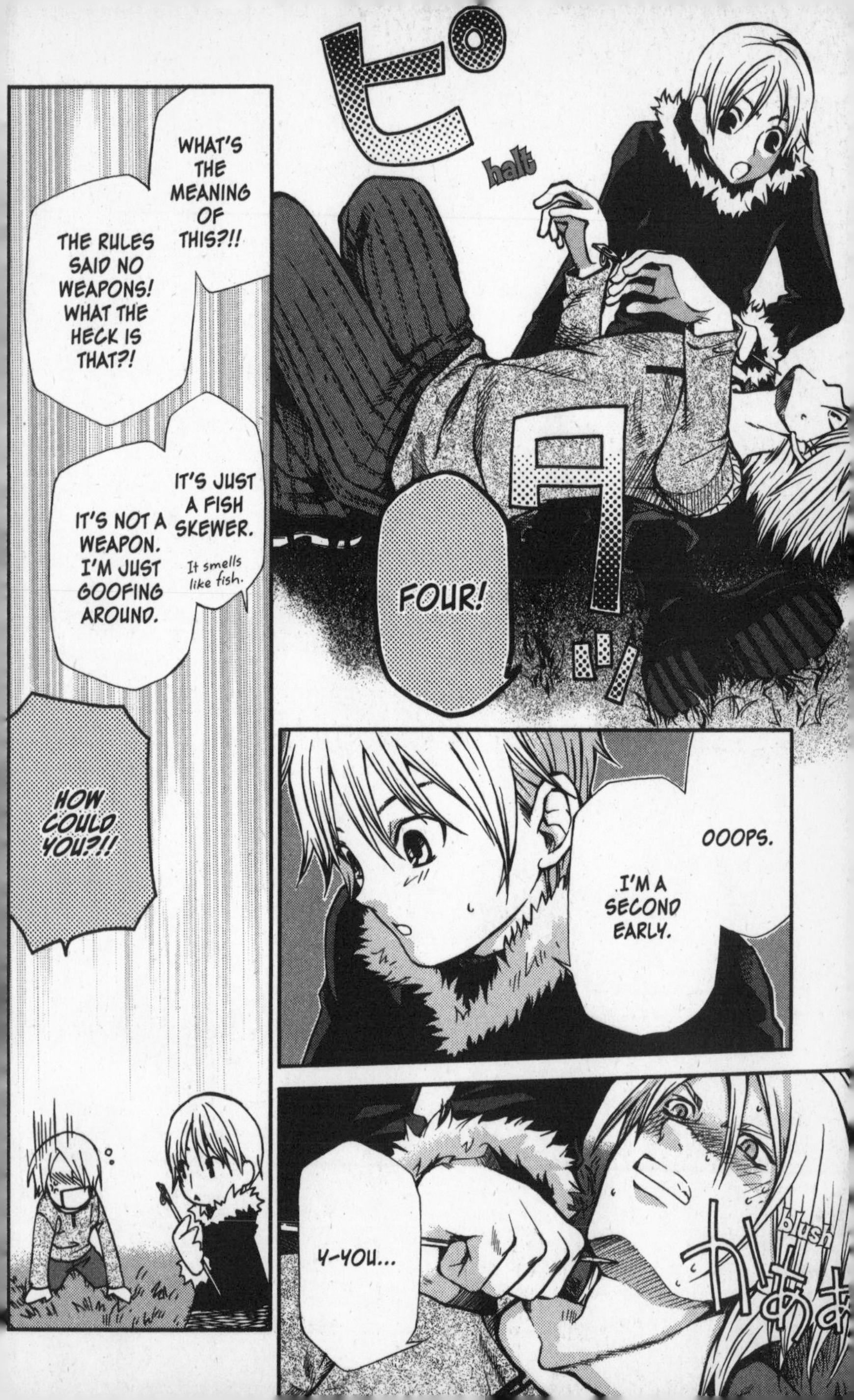

ピ
halt
FOUR!
OOOPS.
I'M A SECOND EARLY.
Y-YOU...
blush
WHAT'S THE MEANING OF THIS?!!
THE RULES SAID NO WEAPONS! WHAT THE HECK IS THAT?!
IT'S JUST A FISH SKEWER.
It smells like fish.
IT'S NOT A WEAPON. I'M JUST GOOFING AROUND.
HOW COULD YOU?!!

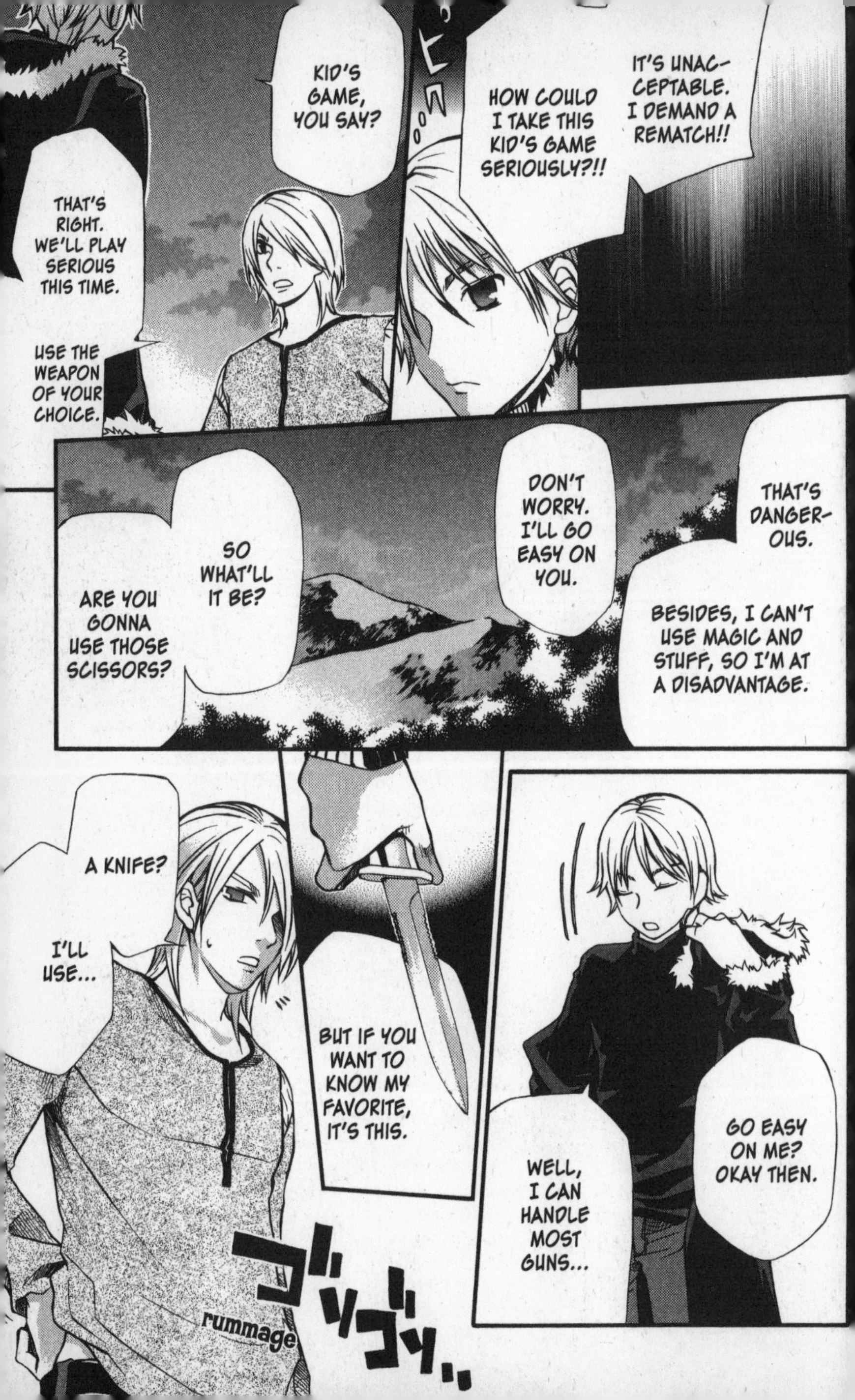
IT'S UNACCEPTABLE. I DEMAND A REMATCH!!
HOW COULD I TAKE THIS KID'S GAME SERIOUSLY?!!
KID'S GAME, YOU SAY?
THAT'S RIGHT. WE'LL PLAY SERIOUS THIS TIME.
USE THE WEAPON OF YOUR CHOICE.
THAT'S DANGEROUS.
BESIDES, I CAN'T USE MAGIC AND STUFF, SO I'M AT A DISADVANTAGE.
DON'T WORRY. I'LL GO EASY ON YOU.
SO WHAT'LL IT BE?
ARE YOU GONNA USE THOSE SCISSORS?
GO EASY ON ME? OKAY THEN.
WELL, I CAN HANDLE MOST GUNS...
I'LL USE...
rummage
BUT IF YOU WANT TO KNOW MY FAVORITE, IT'S THIS.
A KNIFE?

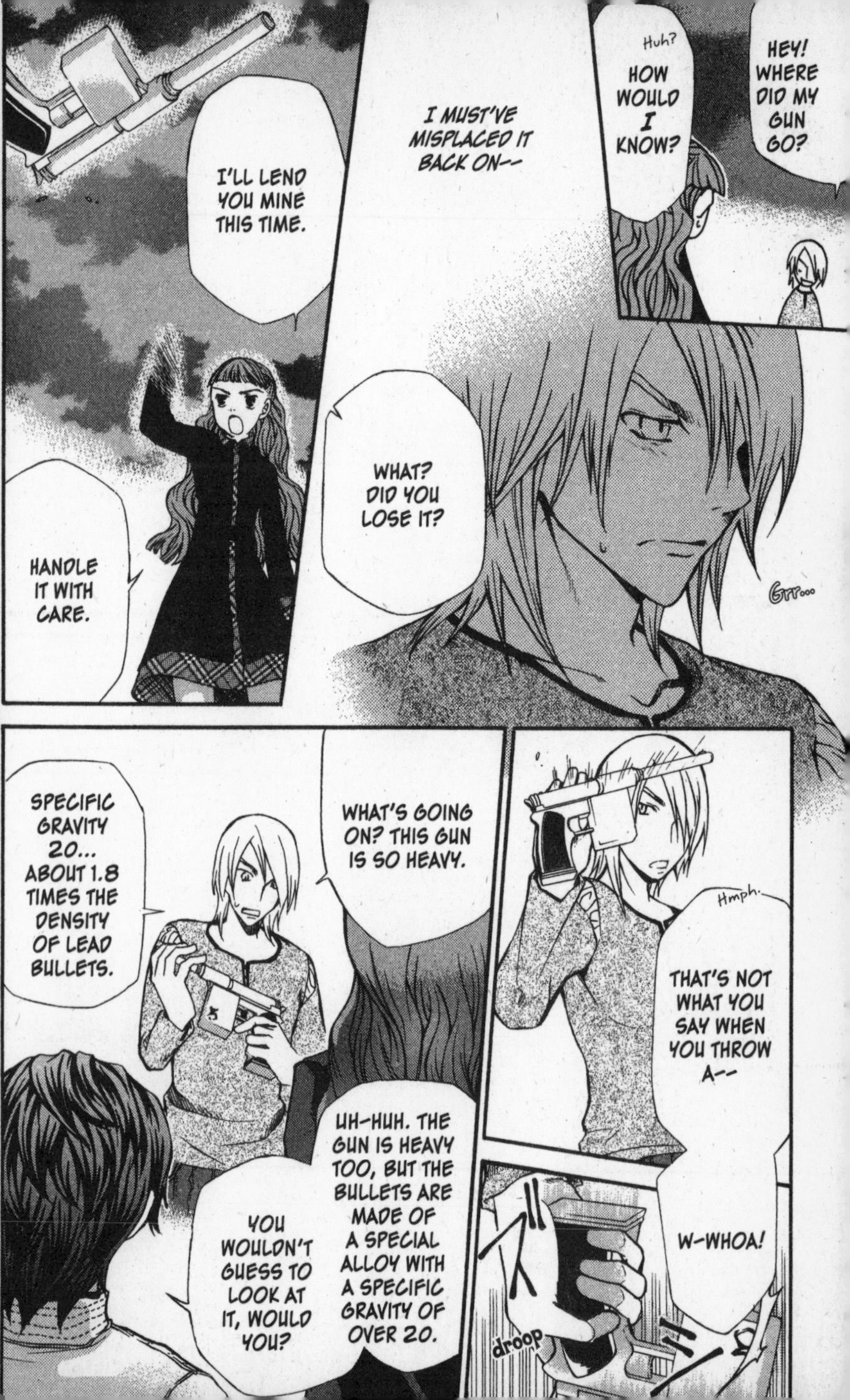
HEY! WHERE DID MY GUN GO?
Huh?
HOW WOULD I KNOW?
I MUST'VE MISPLACED IT BACK ON--
WHAT? DID YOU LOSE IT?
Grr...
I'LL LEND YOU MINE THIS TIME.
HANDLE IT WITH CARE.
Hmph.
THAT'S NOT WHAT YOU SAY WHEN YOU THROW A--
W-WHOA!
droop
WHAT'S GOING ON? THIS GUN IS SO HEAVY.
UH-HUH. THE GUN IS HEAVY TOO, BUT THE BULLETS ARE MADE OF A SPECIAL ALLOY WITH A SPECIFIC GRAVITY OF OVER 20.
YOU WOULDN'T GUESS TO LOOK AT IT, WOULD YOU?
SPECIFIC GRAVITY 20... ABOUT 1.8 TIMES THE DENSITY OF LEAD BULLETS.

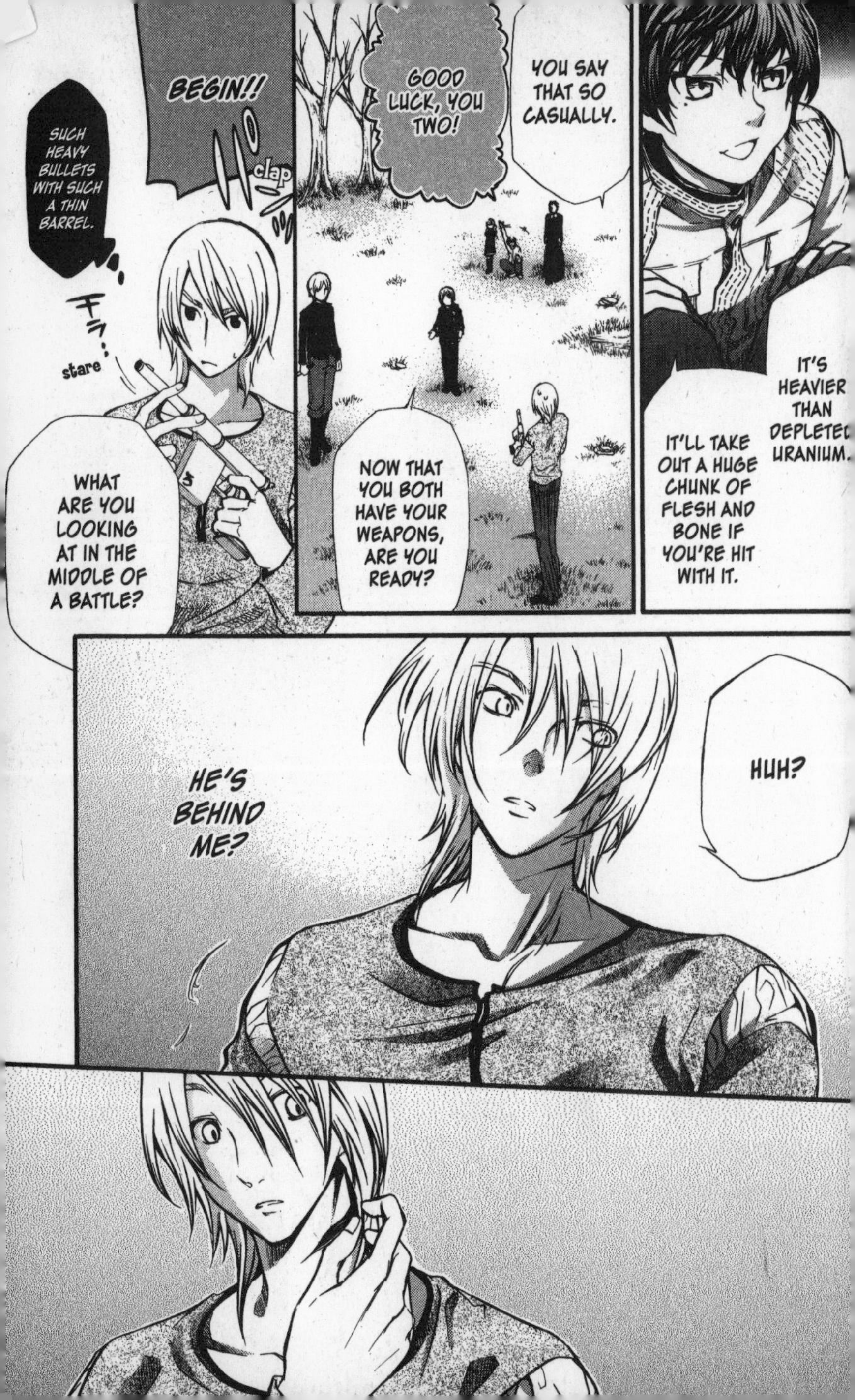
IT'S HEAVIER THAN DEPLETED URANIUM.
IT'LL TAKE OUT A HUGE CHUNK OF FLESH AND BONE IF YOU'RE HIT WITH IT.
YOU SAY THAT SO CASUALLY.
GOOD LUCK, YOU TWO!
NOW THAT YOU BOTH HAVE YOUR WEAPONS, ARE YOU READY?
BEGIN!!
clap
SUCH HEAVY BULLETS WITH SUCH A THIN BARREL.
チラ…
stare
WHAT ARE YOU LOOKING AT IN THE MIDDLE OF A BATTLE?
HUH?
HE'S BEHIND ME?

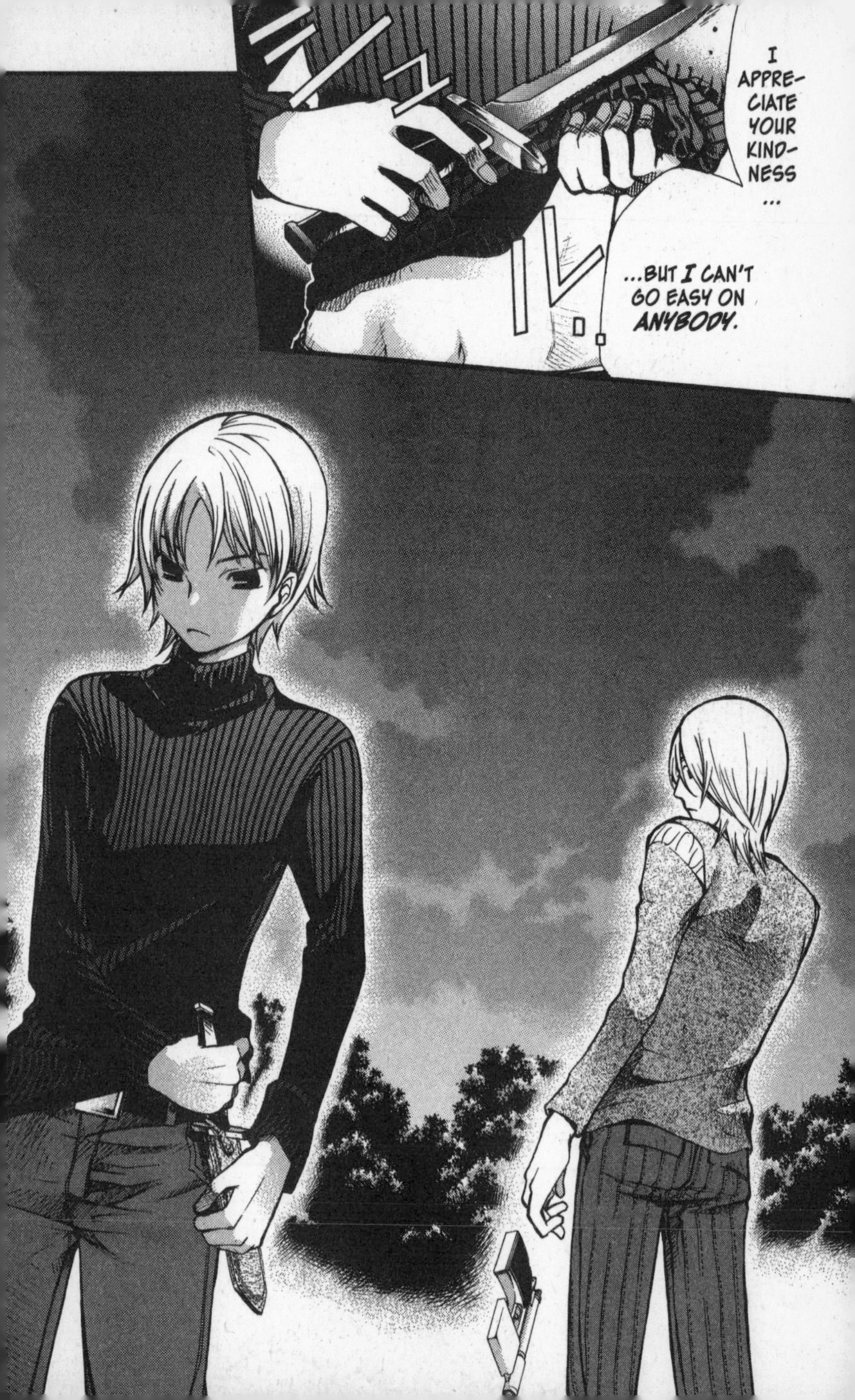
I APPRECIATE YOUR KINDNESS...
...BUT I CAN'T GO EASY ON ANYBODY.

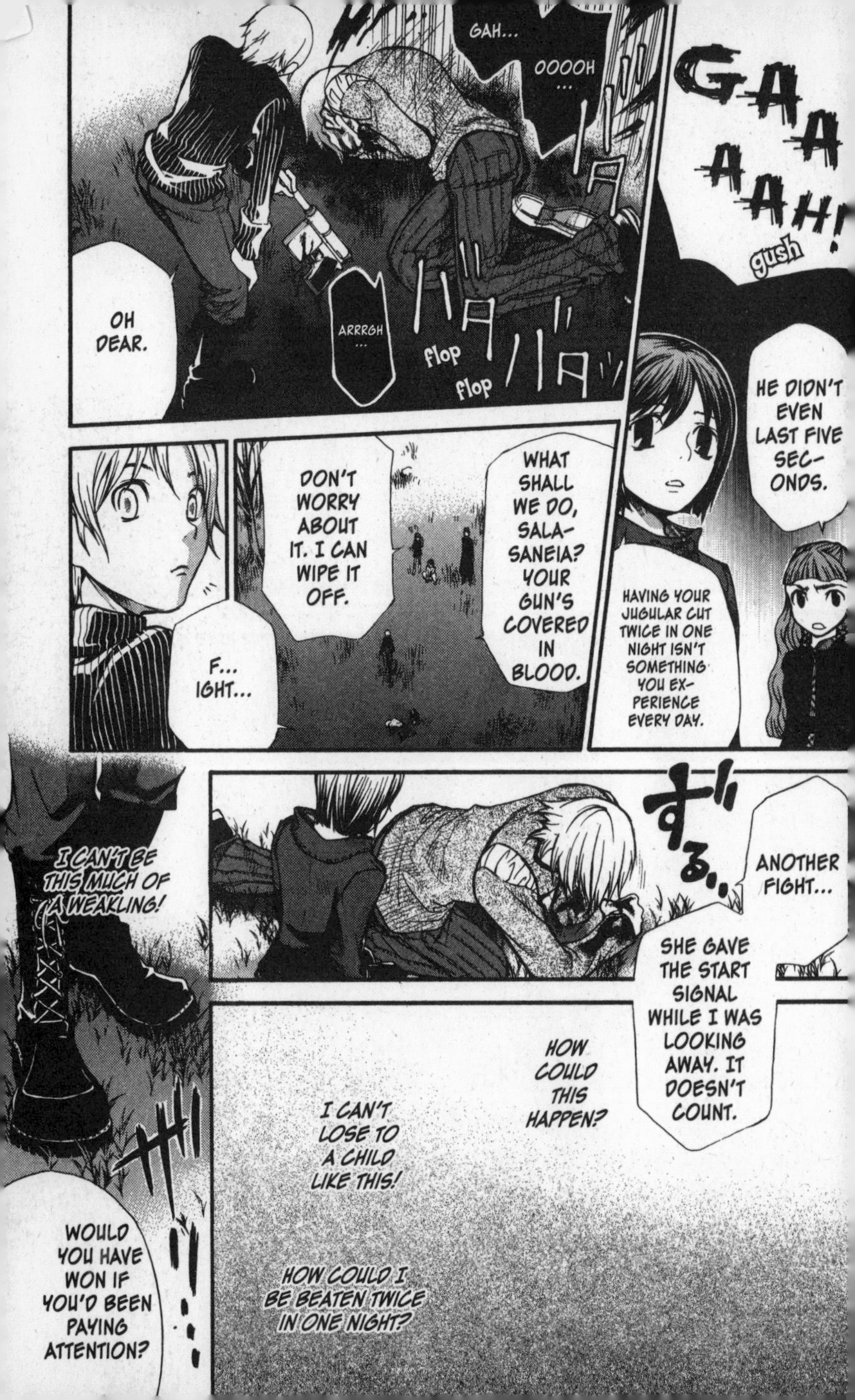
GAAAAAH!
gush
GAH...
OOOOH...
ARRRGH...
flop
flop
OH DEAR.
HE DIDN'T EVEN LAST FIVE SECONDS.
HAVING YOUR JUGULAR CUT TWICE IN ONE NIGHT ISN'T SOMETHING YOU EXPERIENCE EVERY DAY.
WHAT SHALL WE DO, SALASANEIA? YOUR GUN'S COVERED IN BLOOD.
DON'T WORRY ABOUT IT. I CAN WIPE IT OFF.
F... IGHT...
ANOTHER FIGHT...
する..
I CAN'T BE THIS MUCH OF A WEAKLING!
SHE GAVE THE START SIGNAL WHILE I WAS LOOKING AWAY. IT DOESN'T COUNT.
HOW COULD THIS HAPPEN?
I CAN'T LOSE TO A CHILD LIKE THIS!
HOW COULD I BE BEATEN TWICE IN ONE NIGHT?
WOULD YOU HAVE WON IF YOU'D BEEN PAYING ATTENTION?

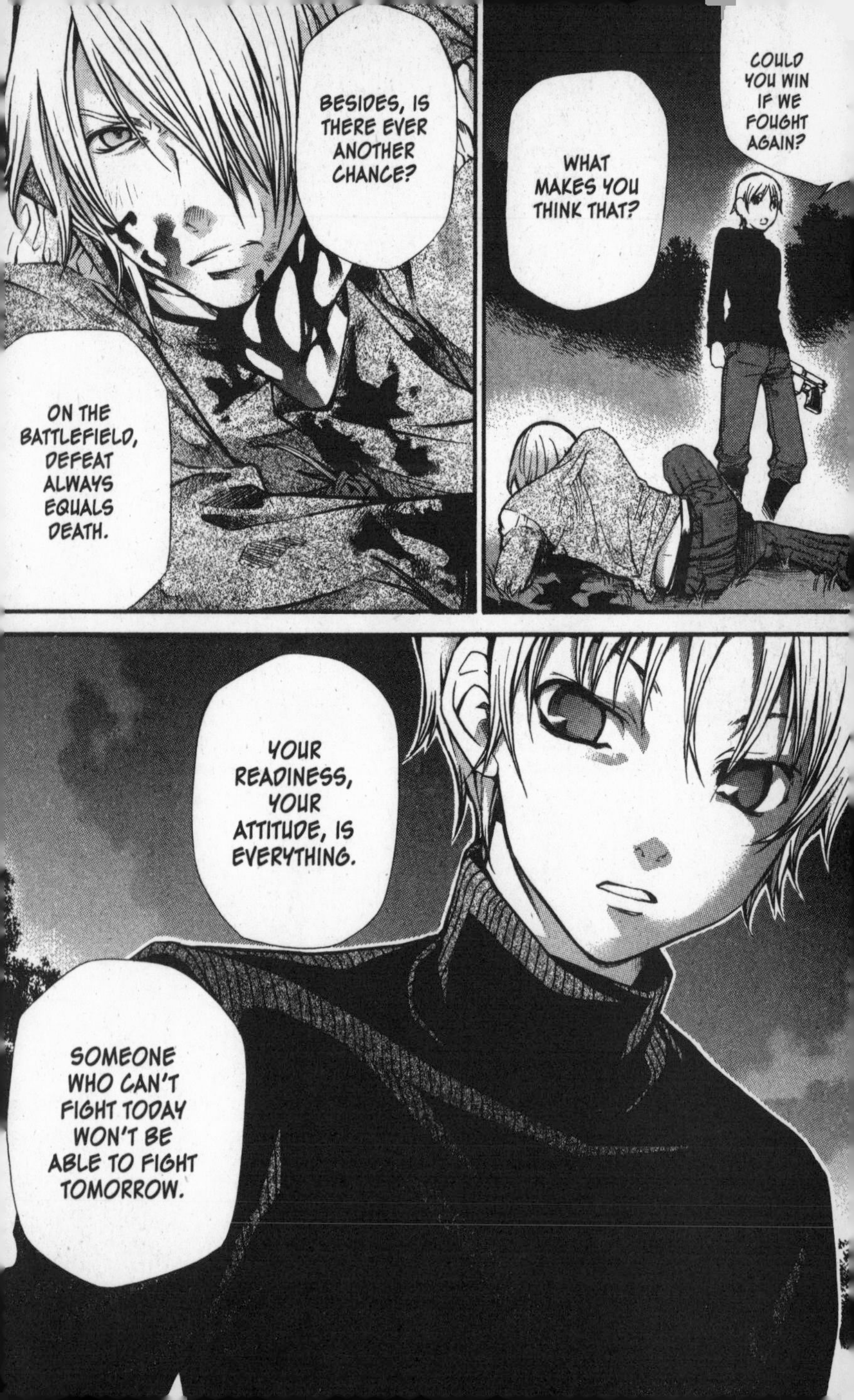
COULD YOU WIN IF WE FOUGHT AGAIN?
WHAT MAKES YOU THINK THAT?
BESIDES, IS THERE EVER ANOTHER CHANCE?
ON THE BATTLEFIELD, DEFEAT ALWAYS EQUALS DEATH.
YOUR READINESS,
YOUR ATTITUDE, IS EVERYTHING.
SOMEONE WHO CAN'T FIGHT TODAY
WON'T BE ABLE TO FIGHT TOMORROW.

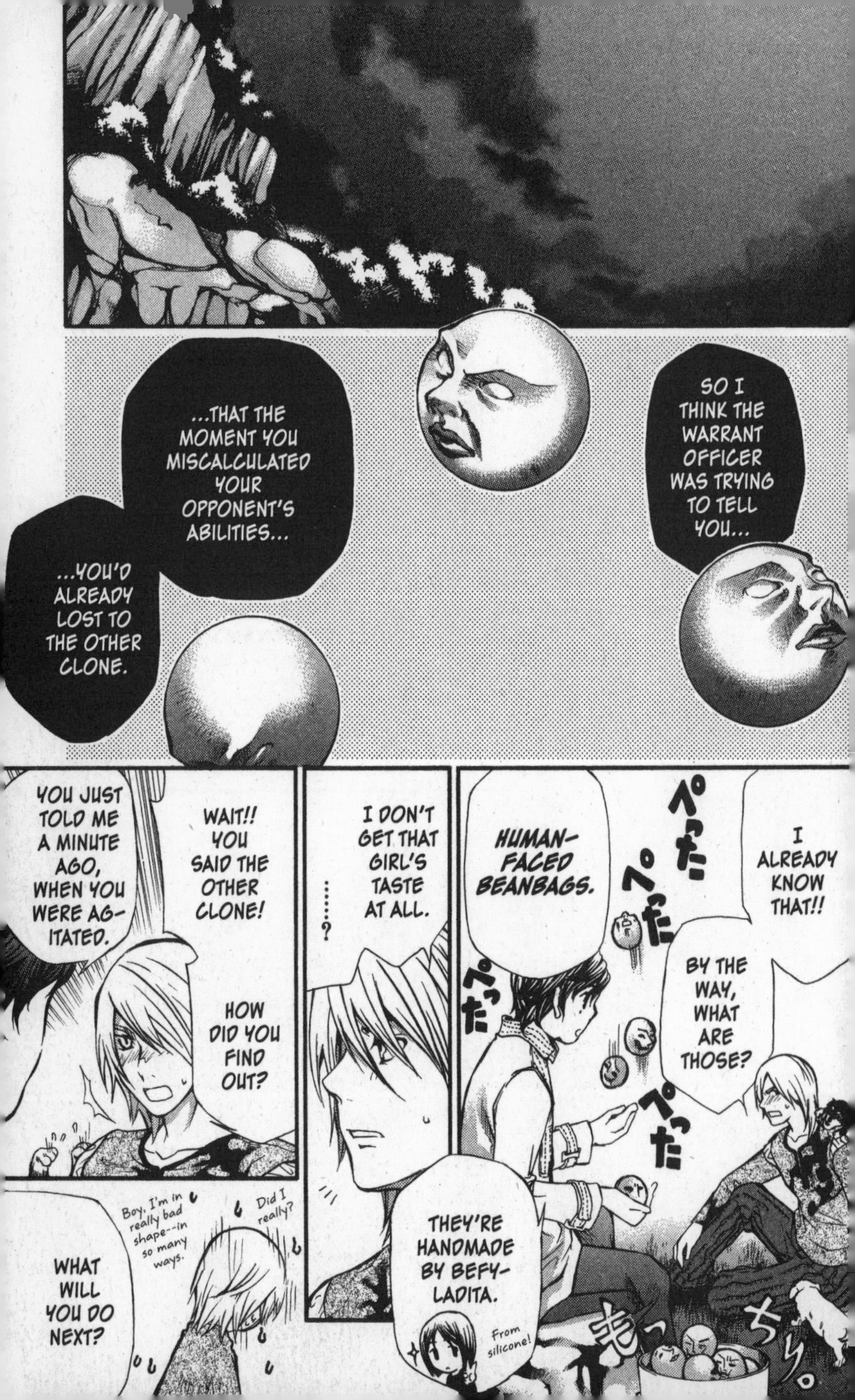

SO I THINK THE WARRANT OFFICER WAS TRYING TO TELL YOU...
...THAT THE MOMENT YOU MISCALCULATED YOUR OPPONENT'S ABILITIES...
...YOU'D ALREADY LOST TO THE OTHER CLONE.
I ALREADY KNOW THAT!!
ぺったぺった
BY THE WAY, WHAT ARE THOSE?
HUMAN-FACED BEANBAGS.
ぺった
ぺった
THEY'RE HANDMADE BY BEFY-LADITA.
From silicone!
もっちり。
I DON'T GET THAT GIRL'S TASTE AT ALL.
......?
WAIT!! YOU SAID THE OTHER CLONE!
HOW DID YOU FIND OUT?
YOU JUST TOLD ME A MINUTE AGO, WHEN YOU WERE AGITATED.
Did I really?
Boy, I'm in really bad shape--in so many ways.
WHAT WILL YOU DO NEXT?

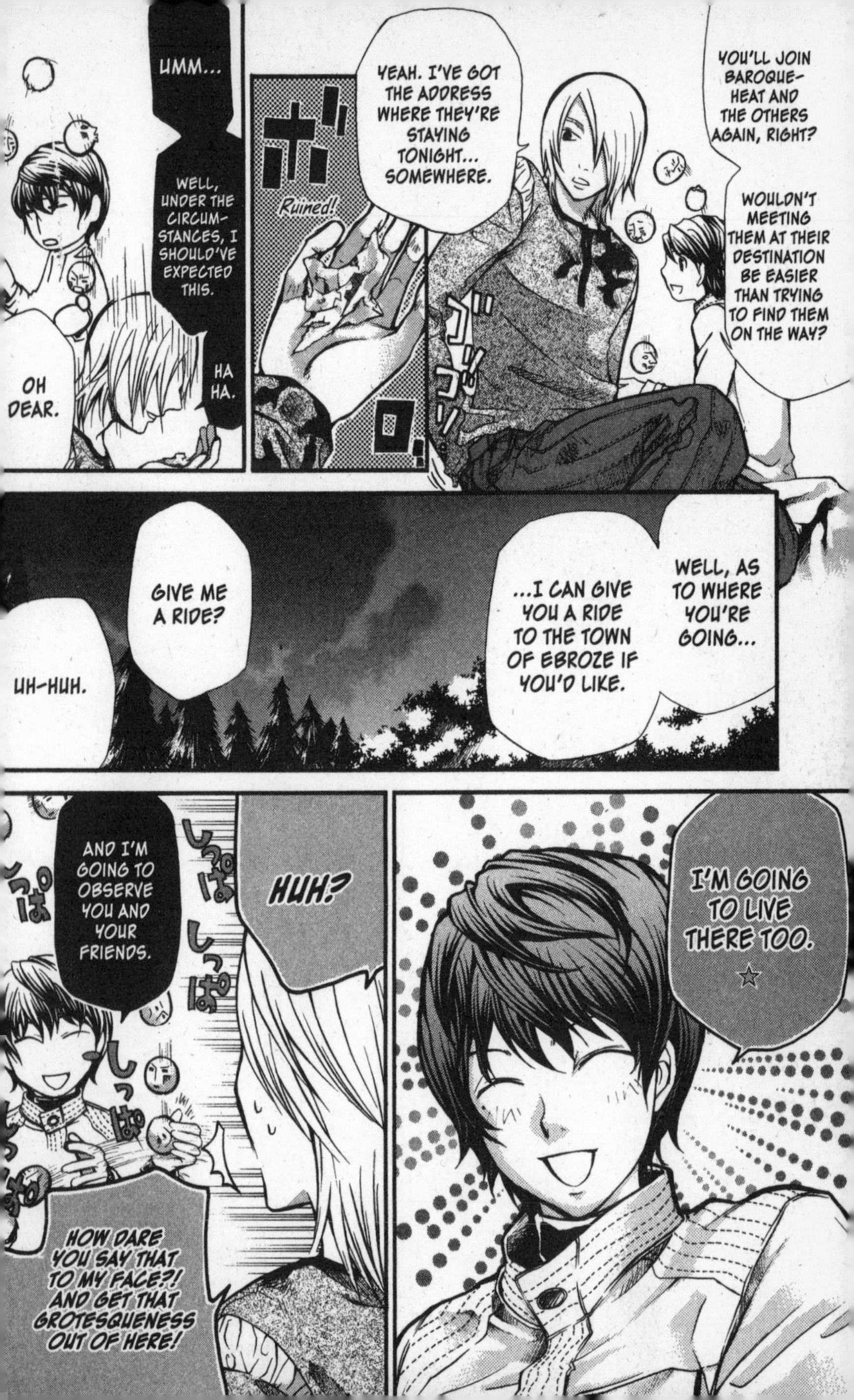
YOU'LL JOIN BAROQUE-HEAT AND THE OTHERS AGAIN, RIGHT?
WOULDN'T MEETING THEM AT THEIR DESTINATION BE EASIER THAN TRYING TO FIND THEM ON THE WAY?
YEAH. I'VE GOT THE ADDRESS WHERE THEY'RE STAYING TONIGHT... SOMEWHERE.
Ruined!
UMM...
WELL, UNDER THE CIRCUMSTANCES, I SHOULD'VE EXPECTED THIS.
HA HA.
OH DEAR.
WELL, AS TO WHERE YOU'RE GOING...
...I CAN GIVE YOU A RIDE TO THE TOWN OF EBROZE IF YOU'D LIKE.
GIVE ME A RIDE?
UH-HUH.
I'M GOING TO LIVE THERE TOO. ☆
HUH?
AND I'M GOING TO OBSERVE YOU AND YOUR FRIENDS.
HOW DARE YOU SAY THAT TO MY FACE?! AND GET THAT GROTESQUENESS OUT OF HERE!

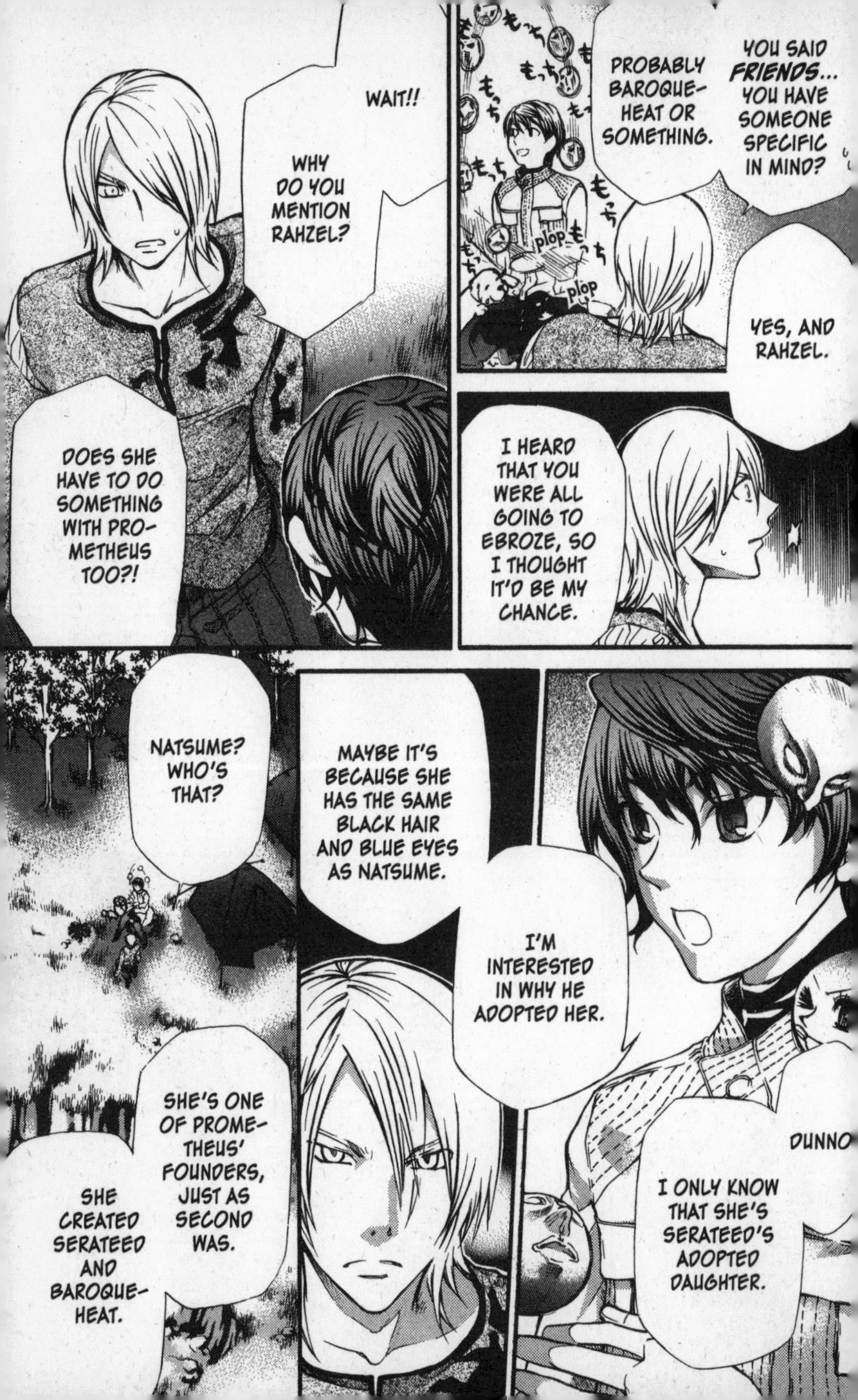

YOU SAID *FRIENDS*... YOU HAVE SOMEONE SPECIFIC IN MIND?
PROBABLY BAROQUE-HEAT OR SOMETHING.
もっち
plop
plop
YES, AND RAHZEL.
I HEARD THAT YOU WERE ALL GOING TO EBROZE, SO I THOUGHT IT'D BE MY CHANCE.
WAIT!!
WHY DO YOU MENTION RAHZEL?
DOES SHE HAVE TO DO SOMETHING WITH PRO-METHEUS TOO?!
DUNNO
I ONLY KNOW THAT SHE'S SERATEED'S ADOPTED DAUGHTER.
I'M INTERESTED IN WHY HE ADOPTED HER.
MAYBE IT'S BECAUSE SHE HAS THE SAME BLACK HAIR AND BLUE EYES AS NATSUME.
NATSUME? WHO'S THAT?
SHE'S ONE OF PROME-THEUS' FOUNDERS, JUST AS SECOND WAS.
SHE CREATED SERATEED AND BAROQUE-HEAT.

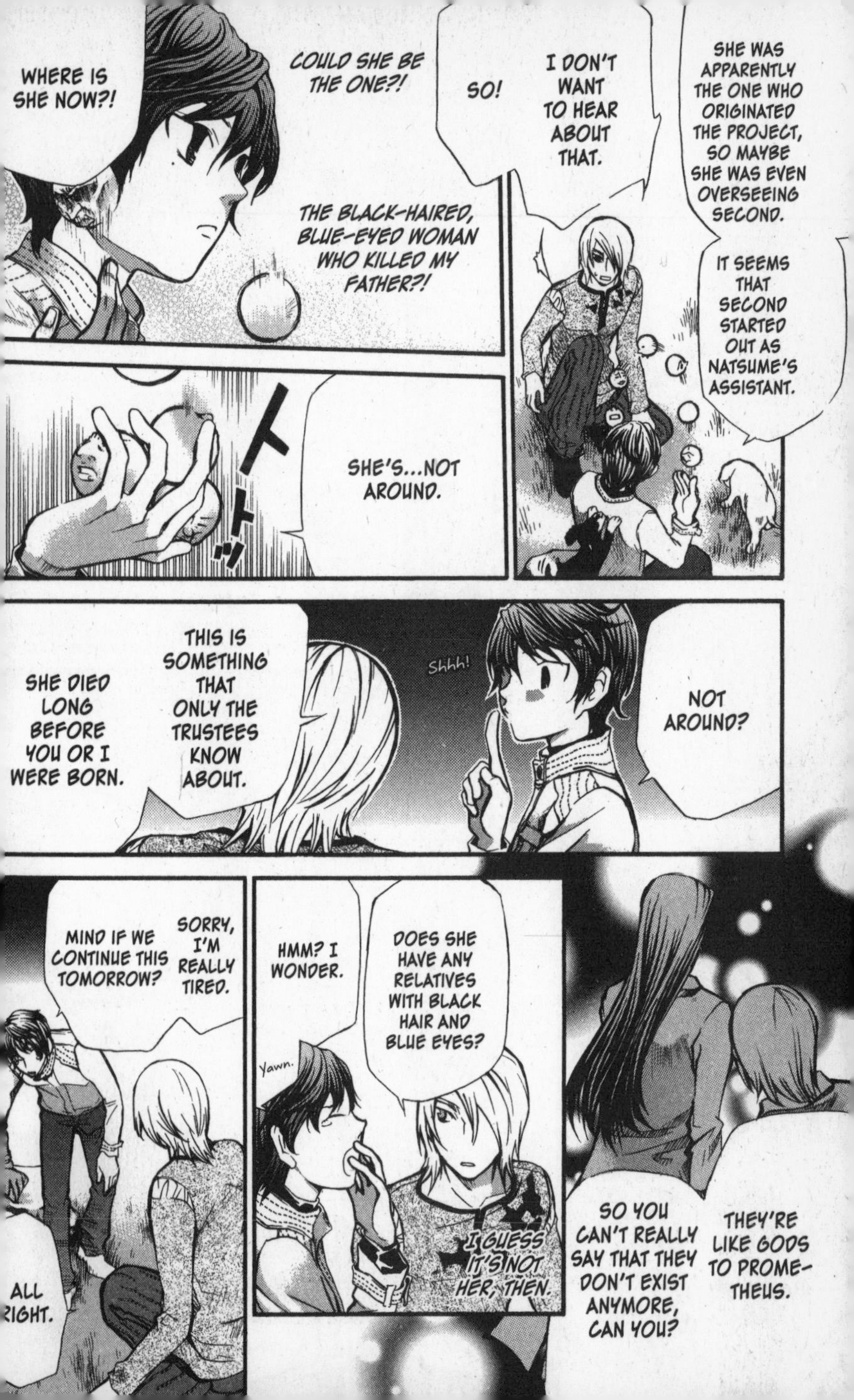
SHE WAS APPARENTLY THE ONE WHO ORIGINATED THE PROJECT, SO MAYBE SHE WAS EVEN OVERSEEING SECOND.
IT SEEMS THAT SECOND STARTED OUT AS NATSUME'S ASSISTANT.
I DON'T WANT TO HEAR ABOUT THAT.
SO!
COULD SHE BE THE ONE?!
THE BLACK-HAIRED, BLUE-EYED WOMAN WHO KILLED MY FATHER?!
WHERE IS SHE NOW?!
SHE'S...NOT AROUND.
トトッ
NOT AROUND?
Shhh!
THIS IS SOMETHING THAT ONLY THE TRUSTEES KNOW ABOUT.
SHE DIED LONG BEFORE YOU OR I WERE BORN.
THEY'RE LIKE GODS TO PROMETHEUS.
SO YOU CAN'T REALLY SAY THAT THEY DON'T EXIST ANYMORE, CAN YOU?
DOES SHE HAVE ANY RELATIVES WITH BLACK HAIR AND BLUE EYES?
HMM? I WONDER.
Yawn.
I GUESS IT'S NOT HER, THEN.
SORRY, I'M REALLY TIRED.
MIND IF WE CONTINUE THIS TOMORROW?
ALL RIGHT.

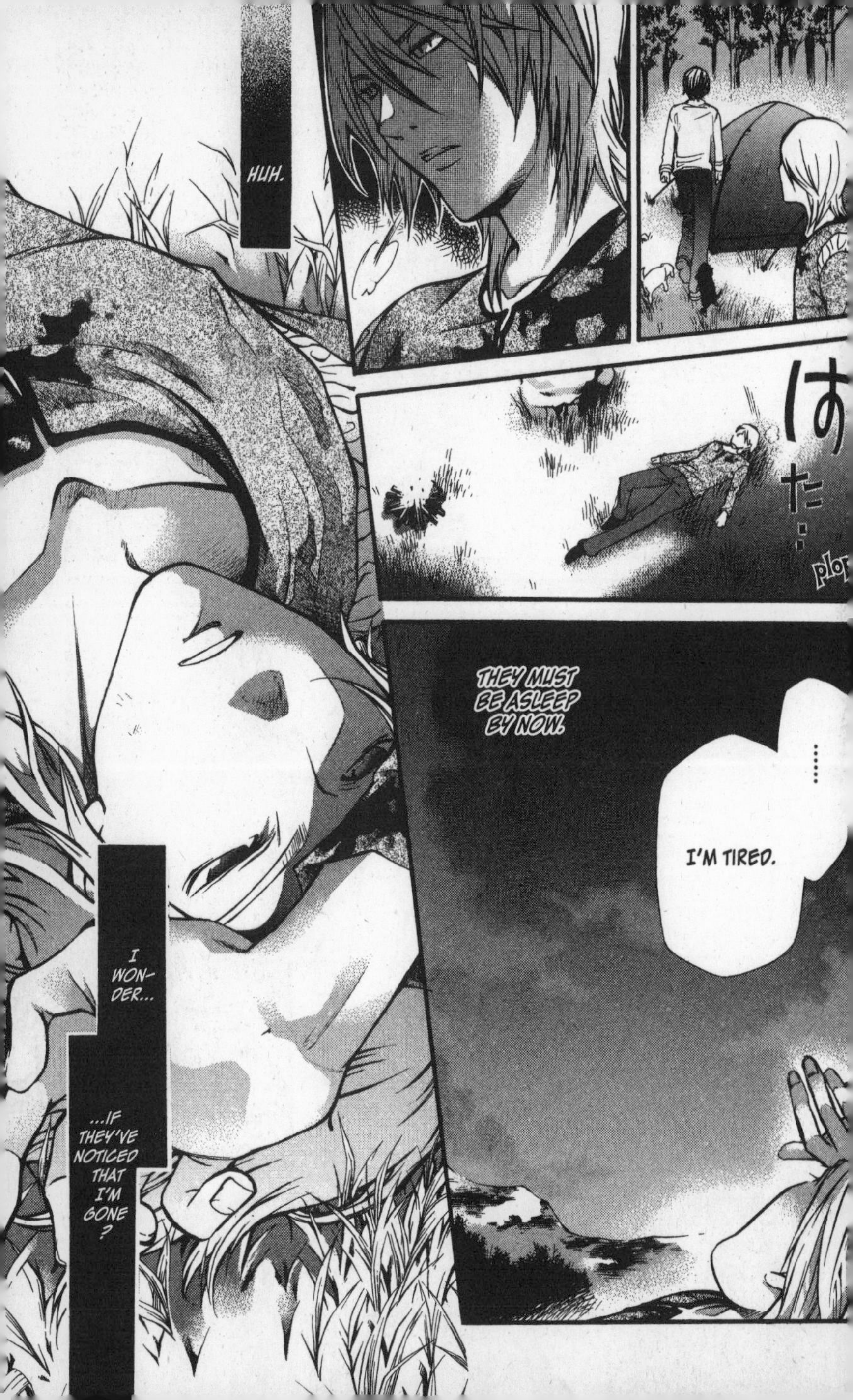
はた・・
plop
HUH.
THEY MUST BE ASLEEP BY NOW.
......
I'M TIRED.
I WONDER...
...IF THEY'VE NOTICED THAT I'M GONE?

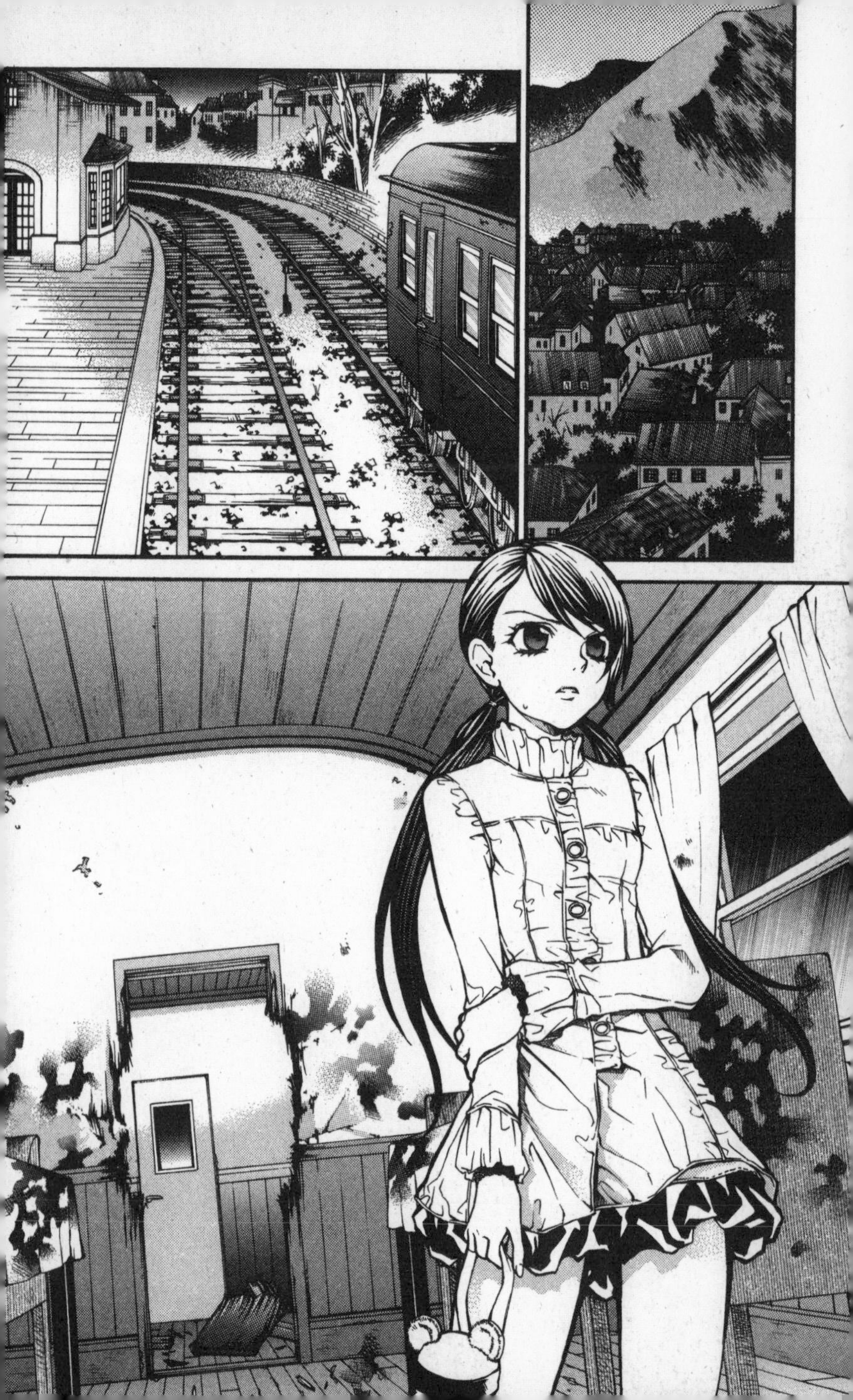

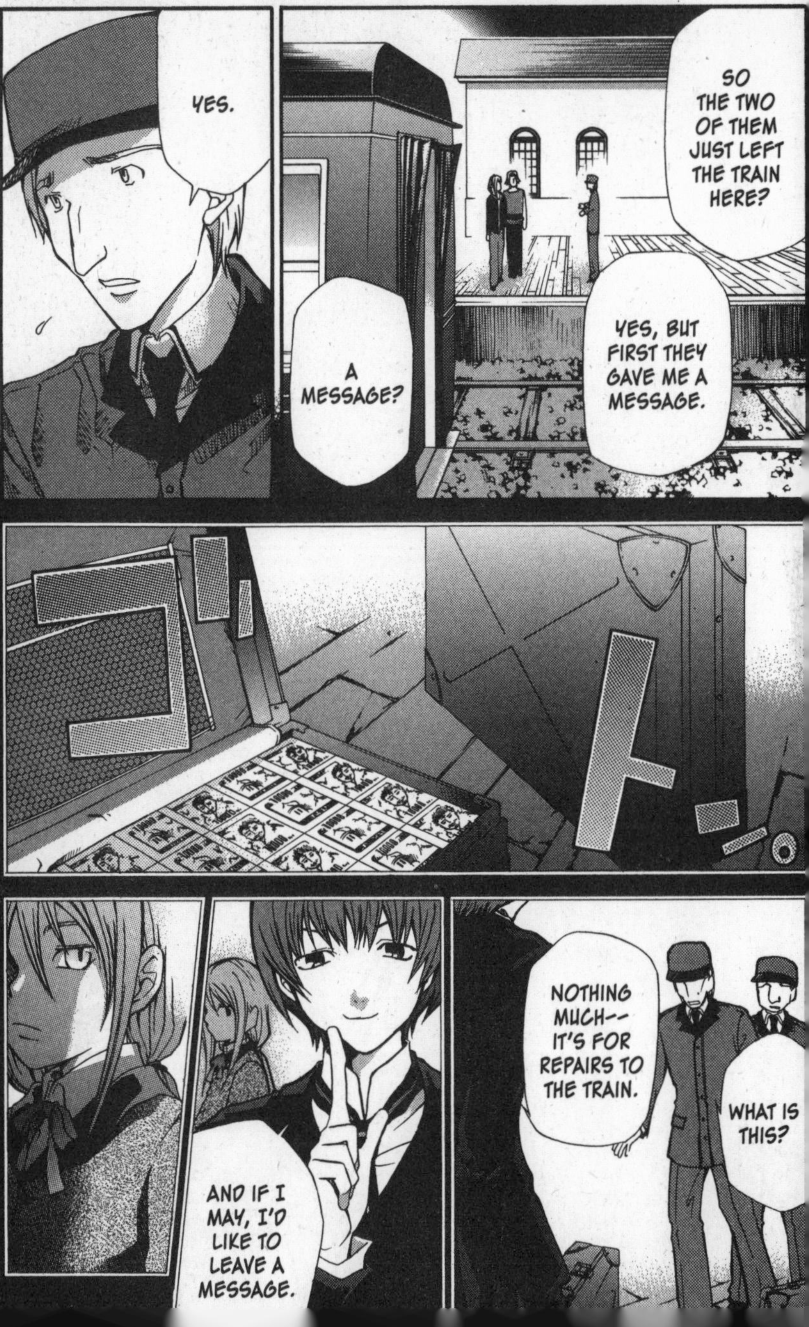
SO THE TWO OF THEM JUST LEFT THE TRAIN HERE?
YES, BUT FIRST THEY GAVE ME A MESSAGE.
A MESSAGE?
YES.
ゴト
WHAT IS THIS?
NOTHING MUCH-- IT'S FOR REPAIRS TO THE TRAIN.
AND IF I MAY, I'D LIKE TO LEAVE A MESSAGE.

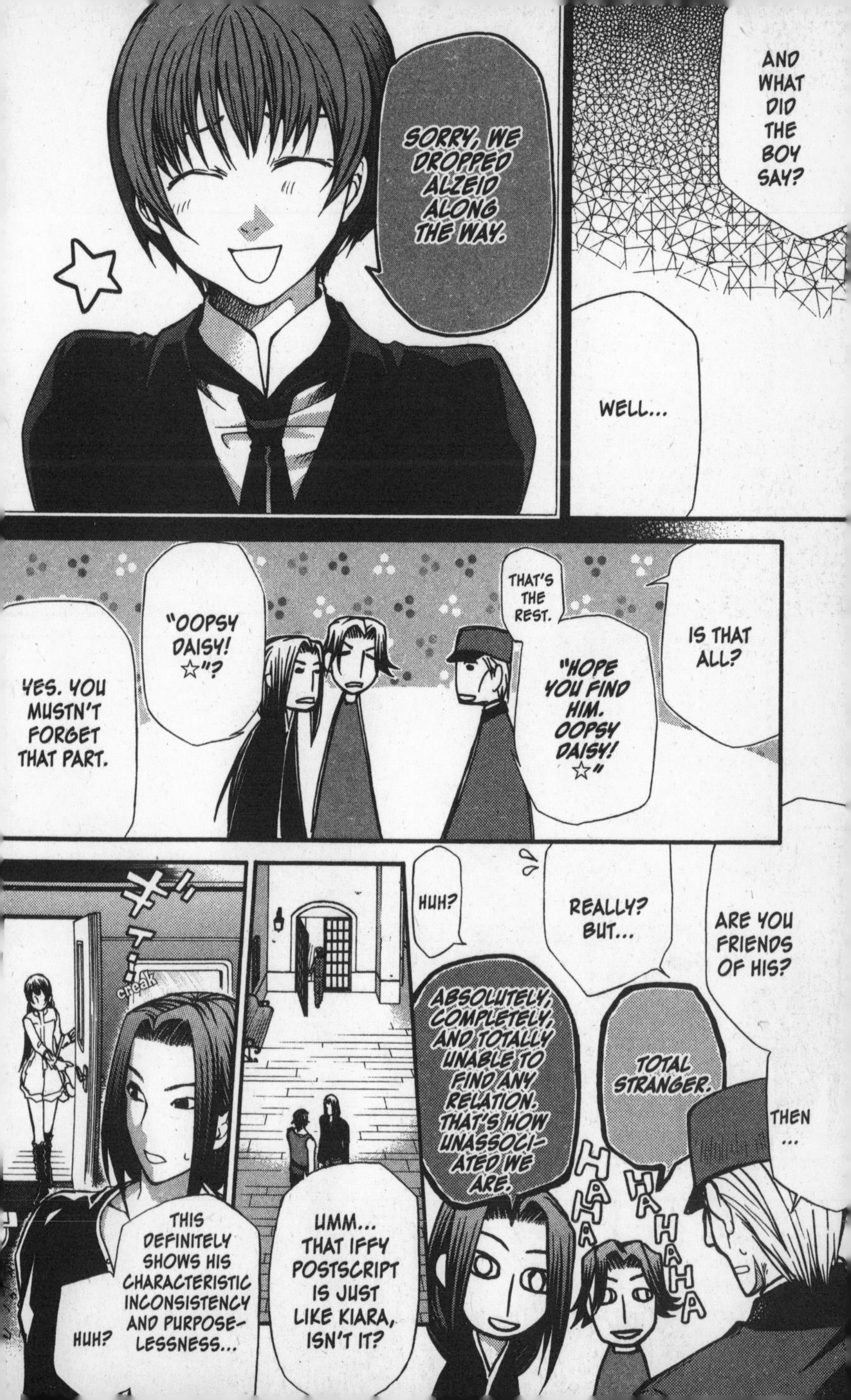

AND WHAT DID THE BOY SAY?
WELL...
SORRY, WE DROPPED ALZEID ALONG THE WAY.
IS THAT ALL?
THAT'S THE REST.
"HOPE YOU FIND HIM. OOPSY DAISY! ☆"
"OOPSY DAISY! ☆"?
YES. YOU MUSTN'T FORGET THAT PART.
ARE YOU FRIENDS OF HIS?
REALLY? BUT...
HUH?
THEN ...
TOTAL STRANGER.
ABSOLUTELY, COMPLETELY, AND TOTALLY UNABLE TO FIND ANY RELATION. THAT'S HOW UNASSOCIATED WE ARE.
HAHAHA
HAHAHAHAHA
UMM... THAT IFFY POSTSCRIPT IS JUST LIKE KIARA, ISN'T IT?
THIS DEFINITELY SHOWS HIS CHARACTERISTIC INCONSISTENCY AND PURPOSELESSNESS...
HUH?
creak

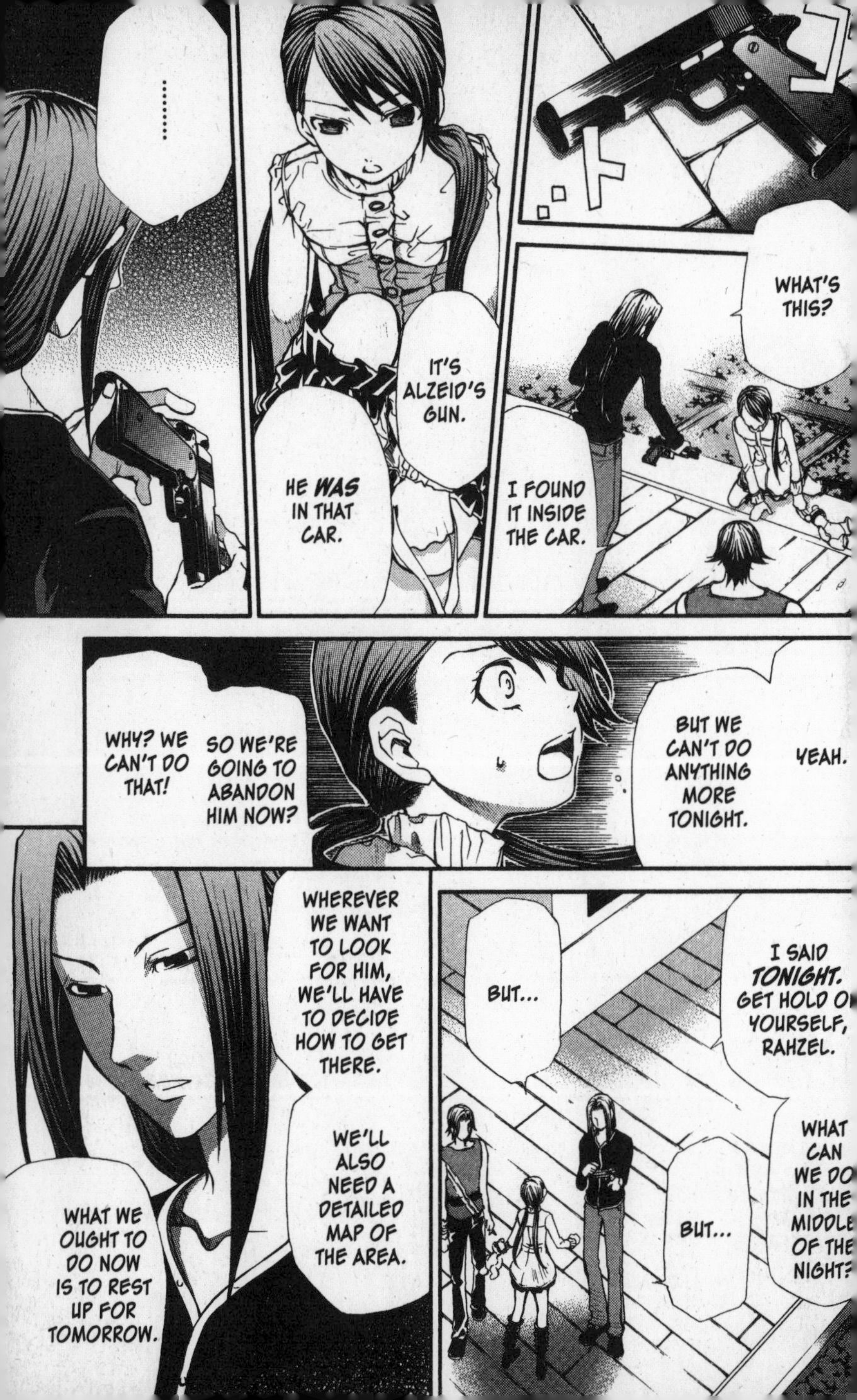
WHAT'S THIS?
I FOUND IT INSIDE THE CAR.
IT'S ALZEID'S GUN.
HE *WAS* IN THAT CAR.
......
YEAH.
BUT WE CAN'T DO ANYTHING MORE TONIGHT.
SO WE'RE GOING TO ABANDON HIM NOW?
WHY? WE CAN'T DO THAT!
I SAID *TONIGHT.* GET HOLD O YOURSELF, RAHZEL.
BUT...
WHAT CAN WE DO IN THE MIDDLE OF THE NIGHT?
BUT...
WHEREVER WE WANT TO LOOK FOR HIM, WE'LL HAVE TO DECIDE HOW TO GET THERE.
WE'LL ALSO NEED A DETAILED MAP OF THE AREA.
WHAT WE OUGHT TO DO NOW IS TO REST UP FOR TOMORROW.

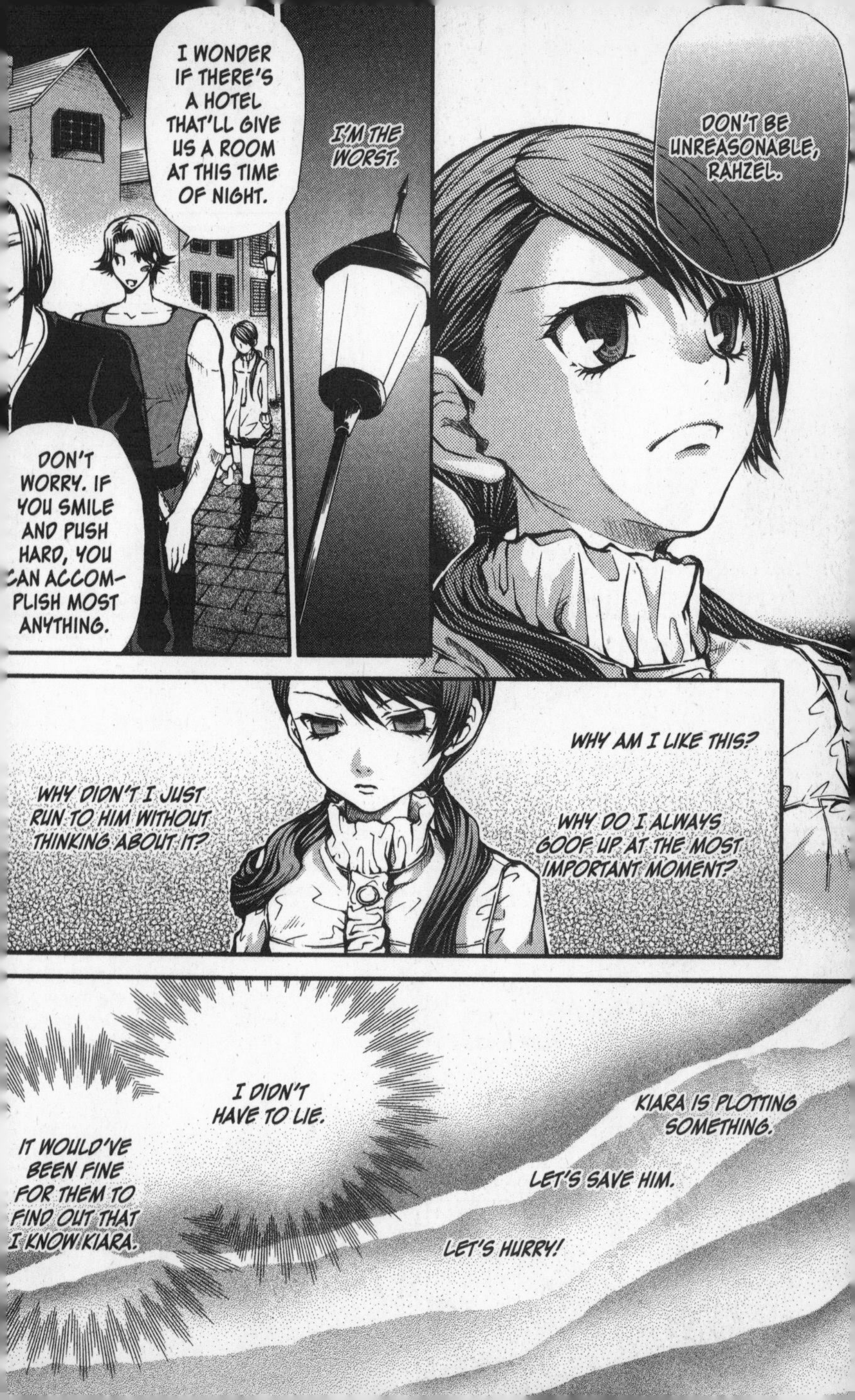
DON'T BE UNREASONABLE, RAHZEL.
I'M THE WORST.
I WONDER IF THERE'S A HOTEL THAT'LL GIVE US A ROOM AT THIS TIME OF NIGHT.
DON'T WORRY. IF YOU SMILE AND PUSH HARD, YOU CAN ACCOMPLISH MOST ANYTHING.
WHY AM I LIKE THIS?
WHY DO I ALWAYS GOOF UP AT THE MOST IMPORTANT MOMENT?
WHY DIDN'T I JUST RUN TO HIM WITHOUT THINKING ABOUT IT?
KIARA IS PLOTTING SOMETHING.
LET'S SAVE HIM.
LET'S HURRY!
I DIDN'T HAVE TO LIE.
IT WOULD'VE BEEN FINE FOR THEM TO FIND OUT THAT I KNOW KIARA.

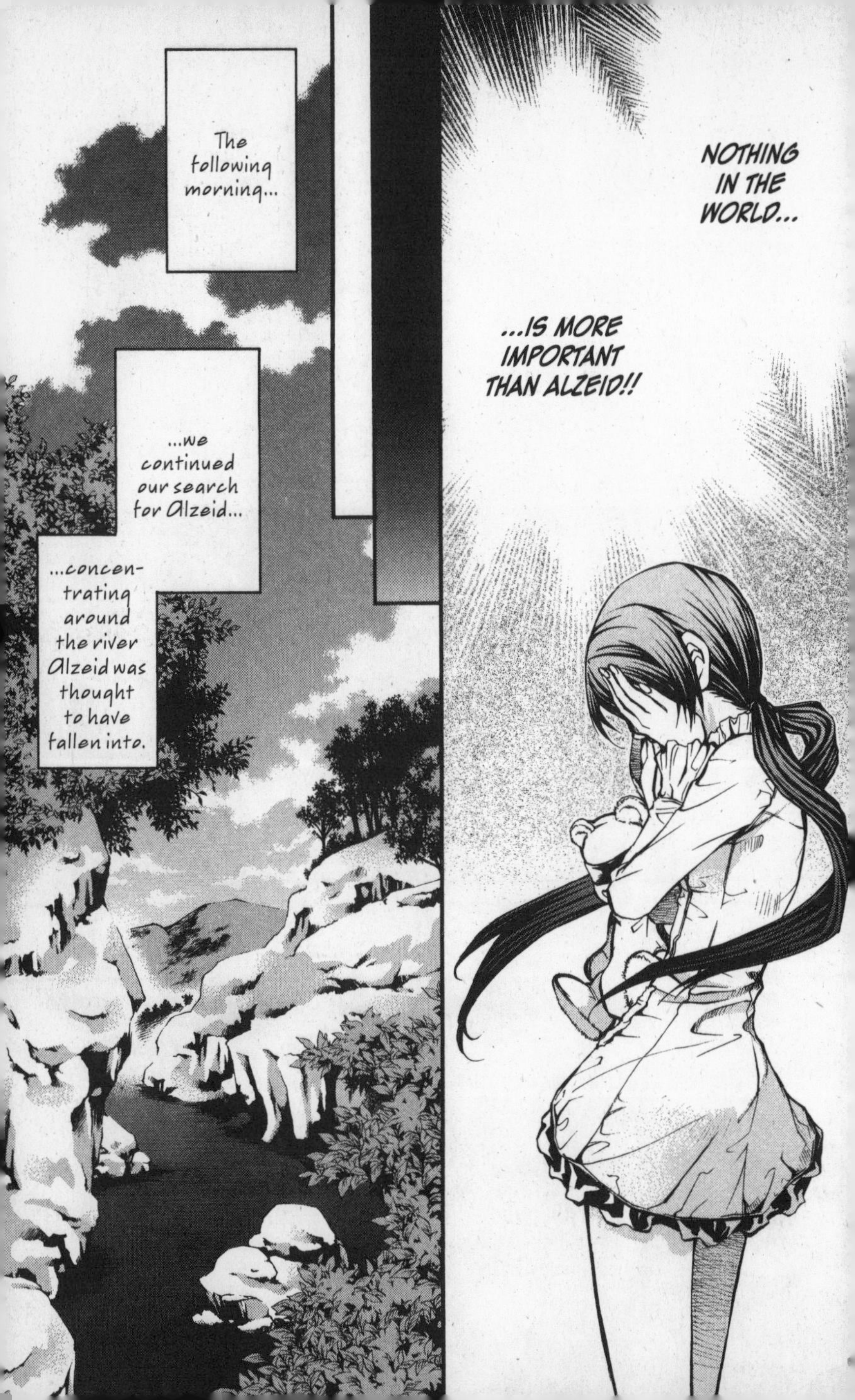
NOTHING IN THE WORLD...
...IS MORE IMPORTANT THAN ALZEID!!
The following morning...
...we continued our search for Alzeid...
...concentrating around the river Alzeid was thought to have fallen into.

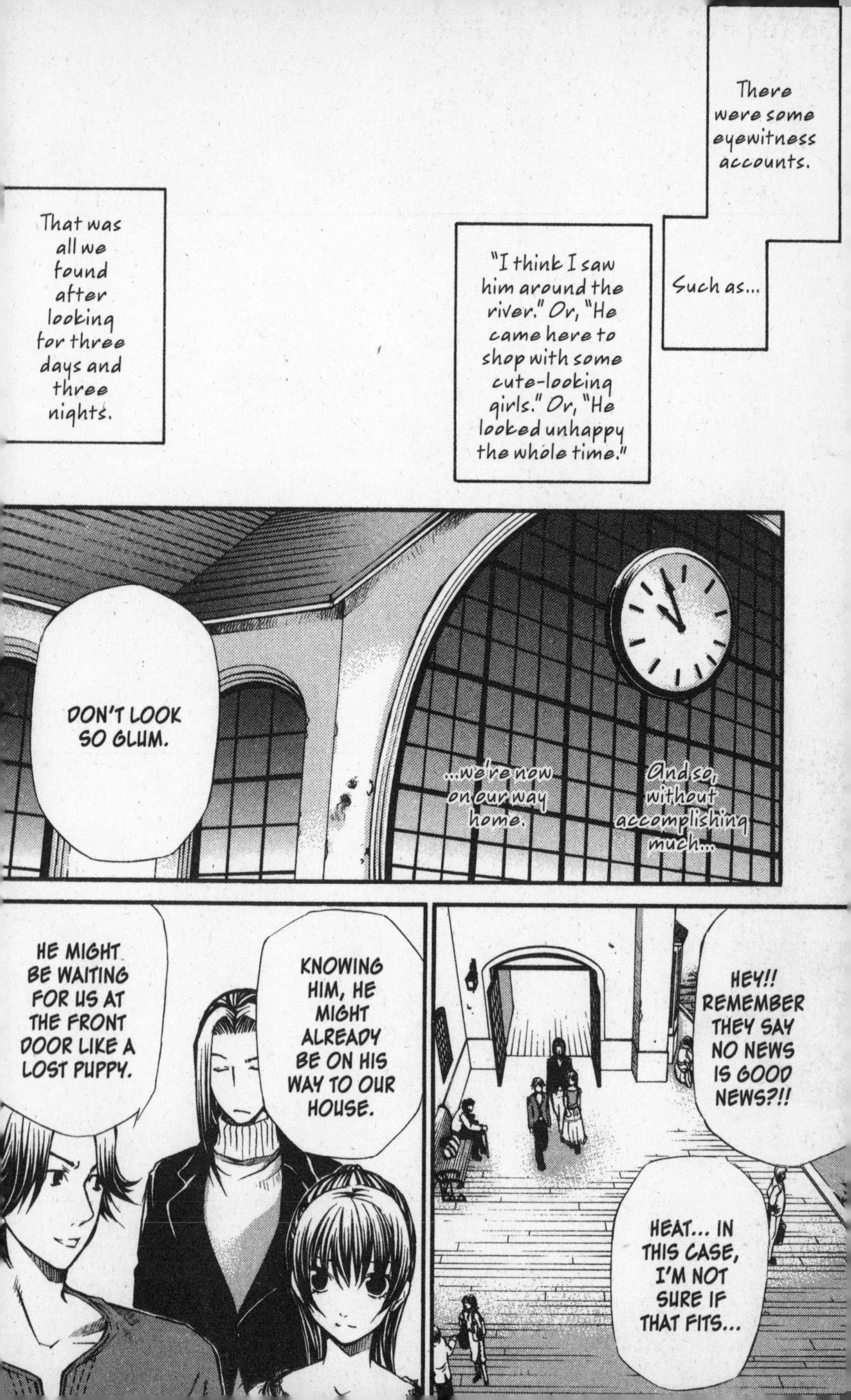
There were some eyewitness accounts.
Such as...
"I think I saw him around the river." Or, "He came here to shop with some cute-looking girls." Or, "He looked unhappy the whole time."
That was all we found after looking for three days and three nights.
And so, without accomplishing much...
...we're now on our way home.
DON'T LOOK SO GLUM.
HEY!! REMEMBER THEY SAY NO NEWS IS GOOD NEWS?!!
HEAT... IN THIS CASE, I'M NOT SURE IF THAT FITS...
KNOWING HIM, HE MIGHT ALREADY BE ON HIS WAY TO OUR HOUSE.
HE MIGHT BE WAITING FOR US AT THE FRONT DOOR LIKE A LOST PUPPY.

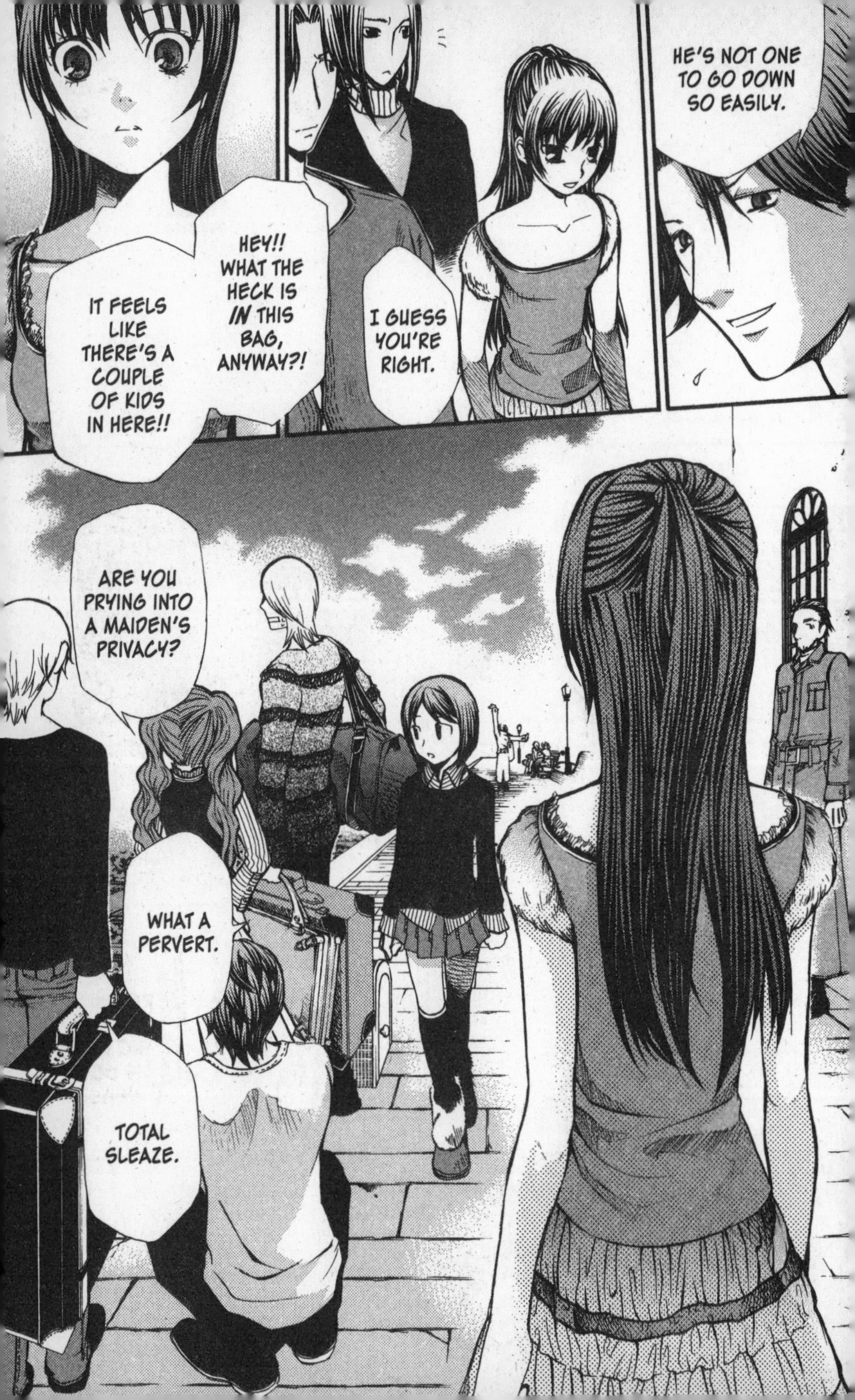
HE'S NOT ONE TO GO DOWN SO EASILY.
I GUESS YOU'RE RIGHT.
HEY!! WHAT THE HECK IS *IN* THIS BAG, ANYWAY?!
IT FEELS LIKE THERE'S A COUPLE OF KIDS IN HERE!!
ARE YOU PRYING INTO A MAIDEN'S PRIVACY?
WHAT A PERVERT.
TOTAL SLEAZE.

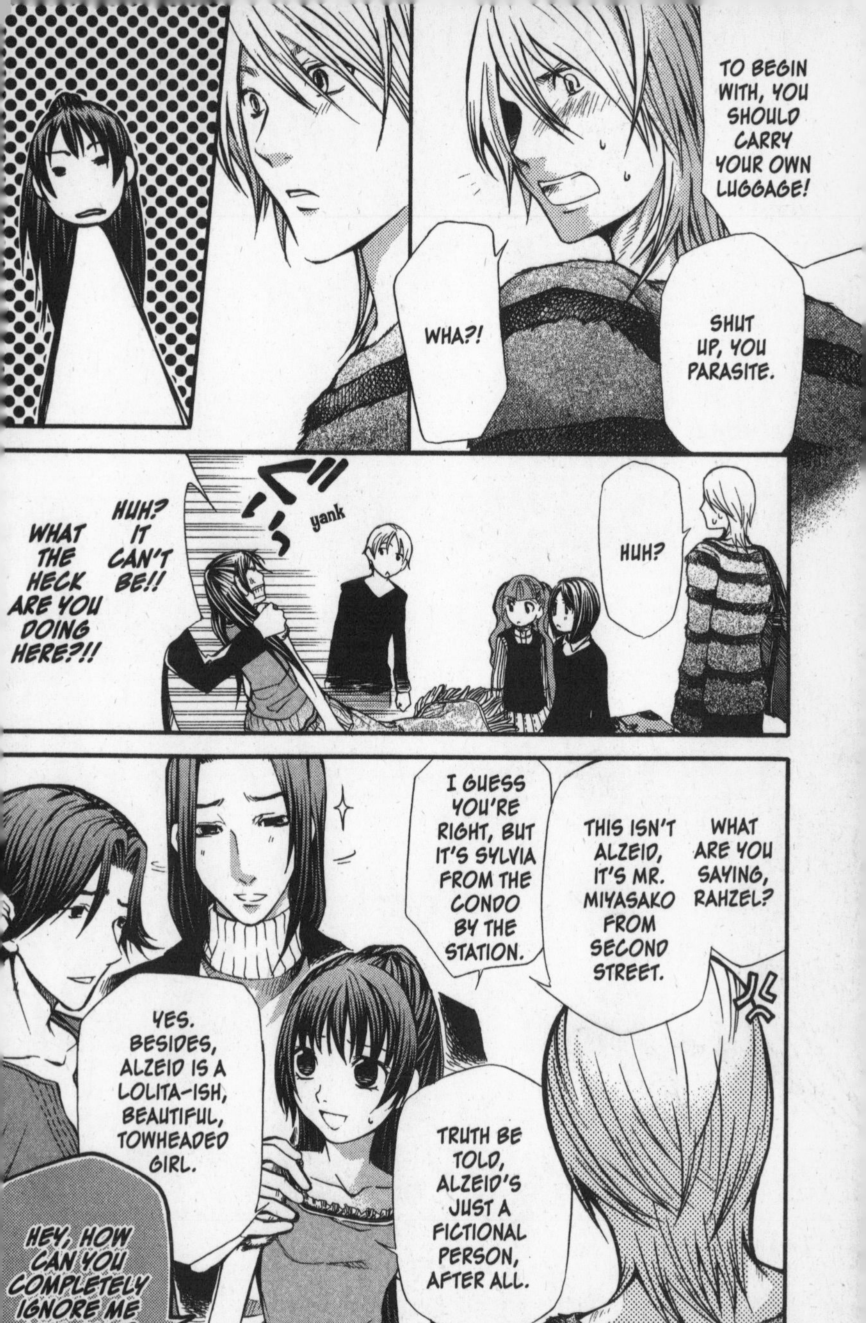
TO BEGIN WITH, YOU SHOULD CARRY YOUR OWN LUGGAGE!
SHUT UP, YOU PARASITE.
WHA?!
HUH?
yank
HUH? IT CAN'T BE!!
WHAT THE HECK ARE YOU DOING HERE?!!
WHAT ARE YOU SAYING, RAHZEL?
THIS ISN'T ALZEID, IT'S MR. MIYASAKO FROM SECOND STREET.
I GUESS YOU'RE RIGHT, BUT IT'S SYLVIA FROM THE CONDO BY THE STATION.
TRUTH BE TOLD, ALZEID'S JUST A FICTIONAL PERSON, AFTER ALL.
YES. BESIDES, ALZEID IS A LOLITA-ISH, BEAUTIFUL, TOWHEADED GIRL.
HEY, HOW CAN YOU COMPLETELY IGNORE ME LIKE THAT?

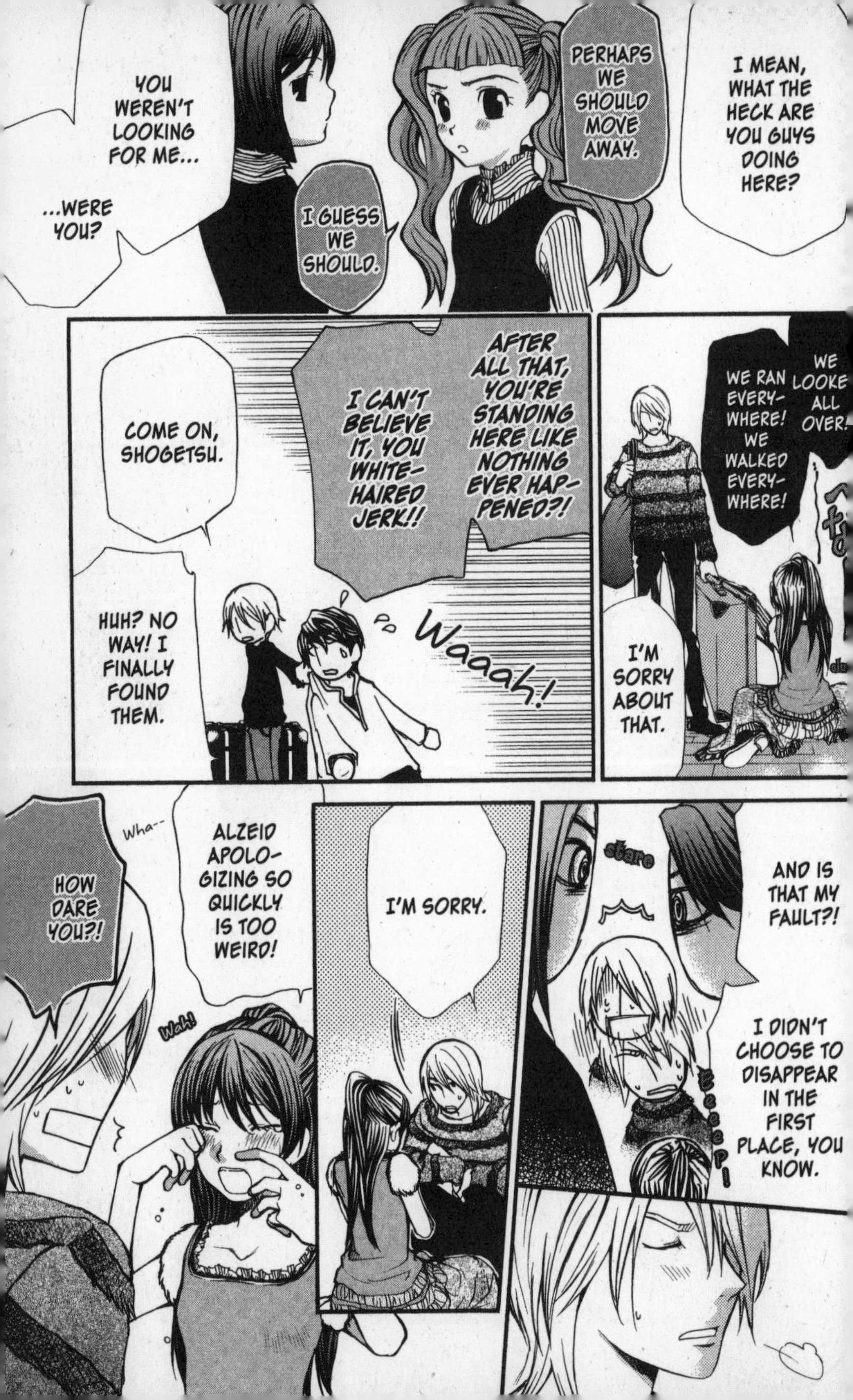
I MEAN, WHAT THE HECK ARE YOU GUYS DOING HERE?
PERHAPS WE SHOULD MOVE AWAY.
I GUESS WE SHOULD.
YOU WEREN'T LOOKING FOR ME...
...WERE YOU?
WE LOOKE ALL OVER!
WE RAN EVERY-WHERE! WE WALKED EVERY-WHERE!
I'M SORRY ABOUT THAT.
AFTER ALL THAT, YOU'RE STANDING HERE LIKE NOTHING EVER HAP-PENED?!
I CAN'T BELIEVE IT, YOU WHITE-HAIRED JERK!!
COME ON, SHOGETSU.
Waaah!
HUH? NO WAY! I FINALLY FOUND THEM.
stare
AND IS THAT MY FAULT?!
Beeep!
I DIDN'T CHOOSE TO DISAPPEAR IN THE FIRST PLACE, YOU KNOW.
I'M SORRY.
ALZEID APOLO-GIZING SO QUICKLY IS TOO WEIRD!
Wha--
HOW DARE YOU?!
Wah!

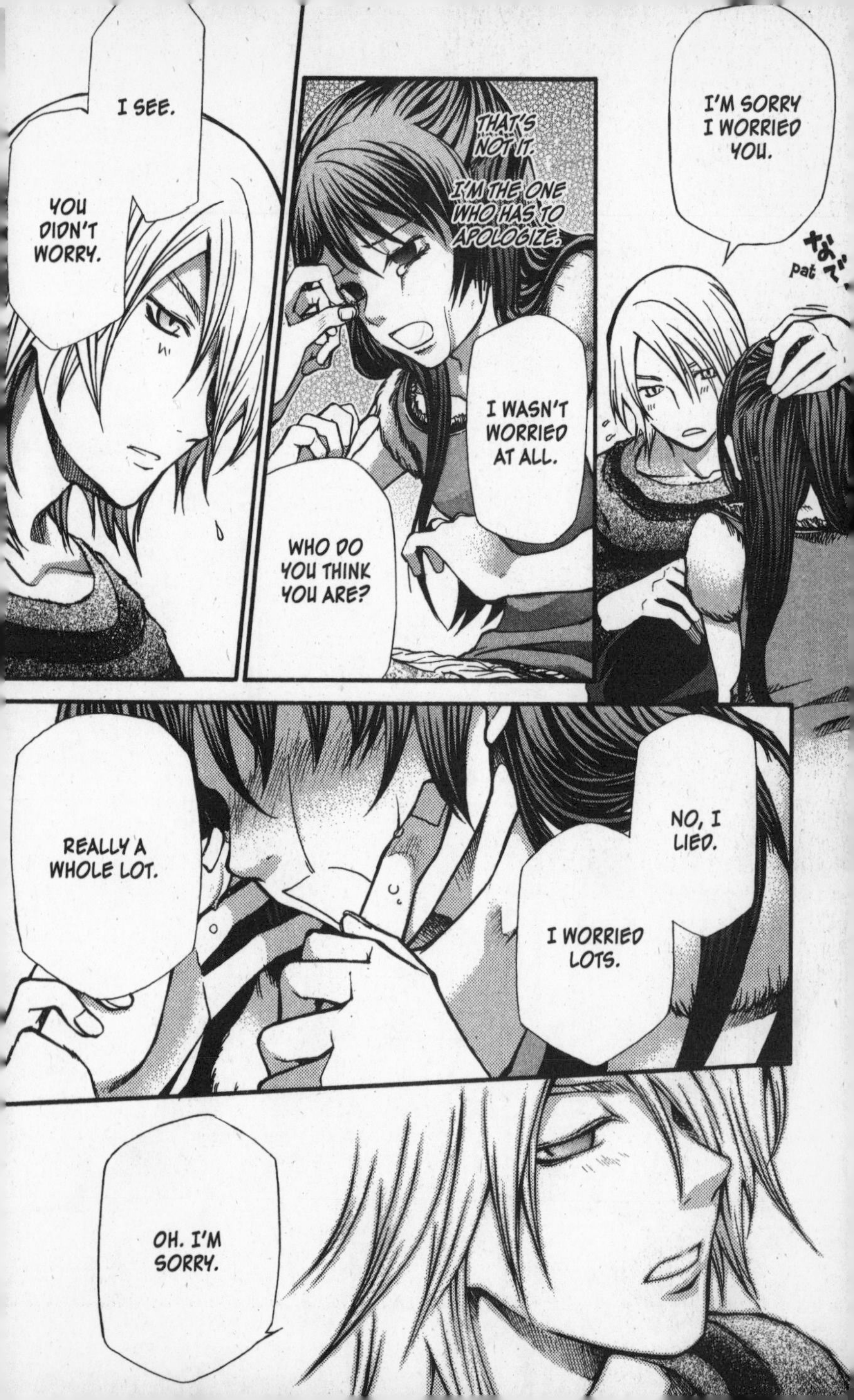
I'M SORRY I WORRIED YOU.
なで pat
THAT'S NOT IT.
I'M THE ONE WHO HAS TO APOLOGIZE.
I WASN'T WORRIED AT ALL.
WHO DO YOU THINK YOU ARE?
I SEE.
YOU DIDN'T WORRY.
NO, I LIED.
I WORRIED LOTS.
REALLY A WHOLE LOT.
OH. I'M SORRY.

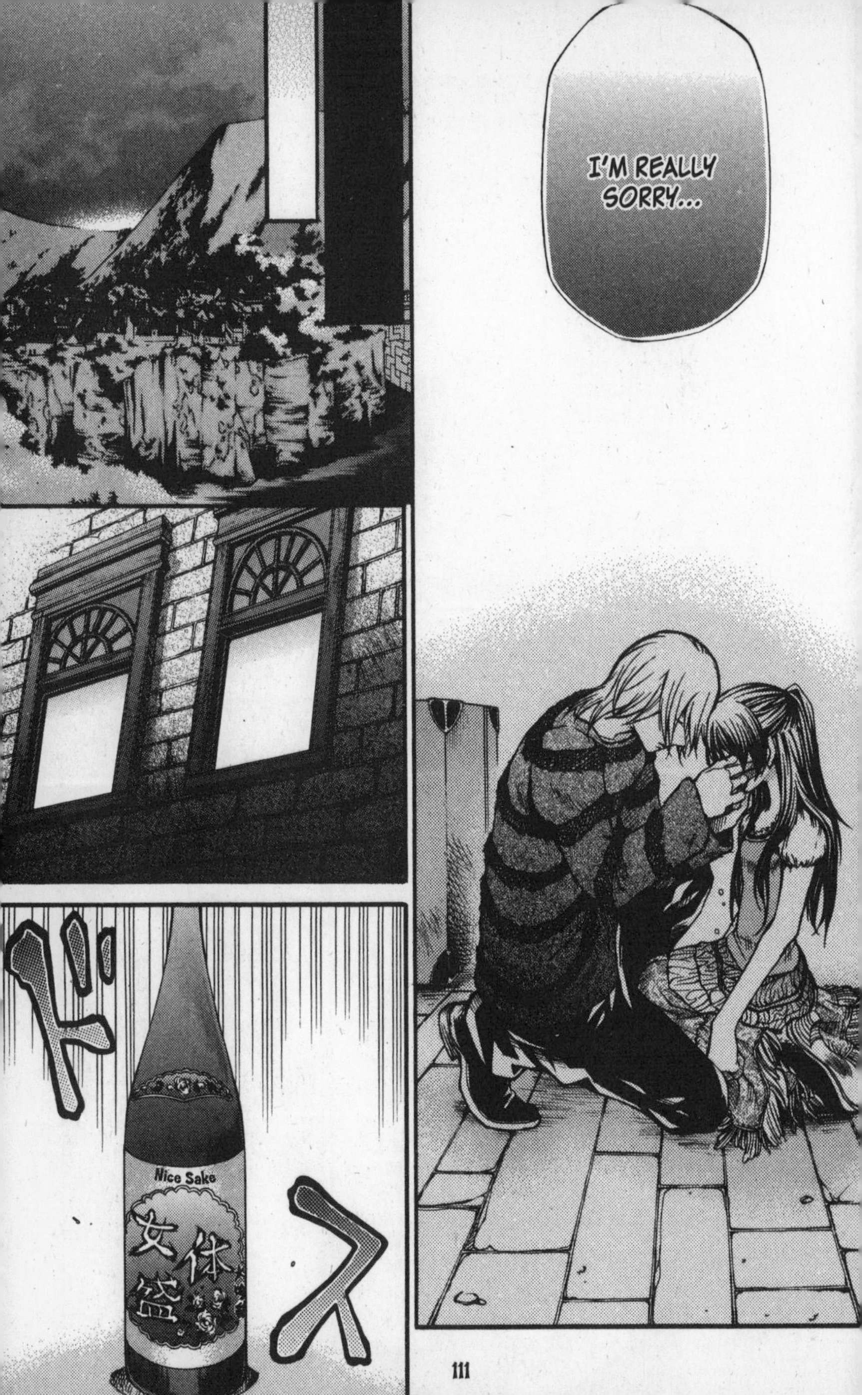
I'M REALLY SORRY...
ドス
Nice Sake
女体盛

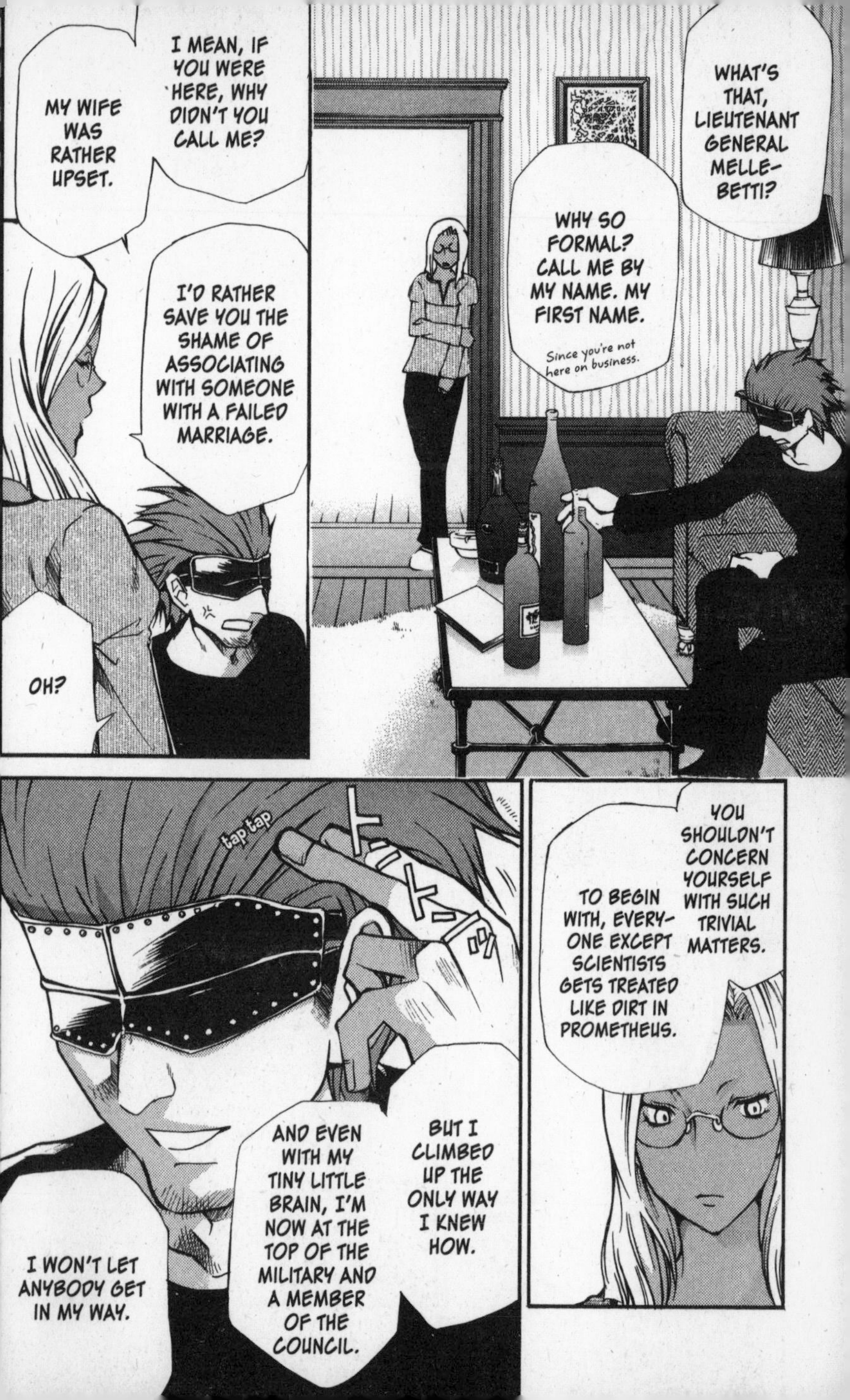
WHAT'S THAT, LIEUTENANT GENERAL MELLE-BETTI?
WHY SO FORMAL? CALL ME BY MY NAME. MY FIRST NAME.
Since you're not here on business.
I MEAN, IF YOU WERE HERE, WHY DIDN'T YOU CALL ME?
MY WIFE WAS RATHER UPSET.
I'D RATHER SAVE YOU THE SHAME OF ASSOCIATING WITH SOMEONE WITH A FAILED MARRIAGE.
OH?
YOU SHOULDN'T CONCERN YOURSELF WITH SUCH TRIVIAL MATTERS.
TO BEGIN WITH, EVERY-ONE EXCEPT SCIENTISTS GETS TREATED LIKE DIRT IN PROMETHEUS.
tap tap
BUT I CLIMBED UP THE ONLY WAY I KNEW HOW.
AND EVEN WITH MY TINY LITTLE BRAIN, I'M NOW AT THE TOP OF THE MILITARY AND A MEMBER OF THE COUNCIL.
I WON'T LET ANYBODY GET IN MY WAY.

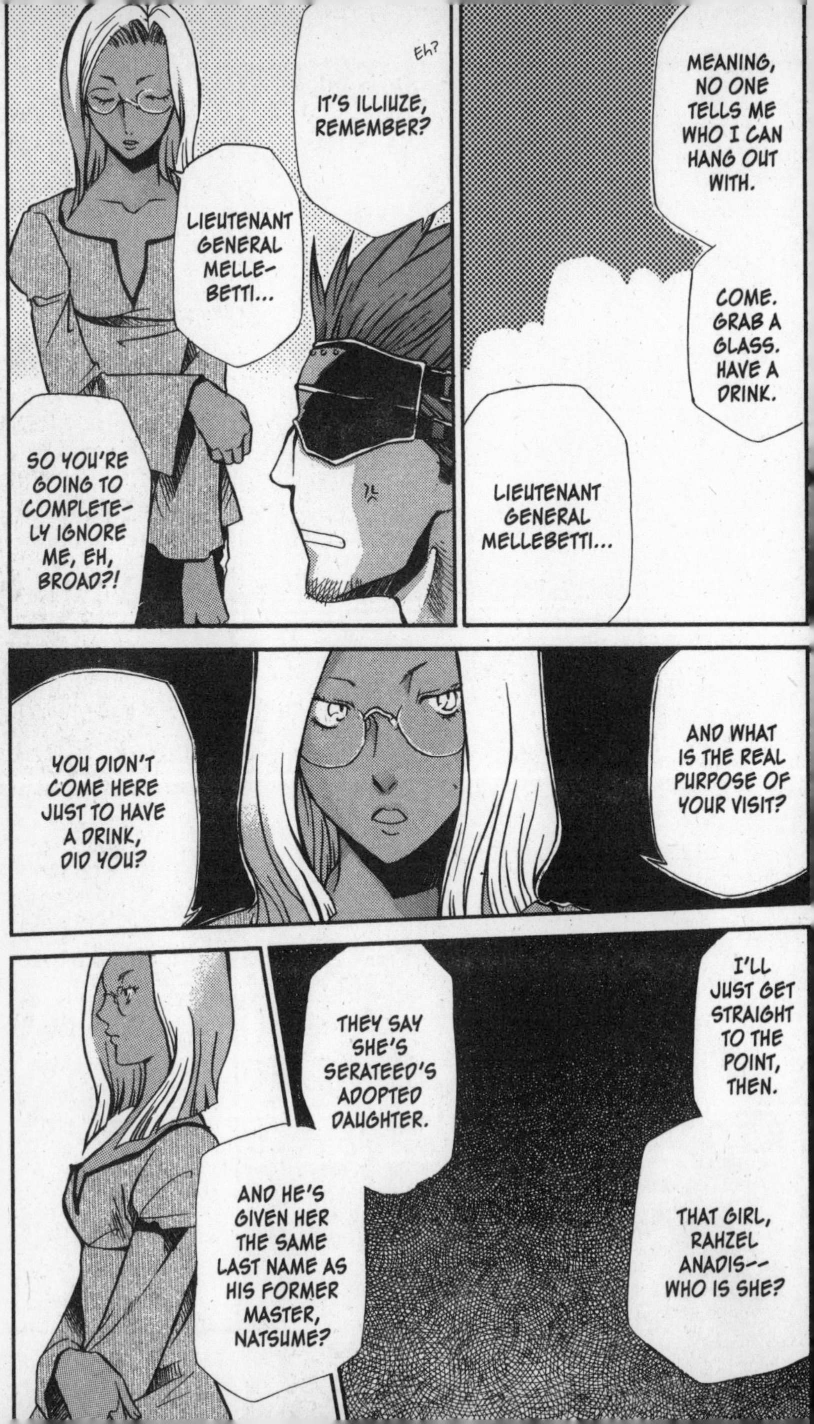
MEANING, NO ONE TELLS ME WHO I CAN HANG OUT WITH.
COME. GRAB A GLASS. HAVE A DRINK.
LIEUTENANT GENERAL MELLEBETTI...
Eh?
IT'S ILLIUZE, REMEMBER?
LIEUTENANT GENERAL MELLE-BETTI...
SO YOU'RE GOING TO COMPLETE-LY IGNORE ME, EH, BROAD?!
AND WHAT IS THE REAL PURPOSE OF YOUR VISIT?
YOU DIDN'T COME HERE JUST TO HAVE A DRINK, DID YOU?
I'LL JUST GET STRAIGHT TO THE POINT, THEN.
THAT GIRL, RAHZEL ANADIS--WHO IS SHE?
THEY SAY SHE'S SERATEED'S ADOPTED DAUGHTER.
AND HE'S GIVEN HER THE SAME LAST NAME AS HIS FORMER MASTER, NATSUME?

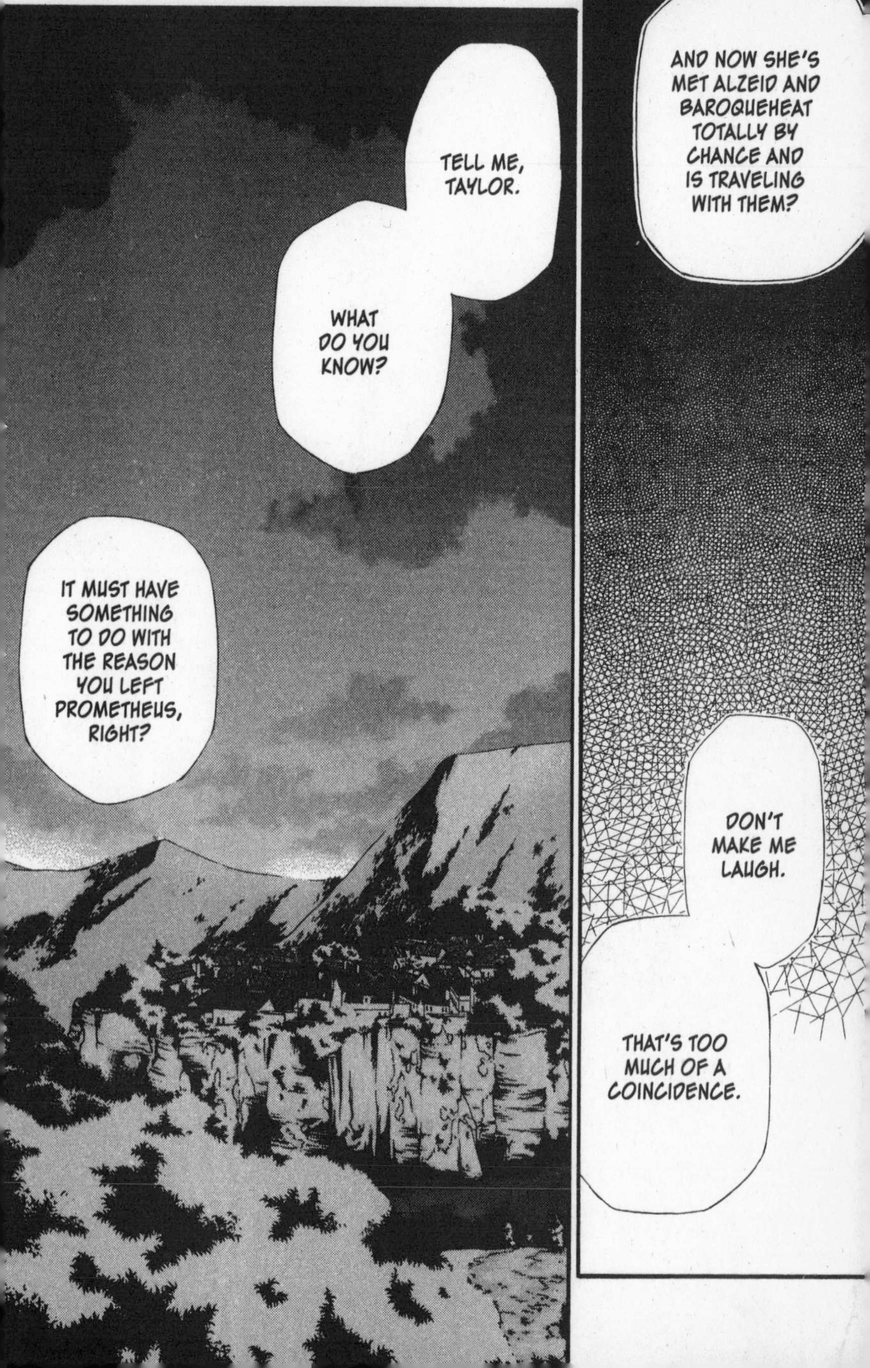
AND NOW SHE'S MET ALZEID AND BAROQUEHEAT TOTALLY BY CHANCE AND IS TRAVELING WITH THEM?
DON'T MAKE ME LAUGH.
THAT'S TOO MUCH OF A COINCIDENCE.
TELL ME, TAYLOR.
WHAT DO YOU KNOW?
IT MUST HAVE SOMETHING TO DO WITH THE REASON YOU LEFT PROMETHEUS, RIGHT?

"I'm home."

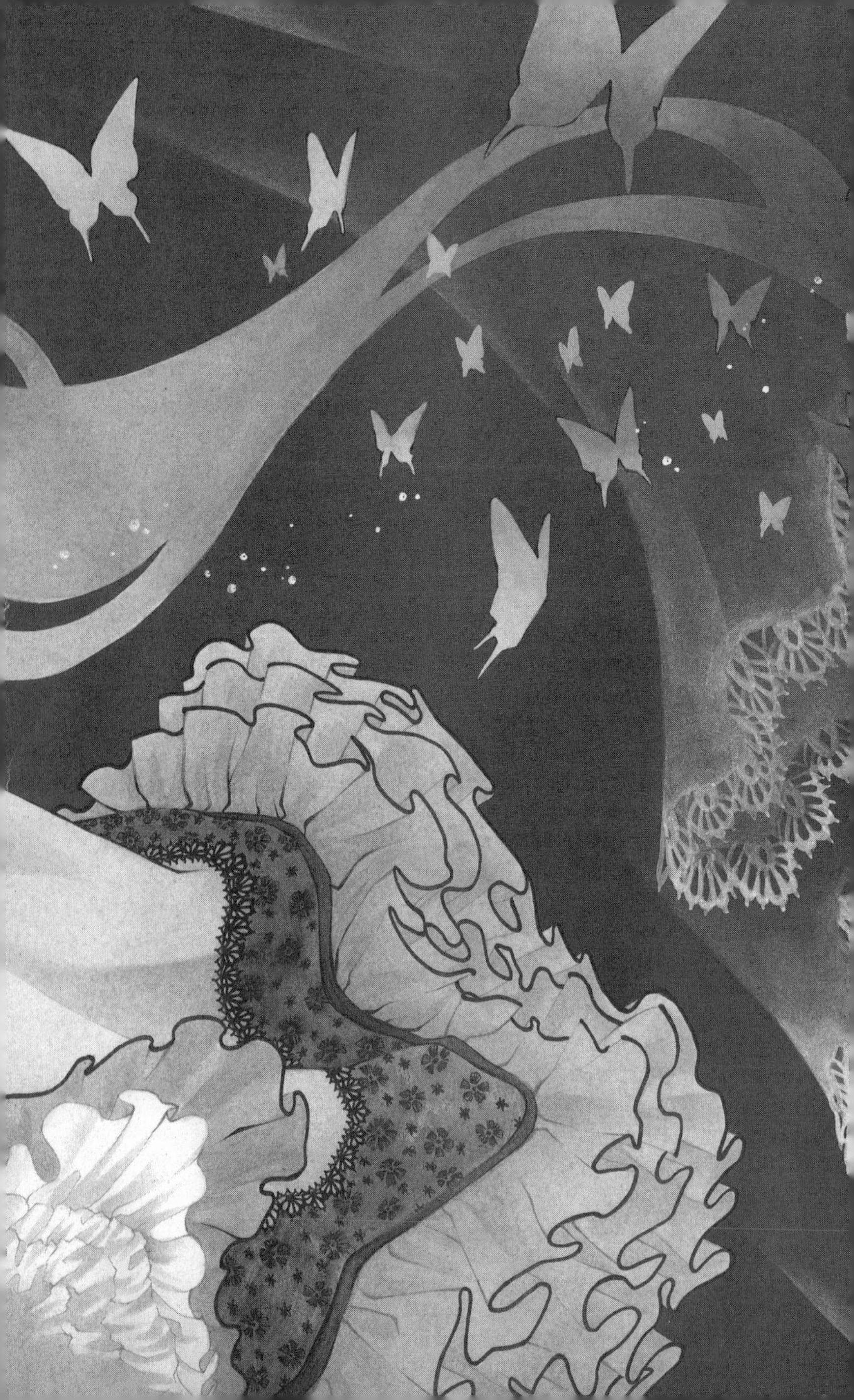

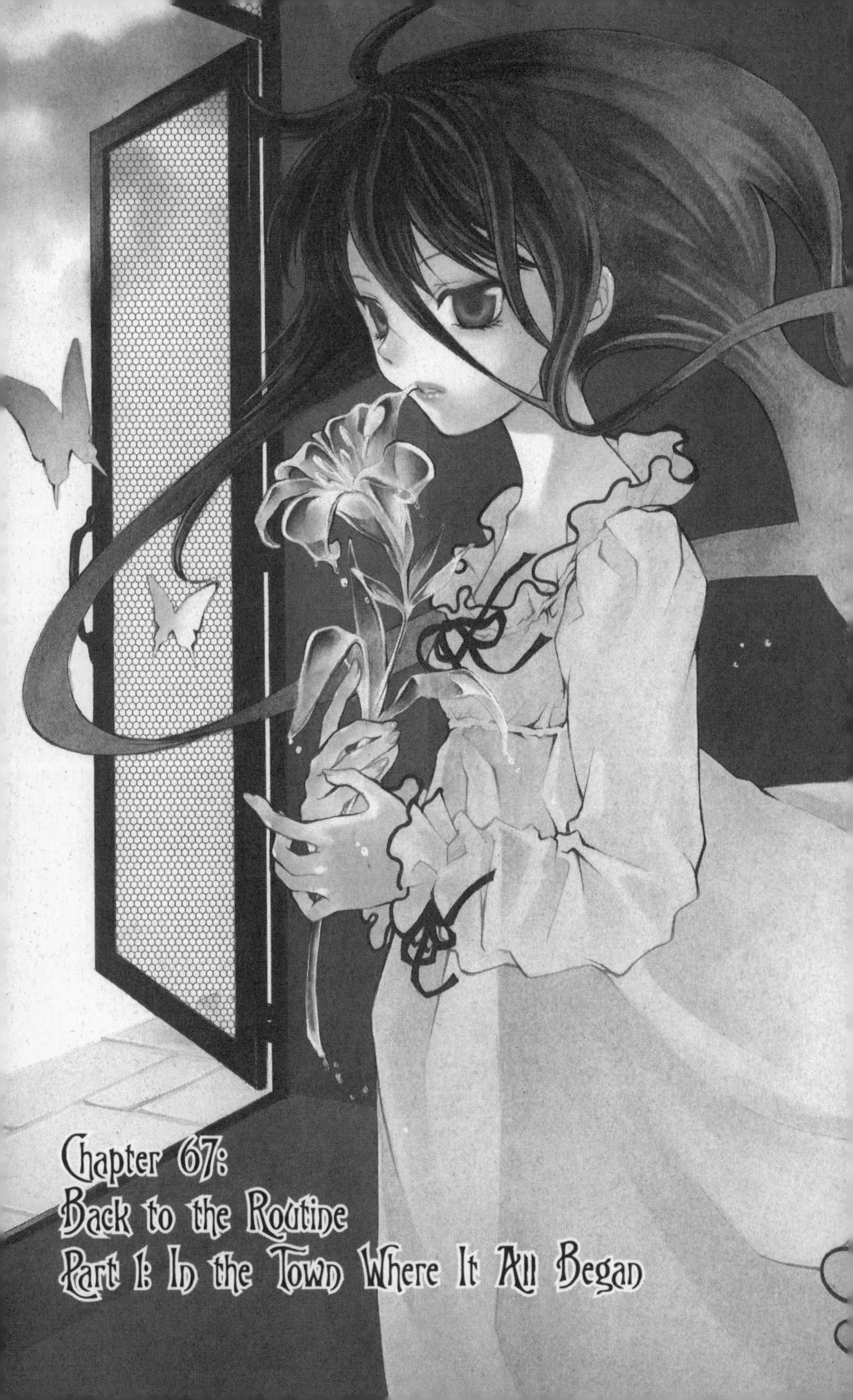
Chapter 67:
Back to the Routine
Part 1: In the Town Where It All Began

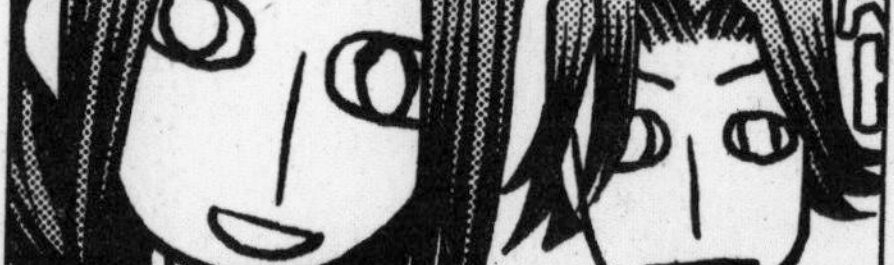
A
HA

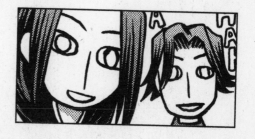

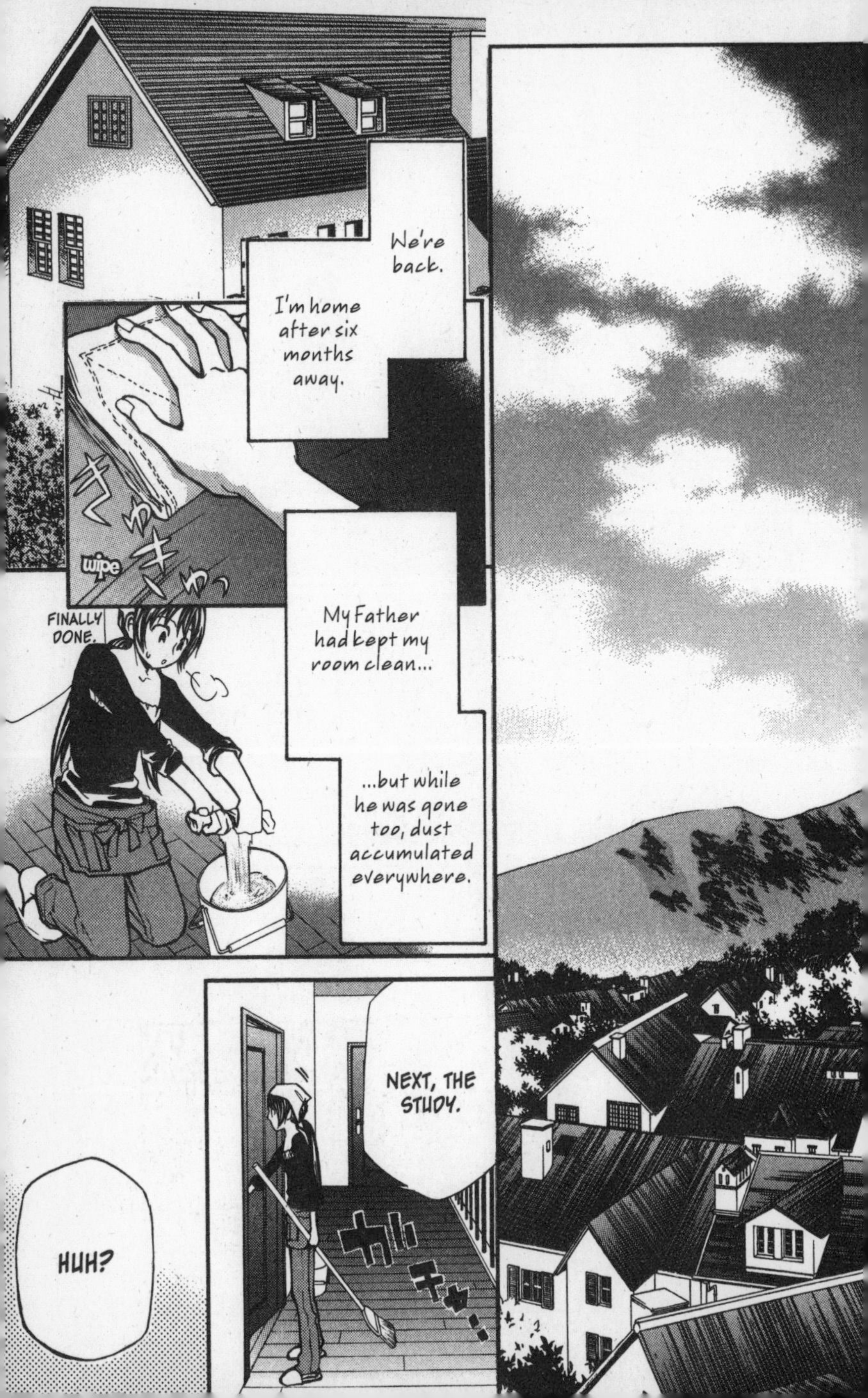

We're back.
I'm home after six months away.
wipe
FINALLY DONE.
My Father had kept my room clean...
...but while he was gone too, dust accumulated everywhere.
NEXT, THE STUDY.
HUH?

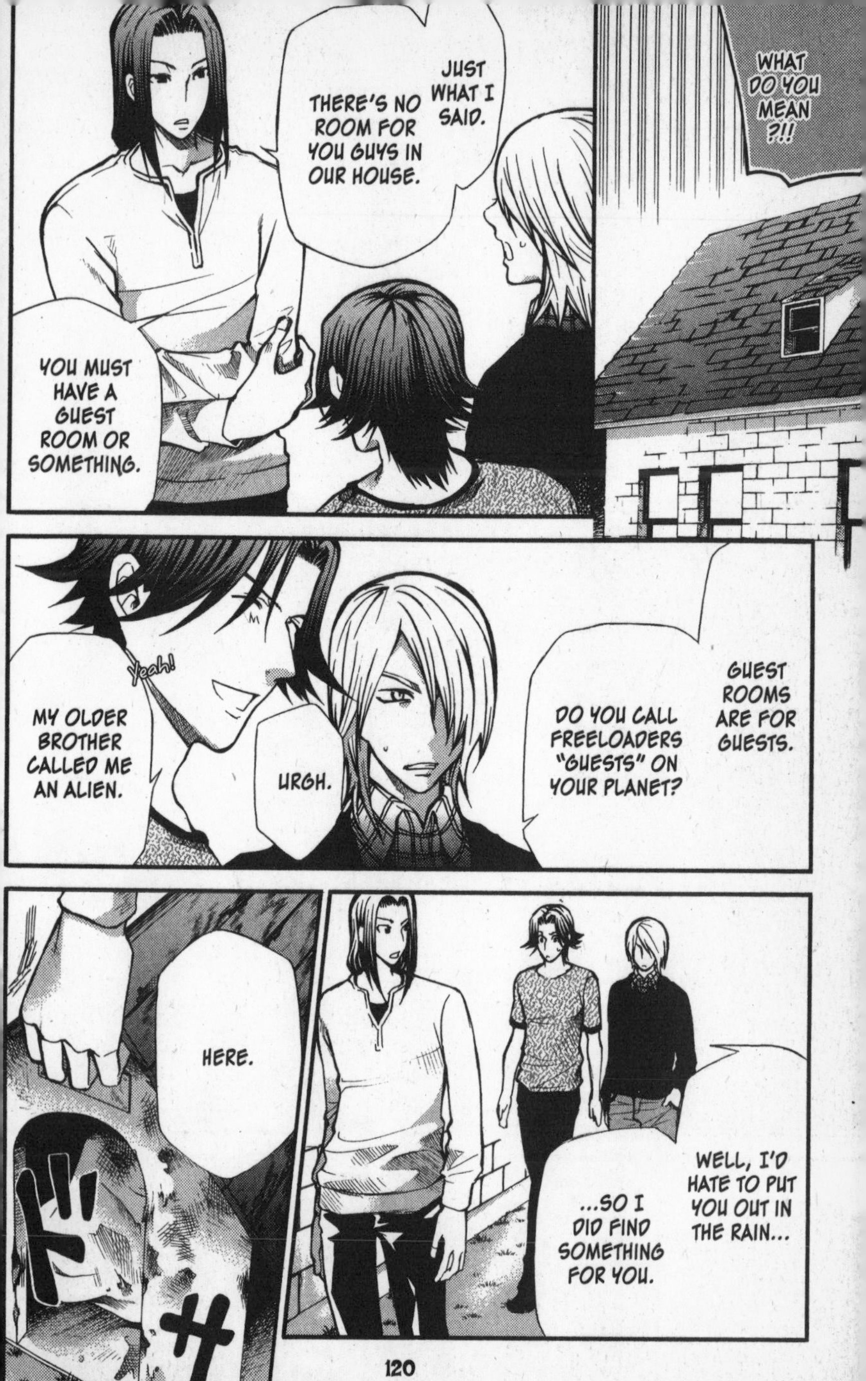
WHAT DO YOU MEAN ?!!
JUST WHAT I SAID.
THERE'S NO ROOM FOR YOU GUYS IN OUR HOUSE.
YOU MUST HAVE A GUEST ROOM OR SOMETHING.
GUEST ROOMS ARE FOR GUESTS.
DO YOU CALL FREELOADERS "GUESTS" ON YOUR PLANET?
URGH.
Yeah!
MY OLDER BROTHER CALLED ME AN ALIEN.
WELL, I'D HATE TO PUT YOU OUT IN THE RAIN...
...SO I DID FIND SOMETHING FOR YOU.
HERE.
ドサ

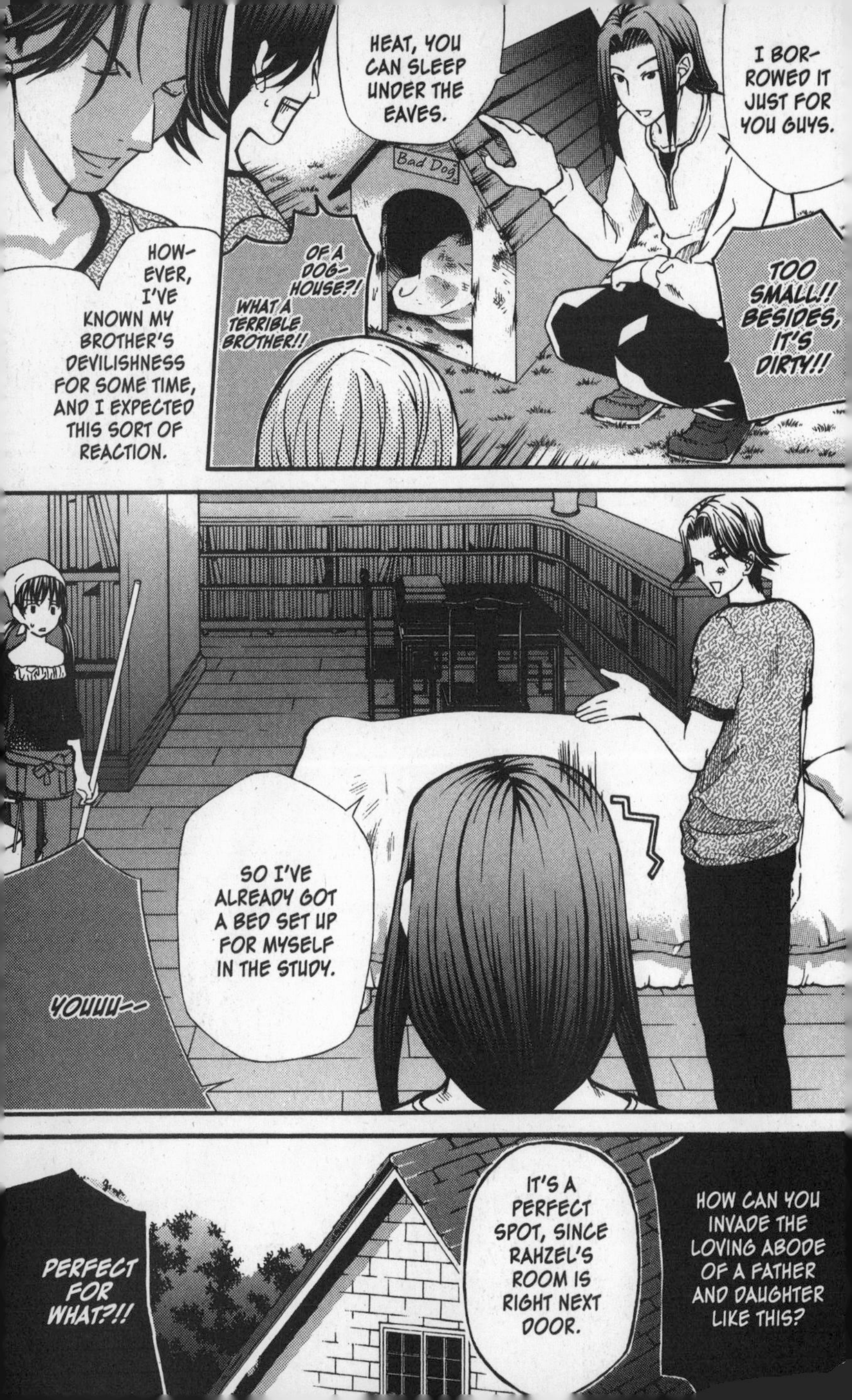
I BOR-ROWED IT JUST FOR YOU GUYS.
HEAT, YOU CAN SLEEP UNDER THE EAVES.
Bad Dog
TOO SMALL!! BESIDES, IT'S DIRTY!!
OF A DOG-HOUSE?!
WHAT A TERRIBLE BROTHER!!
HOW-EVER, I'VE KNOWN MY BROTHER'S DEVILISHNESS FOR SOME TIME, AND I EXPECTED THIS SORT OF REACTION.
SO I'VE ALREADY GOT A BED SET UP FOR MYSELF IN THE STUDY.
YOUUU--
HOW CAN YOU INVADE THE LOVING ABODE OF A FATHER AND DAUGHTER LIKE THIS?
IT'S A PERFECT SPOT, SINCE RAHZEL'S ROOM IS RIGHT NEXT DOOR.
PERFECT FOR WHAT?!!

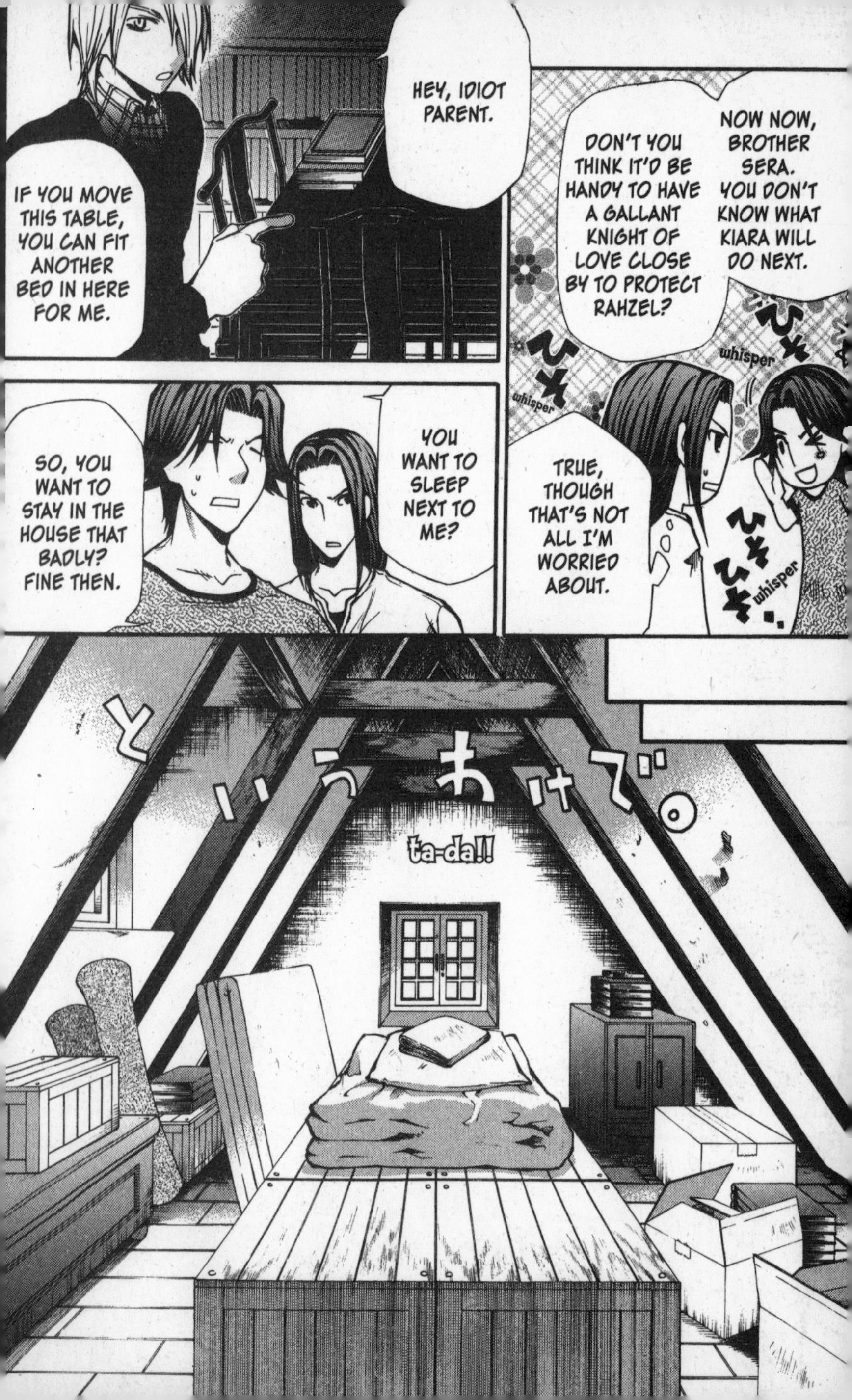
HEY, IDIOT PARENT.
IF YOU MOVE THIS TABLE, YOU CAN FIT ANOTHER BED IN HERE FOR ME.
SO, YOU WANT TO STAY IN THE HOUSE THAT BADLY? FINE THEN.
YOU WANT TO SLEEP NEXT TO ME?
DON'T YOU THINK IT'D BE HANDY TO HAVE A GALLANT KNIGHT OF LOVE CLOSE BY TO PROTECT RAHZEL?
NOW NOW, BROTHER SERA. YOU DON'T KNOW WHAT KIARA WILL DO NEXT.
ひそ whisper
ひそ whisper
TRUE, THOUGH THAT'S NOT ALL I'M WORRIED ABOUT.
ひそひそ whisper
というわけで。
ta-da!!

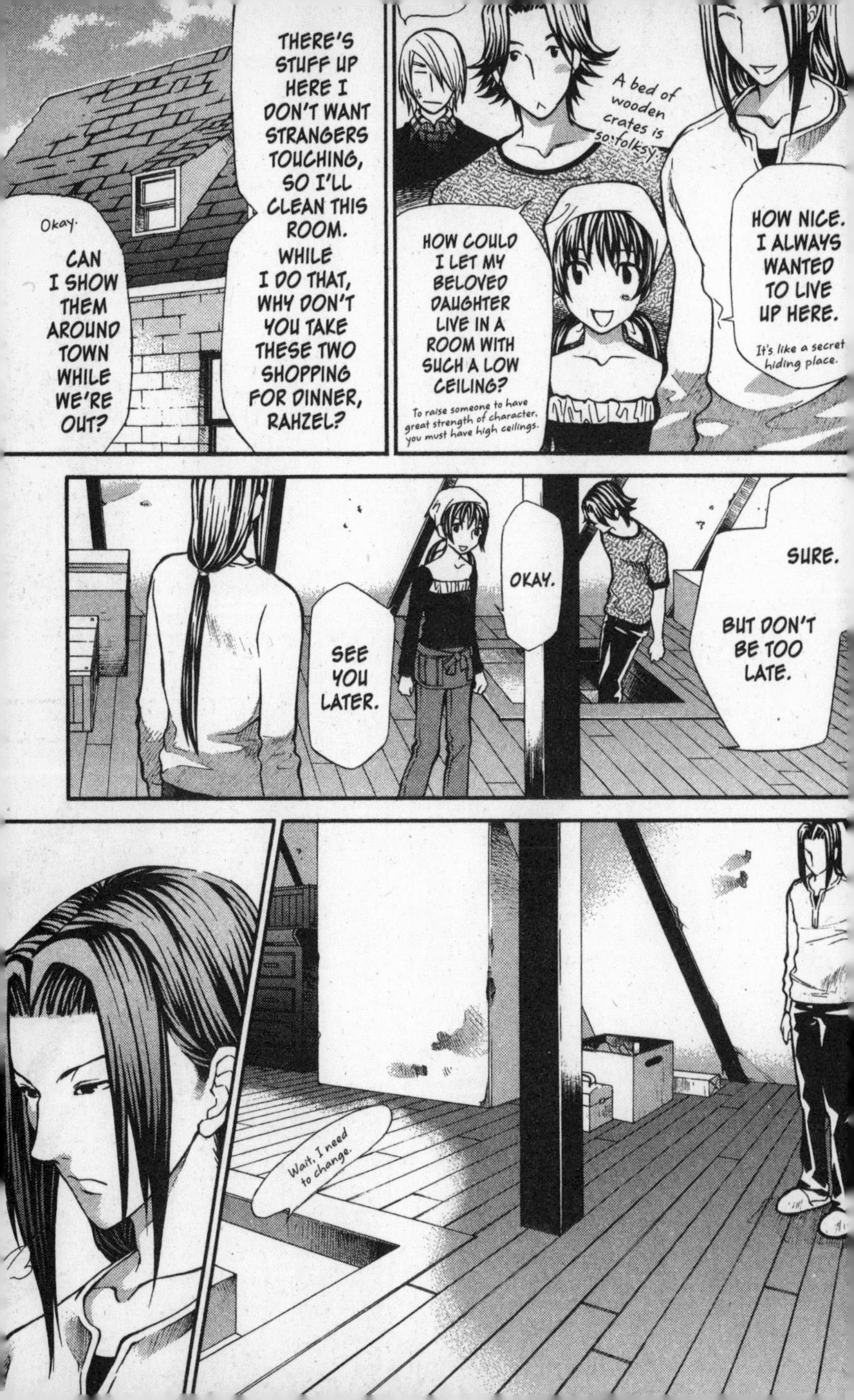
HOW NICE. I ALWAYS WANTED TO LIVE UP HERE.
It's like a secret hiding place.
A bed of wooden crates is so folksy.
HOW COULD I LET MY BELOVED DAUGHTER LIVE IN A ROOM WITH SUCH A LOW CEILING?
To raise someone to have great strength of character, you must have high ceilings.
THERE'S STUFF UP HERE I DON'T WANT STRANGERS TOUCHING, SO I'LL CLEAN THIS ROOM. WHILE I DO THAT, WHY DON'T YOU TAKE THESE TWO SHOPPING FOR DINNER, RAHZEL?
CAN I SHOW THEM AROUND TOWN WHILE WE'RE OUT?
Okay.
SURE.
BUT DON'T BE TOO LATE.
OKAY.
SEE YOU LATER.
Wait, I need to change.

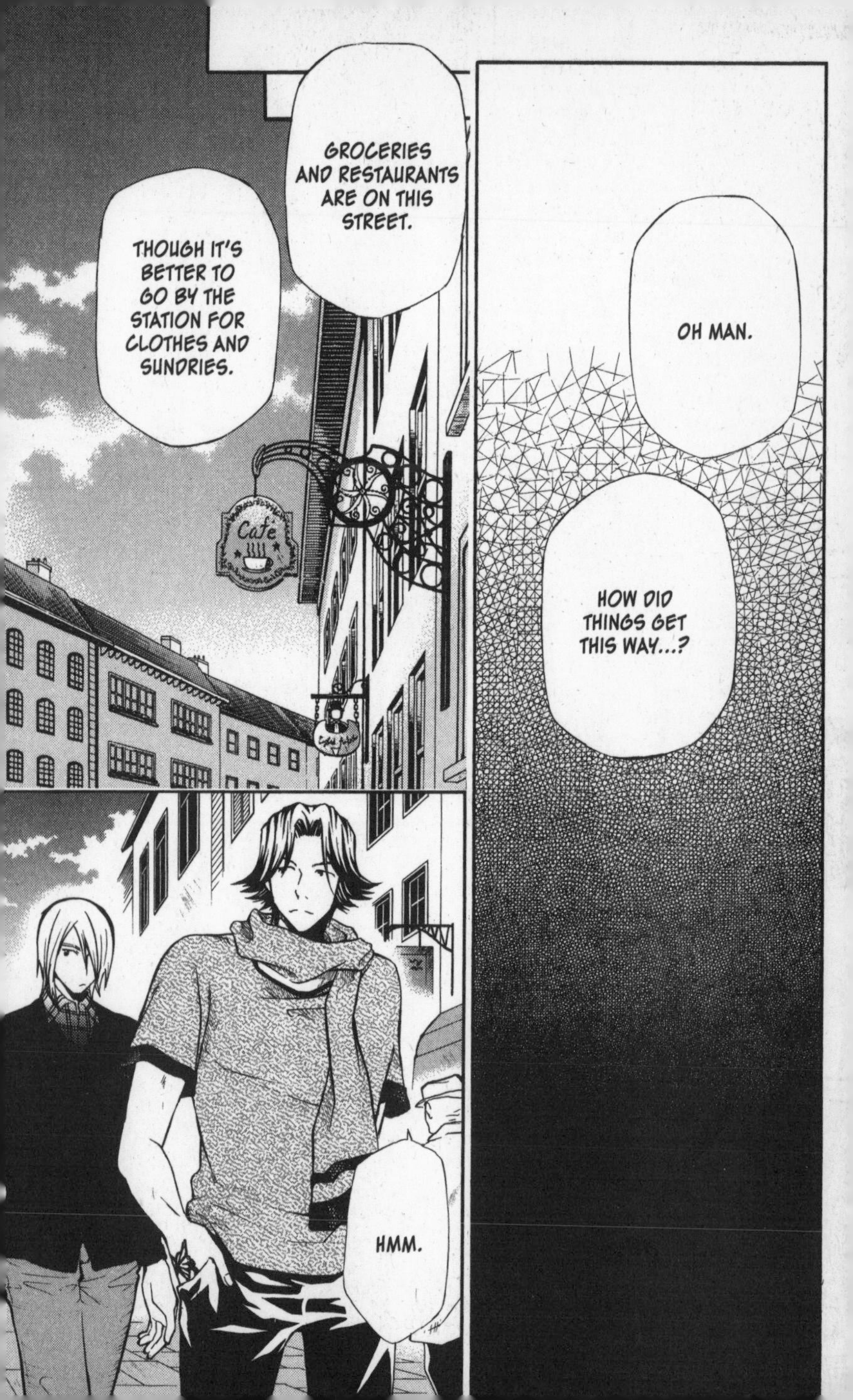
OH MAN.
HOW DID THINGS GET THIS WAY...?
GROCERIES AND RESTAURANTS ARE ON THIS STREET.
THOUGH IT'S BETTER TO GO BY THE STATION FOR CLOTHES AND SUNDRIES.
Café
HMM.

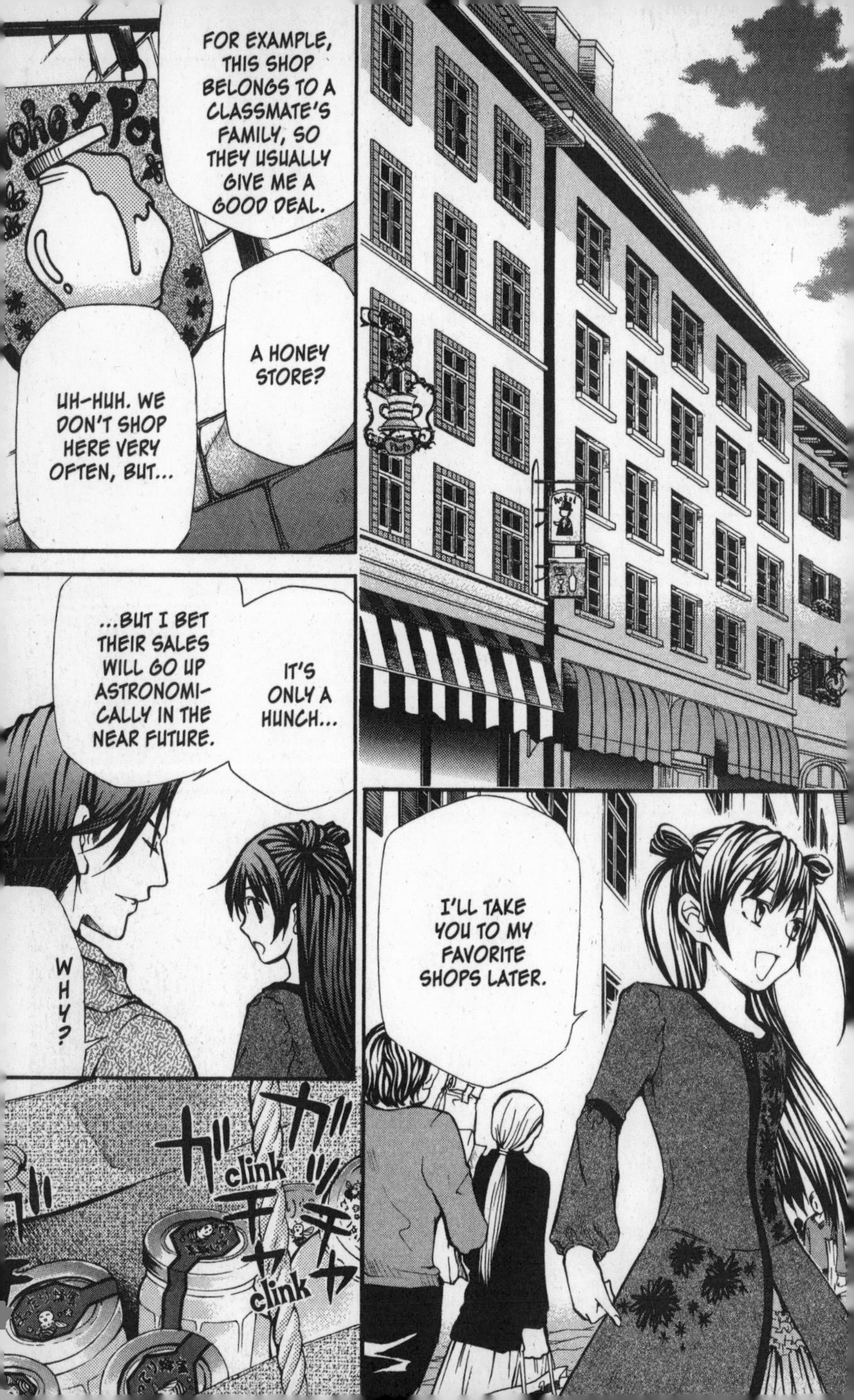

FOR EXAMPLE, THIS SHOP BELONGS TO A CLASSMATE'S FAMILY, SO THEY USUALLY GIVE ME A GOOD DEAL.
A HONEY STORE?
UH-HUH. WE DON'T SHOP HERE VERY OFTEN, BUT...
...BUT I BET THEIR SALES WILL GO UP ASTRONOMI-CALLY IN THE NEAR FUTURE.
IT'S ONLY A HUNCH...
WHY?
I'LL TAKE YOU TO MY FAVORITE SHOPS LATER.
clink
clink

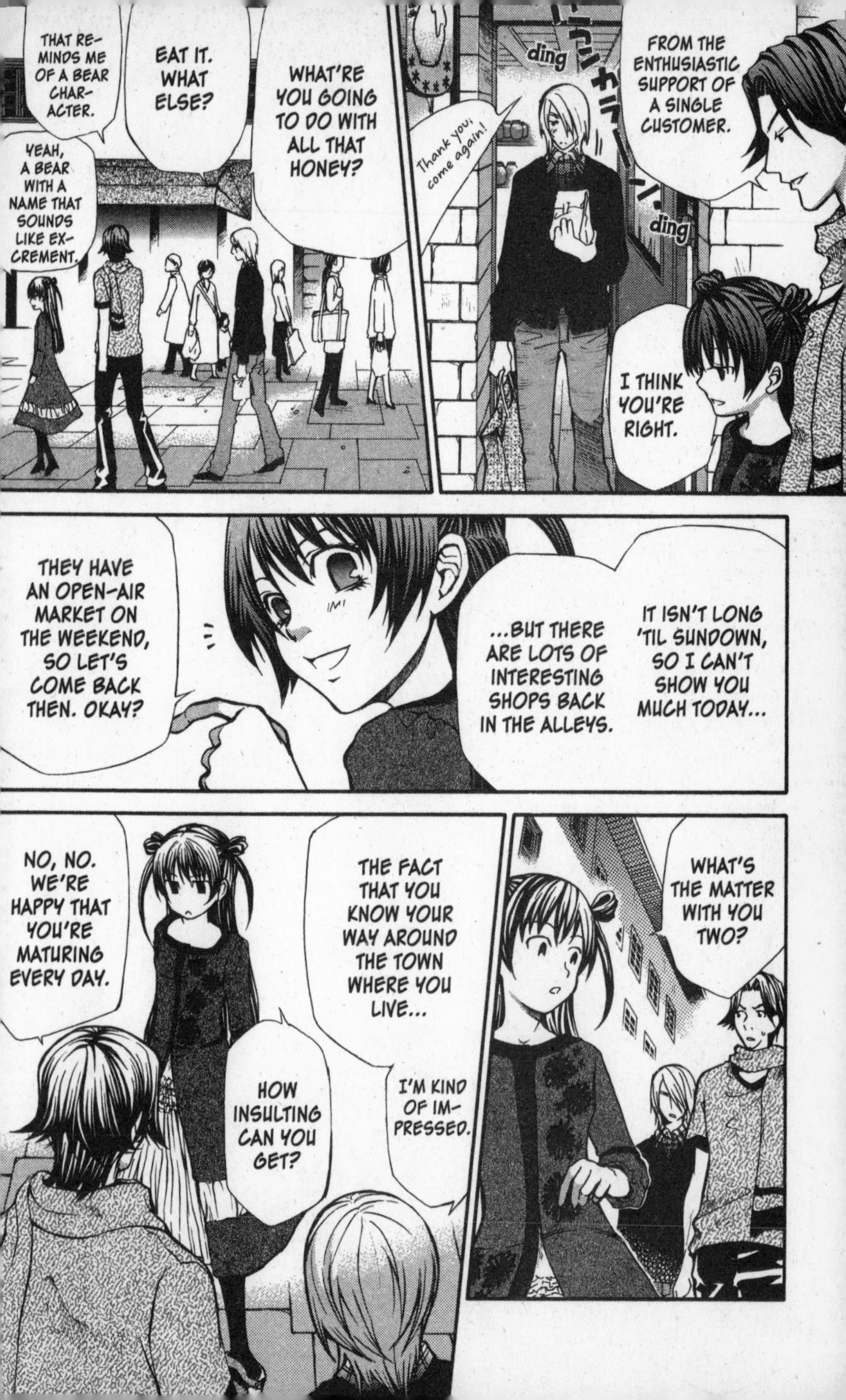
FROM THE ENTHUSIASTIC SUPPORT OF A SINGLE CUSTOMER.
ding
ding
Thank you; come again!
I THINK YOU'RE RIGHT.
WHAT'RE YOU GOING TO DO WITH ALL THAT HONEY?
EAT IT. WHAT ELSE?
THAT RE-MINDS ME OF A BEAR CHAR-ACTER.
YEAH, A BEAR WITH A NAME THAT SOUNDS LIKE EX-CREMENT.
IT ISN'T LONG 'TIL SUNDOWN, SO I CAN'T SHOW YOU MUCH TODAY...
...BUT THERE ARE LOTS OF INTERESTING SHOPS BACK IN THE ALLEYS.
THEY HAVE AN OPEN-AIR MARKET ON THE WEEKEND, SO LET'S COME BACK THEN. OKAY?
WHAT'S THE MATTER WITH YOU TWO?
THE FACT THAT YOU KNOW YOUR WAY AROUND THE TOWN WHERE YOU LIVE...
I'M KIND OF IM-PRESSED.
HOW INSULTING CAN YOU GET?
NO, NO. WE'RE HAPPY THAT YOU'RE MATURING EVERY DAY.

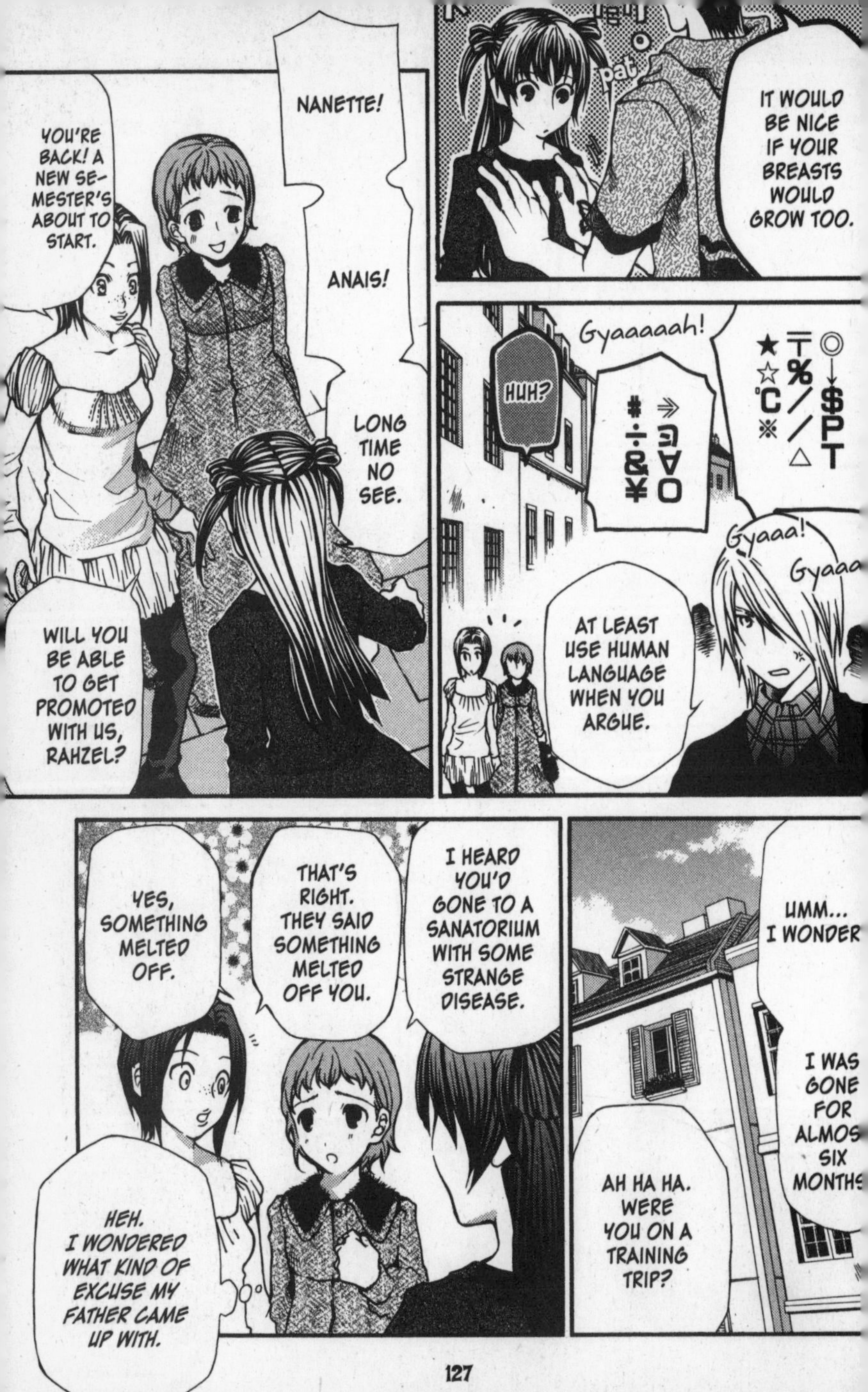
pat
IT WOULD BE NICE IF YOUR BREASTS WOULD GROW TOO.
Gyaaaaah!
◎↓$PT
〒%//△
★☆℃※
⇒ヨ∀O
#÷&¥
HUH?
Gyaaa!
Gyaaa
AT LEAST USE HUMAN LANGUAGE WHEN YOU ARGUE.
NANETTE!
ANAIS!
LONG TIME NO SEE.
YOU'RE BACK! A NEW SE-MESTER'S ABOUT TO START.
WILL YOU BE ABLE TO GET PROMOTED WITH US, RAHZEL?
UMM... I WONDER
I WAS GONE FOR ALMOS SIX MONTHS
AH HA HA. WERE YOU ON A TRAINING TRIP?
I HEARD YOU'D GONE TO A SANATORIUM WITH SOME STRANGE DISEASE.
THAT'S RIGHT. THEY SAID SOMETHING MELTED OFF YOU.
YES, SOMETHING MELTED OFF.
HEH. I WONDERED WHAT KIND OF EXCUSE MY FATHER CAME UP WITH.

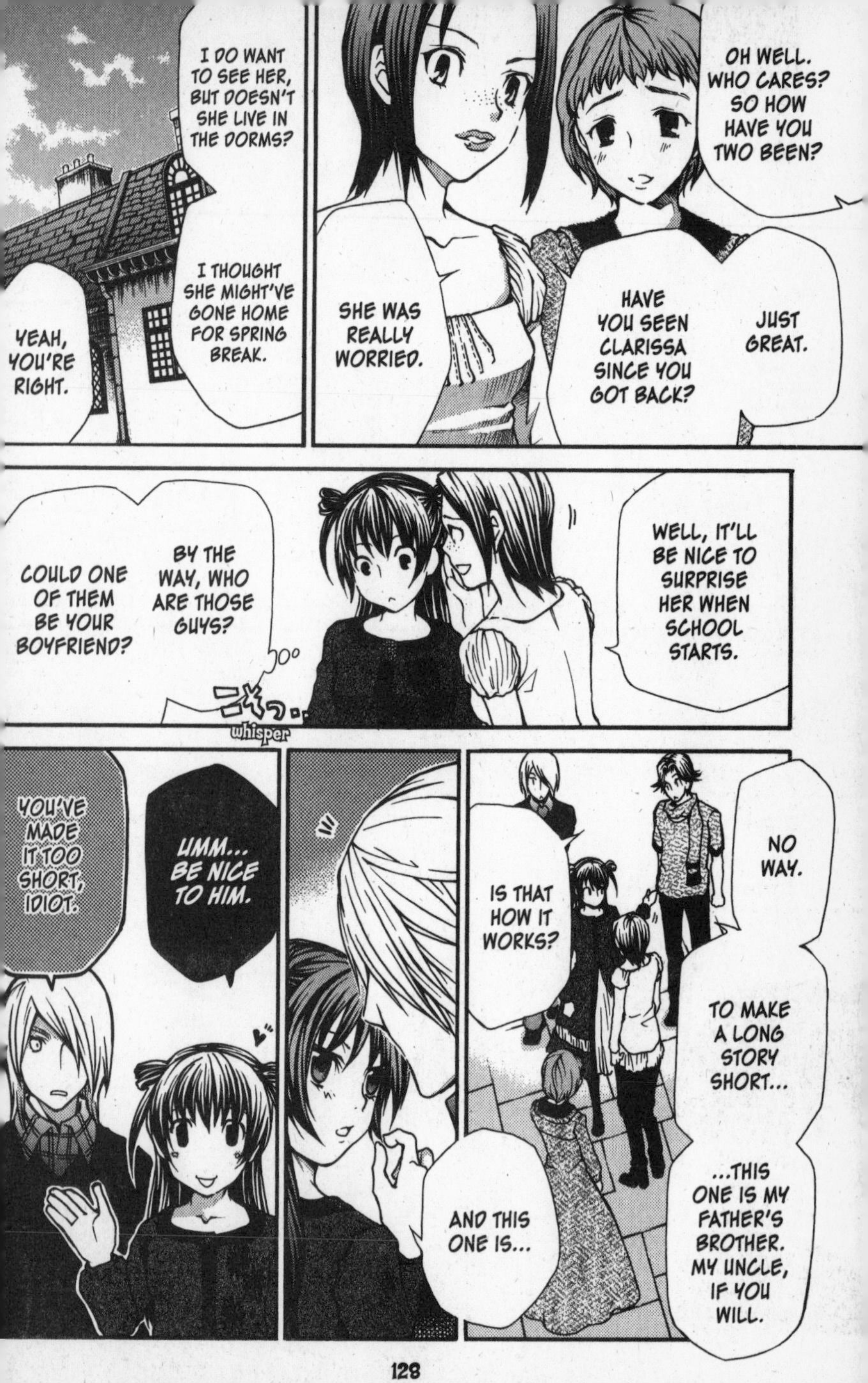
OH WELL. WHO CARES? SO HOW HAVE YOU TWO BEEN?
JUST GREAT.
HAVE YOU SEEN CLARISSA SINCE YOU GOT BACK?
SHE WAS REALLY WORRIED.
I DO WANT TO SEE HER, BUT DOESN'T SHE LIVE IN THE DORMS?
I THOUGHT SHE MIGHT'VE GONE HOME FOR SPRING BREAK.
YEAH, YOU'RE RIGHT.
WELL, IT'LL BE NICE TO SURPRISE HER WHEN SCHOOL STARTS.
BY THE WAY, WHO ARE THOSE GUYS?
COULD ONE OF THEM BE YOUR BOYFRIEND?
whisper
NO WAY.
TO MAKE A LONG STORY SHORT...
...THIS ONE IS MY FATHER'S BROTHER. MY UNCLE, IF YOU WILL.
IS THAT HOW IT WORKS?
AND THIS ONE IS...
UMM... BE NICE TO HIM.
YOU'VE MADE IT TOO SHORT, IDIOT.

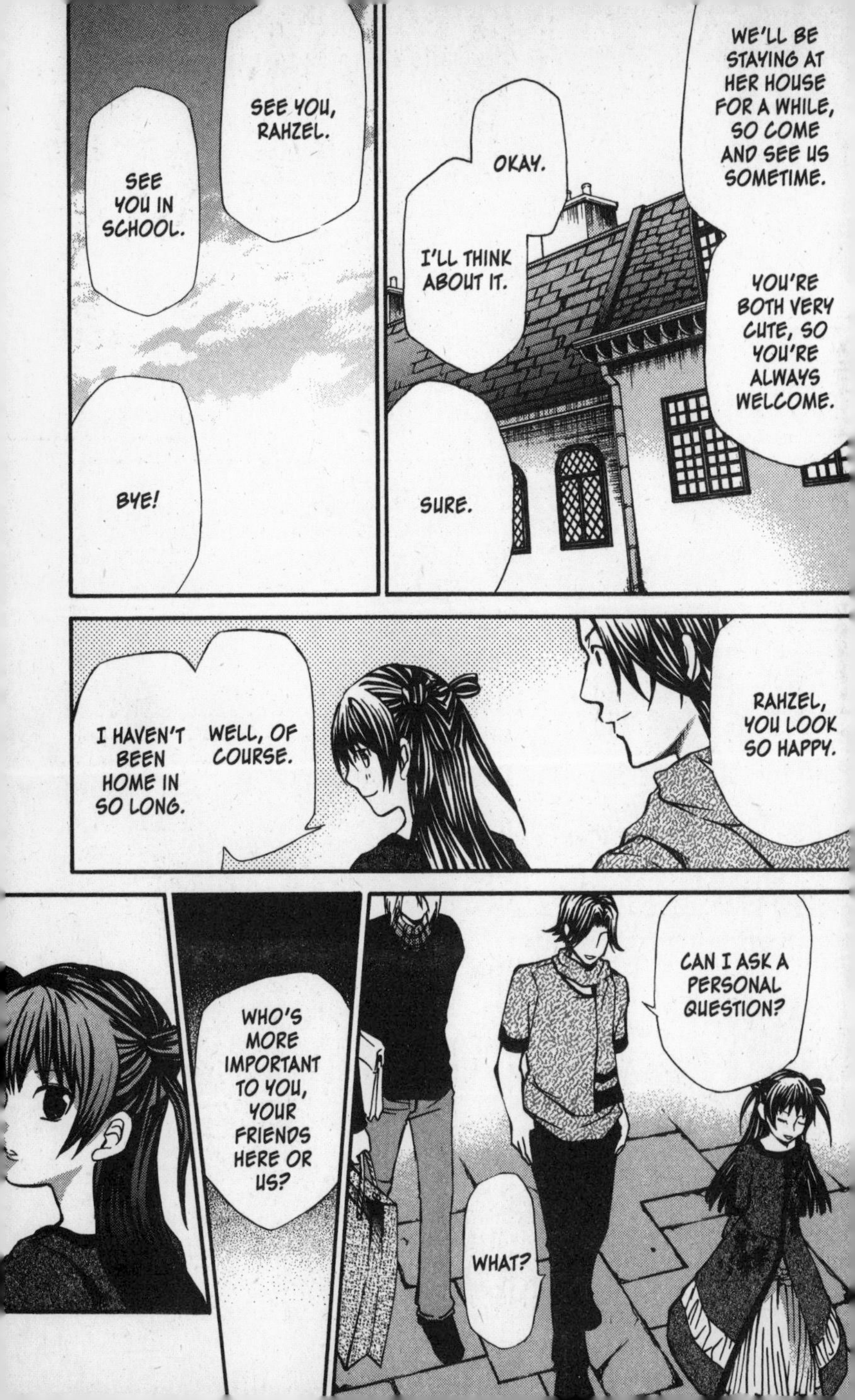
WE'LL BE STAYING AT HER HOUSE FOR A WHILE, SO COME AND SEE US SOMETIME.
YOU'RE BOTH VERY CUTE, SO YOU'RE ALWAYS WELCOME.
OKAY.
I'LL THINK ABOUT IT.
SURE.
SEE YOU, RAHZEL.
SEE YOU IN SCHOOL.
BYE!
RAHZEL, YOU LOOK SO HAPPY.
WELL, OF COURSE.
I HAVEN'T BEEN HOME IN SO LONG.
CAN I ASK A PERSONAL QUESTION?
WHAT?
WHO'S MORE IMPORTANT TO YOU, YOUR FRIENDS HERE OR US?

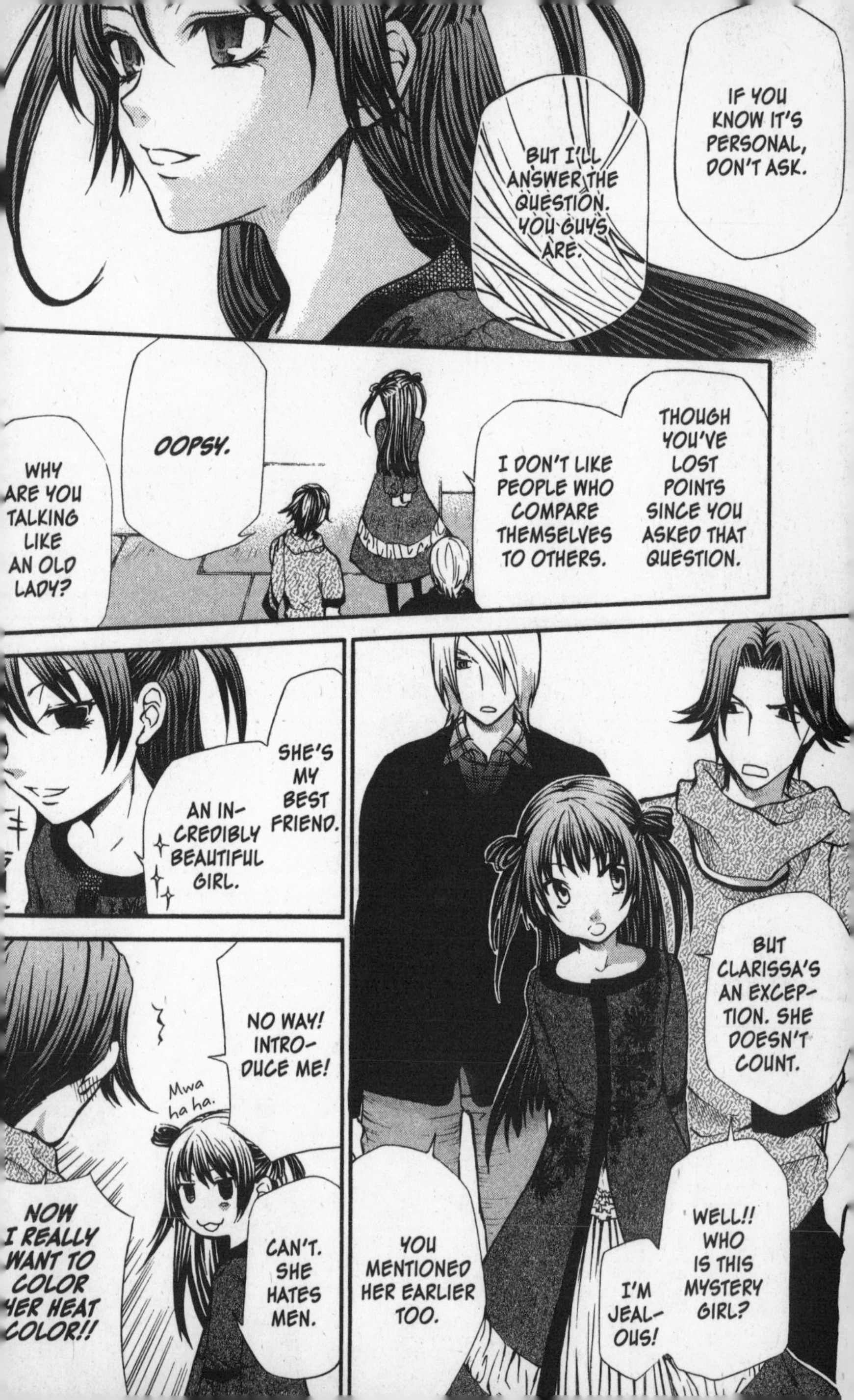
IF YOU KNOW IT'S PERSONAL, DON'T ASK.
BUT I'LL ANSWER THE QUESTION. YOU GUYS ARE.
THOUGH YOU'VE LOST POINTS SINCE YOU ASKED THAT QUESTION.
I DON'T LIKE PEOPLE WHO COMPARE THEMSELVES TO OTHERS.
OOPSY.
WHY ARE YOU TALKING LIKE AN OLD LADY?
BUT CLARISSA'S AN EXCEPTION. SHE DOESN'T COUNT.
SHE'S MY BEST FRIEND.
AN INCREDIBLY BEAUTIFUL GIRL.
WELL!! WHO IS THIS MYSTERY GIRL?
I'M JEALOUS!
YOU MENTIONED HER EARLIER TOO.
NO WAY! INTRODUCE ME!
CAN'T. SHE HATES MEN.
Mwa ha ha.
NOW I REALLY WANT TO COLOR HER HEAT COLOR!!

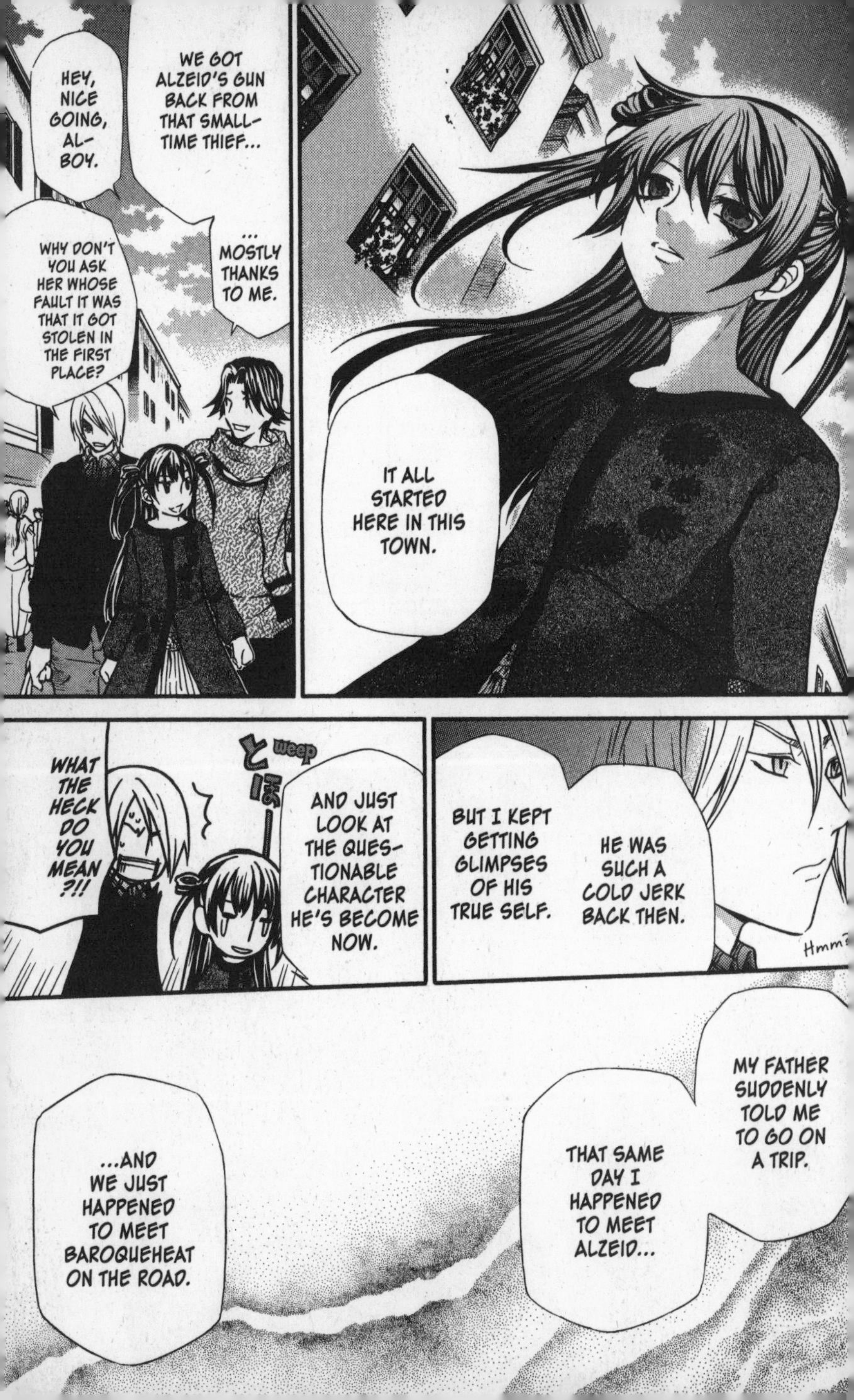
IT ALL STARTED HERE IN THIS TOWN.
WE GOT ALZEID'S GUN BACK FROM THAT SMALL-TIME THIEF...
HEY, NICE GOING, AL-BOY.
...MOSTLY THANKS TO ME.
WHY DON'T YOU ASK HER WHOSE FAULT IT WAS THAT IT GOT STOLEN IN THE FIRST PLACE?
HE WAS SUCH A COLD JERK BACK THEN.
BUT I KEPT GETTING GLIMPSES OF HIS TRUE SELF.
AND JUST LOOK AT THE QUESTIONABLE CHARACTER HE'S BECOME NOW.
weep
WHAT THE HECK DO YOU MEAN?!!
MY FATHER SUDDENLY TOLD ME TO GO ON A TRIP.
THAT SAME DAY I HAPPENED TO MEET ALZEID...
...AND WE JUST HAPPENED TO MEET BAROQUEHEAT ON THE ROAD.

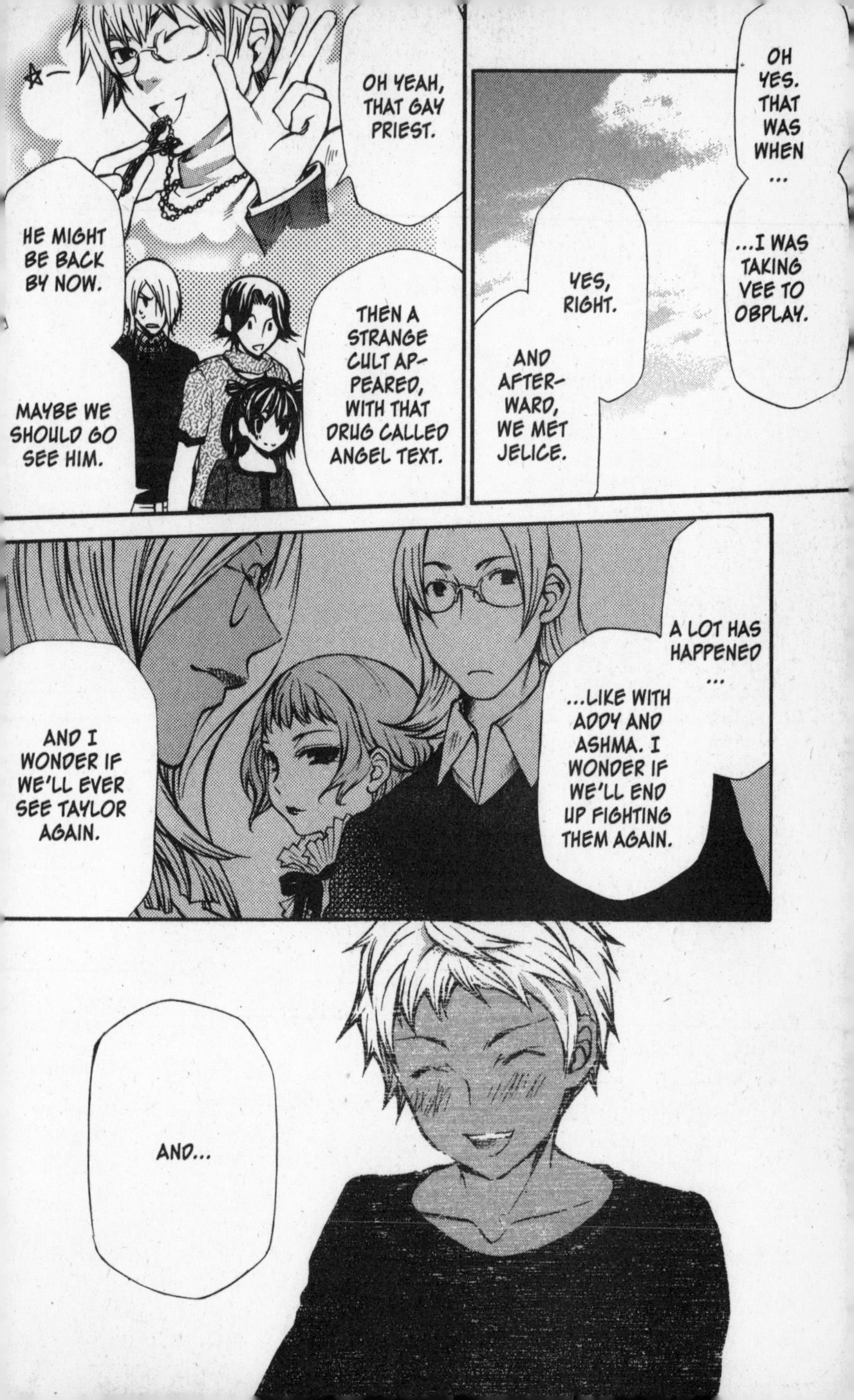
OH YES. THAT WAS WHEN ...
...I WAS TAKING VEE TO OBPLAY.
YES, RIGHT.
AND AFTER-WARD, WE MET JELICE.
OH YEAH, THAT GAY PRIEST.
THEN A STRANGE CULT AP-PEARED, WITH THAT DRUG CALLED ANGEL TEXT.
HE MIGHT BE BACK BY NOW.
MAYBE WE SHOULD GO SEE HIM.
A LOT HAS HAPPENED ...
...LIKE WITH ADDY AND ASHMA. I WONDER IF WE'LL END UP FIGHTING THEM AGAIN.
AND I WONDER IF WE'LL EVER SEE TAYLOR AGAIN.
AND...

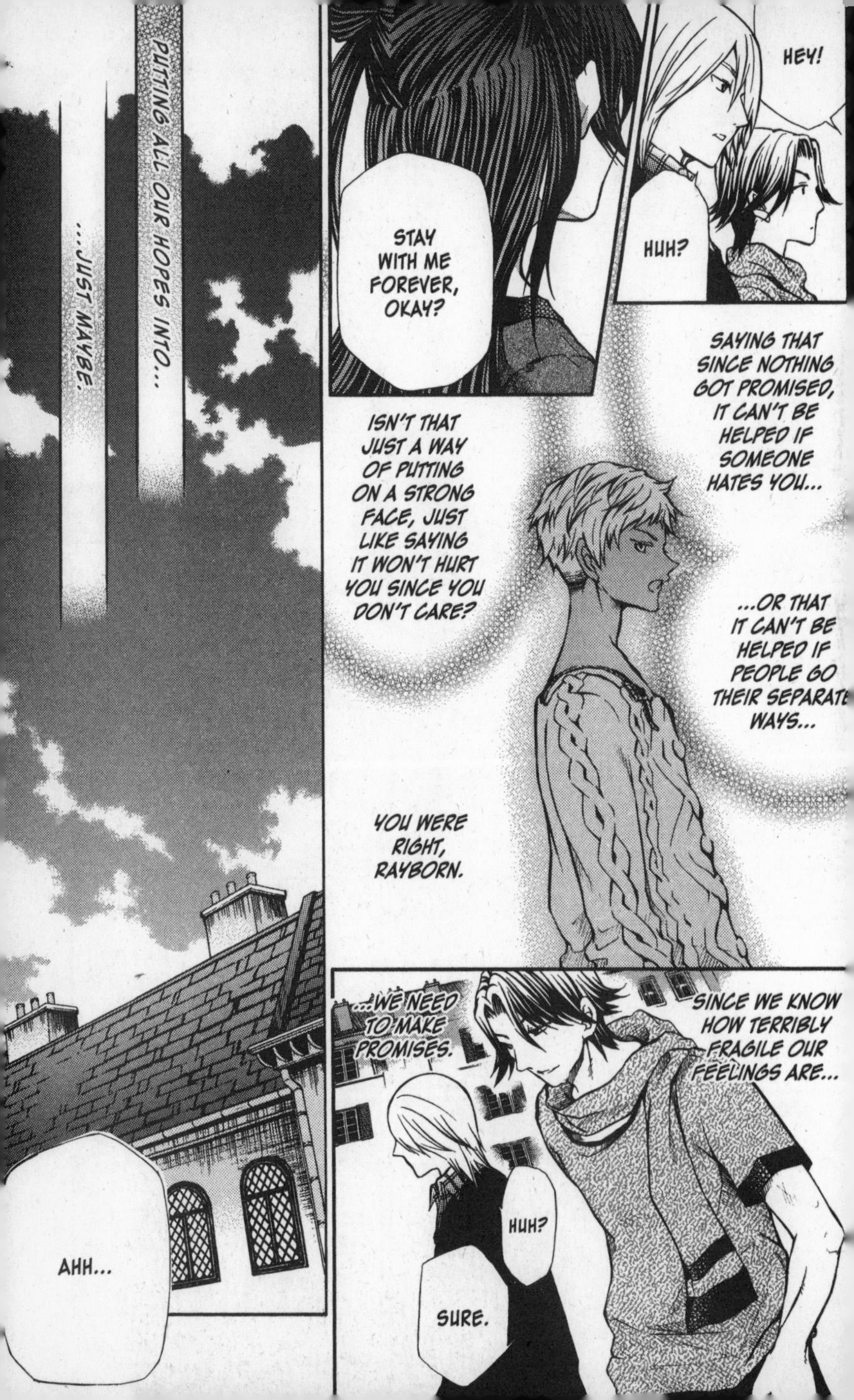
HEY!
HUH?
STAY WITH ME FOREVER, OKAY?
SAYING THAT SINCE NOTHING GOT PROMISED, IT CAN'T BE HELPED IF SOMEONE HATES YOU...
...OR THAT IT CAN'T BE HELPED IF PEOPLE GO THEIR SEPARATE WAYS...
ISN'T THAT JUST A WAY OF PUTTING ON A STRONG FACE, JUST LIKE SAYING IT WON'T HURT YOU SINCE YOU DON'T CARE?
YOU WERE RIGHT, RAYBORN.
SINCE WE KNOW HOW TERRIBLY FRAGILE OUR FEELINGS ARE...
...WE NEED TO MAKE PROMISES.
HUH?
SURE.
PUTTING ALL OUR HOPES INTO...
...JUST MAYBE.
AHH...

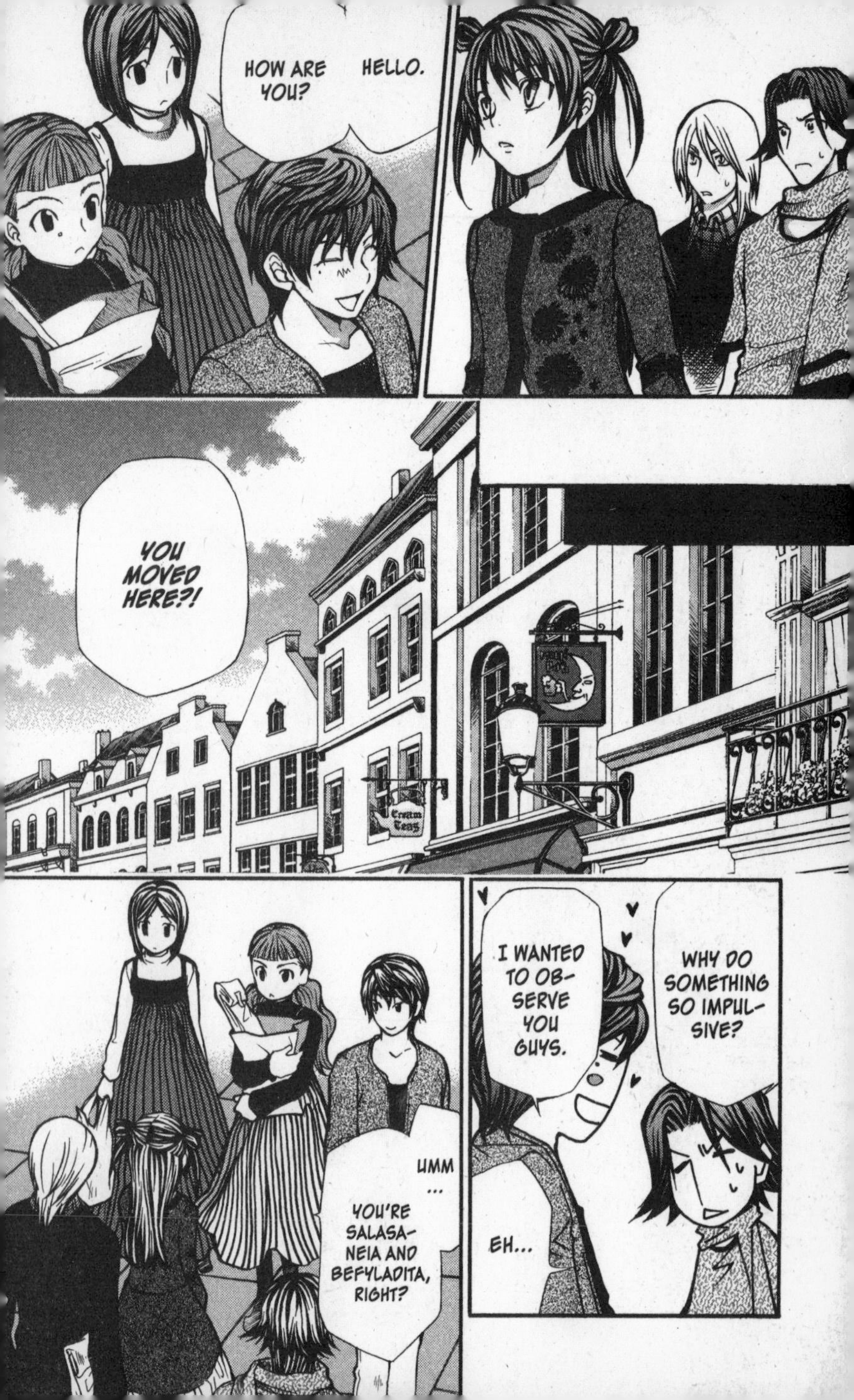
HELLO.
HOW ARE YOU?
YOU MOVED HERE?!
WHY DO SOMETHING SO IMPUL-SIVE?
I WANTED TO OB-SERVE YOU GUYS.
EH...
UMM ...
YOU'RE SALASA-NEIA AND BEFYLADITA, RIGHT?

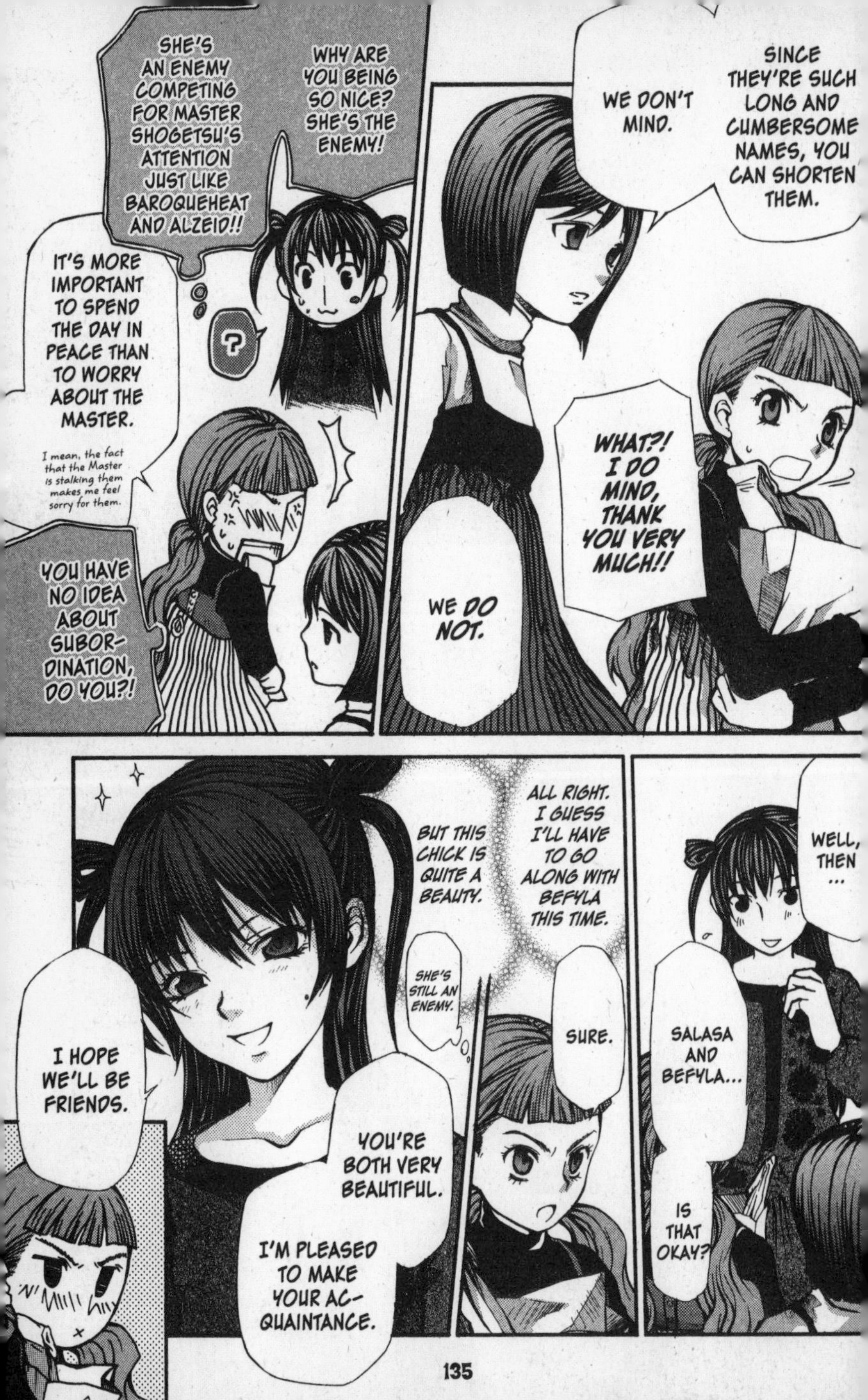
SINCE THEY'RE SUCH LONG AND CUMBERSOME NAMES, YOU CAN SHORTEN THEM.
WE DON'T MIND.
WHAT?! I DO MIND, THANK YOU VERY MUCH!!
WE DO NOT.
WHY ARE YOU BEING SO NICE? SHE'S THE ENEMY!
SHE'S AN ENEMY COMPETING FOR MASTER SHOGETSU'S ATTENTION JUST LIKE BAROQUEHEAT AND ALZEID!!
?
IT'S MORE IMPORTANT TO SPEND THE DAY IN PEACE THAN TO WORRY ABOUT THE MASTER.
I mean, the fact that the Master is stalking them makes me feel sorry for them.
YOU HAVE NO IDEA ABOUT SUBOR-DINATION, DO YOU?!
WELL, THEN...
SALASA AND BEFYLA...
IS THAT OKAY?
SURE.
ALL RIGHT. I GUESS I'LL HAVE TO GO ALONG WITH BEFYLA THIS TIME.
SHE'S STILL AN ENEMY.
BUT THIS CHICK IS QUITE A BEAUTY.
YOU'RE BOTH VERY BEAUTIFUL.
I'M PLEASED TO MAKE YOUR AC-QUAINTANCE.
I HOPE WE'LL BE FRIENDS.

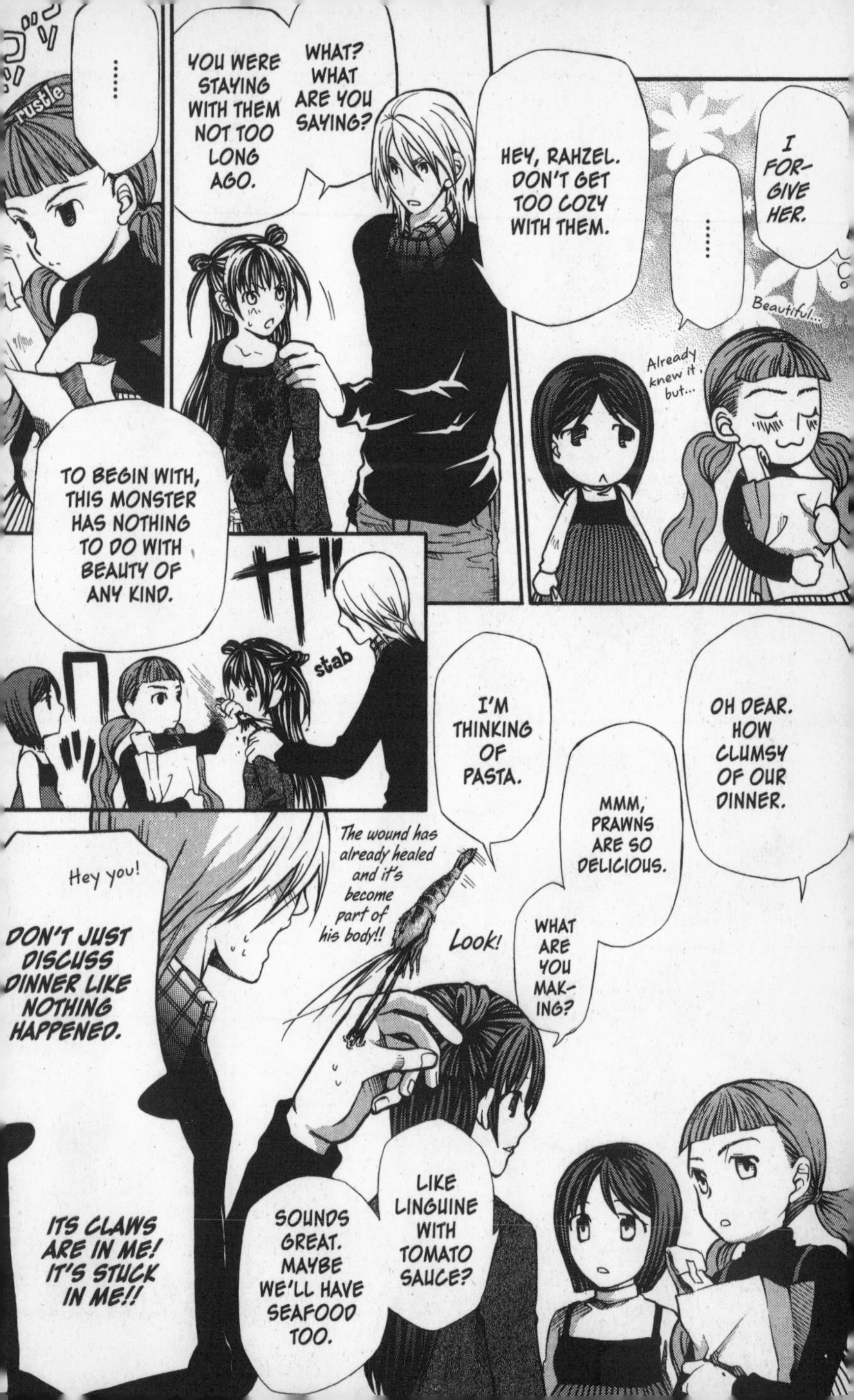
I FORGIVE HER.
......
Beautiful...
Already knew it, but...
HEY, RAHZEL. DON'T GET TOO COZY WITH THEM.
WHAT? WHAT ARE YOU SAYING?
YOU WERE STAYING WITH THEM NOT TOO LONG AGO.
......
rustle
TO BEGIN WITH, THIS MONSTER HAS NOTHING TO DO WITH BEAUTY OF ANY KIND.
stab
OH DEAR. HOW CLUMSY OF OUR DINNER.
I'M THINKING OF PASTA.
MMM, PRAWNS ARE SO DELICIOUS.
WHAT ARE YOU MAKING?
Look!
The wound has already healed and it's become part of his body!!
LIKE LINGUINE WITH TOMATO SAUCE?
SOUNDS GREAT. MAYBE WE'LL HAVE SEAFOOD TOO.
Hey you!
DON'T JUST DISCUSS DINNER LIKE NOTHING HAPPENED.
ITS CLAWS ARE IN ME! IT'S STUCK IN ME!!

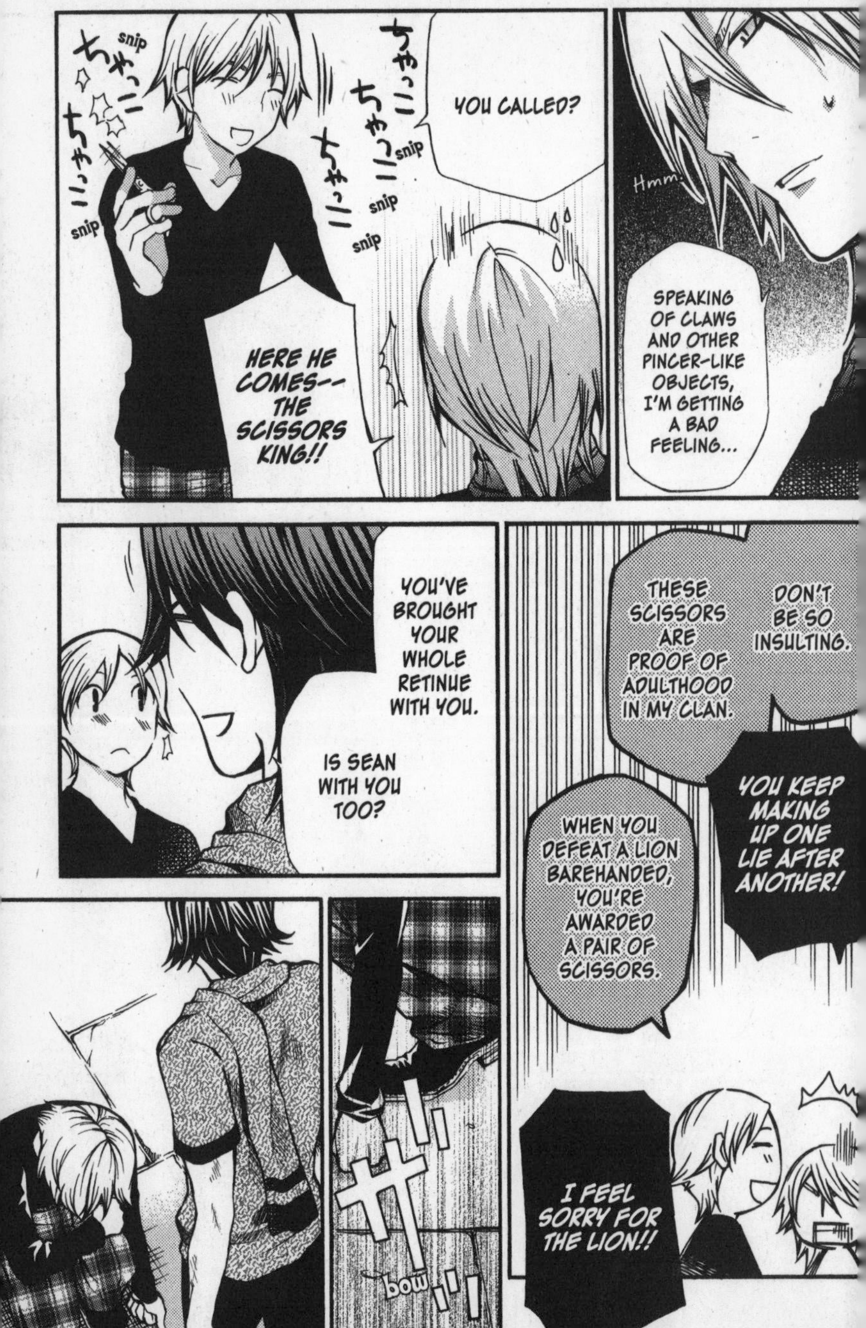
Hmm.
SPEAKING OF CLAWS AND OTHER PINCER-LIKE OBJECTS, I'M GETTING A BAD FEELING...
ちゃっこ ちゃっこ ちゃっこ
snip
snip
snip
YOU CALLED?
ちゃっこ ちゃっちゃっこ
snip
snip
HERE HE COMES-- THE SCISSORS KING!!
DON'T BE SO INSULTING.
THESE SCISSORS ARE PROOF OF ADULTHOOD IN MY CLAN.
YOU KEEP MAKING UP ONE LIE AFTER ANOTHER!
WHEN YOU DEFEAT A LION BAREHANDED, YOU'RE AWARDED A PAIR OF SCISSORS.
YOU'VE BROUGHT YOUR WHOLE RETINUE WITH YOU.
IS SEAN WITH YOU TOO?
I FEEL SORRY FOR THE LION!!
bow

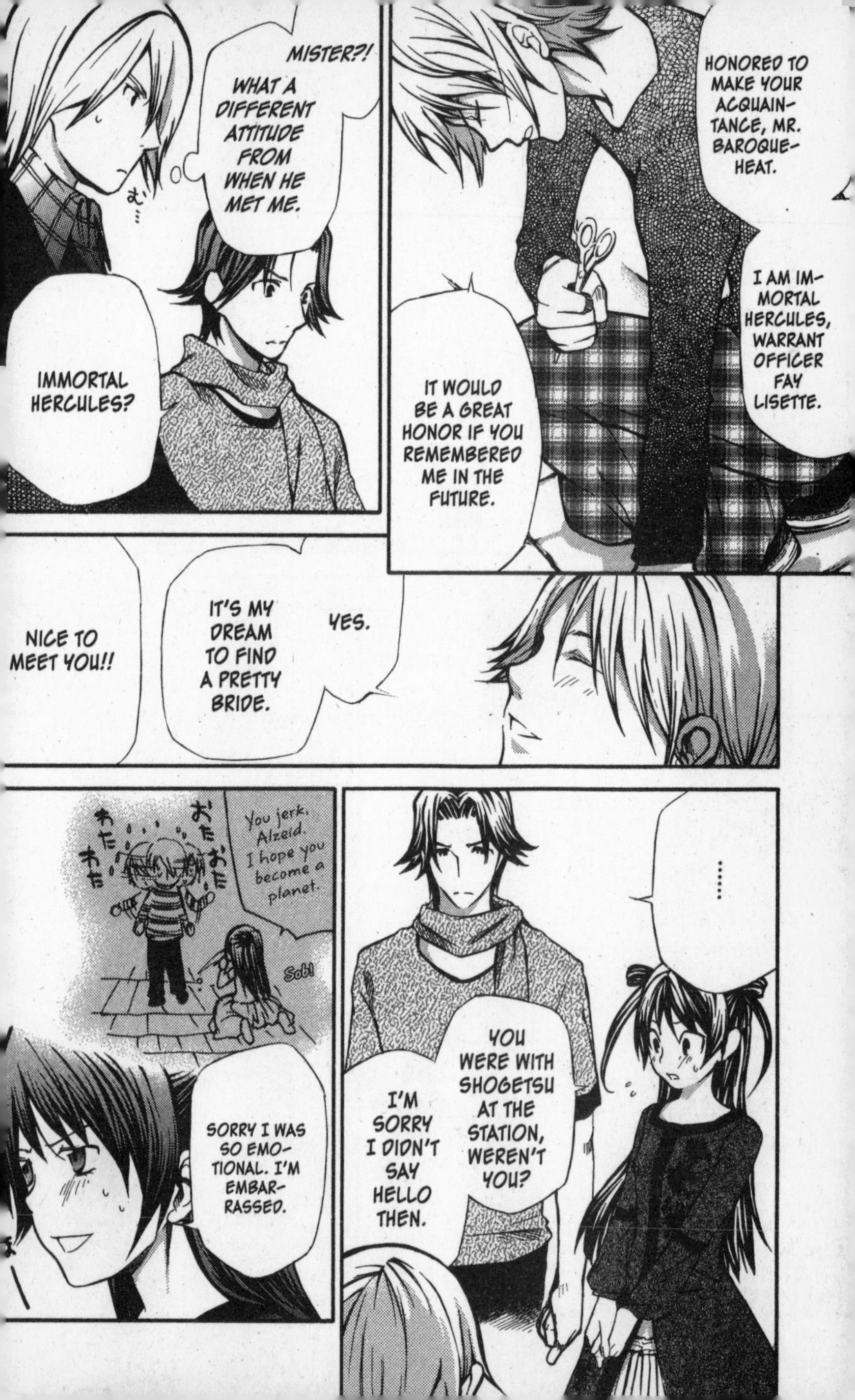
HONORED TO MAKE YOUR ACQUAINTANCE, MR. BAROQUEHEAT.
I AM IMMORTAL HERCULES, WARRANT OFFICER FAY LISETTE.
IT WOULD BE A GREAT HONOR IF YOU REMEMBERED ME IN THE FUTURE.
MISTER?!
WHAT A DIFFERENT ATTITUDE FROM WHEN HE MET ME.
IMMORTAL HERCULES?
YES.
IT'S MY DREAM TO FIND A PRETTY BRIDE.
NICE TO MEET YOU!!
......
YOU WERE WITH SHOGETSU AT THE STATION, WEREN'T YOU?
I'M SORRY I DIDN'T SAY HELLO THEN.
You jerk, Alzeid. I hope you become a planet.
おたおた
わたわた
Sob!
SORRY I WAS SO EMOTIONAL. I'M EMBARRASSED.

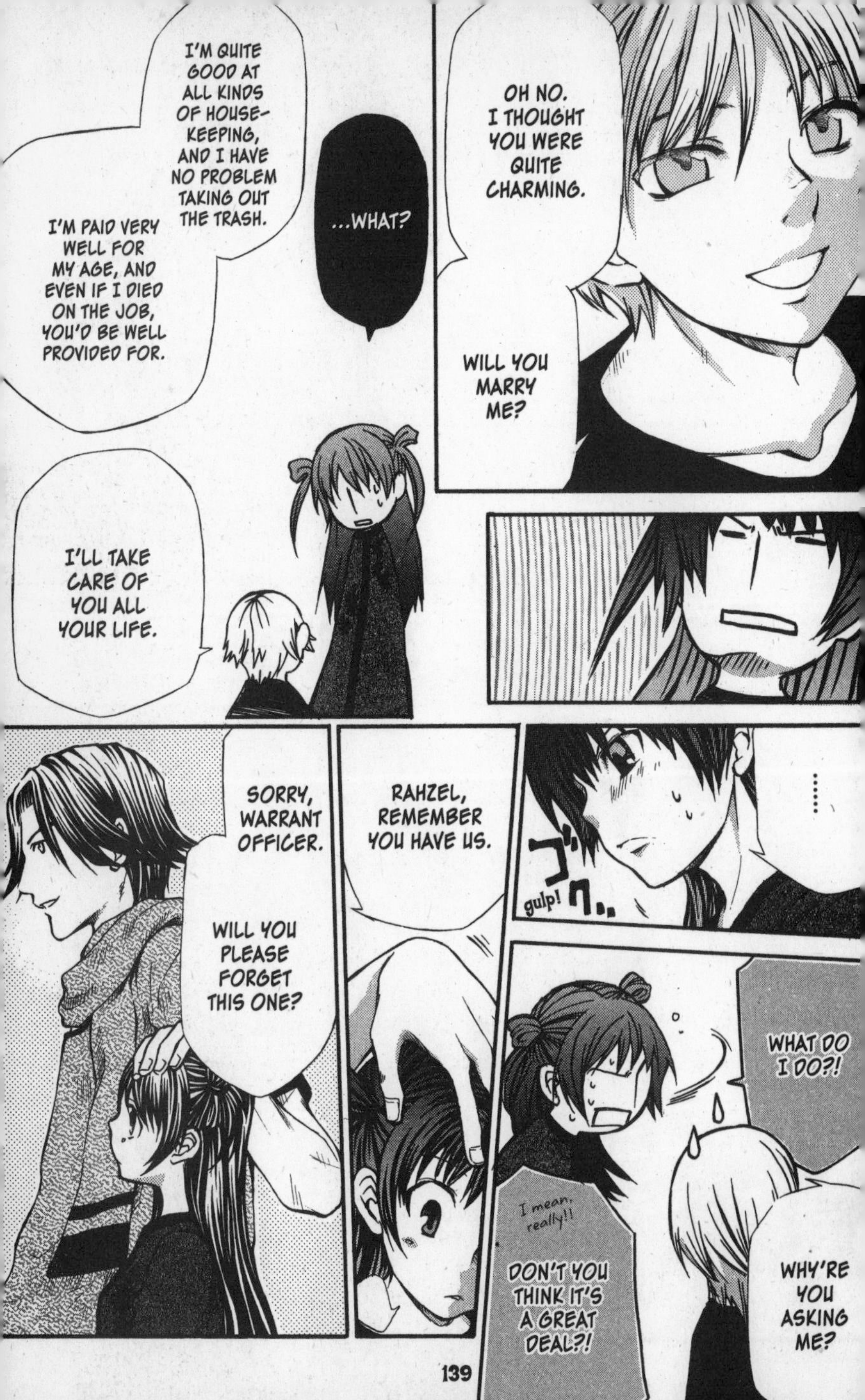

OH NO. I THOUGHT YOU WERE QUITE CHARMING.
WILL YOU MARRY ME?
...WHAT?
I'M QUITE GOOD AT ALL KINDS OF HOUSE-KEEPING, AND I HAVE NO PROBLEM TAKING OUT THE TRASH.
I'M PAID VERY WELL FOR MY AGE, AND EVEN IF I DIED ON THE JOB, YOU'D BE WELL PROVIDED FOR.
I'LL TAKE CARE OF YOU ALL YOUR LIFE.
......
gulp!
RAHZEL, REMEMBER YOU HAVE US.
SORRY, WARRANT OFFICER.
WILL YOU PLEASE FORGET THIS ONE?
WHAT DO I DO?!
WHY'RE YOU ASKING ME?
I mean, really!!
DON'T YOU THINK IT'S A GREAT DEAL?!

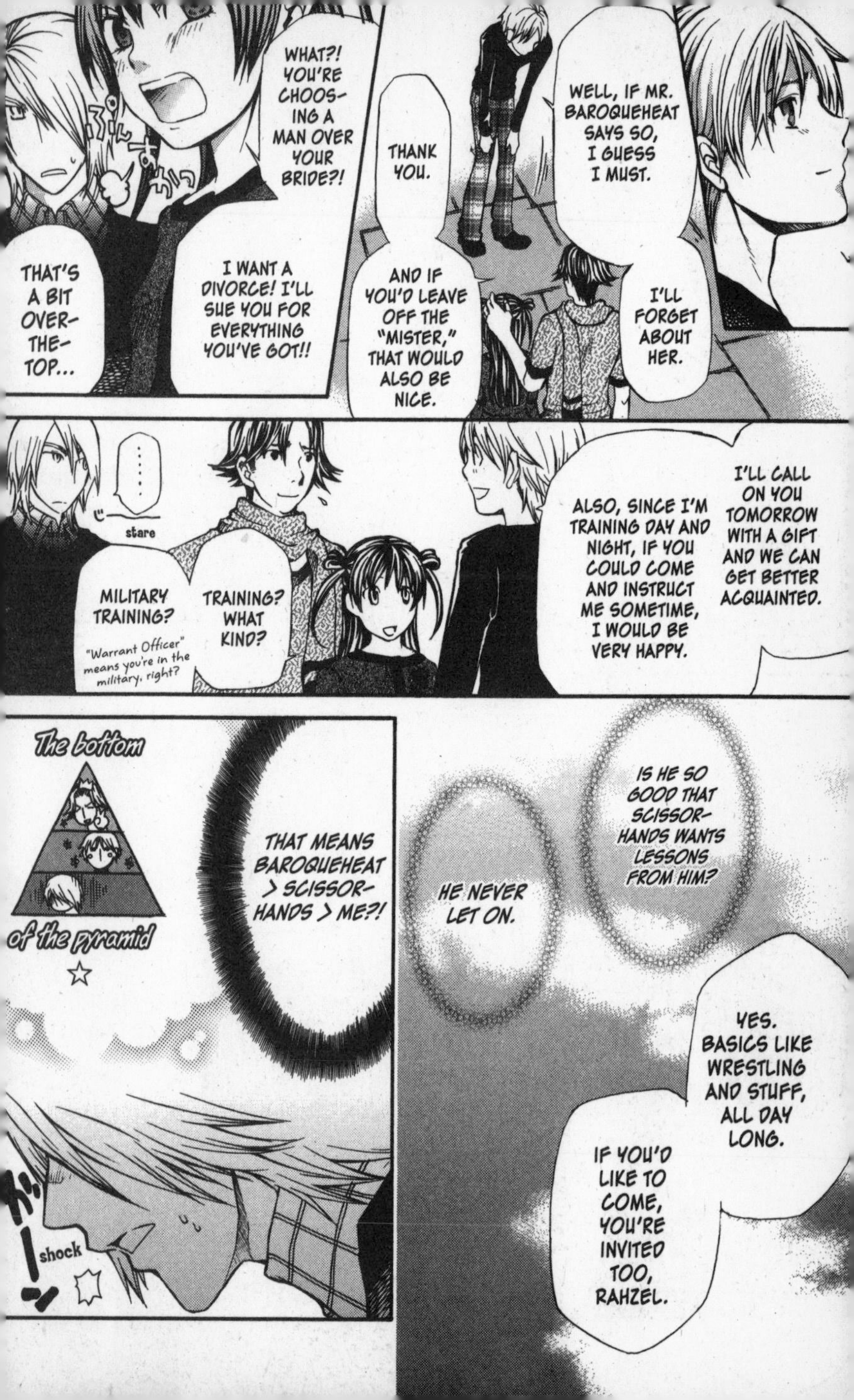
WELL, IF MR. BAROQUEHEAT SAYS SO, I GUESS I MUST.
I'LL FORGET ABOUT HER.
THANK YOU.
AND IF YOU'D LEAVE OFF THE "MISTER," THAT WOULD ALSO BE NICE.
WHAT?! YOU'RE CHOOSING A MAN OVER YOUR BRIDE?!
I WANT A DIVORCE! I'LL SUE YOU FOR EVERYTHING YOU'VE GOT!!
THAT'S A BIT OVER-THE-TOP...
I'LL CALL ON YOU TOMORROW WITH A GIFT AND WE CAN GET BETTER ACQUAINTED.
ALSO, SINCE I'M TRAINING DAY AND NIGHT, IF YOU COULD COME AND INSTRUCT ME SOMETIME, I WOULD BE VERY HAPPY.
TRAINING? WHAT KIND?
MILITARY TRAINING?
"Warrant Officer" means you're in the military, right?
......
stare
YES. BASICS LIKE WRESTLING AND STUFF, ALL DAY LONG.
IF YOU'D LIKE TO COME, YOU'RE INVITED TOO, RAHZEL.
IS HE SO GOOD THAT SCISSORHANDS WANTS LESSONS FROM HIM?
HE NEVER LET ON.
THAT MEANS BAROQUEHEAT > SCISSORHANDS > ME?!
The bottom of the pyramid ☆
shock

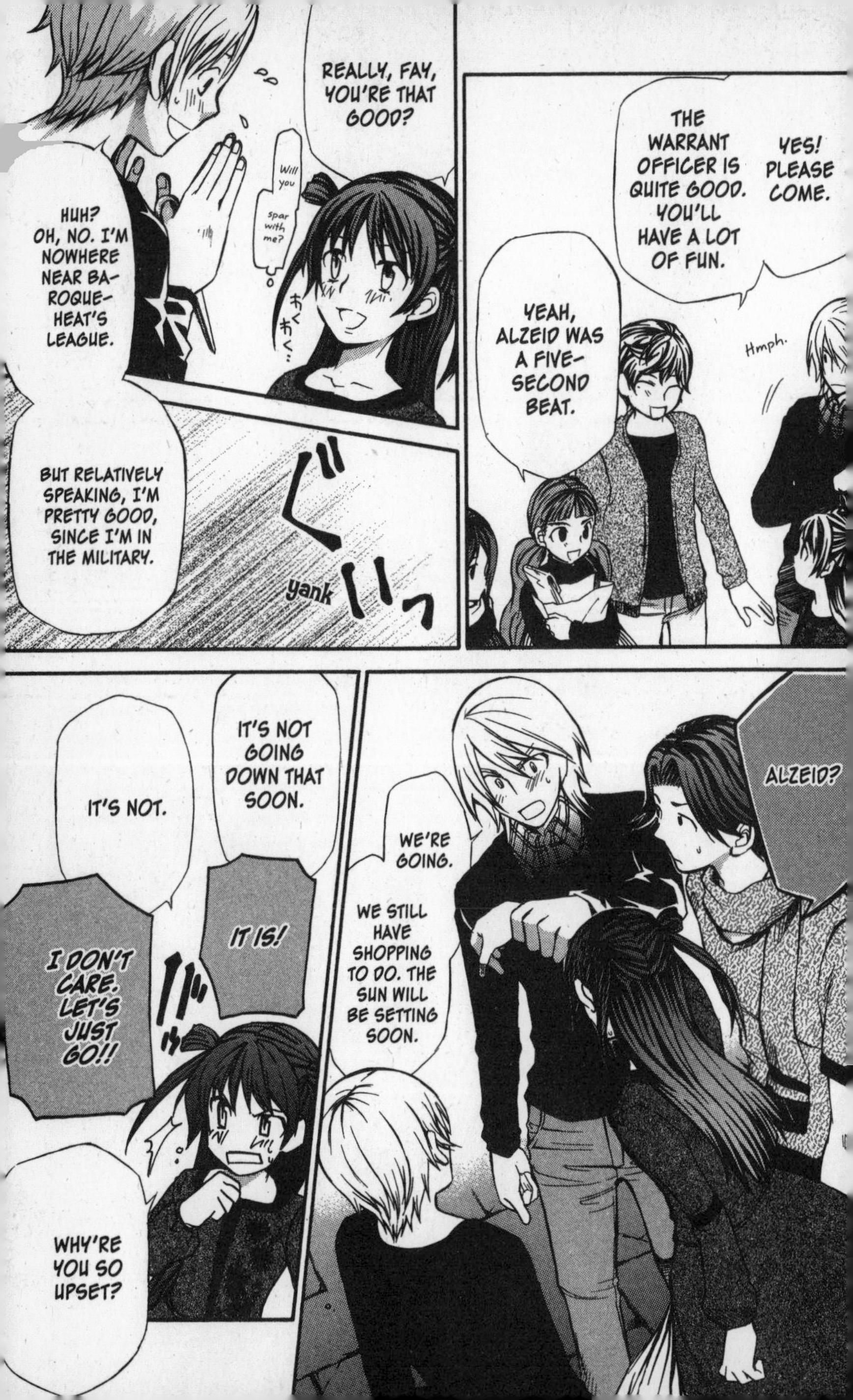

YES! PLEASE COME.
THE WARRANT OFFICER IS QUITE GOOD. YOU'LL HAVE A LOT OF FUN.
YEAH, ALZEID WAS A FIVE-SECOND BEAT.
Hmph.
REALLY, FAY, YOU'RE THAT GOOD?
Will you spar with me?
HUH? OH, NO. I'M NOWHERE NEAR BAROQUE-HEAT'S LEAGUE.
BUT RELATIVELY SPEAKING, I'M PRETTY GOOD, SINCE I'M IN THE MILITARY.
yank
ALZEID?
WE'RE GOING.
WE STILL HAVE SHOPPING TO DO. THE SUN WILL BE SETTING SOON.
IT'S NOT GOING DOWN THAT SOON.
IT'S NOT.
IT IS!
I DON'T CARE. LET'S JUST GO!!
WHY'RE YOU SO UPSET?

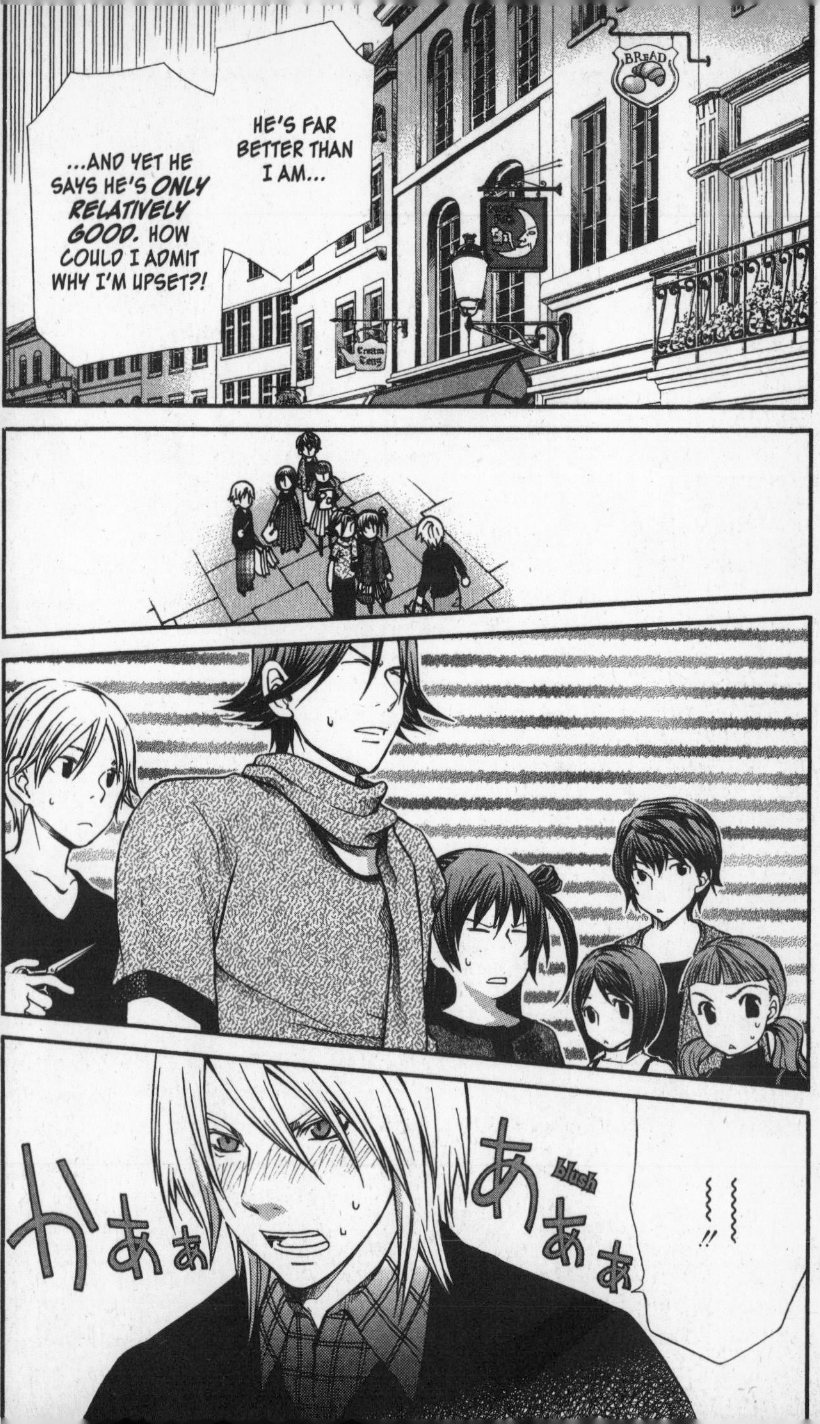
BREAD
HE'S FAR BETTER THAN I AM...
...AND YET HE SAYS HE'S *ONLY RELATIVELY GOOD.* HOW COULD I ADMIT WHY I'M UPSET?!
ああぁ
blush
わあぁ
!!

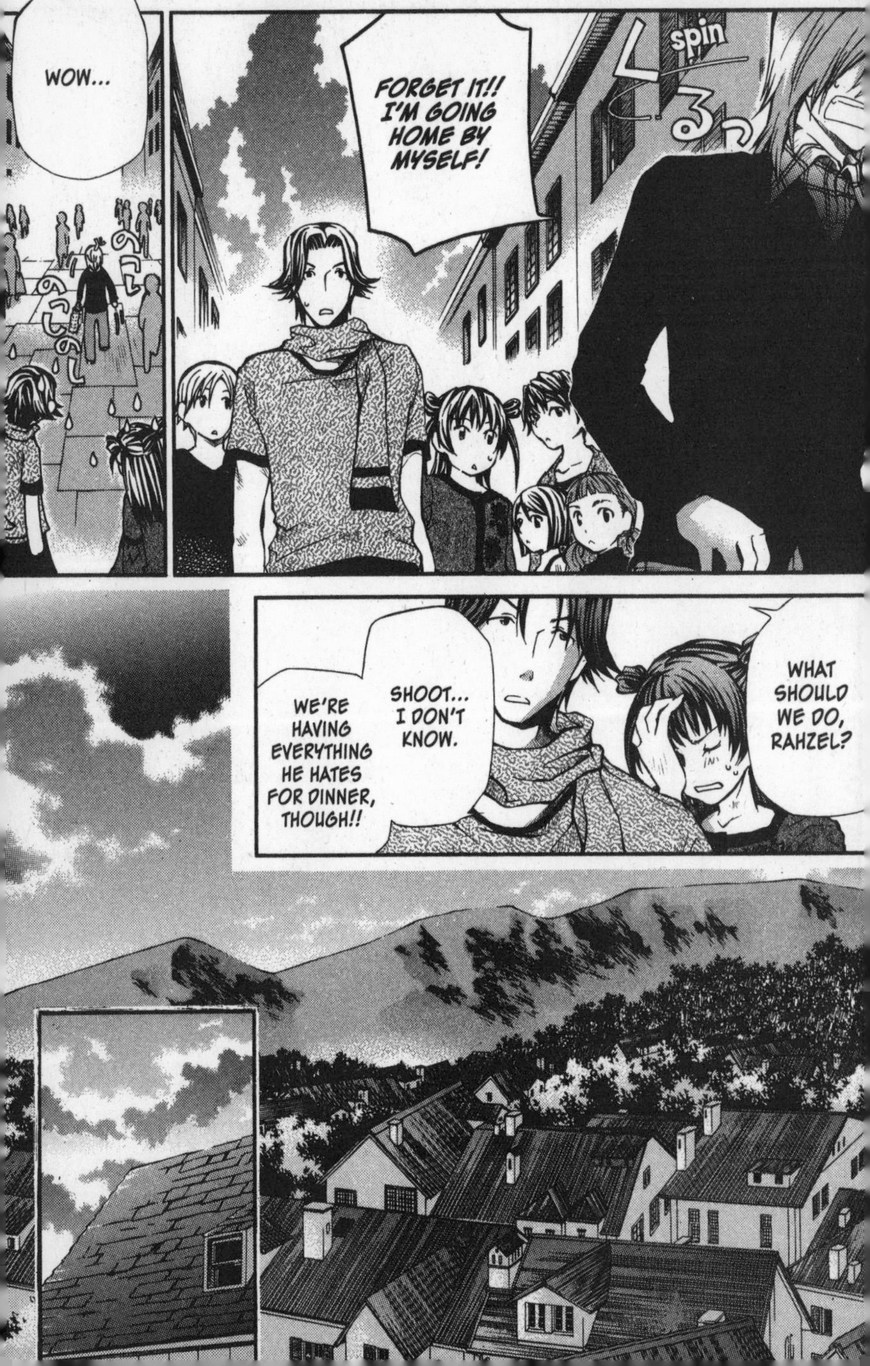
spin
FORGET IT!! I'M GOING HOME BY MYSELF!
WOW...
WHAT SHOULD WE DO, RAHZEL?
SHOOT... I DON'T KNOW.
WE'RE HAVING EVERYTHING HE HATES FOR DINNER, THOUGH!!

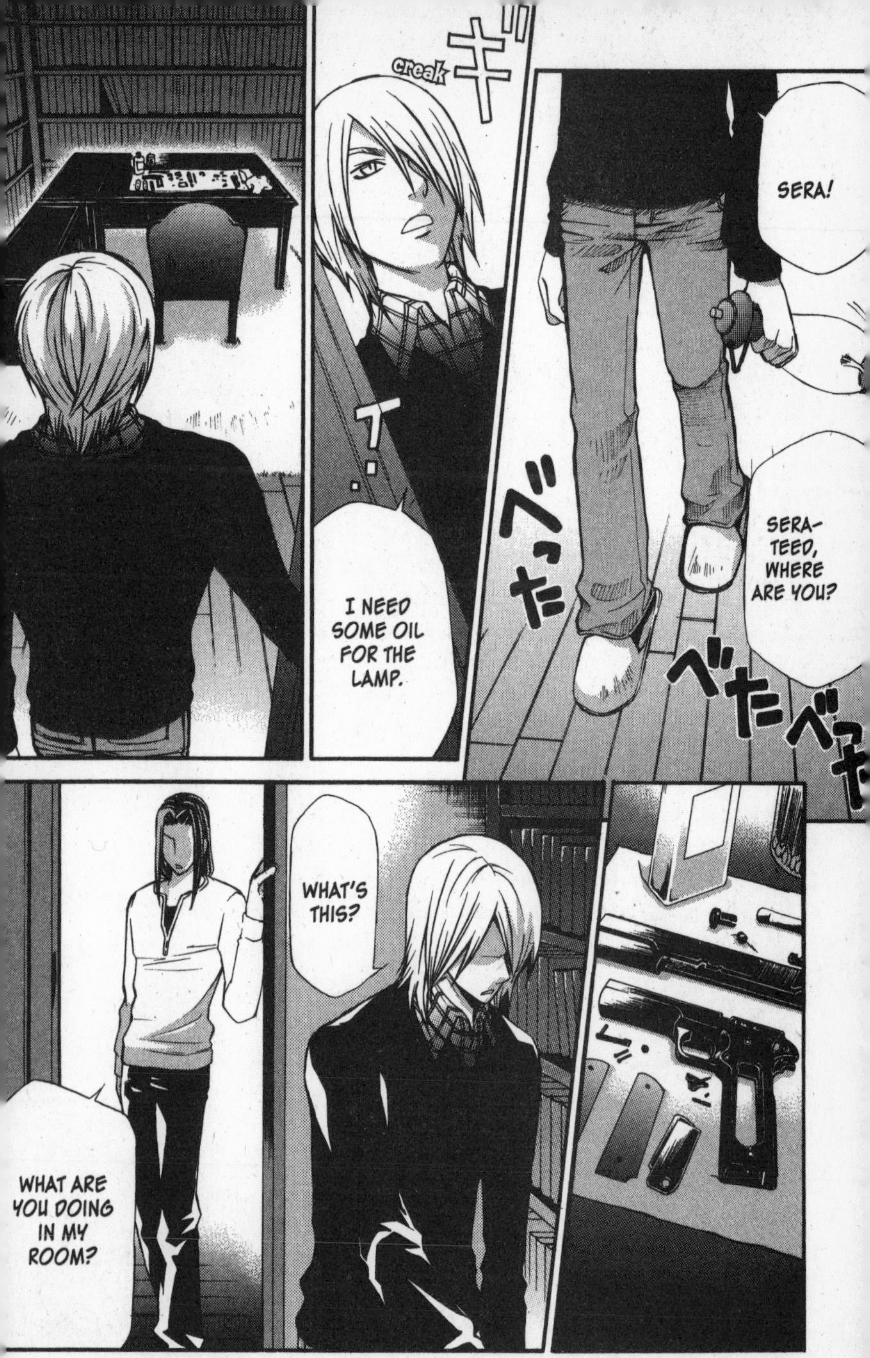
SERA!
SERA-TEED, WHERE ARE YOU?
creak
I NEED SOME OIL FOR THE LAMP.
WHAT'S THIS?
WHAT ARE YOU DOING IN MY ROOM?

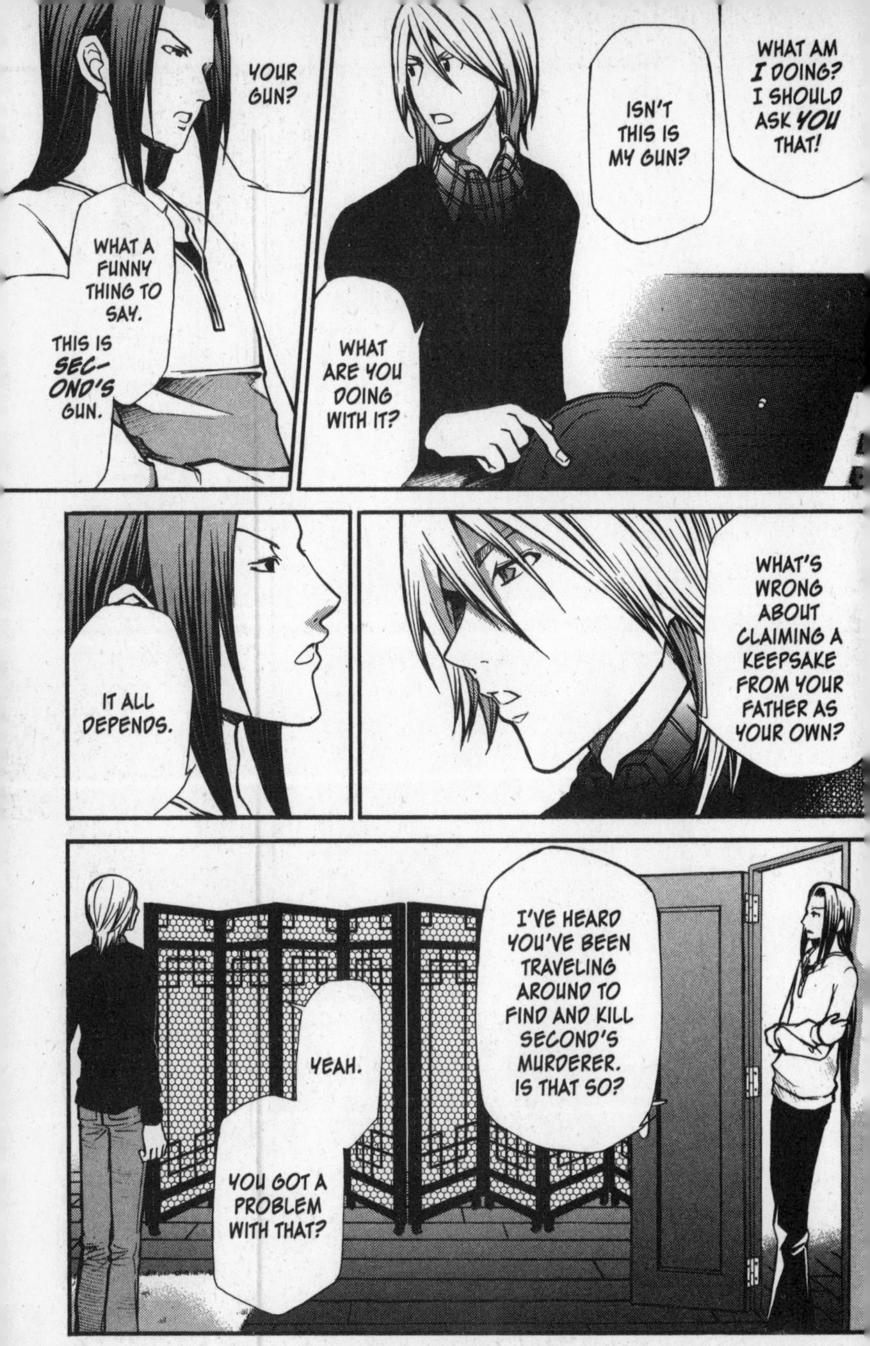
WHAT AM I DOING? I SHOULD ASK YOU THAT!
ISN'T THIS IS MY GUN?
WHAT ARE YOU DOING WITH IT?
YOUR GUN?
WHAT A FUNNY THING TO SAY.
THIS IS SEC-OND'S GUN.
WHAT'S WRONG ABOUT CLAIMING A KEEPSAKE FROM YOUR FATHER AS YOUR OWN?
IT ALL DEPENDS.
I'VE HEARD YOU'VE BEEN TRAVELING AROUND TO FIND AND KILL SECOND'S MURDERER. IS THAT SO?
YEAH.
YOU GOT A PROBLEM WITH THAT?

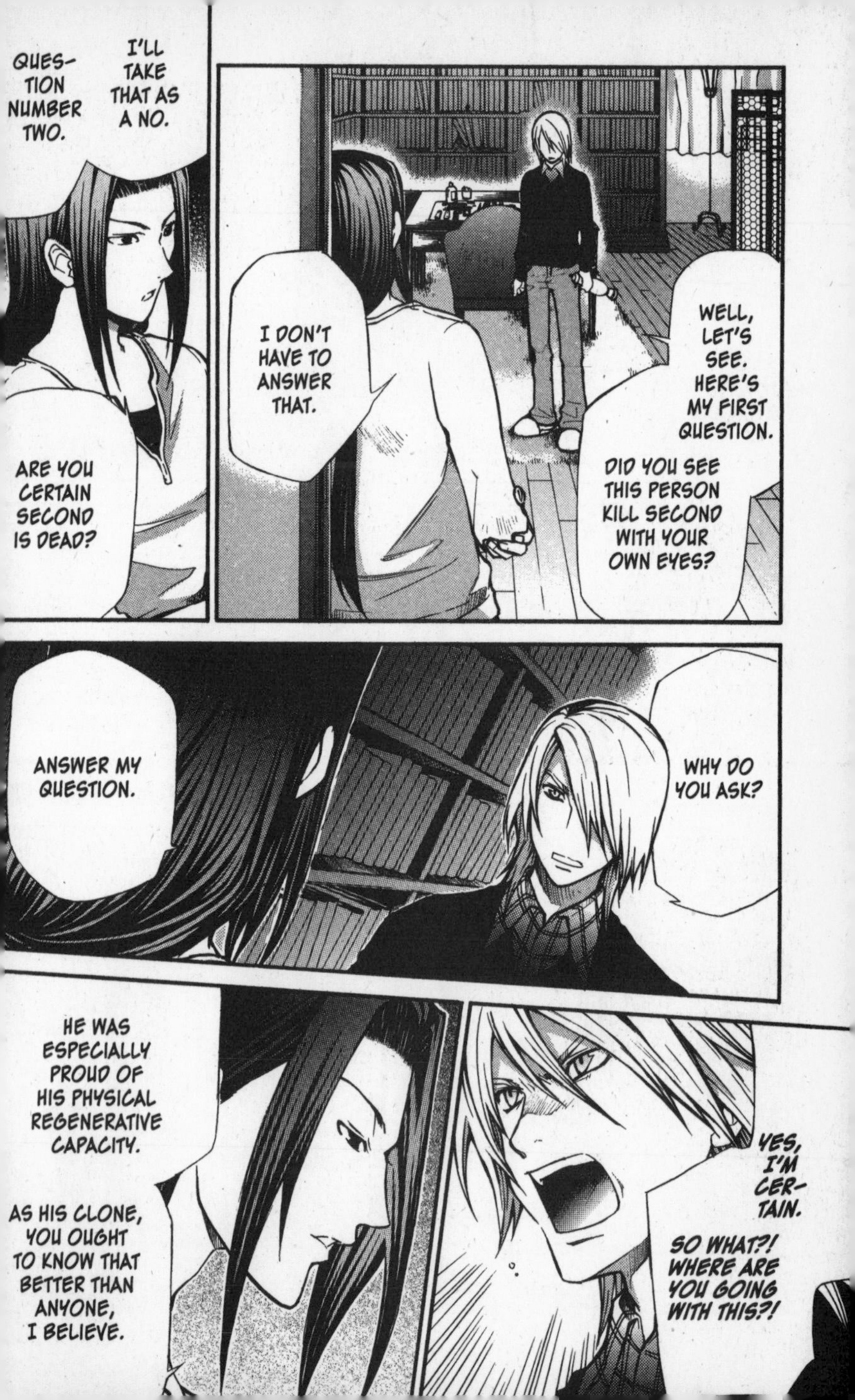
WELL, LET'S SEE. HERE'S MY FIRST QUESTION.
DID YOU SEE THIS PERSON KILL SECOND WITH YOUR OWN EYES?
I DON'T HAVE TO ANSWER THAT.
I'LL TAKE THAT AS A NO.
QUES-TION NUMBER TWO.
ARE YOU CERTAIN SECOND IS DEAD?
WHY DO YOU ASK?
ANSWER MY QUESTION.
YES, I'M CER-TAIN.
SO WHAT?! WHERE ARE YOU GOING WITH THIS?!
HE WAS ESPECIALLY PROUD OF HIS PHYSICAL REGENERATIVE CAPACITY.
AS HIS CLONE, YOU OUGHT TO KNOW THAT BETTER THAN ANYONE, I BELIEVE.

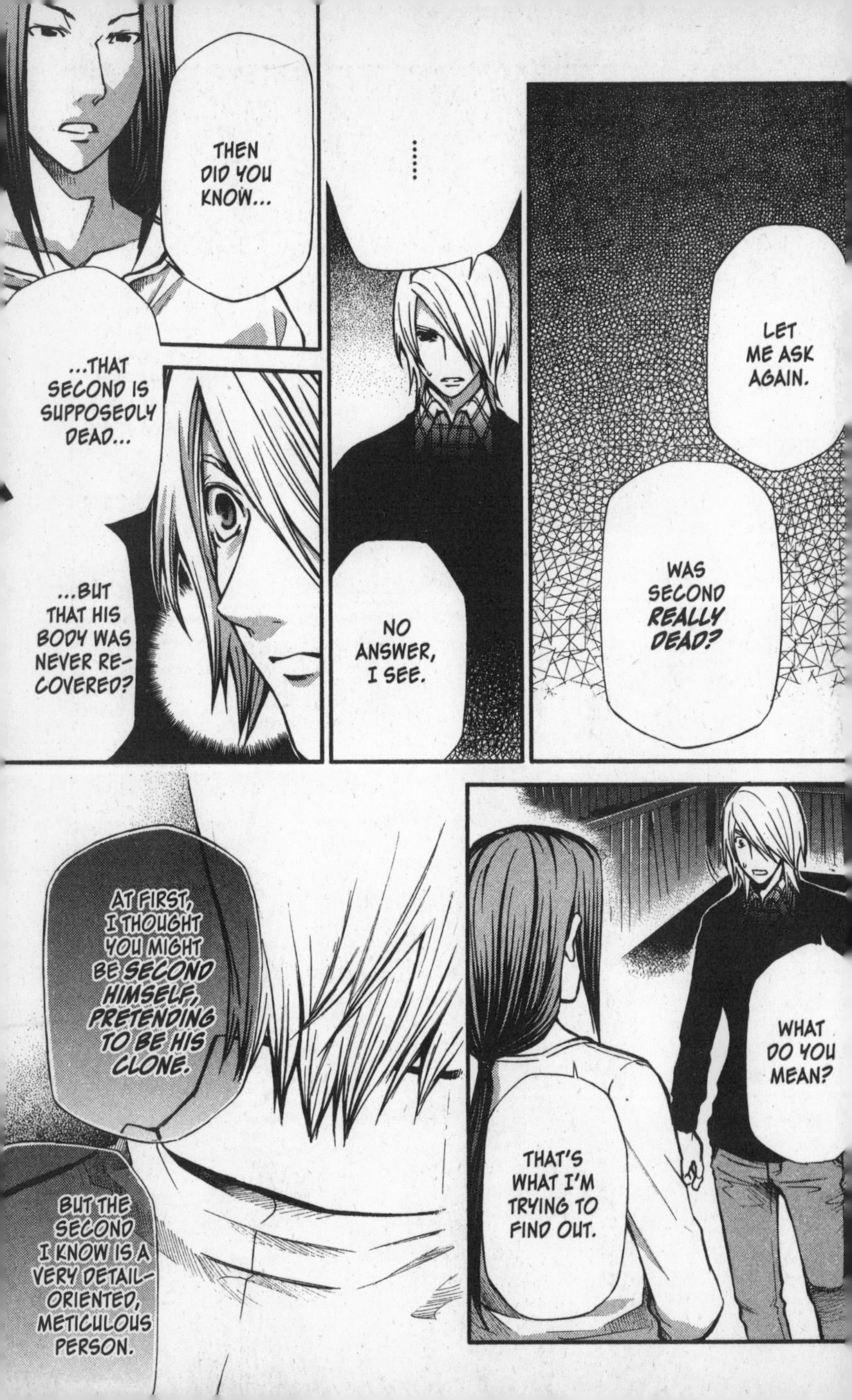
LET ME ASK AGAIN.
WAS SECOND REALLY DEAD?
......
NO ANSWER, I SEE.
THEN DID YOU KNOW...
...THAT SECOND IS SUPPOSEDLY DEAD...
...BUT THAT HIS BODY WAS NEVER RE-COVERED?
WHAT DO YOU MEAN?
THAT'S WHAT I'M TRYING TO FIND OUT.
AT FIRST, I THOUGHT YOU MIGHT BE SECOND HIMSELF, PRETENDING TO BE HIS CLONE.
BUT THE SECOND I KNOW IS A VERY DETAIL-ORIENTED, METICULOUS PERSON.

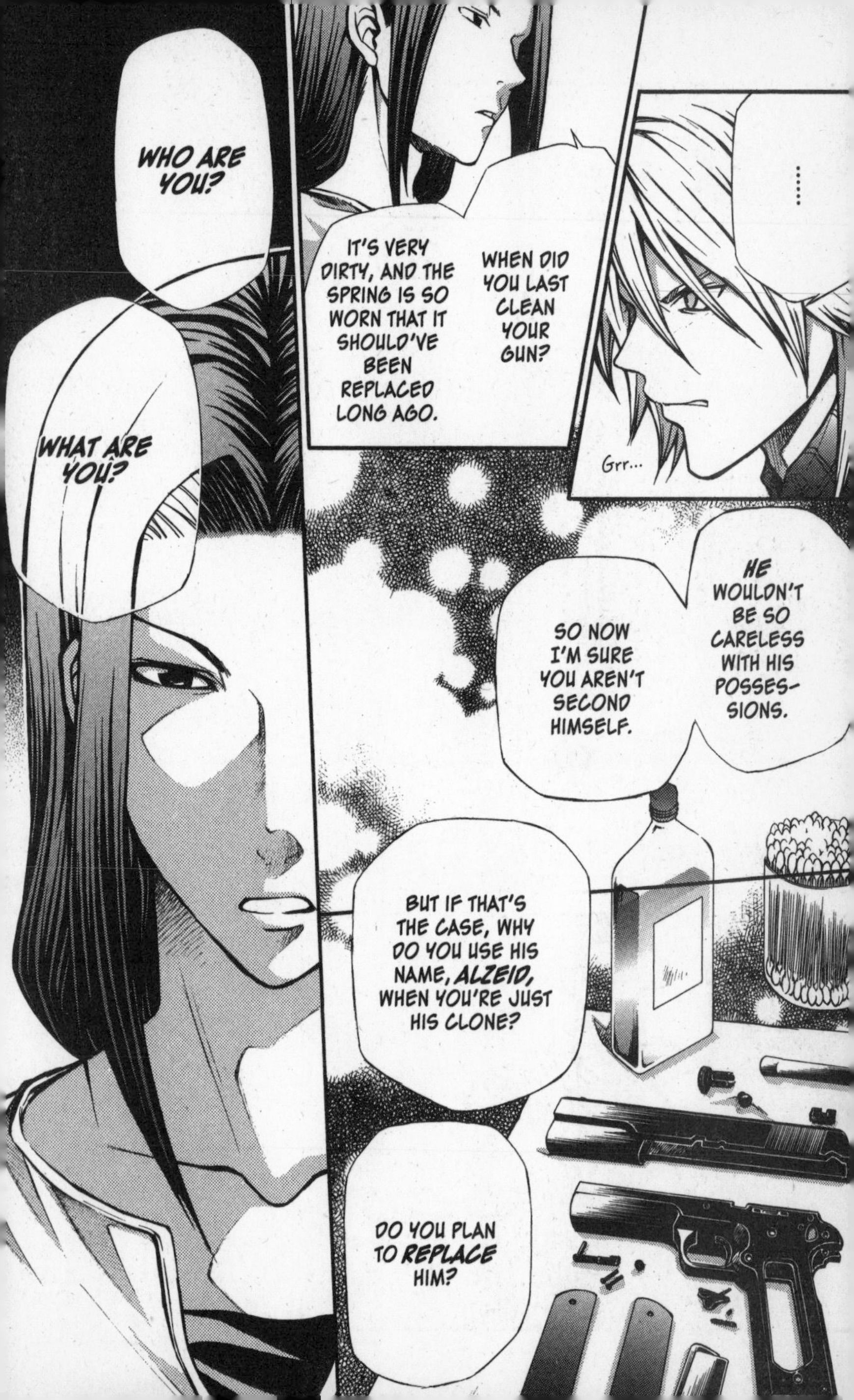
......
Grr...
WHEN DID YOU LAST CLEAN YOUR GUN?
IT'S VERY DIRTY, AND THE SPRING IS SO WORN THAT IT SHOULD'VE BEEN REPLACED LONG AGO.
HE WOULDN'T BE SO CARELESS WITH HIS POSSES-SIONS.
SO NOW I'M SURE YOU AREN'T SECOND HIMSELF.
BUT IF THAT'S THE CASE, WHY DO YOU USE HIS NAME, ALZEID, WHEN YOU'RE JUST HIS CLONE?
DO YOU PLAN TO REPLACE HIM?
WHO ARE YOU?
WHAT ARE YOU?

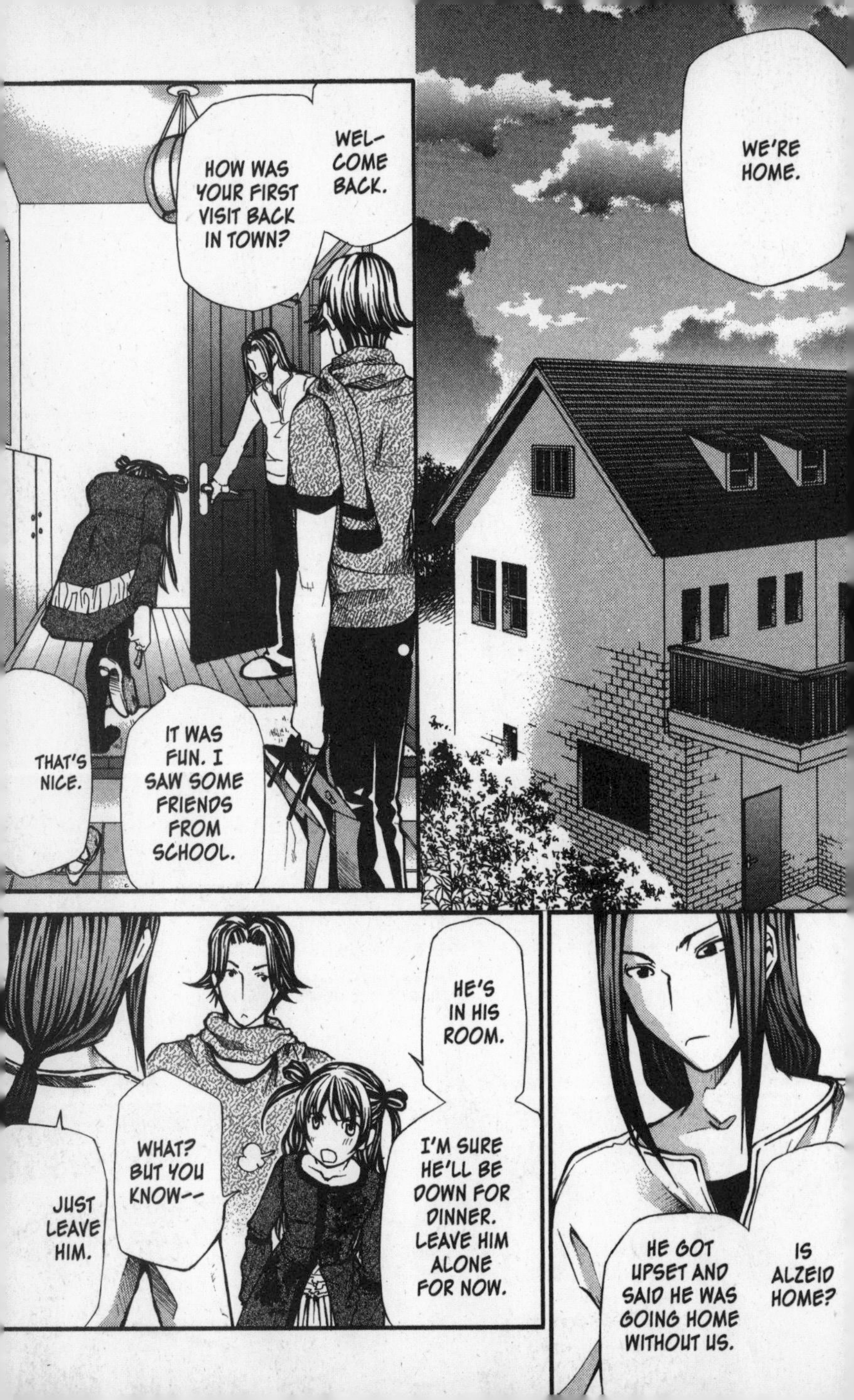
WE'RE HOME.
WEL-COME BACK.
HOW WAS YOUR FIRST VISIT BACK IN TOWN?
IT WAS FUN. I SAW SOME FRIENDS FROM SCHOOL.
THAT'S NICE.
IS ALZEID HOME?
HE GOT UPSET AND SAID HE WAS GOING HOME WITHOUT US.
HE'S IN HIS ROOM.
I'M SURE HE'LL BE DOWN FOR DINNER. LEAVE HIM ALONE FOR NOW.
WHAT? BUT YOU KNOW--
JUST LEAVE HIM.

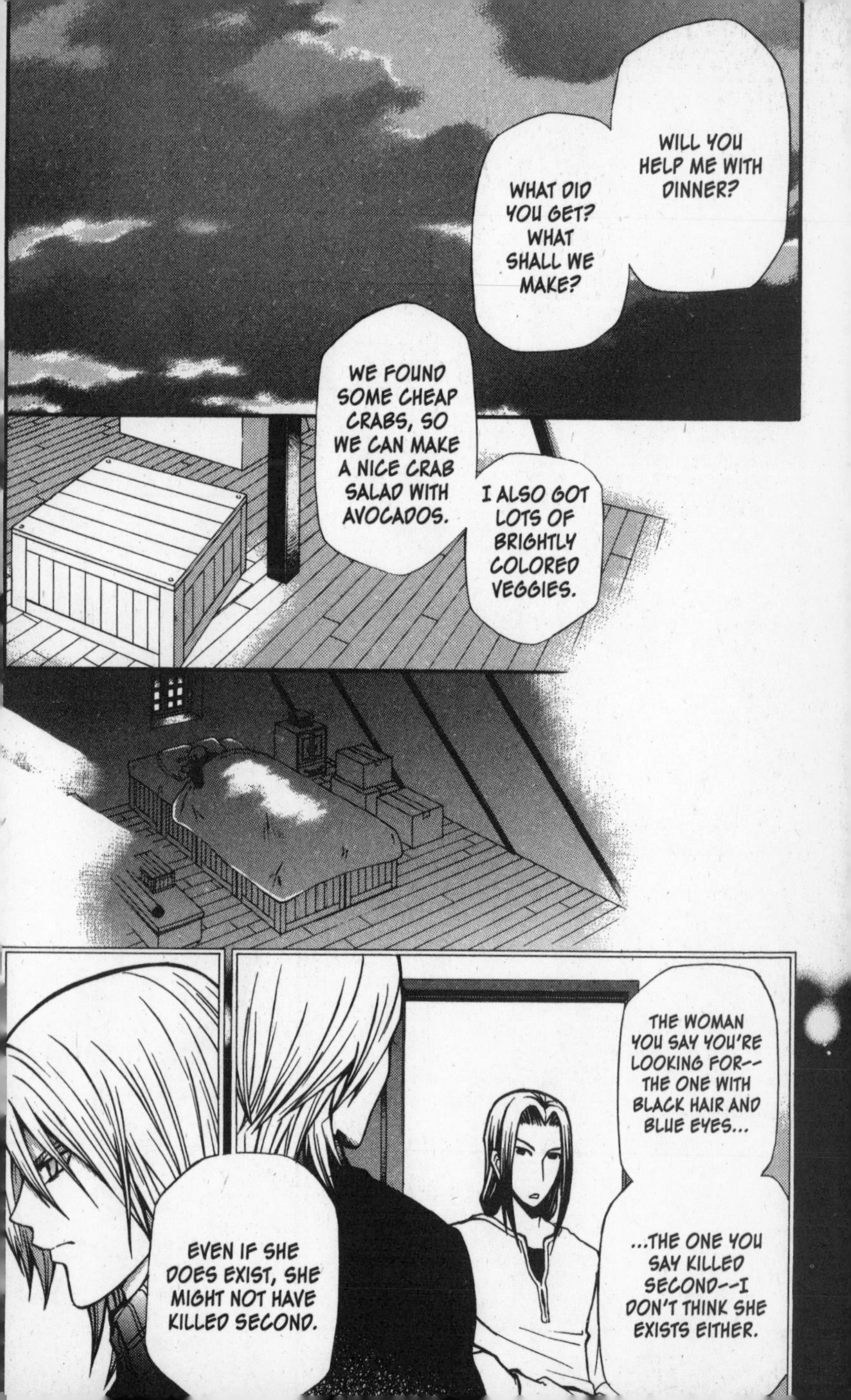
WILL YOU HELP ME WITH DINNER?
WHAT DID YOU GET? WHAT SHALL WE MAKE?
WE FOUND SOME CHEAP CRABS, SO WE CAN MAKE A NICE CRAB SALAD WITH AVOCADOS.
I ALSO GOT LOTS OF BRIGHTLY COLORED VEGGIES.
THE WOMAN YOU SAY YOU'RE LOOKING FOR-- THE ONE WITH BLACK HAIR AND BLUE EYES...
...THE ONE YOU SAY KILLED SECOND--I DON'T THINK SHE EXISTS EITHER.
EVEN IF SHE DOES EXIST, SHE MIGHT NOT HAVE KILLED SECOND.

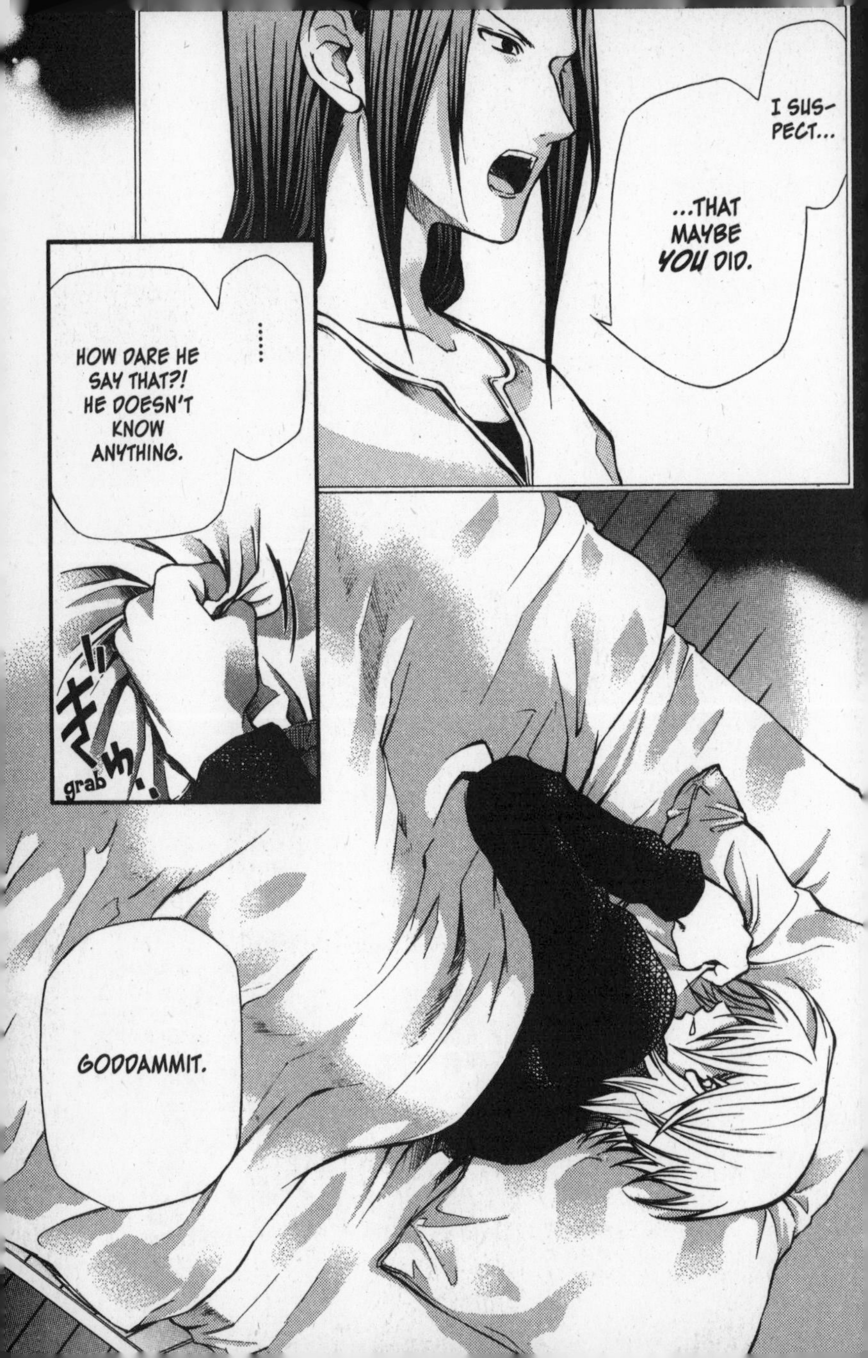
I SUS-PECT...
...THAT MAYBE YOU DID.
......
HOW DARE HE SAY THAT?! HE DOESN'T KNOW ANYTHING.
grab
GODDAMMIT.

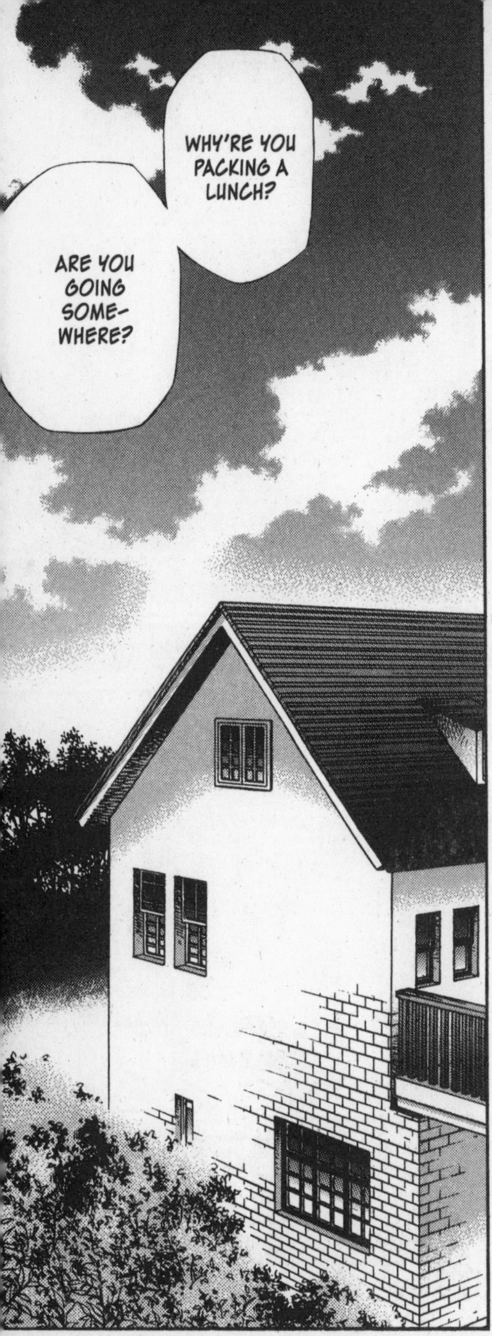
WHY'RE YOU PACKING A LUNCH?
ARE YOU GOING SOME-WHERE?

Chapter 68: Back to the Routin Part 2: "I will leave you behind."

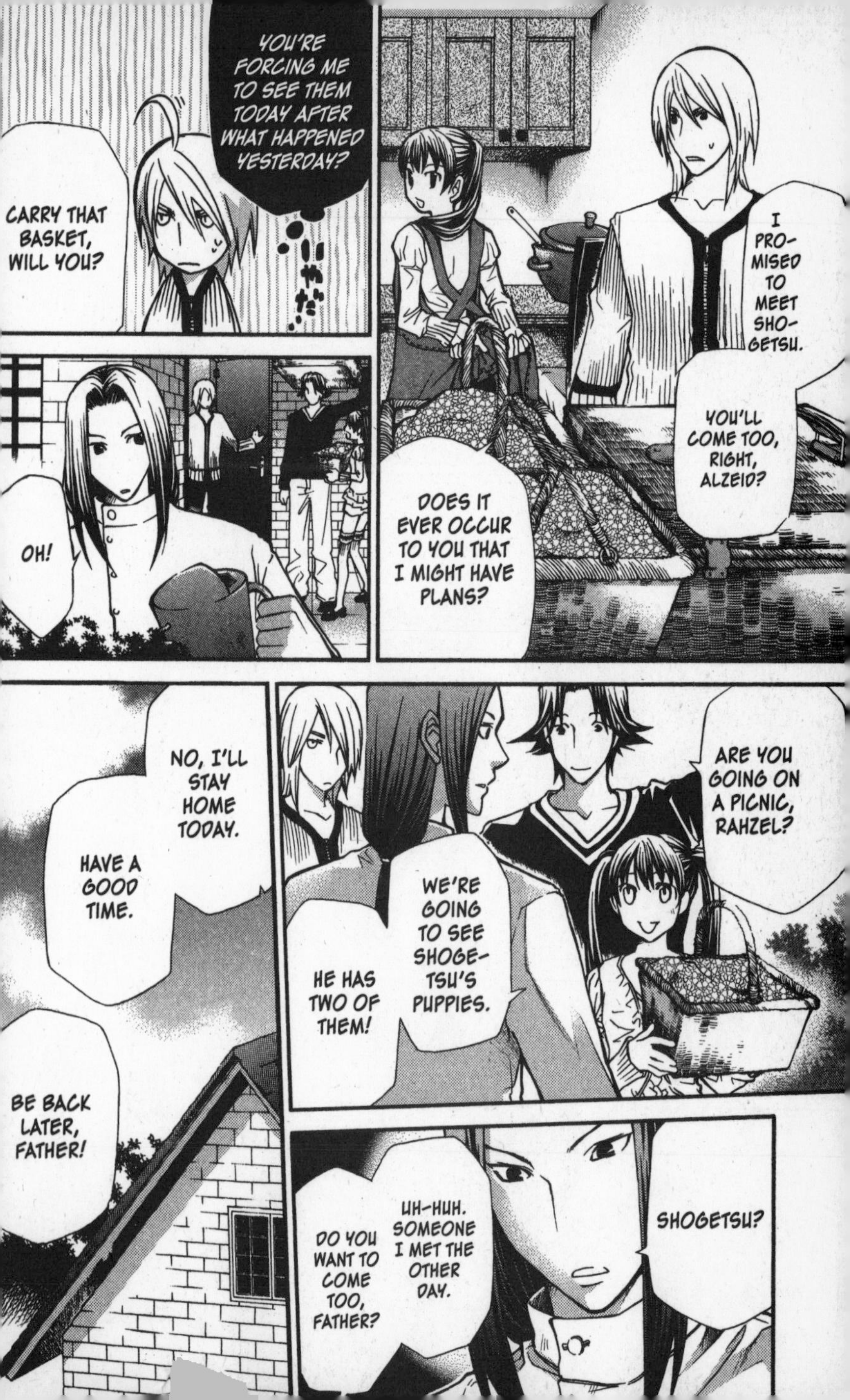
I PROMISED TO MEET SHOGETSU.
YOU'LL COME TOO, RIGHT, ALZEID?
DOES IT EVER OCCUR TO YOU THAT I MIGHT HAVE PLANS?
YOU'RE FORCING ME TO SEE THEM TODAY AFTER WHAT HAPPENED YESTERDAY?
いやだ
CARRY THAT BASKET, WILL YOU?
OH!
ARE YOU GOING ON A PICNIC, RAHZEL?
WE'RE GOING TO SEE SHOGETSU'S PUPPIES.
HE HAS TWO OF THEM!
SHOGETSU?
UH-HUH. SOMEONE I MET THE OTHER DAY.
DO YOU WANT TO COME TOO, FATHER?
NO, I'LL STAY HOME TODAY.
HAVE A GOOD TIME.
BE BACK LATER, FATHER!

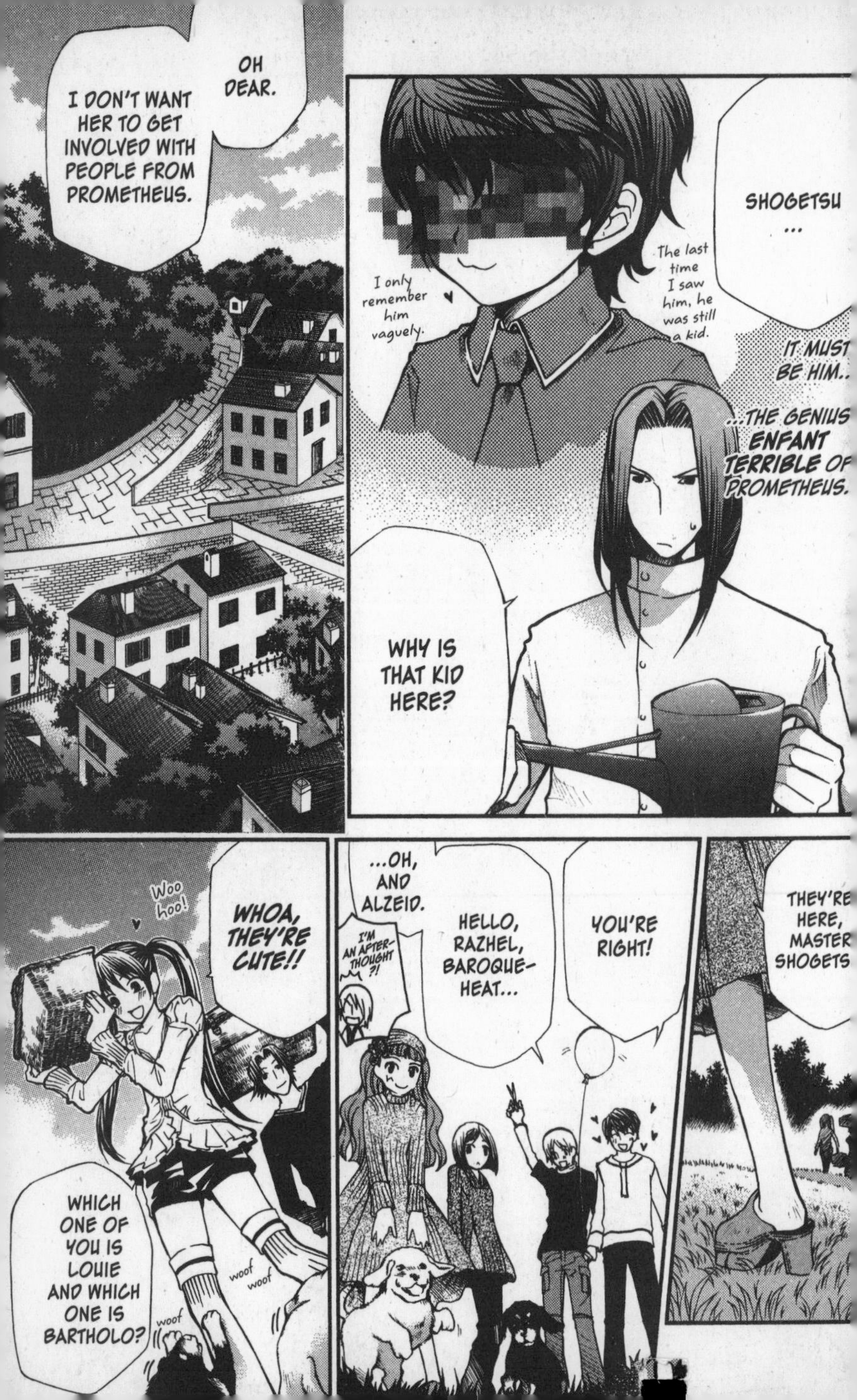
SHOGETSU ...
The last time I saw him, he was still a kid.
I only remember him vaguely.
IT MUST BE HIM...
...THE GENIUS ENFANT TERRIBLE OF PROMETHEUS.
WHY IS THAT KID HERE?
OH DEAR.
I DON'T WANT HER TO GET INVOLVED WITH PEOPLE FROM PROMETHEUS.
THEY'RE HERE, MASTER SHOGETS
YOU'RE RIGHT!
HELLO, RAZHEL, BAROQUE-HEAT...
...OH, AND ALZEID.
I'M AN AFTER-THOUGHT?!
WHOA, THEY'RE CUTE!!
Woo hoo!
WHICH ONE OF YOU IS LOUIE AND WHICH ONE IS BARTHOLO?
woof woof
woof

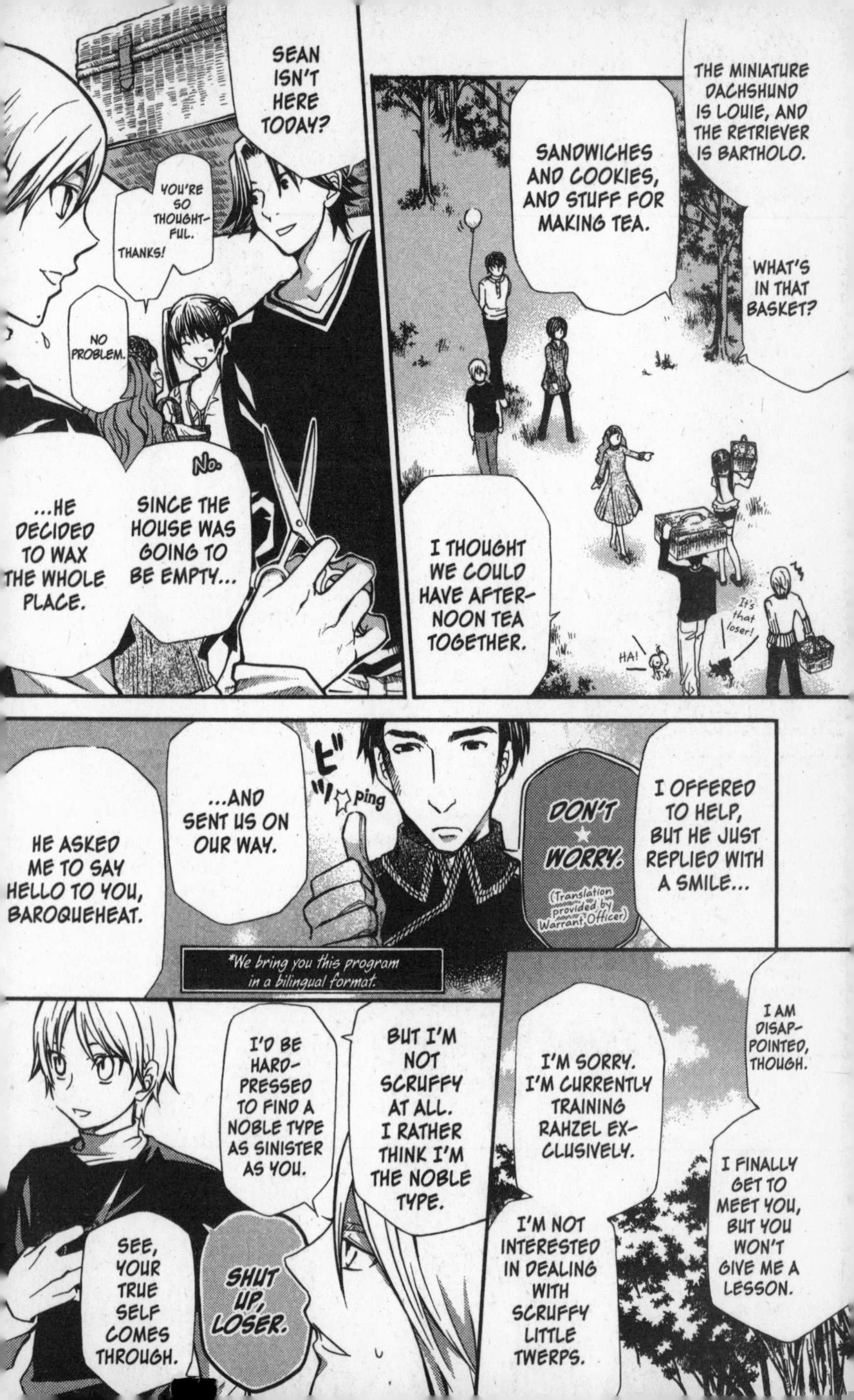
THE MINIATURE DACHSHUND IS LOUIE, AND THE RETRIEVER IS BARTHOLO.
WHAT'S IN THAT BASKET?
SANDWICHES AND COOKIES, AND STUFF FOR MAKING TEA.
I THOUGHT WE COULD HAVE AFTERNOON TEA TOGETHER.
It's that loser!
HA!
SEAN ISN'T HERE TODAY?
YOU'RE SO THOUGHTFUL.
THANKS!
NO PROBLEM.
No.
SINCE THE HOUSE WAS GOING TO BE EMPTY...
...HE DECIDED TO WAX THE WHOLE PLACE.
I OFFERED TO HELP, BUT HE JUST REPLIED WITH A SMILE...
DON'T ★ WORRY.
(Translation provided by Warrant Officer)
ping
...AND SENT US ON OUR WAY.
HE ASKED ME TO SAY HELLO TO YOU, BAROQUEHEAT.
*We bring you this program in a bilingual format.
I AM DISAPPOINTED, THOUGH.
I FINALLY GET TO MEET YOU, BUT YOU WON'T GIVE ME A LESSON.
I'M SORRY. I'M CURRENTLY TRAINING RAHZEL EXCLUSIVELY.
I'M NOT INTERESTED IN DEALING WITH SCRUFFY LITTLE TWERPS.
BUT I'M NOT SCRUFFY AT ALL. I RATHER THINK I'M THE NOBLE TYPE.
I'D BE HARD-PRESSED TO FIND A NOBLE TYPE AS SINISTER AS YOU.
SHUT UP, LOSER.
SEE, YOUR TRUE SELF COMES THROUGH.

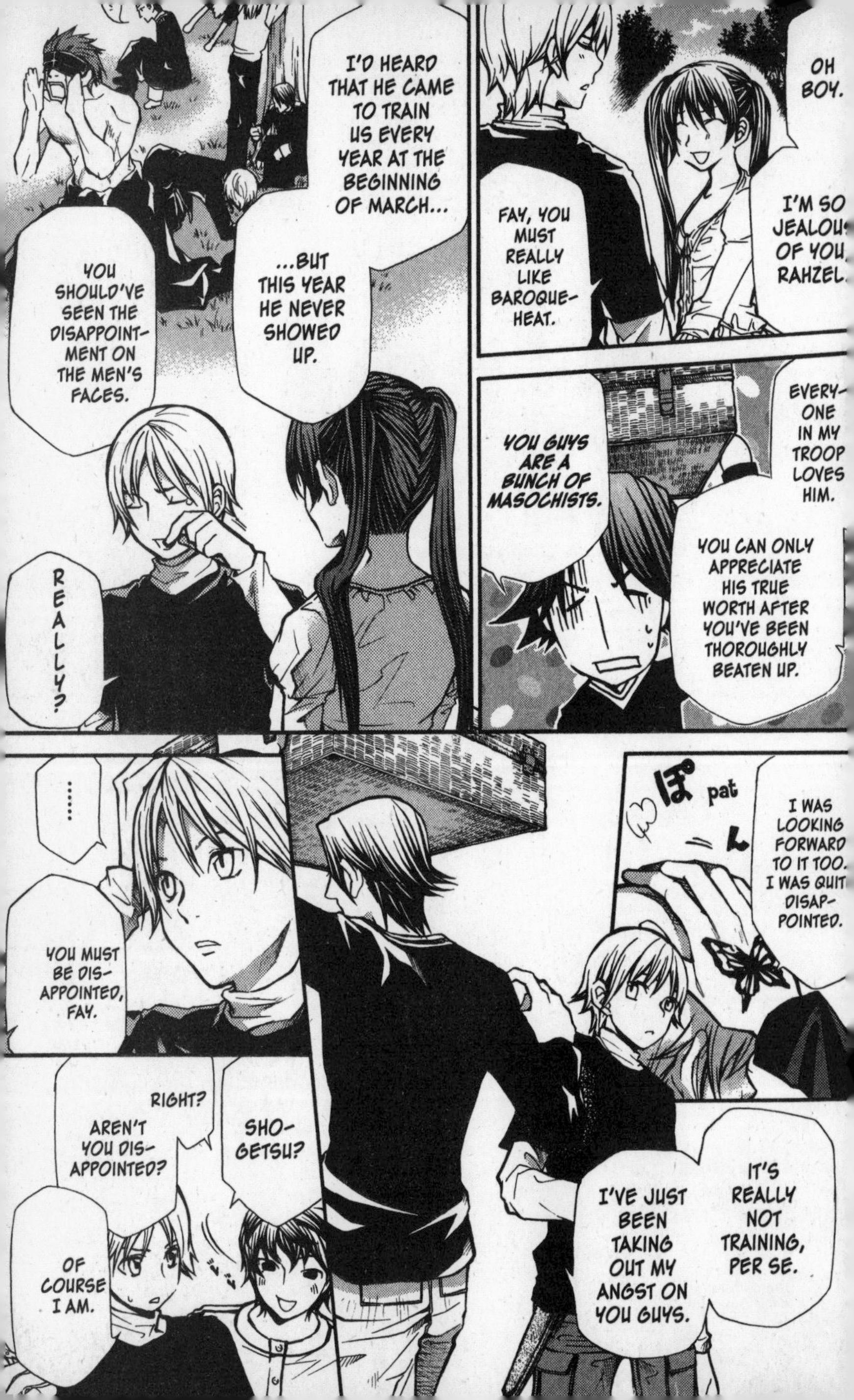

OH BOY.
I'M SO JEALOU OF YOU RAHZEL.
FAY, YOU MUST REALLY LIKE BAROQUE-HEAT.
I'D HEARD THAT HE CAME TO TRAIN US EVERY YEAR AT THE BEGINNING OF MARCH...
...BUT THIS YEAR HE NEVER SHOWED UP.
YOU SHOULD'VE SEEN THE DISAPPOINTMENT ON THE MEN'S FACES.
EVERY-ONE IN MY TROOP LOVES HIM.
YOU CAN ONLY APPRECIATE HIS TRUE WORTH AFTER YOU'VE BEEN THOROUGHLY BEATEN UP.
YOU GUYS ARE A BUNCH OF MASOCHISTS.
REALLY?
ぽん pat
I WAS LOOKING FORWARD TO IT TOO. I WAS QUIT DISAP-POINTED.
......
YOU MUST BE DIS-APPOINTED, FAY.
IT'S REALLY NOT TRAINING, PER SE.
I'VE JUST BEEN TAKING OUT MY ANGST ON YOU GUYS.
SHO-GETSU?
RIGHT?
AREN'T YOU DIS-APPOINTED?
OF COURSE I AM.

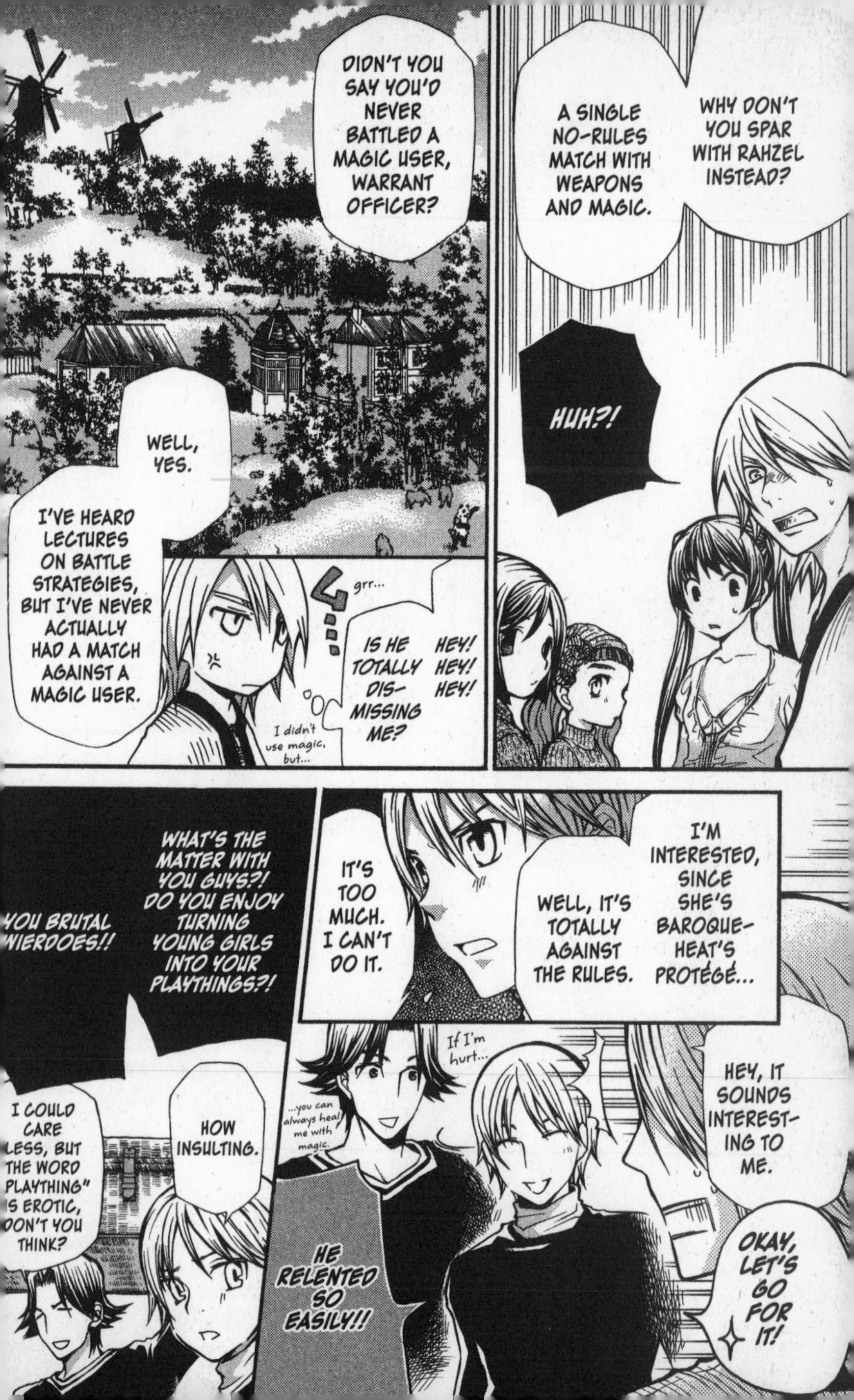

DIDN'T YOU SAY YOU'D NEVER BATTLED A MAGIC USER, WARRANT OFFICER?
WELL, YES.
I'VE HEARD LECTURES ON BATTLE STRATEGIES, BUT I'VE NEVER ACTUALLY HAD A MATCH AGAINST A MAGIC USER.
grr...
HEY! HEY! HEY!
IS HE TOTALLY DIS-MISSING ME?
I didn't use magic, but...
WHY DON'T YOU SPAR WITH RAHZEL INSTEAD?
A SINGLE NO-RULES MATCH WITH WEAPONS AND MAGIC.
HUH?!
I'M INTERESTED, SINCE SHE'S BAROQUE-HEAT'S PROTÉGÉ...
WELL, IT'S TOTALLY AGAINST THE RULES.
IT'S TOO MUCH. I CAN'T DO IT.
WHAT'S THE MATTER WITH YOU GUYS?! DO YOU ENJOY TURNING YOUNG GIRLS INTO YOUR PLAYTHINGS?!
YOU BRUTAL WIERDOES!!
HEY, IT SOUNDS INTERESTING TO ME.
OKAY, LET'S GO FOR IT!
If I'm hurt...
...you can always heal me with magic.
HE RELENTED SO EASILY!!
HOW INSULTING.
I COULD CARE LESS, BUT THE WORD "PLAYTHING" IS EROTIC, DON'T YOU THINK?

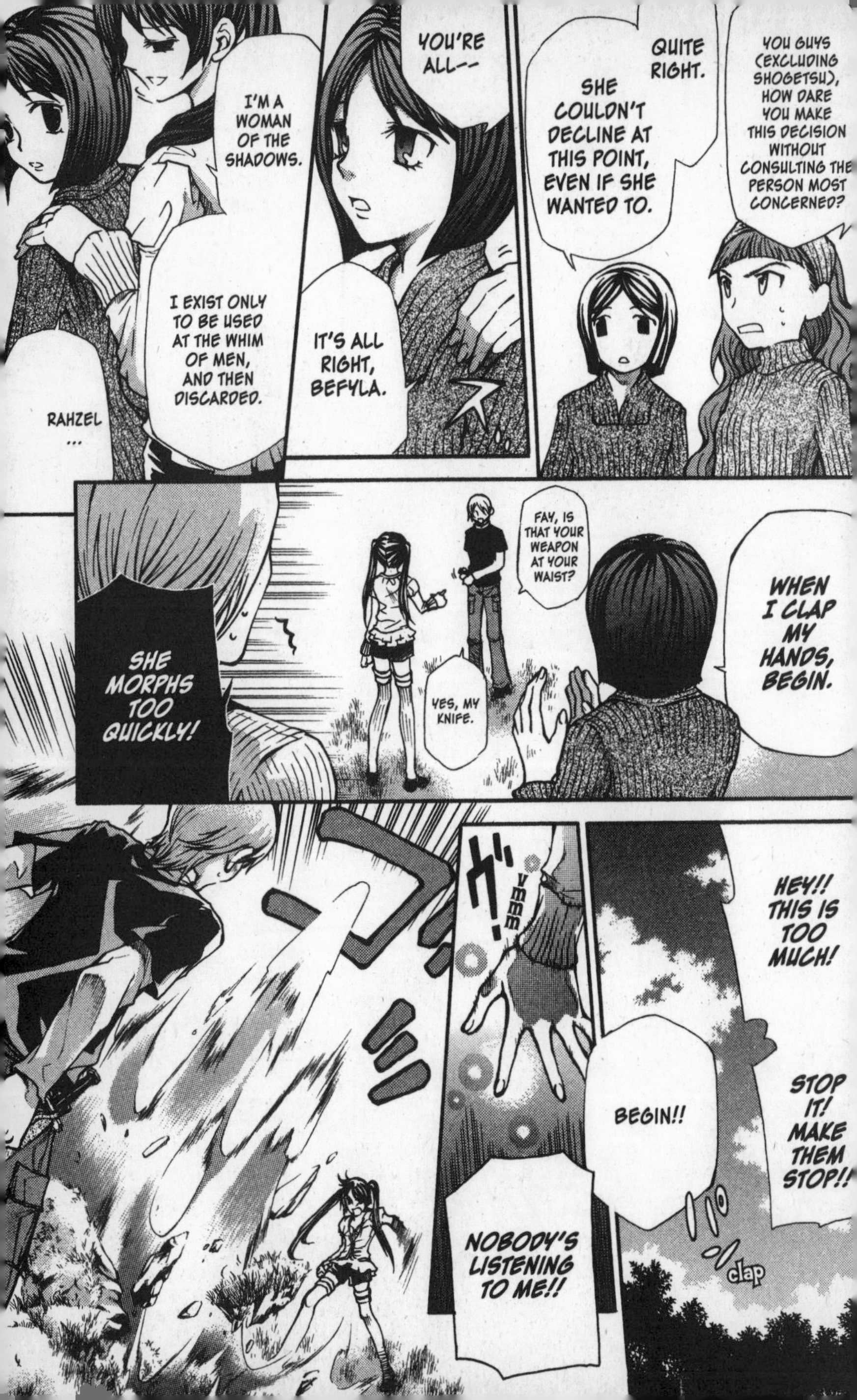
YOU GUYS (EXCLUDING SHOGETSU), HOW DARE YOU MAKE THIS DECISION WITHOUT CONSULTING THE PERSON MOST CONCERNED?
QUITE RIGHT.
SHE COULDN'T DECLINE AT THIS POINT, EVEN IF SHE WANTED TO.
YOU'RE ALL--
IT'S ALL RIGHT, BEFYLA.
I'M A WOMAN OF THE SHADOWS.
I EXIST ONLY TO BE USED AT THE WHIM OF MEN, AND THEN DISCARDED.
RAHZEL...
WHEN I CLAP MY HANDS, BEGIN.
FAY, IS THAT YOUR WEAPON AT YOUR WAIST?
YES, MY KNIFE.
SHE MORPHS TOO QUICKLY!
HEY!! THIS IS TOO MUCH!
STOP IT! MAKE THEM STOP!!
clap
BEGIN!!
NOBODY'S LISTENING TO ME!!
VMMM

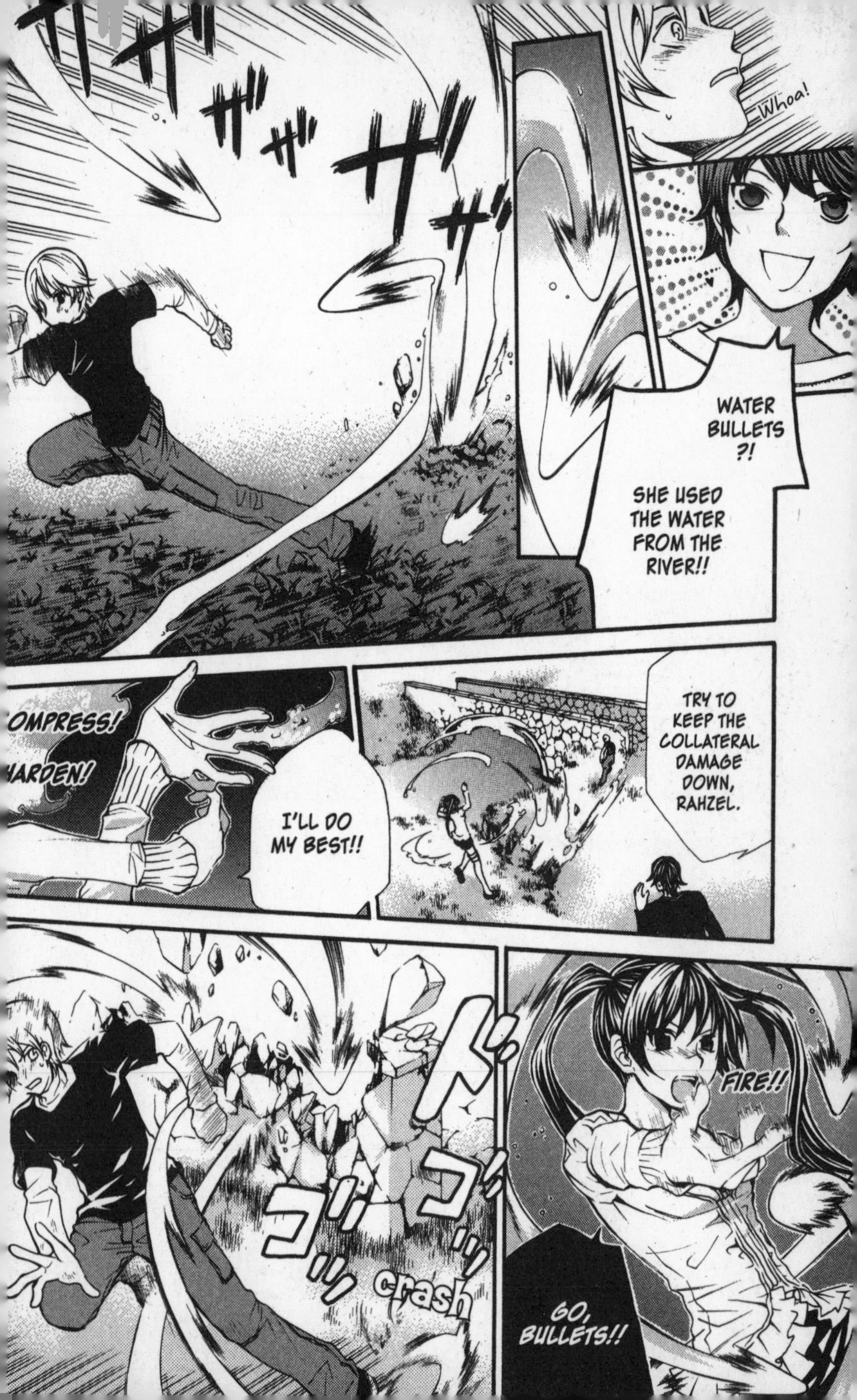
Whoa!
WATER BULLETS ?!
SHE USED THE WATER FROM THE RIVER!!
TRY TO KEEP THE COLLATERAL DAMAGE DOWN, RAHZEL.
I'LL DO MY BEST!!
OMPRESS!
HARDEN!
FIRE!!
GO, BULLETS!!
crash

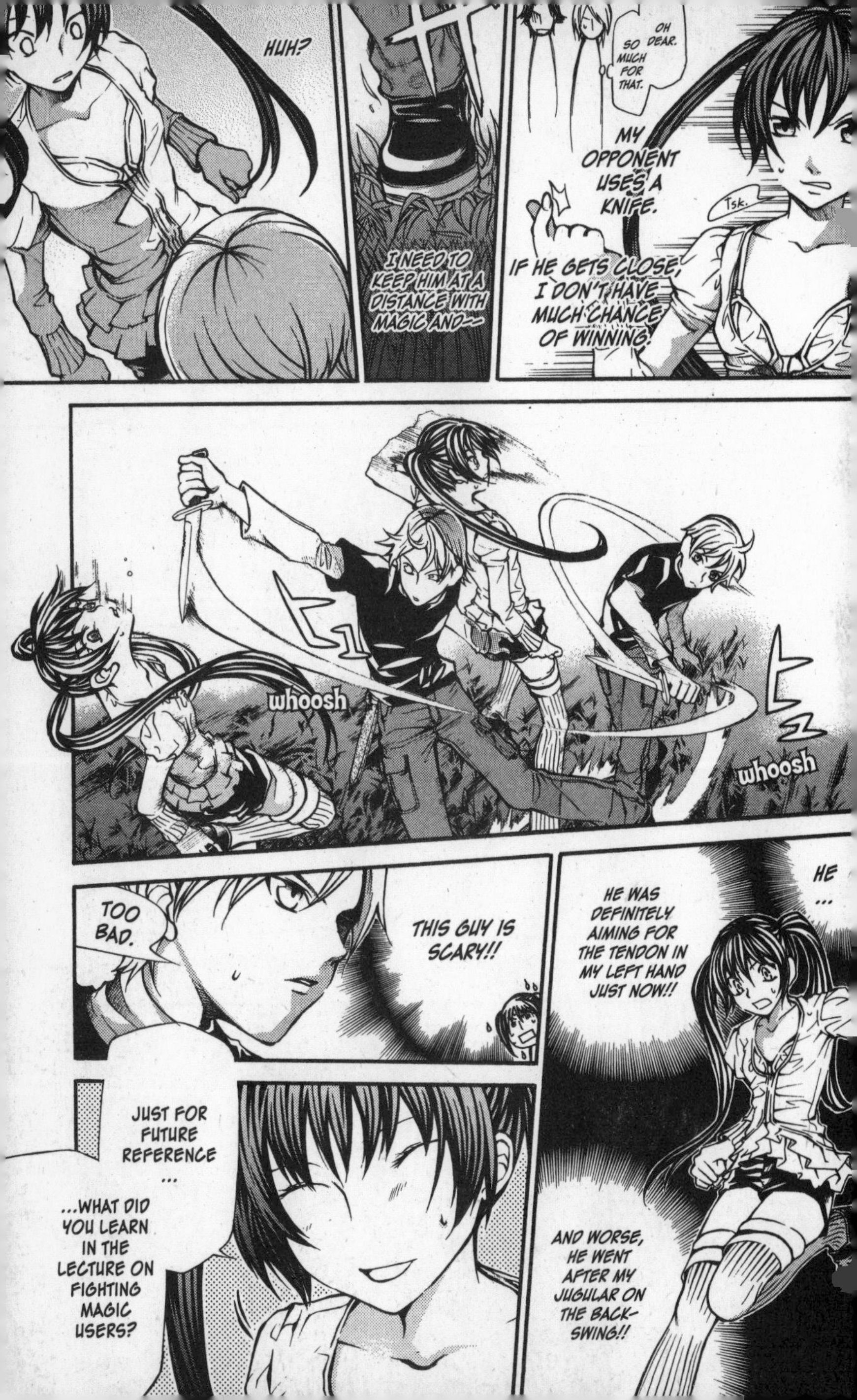
OH DEAR. SO MUCH FOR THAT.
MY OPPONENT USES A KNIFE.
Tsk.
IF HE GETS CLOSE, I DON'T HAVE MUCH CHANCE OF WINNING.
I NEED TO KEEP HIM AT A DISTANCE WITH MAGIC AND--
HUH?
whoosh
whoosh
HE ...
HE WAS DEFINITELY AIMING FOR THE TENDON IN MY LEFT HAND JUST NOW!!
AND WORSE, HE WENT AFTER MY JUGULAR ON THE BACK-SWING!!
THIS GUY IS SCARY!!
TOO BAD.
JUST FOR FUTURE REFERENCE ...
...WHAT DID YOU LEARN IN THE LECTURE ON FIGHTING MAGIC USERS?

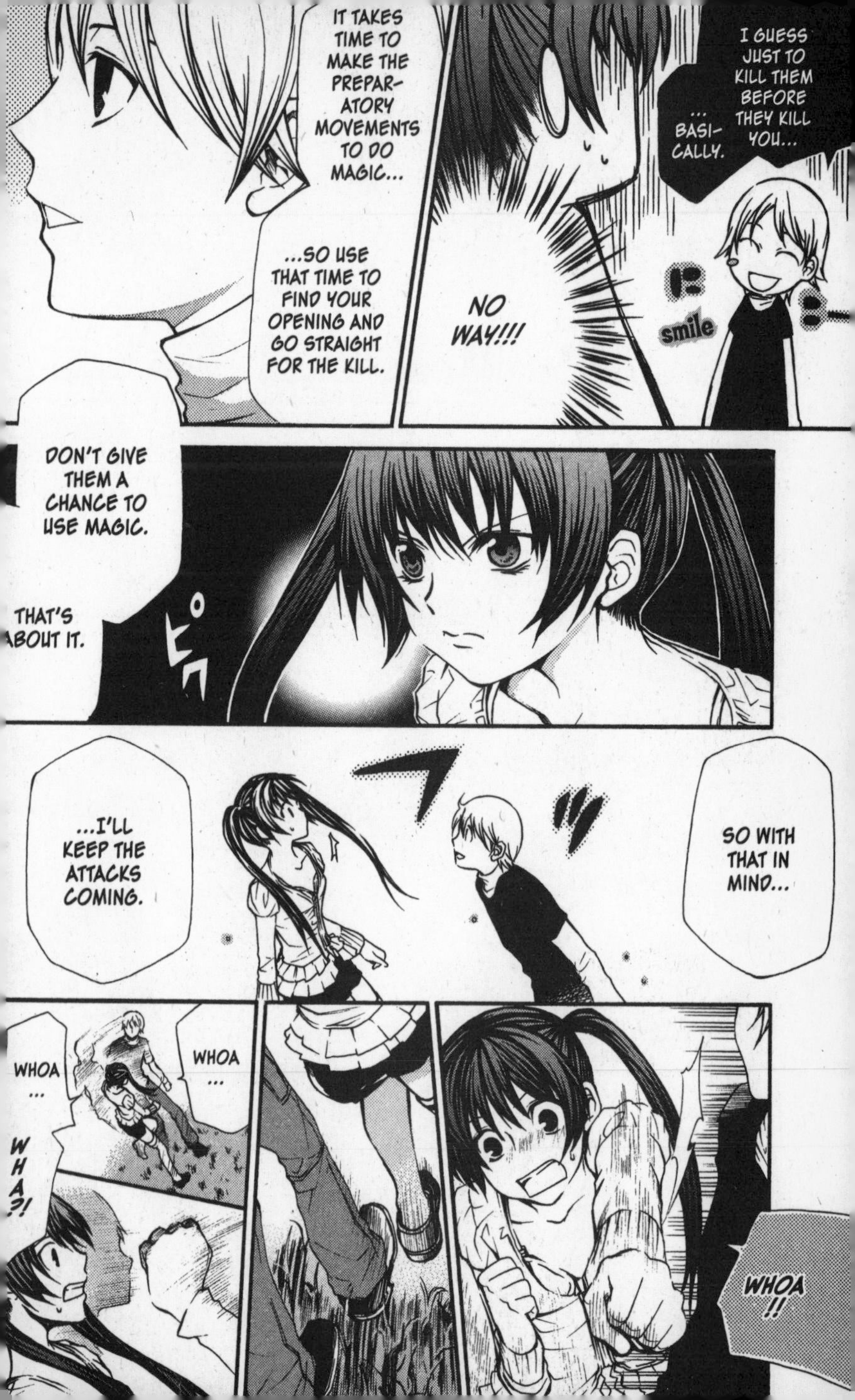

I GUESS JUST TO KILL THEM BEFORE THEY KILL YOU...
...BASI-CALLY.
smile
NO WAY!!!
IT TAKES TIME TO MAKE THE PREPAR-ATORY MOVEMENTS TO DO MAGIC...
...SO USE THAT TIME TO FIND YOUR OPENING AND GO STRAIGHT FOR THE KILL.
DON'T GIVE THEM A CHANCE TO USE MAGIC.
THAT'S ABOUT IT.
SO WITH THAT IN MIND...
...I'LL KEEP THE ATTACKS COMING.
WHOA!!
WHOA...
WHOA...
WHA?!

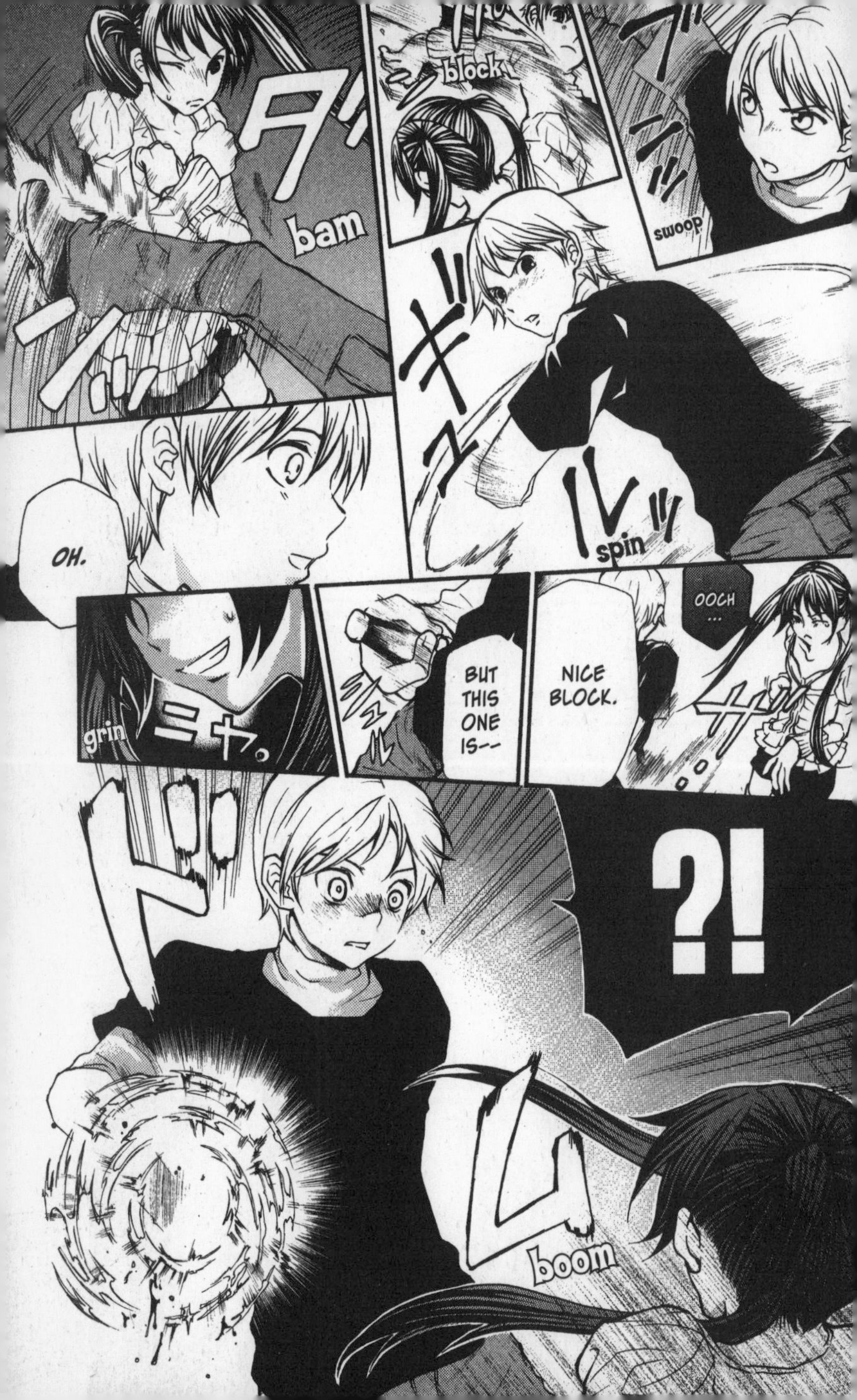

swoop
block
bam
spin
OH.
OOCH ...
NICE BLOCK.
BUT THIS ONE IS--
grin
ニヤ。
?!
boom

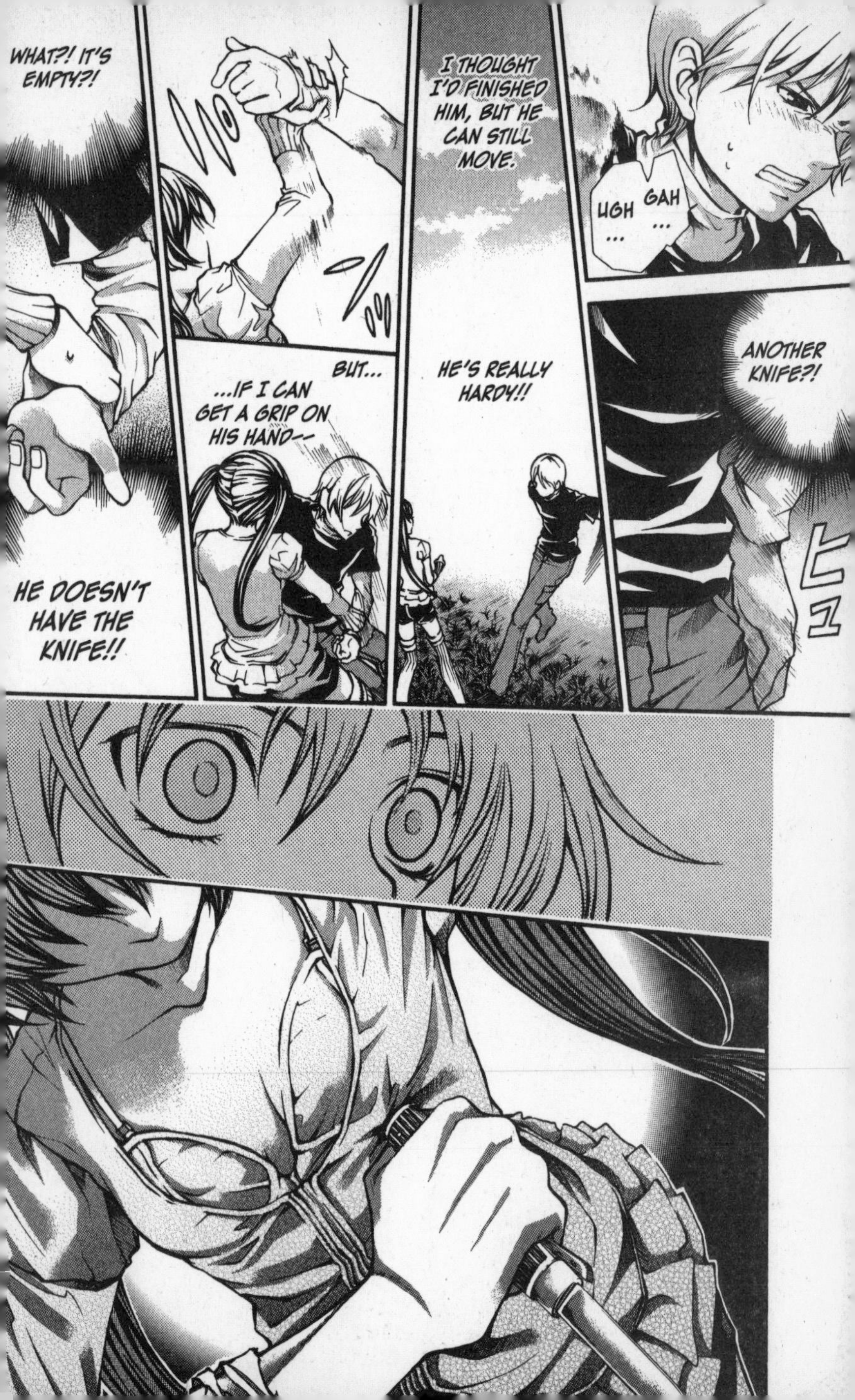
GAH ...
UGH ...
I THOUGHT I'D FINISHED HIM, BUT HE CAN STILL MOVE.
ANOTHER KNIFE?!
ヒュ
HE'S REALLY HARDY!!
BUT...
...IF I CAN GET A GRIP ON HIS HAND--
WHAT?! IT'S EMPTY?!
HE DOESN'T HAVE THE KNIFE!!

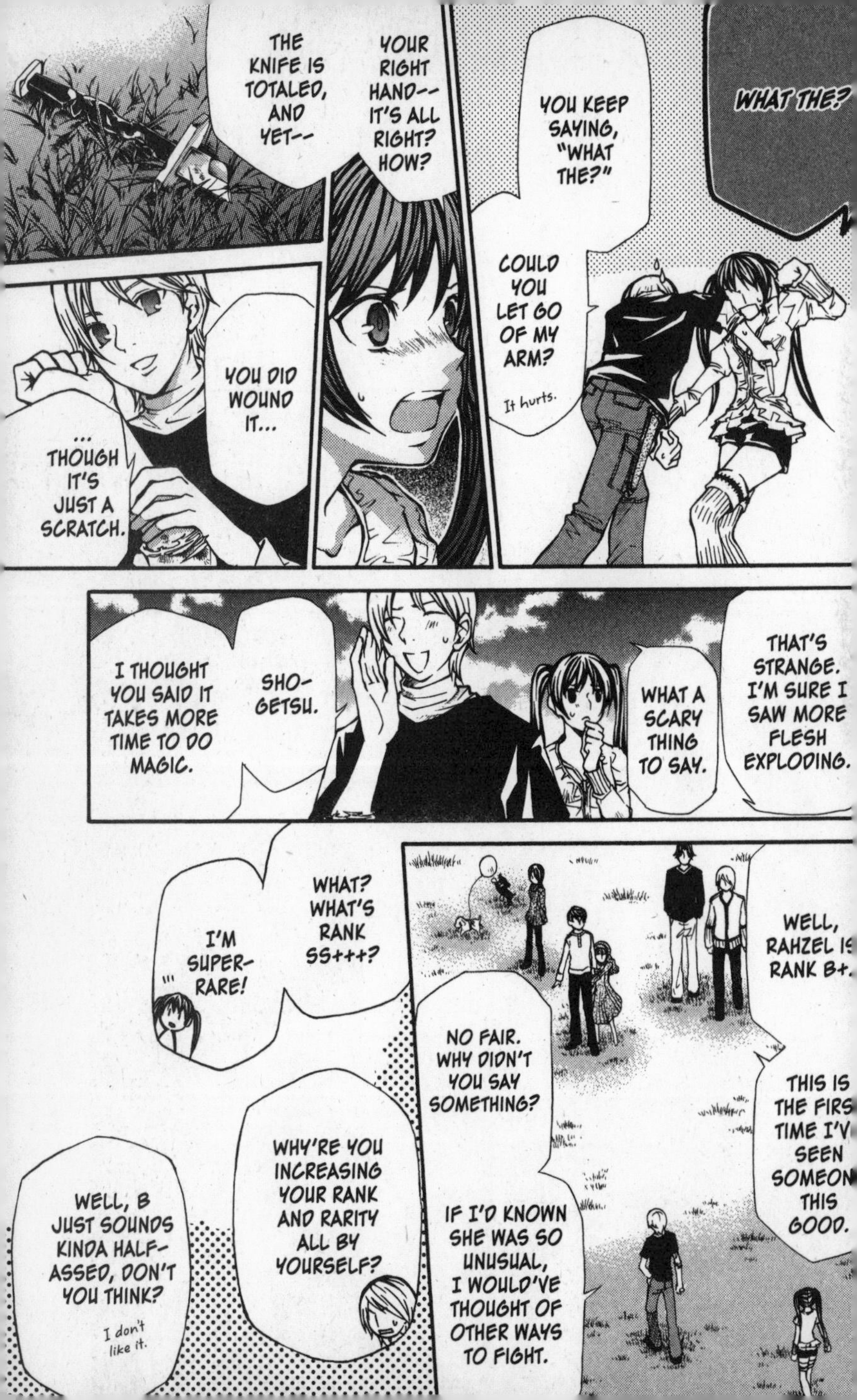
WHAT THE?
YOU KEEP SAYING, "WHAT THE?"
COULD YOU LET GO OF MY ARM?
It hurts.
YOUR RIGHT HAND-- IT'S ALL RIGHT? HOW?
THE KNIFE IS TOTALED, AND YET--
YOU DID WOUND IT...
... THOUGH IT'S JUST A SCRATCH.
THAT'S STRANGE. I'M SURE I SAW MORE FLESH EXPLODING.
WHAT A SCARY THING TO SAY.
SHO-GETSU.
I THOUGHT YOU SAID IT TAKES MORE TIME TO DO MAGIC.
WELL, RAHZEL IS RANK B+.
THIS IS THE FIRS TIME I'V SEEN SOMEON THIS GOOD.
NO FAIR. WHY DIDN'T YOU SAY SOMETHING?
WHAT? WHAT'S RANK SS+++?
I'M SUPER-RARE!
...
IF I'D KNOWN SHE WAS SO UNUSUAL, I WOULD'VE THOUGHT OF OTHER WAYS TO FIGHT.
WHY'RE YOU INCREASING YOUR RANK AND RARITY ALL BY YOURSELF?
WELL, B JUST SOUNDS KINDA HALF-ASSED, DON'T YOU THINK?
I don't like it.

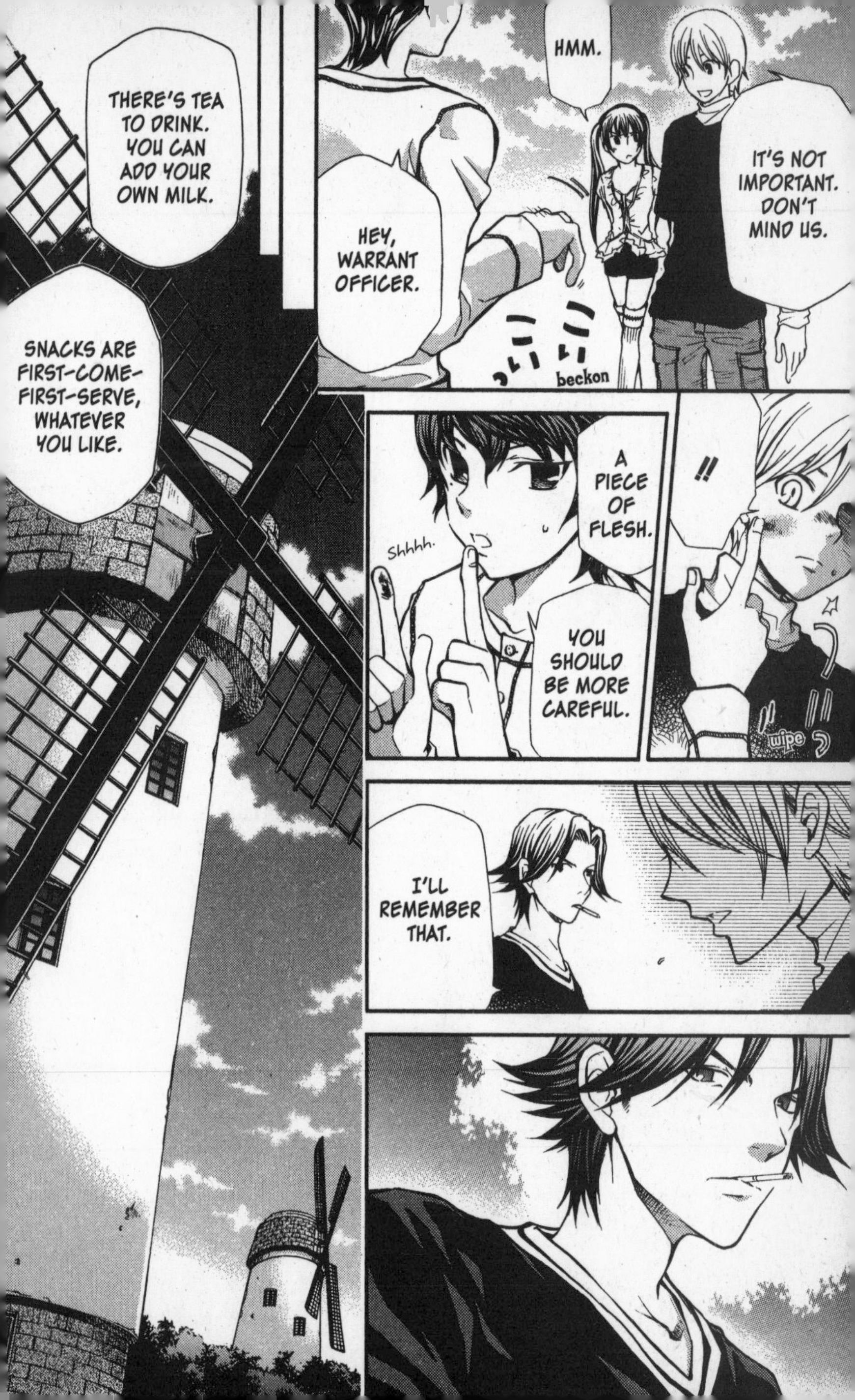

IT'S NOT IMPORTANT. DON'T MIND US.
HMM.
HEY, WARRANT OFFICER.
beckon
A PIECE OF FLESH.
Shhhh.
YOU SHOULD BE MORE CAREFUL.
!!
wipe
I'LL REMEMBER THAT.
THERE'S TEA TO DRINK. YOU CAN ADD YOUR OWN MILK.
SNACKS ARE FIRST-COME-FIRST-SERVE, WHATEVER YOU LIKE.

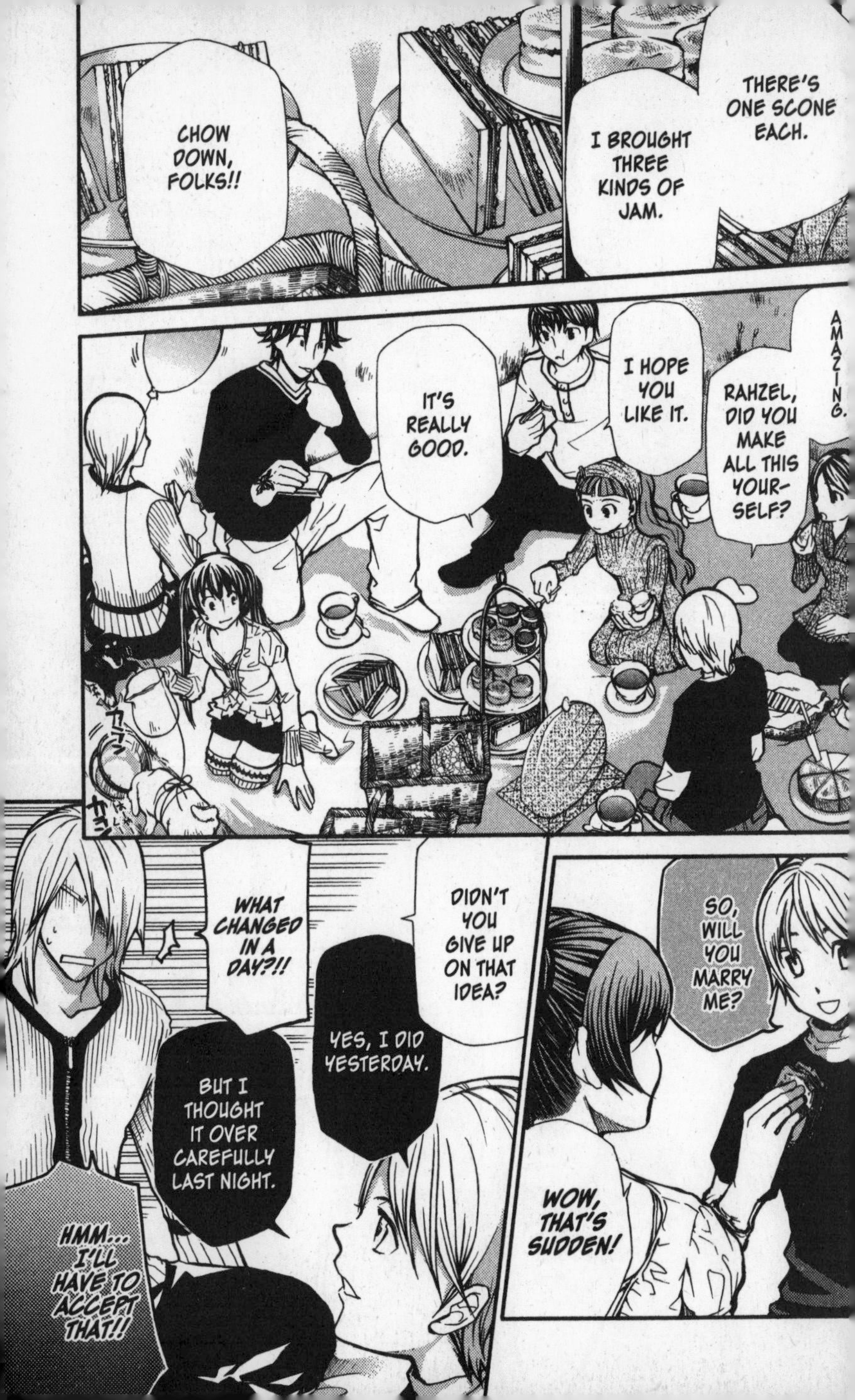
THERE'S ONE SCONE EACH.
I BROUGHT THREE KINDS OF JAM.
CHOW DOWN, FOLKS!!
AMAZING.
RAHZEL, DID YOU MAKE ALL THIS YOUR-SELF?
I HOPE YOU LIKE IT.
IT'S REALLY GOOD.
SO, WILL YOU MARRY ME?
WOW, THAT'S SUDDEN!
DIDN'T YOU GIVE UP ON THAT IDEA?
WHAT CHANGED IN A DAY?!!
YES, I DID YESTERDAY.
BUT I THOUGHT IT OVER CAREFULLY LAST NIGHT.
HMM... I'LL HAVE TO ACCEPT THAT!!

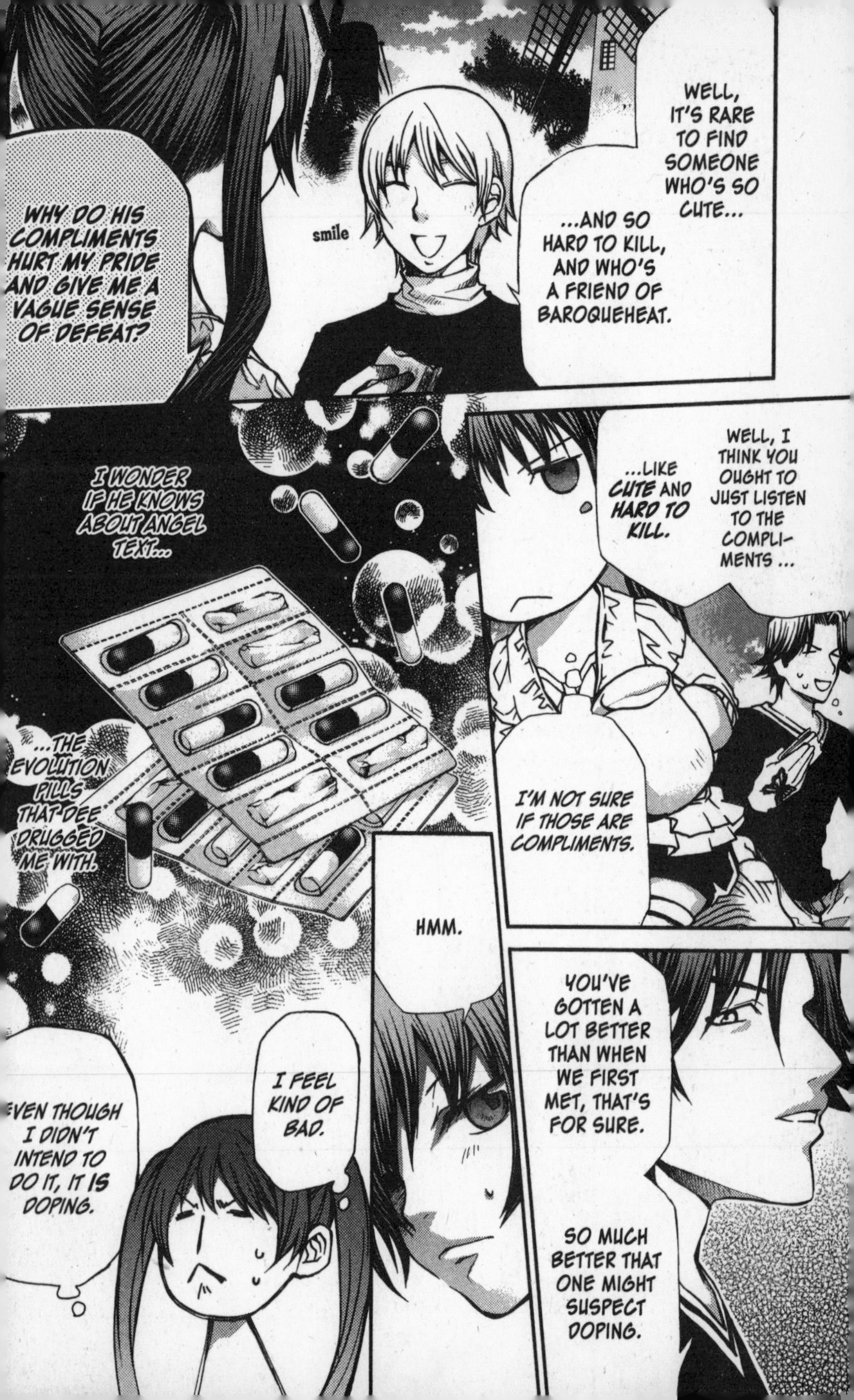
WELL, IT'S RARE TO FIND SOMEONE WHO'S SO CUTE...
...AND SO HARD TO KILL, AND WHO'S A FRIEND OF BAROQUEHEAT.
smile
WHY DO HIS COMPLIMENTS HURT MY PRIDE AND GIVE ME A VAGUE SENSE OF DEFEAT?
WELL, I THINK YOU OUGHT TO JUST LISTEN TO THE COMPLI-MENTS ...
...LIKE CUTE AND HARD TO KILL.
I'M NOT SURE IF THOSE ARE COMPLIMENTS.
I WONDER IF HE KNOWS ABOUT ANGEL TEXT...
...THE EVOLUTION PILLS THAT DEE DRUGGED ME WITH.
YOU'VE GOTTEN A LOT BETTER THAN WHEN WE FIRST MET, THAT'S FOR SURE.
SO MUCH BETTER THAT ONE MIGHT SUSPECT DOPING.
HMM.
I FEEL KIND OF BAD.
EVEN THOUGH I DIDN'T INTEND TO DO IT, IT IS DOPING.

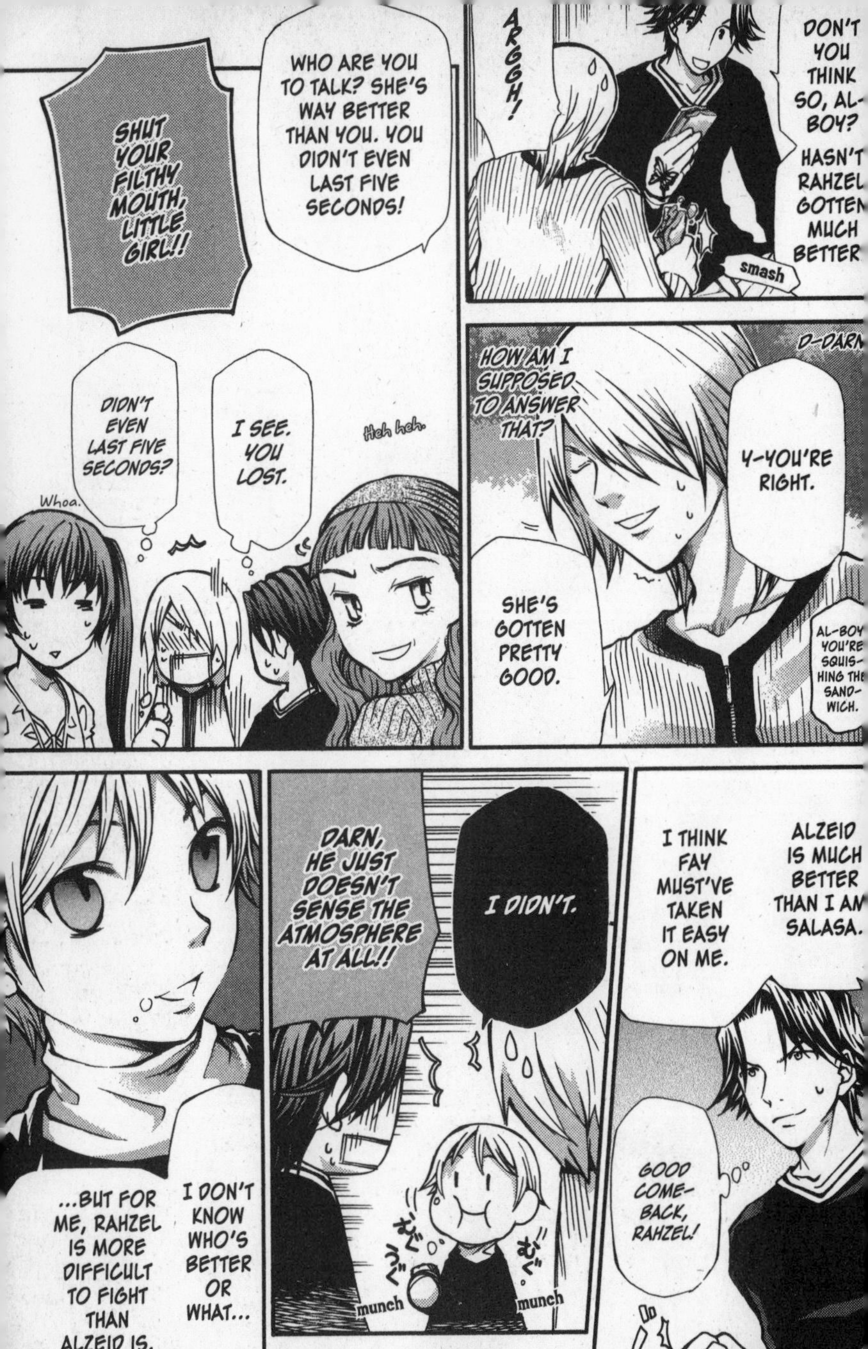
DON'T YOU THINK SO, AL-BOY?
HASN'T RAHZEL GOTTEN MUCH BETTER
ARGGGH!
smash
WHO ARE YOU TO TALK? SHE'S WAY BETTER THAN YOU. YOU DIDN'T EVEN LAST FIVE SECONDS!
SHUT YOUR FILTHY MOUTH, LITTLE GIRL!!
D-DARN
HOW AM I SUPPOSED TO ANSWER THAT?
Y-YOU'RE RIGHT.
SHE'S GOTTEN PRETTY GOOD.
AL-BOY YOU'RE SQUISHING THE SANDWICH.
Heh heh.
I SEE. YOU LOST.
DIDN'T EVEN LAST FIVE SECONDS?
Whoa.
ALZEID IS MUCH BETTER THAN I AM SALASA.
I THINK FAY MUST'VE TAKEN IT EASY ON ME.
GOOD COME-BACK, RAHZEL!
I DIDN'T.
DARN, HE JUST DOESN'T SENSE THE ATMOSPHERE AT ALL!!
munch
munch
I DON'T KNOW WHO'S BETTER OR WHAT...
...BUT FOR ME, RAHZEL IS MORE DIFFICULT TO FIGHT THAN ALZEID IS.

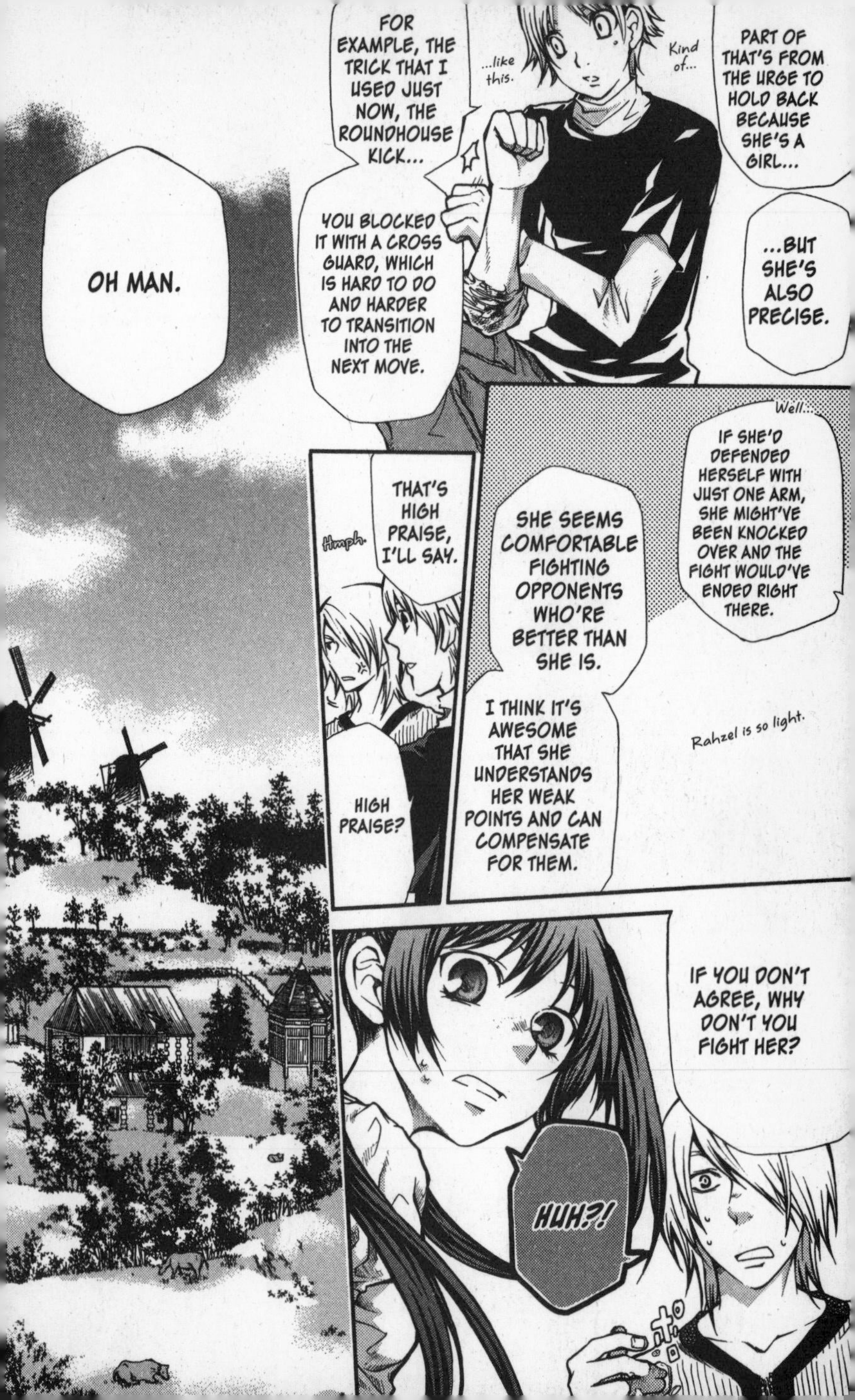
PART OF THAT'S FROM THE URGE TO HOLD BACK BECAUSE SHE'S A GIRL...
Kind of...
...like this.
FOR EXAMPLE, THE TRICK THAT I USED JUST NOW, THE ROUNDHOUSE KICK...
YOU BLOCKED IT WITH A CROSS GUARD, WHICH IS HARD TO DO AND HARDER TO TRANSITION INTO THE NEXT MOVE.
...BUT SHE'S ALSO PRECISE.
OH MAN.
Well...
IF SHE'D DEFENDED HERSELF WITH JUST ONE ARM, SHE MIGHT'VE BEEN KNOCKED OVER AND THE FIGHT WOULD'VE ENDED RIGHT THERE.
SHE SEEMS COMFORTABLE FIGHTING OPPONENTS WHO'RE BETTER THAN SHE IS.
I THINK IT'S AWESOME THAT SHE UNDERSTANDS HER WEAK POINTS AND CAN COMPENSATE FOR THEM.
Rahzel is so light.
THAT'S HIGH PRAISE, I'LL SAY.
Hmph.
HIGH PRAISE?
IF YOU DON'T AGREE, WHY DON'T YOU FIGHT HER?
HUH?!

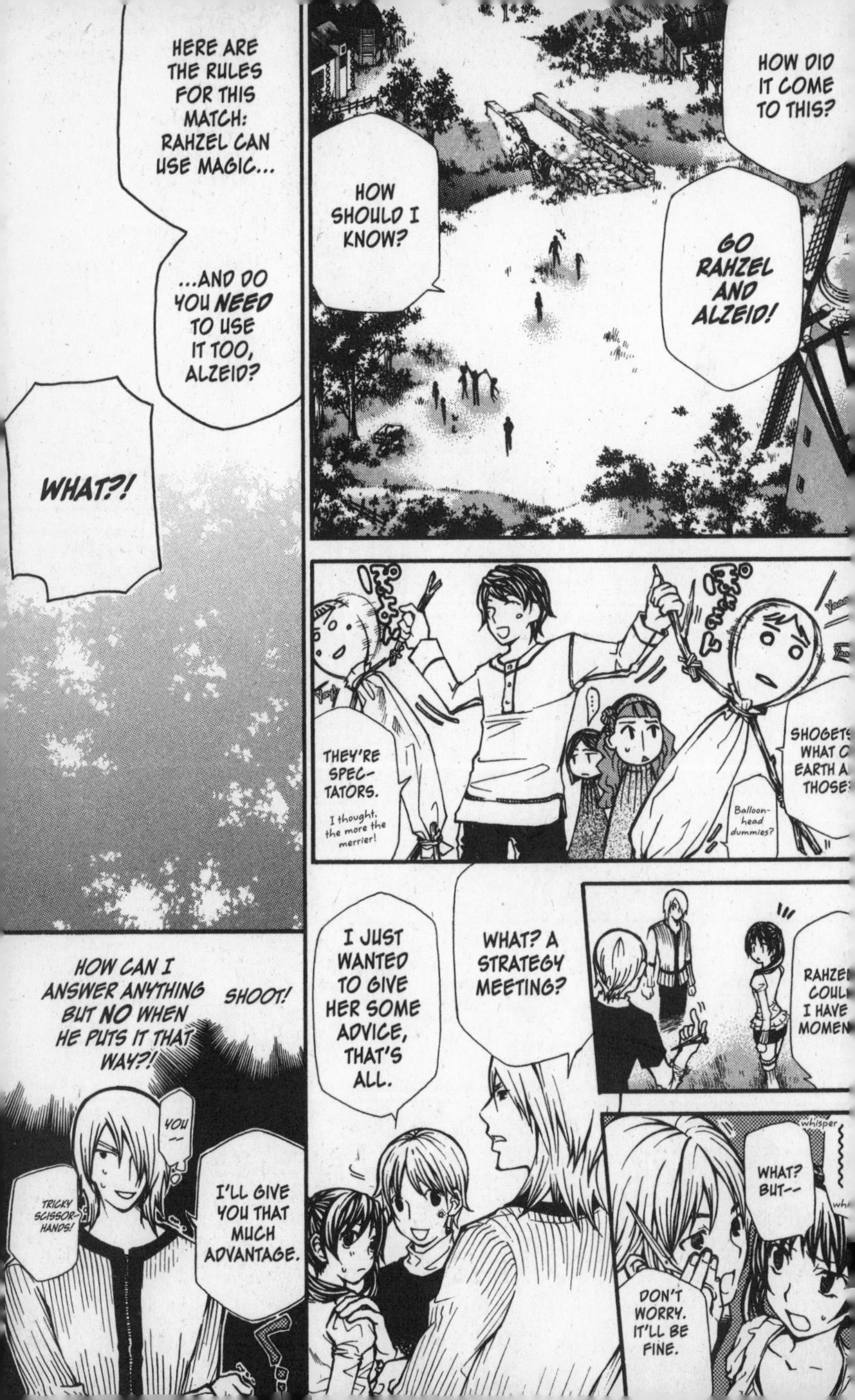
HOW DID IT COME TO THIS?
GO RAHZEL AND ALZEID!
HOW SHOULD I KNOW?
HERE ARE THE RULES FOR THIS MATCH: RAHZEL CAN USE MAGIC...
...AND DO YOU NEED TO USE IT TOO, ALZEID?
WHAT?!
SHOGETS WHAT O EARTH A THOSE
Balloon-head dummies?
THEY'RE SPEC-TATORS.
I thought, the more the merrier!
RAHZEL COUL I HAVE MOMEN
WHAT? A STRATEGY MEETING?
I JUST WANTED TO GIVE HER SOME ADVICE, THAT'S ALL.
whisper
WHAT? BUT--
DON'T WORRY. IT'LL BE FINE.
HOW CAN I ANSWER ANYTHING BUT NO WHEN HE PUTS IT THAT WAY?!
SHOOT!
YOU--
I'LL GIVE YOU THAT MUCH ADVANTAGE.
TRICKY SCISSOR-HANDS!

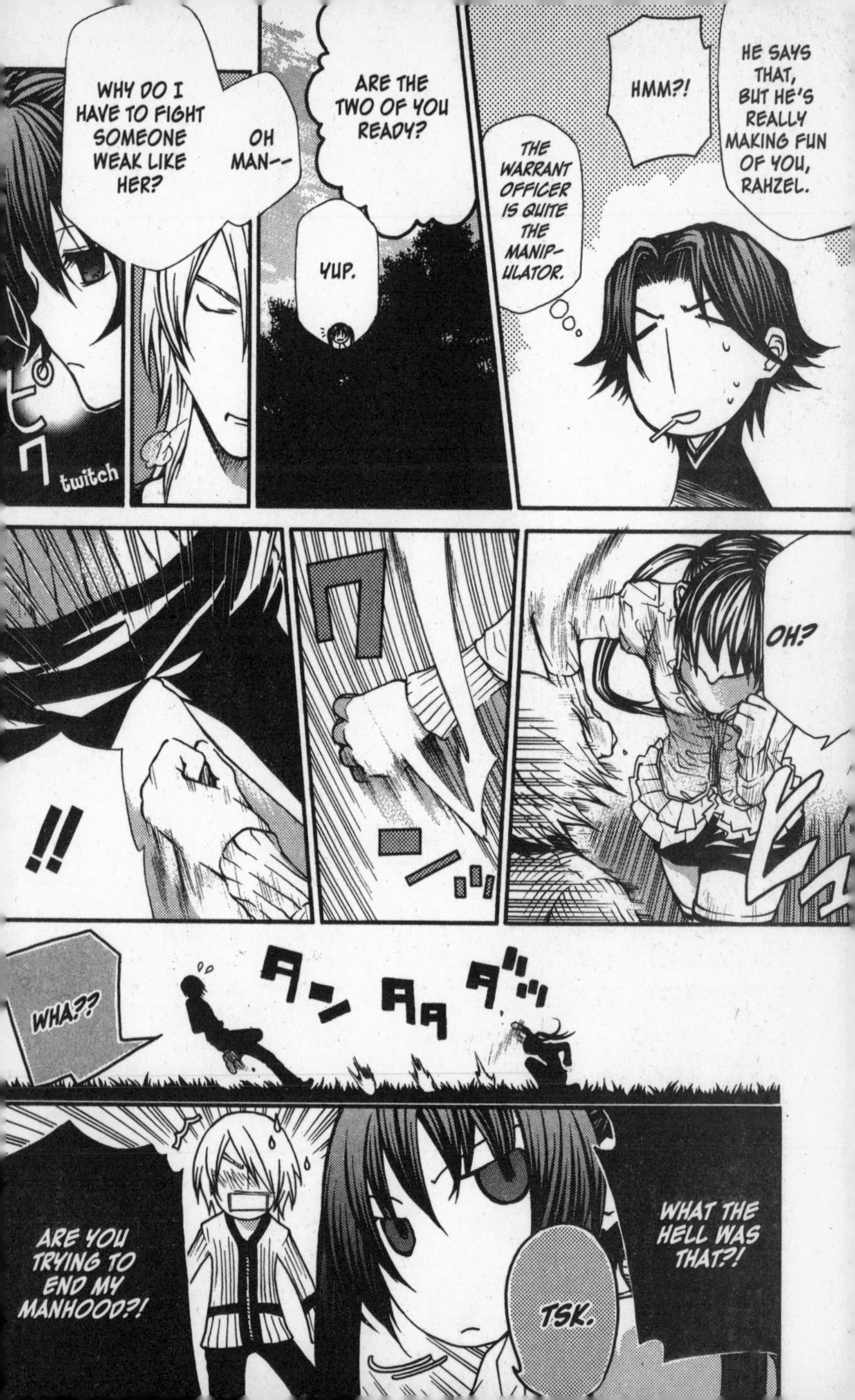
HE SAYS THAT, BUT HE'S REALLY MAKING FUN OF YOU, RAHZEL.
HMM?!
THE WARRANT OFFICER IS QUITE THE MANIPULATOR.
ARE THE TWO OF YOU READY?
YUP.
OH MAN--
WHY DO I HAVE TO FIGHT SOMEONE WEAK LIKE HER?
twitch
OH?
!!
WHA??
WHAT THE HELL WAS THAT?!
TSK.
ARE YOU TRYING TO END MY MANHOOD?!

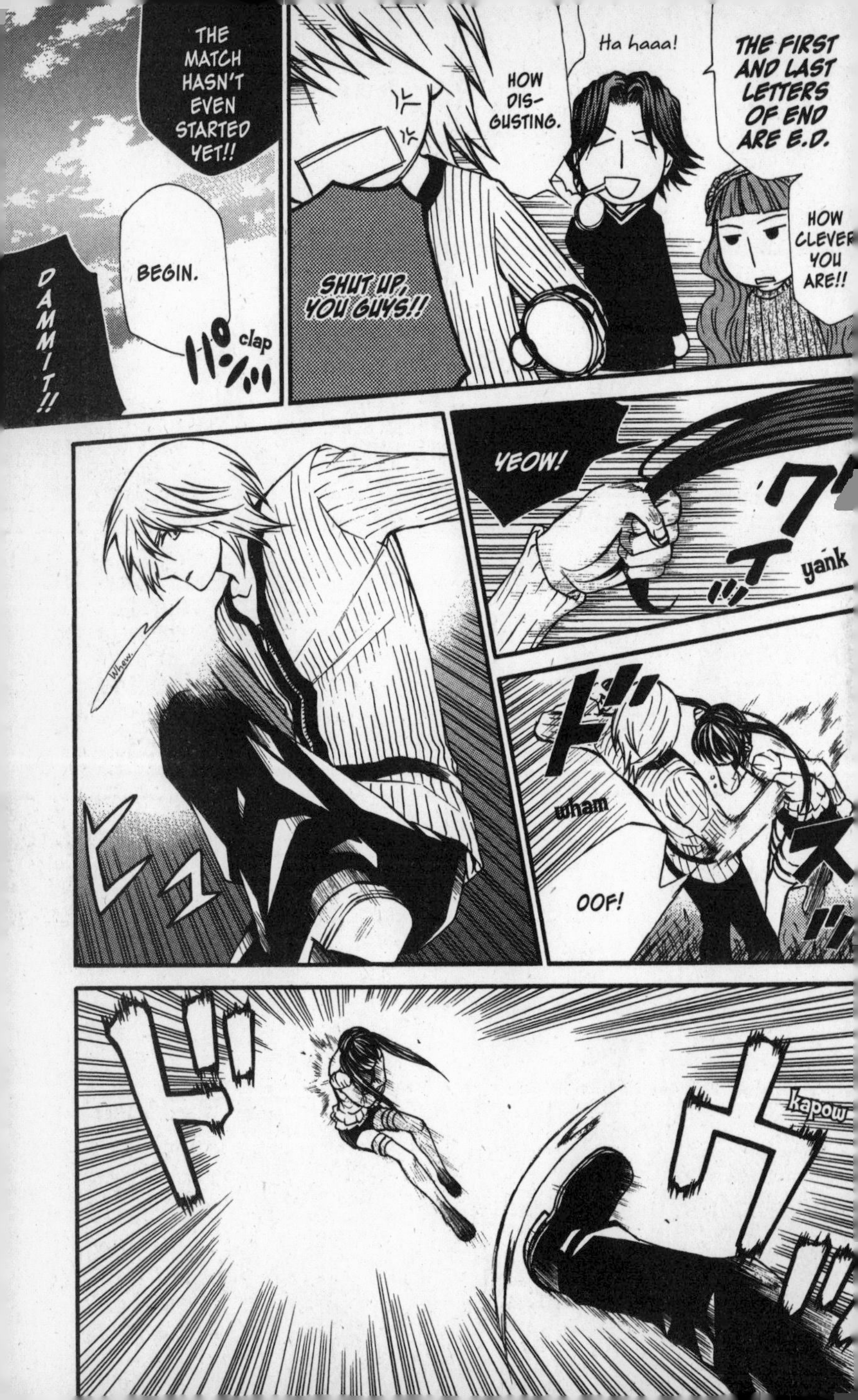
THE FIRST AND LAST LETTERS OF END ARE E.D.
HOW CLEVER YOU ARE!!
Ha haaa!
HOW DIS-GUSTING.
SHUT UP, YOU GUYS!!
THE MATCH HASN'T EVEN STARTED YET!!
BEGIN.
clap
DAMMIT!!
YEOW!
yank
Whew.
wham
OOF!
kapow

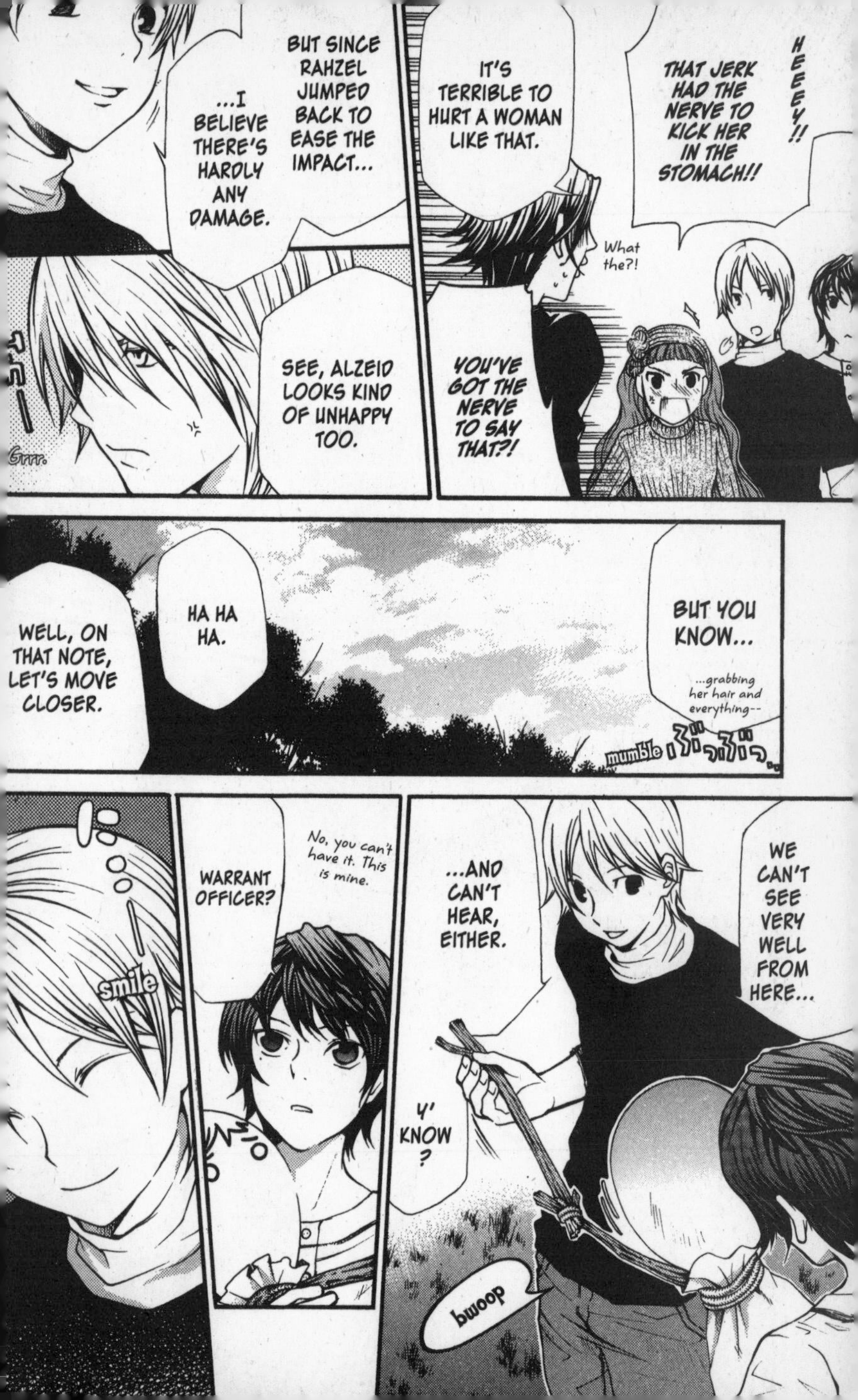
HEEEY!!
THAT JERK HAD THE NERVE TO KICK HER IN THE STOMACH!!
What the?!
IT'S TERRIBLE TO HURT A WOMAN LIKE THAT.
YOU'VE GOT THE NERVE TO SAY THAT?!
BUT SINCE RAHZEL JUMPED BACK TO EASE THE IMPACT...
...I BELIEVE THERE'S HARDLY ANY DAMAGE.
SEE, ALZEID LOOKS KIND OF UNHAPPY TOO.
Grrr.
BUT YOU KNOW...
...grabbing her hair and everything--
mumble
HA HA HA.
WELL, ON THAT NOTE, LET'S MOVE CLOSER.
WE CAN'T SEE VERY WELL FROM HERE...
...AND CAN'T HEAR, EITHER.
Y' KNOW?
bwoop
WARRANT OFFICER?
No, you can't have it. This is mine.
smile

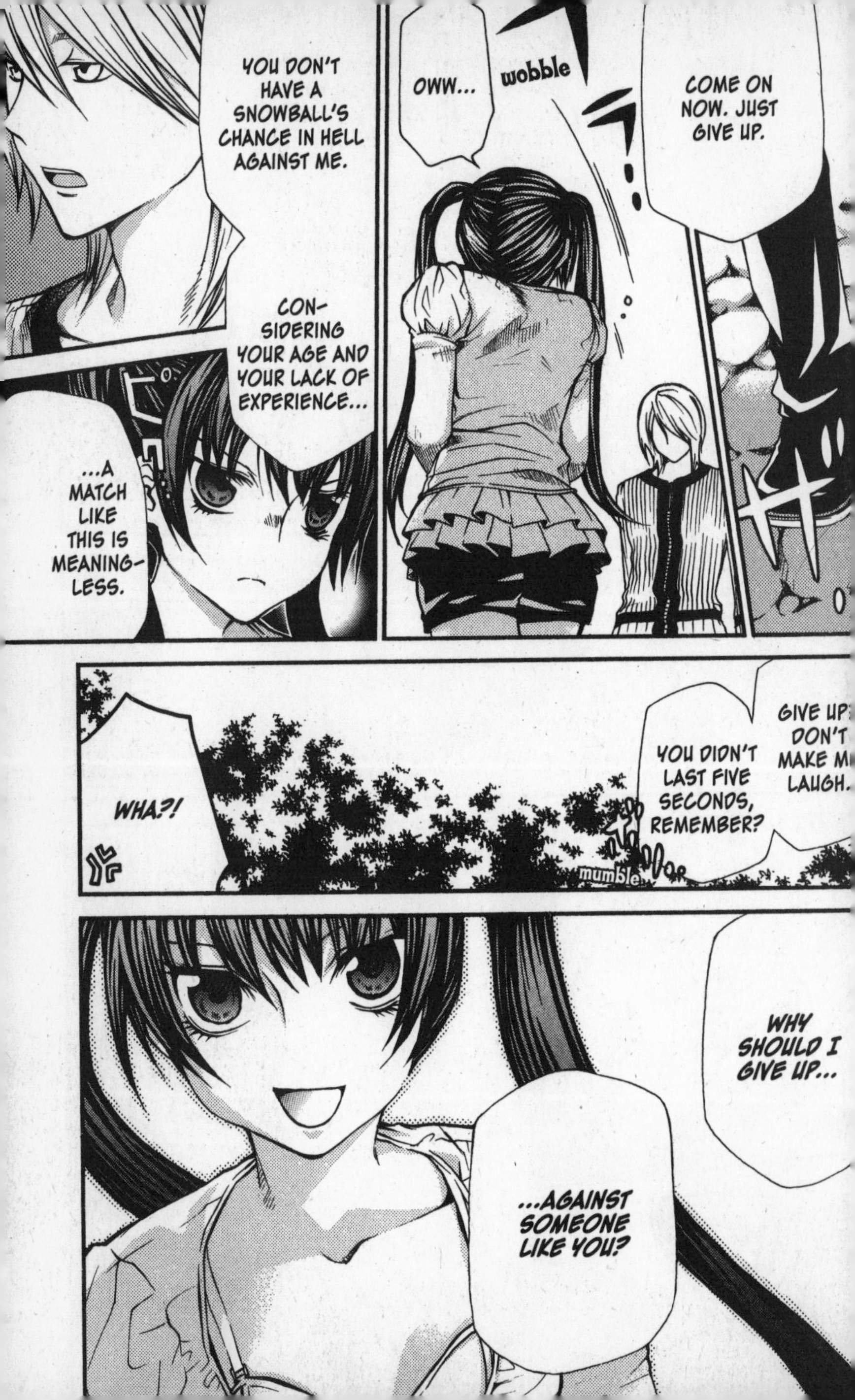
COME ON NOW. JUST GIVE UP.
OWW...
wobble
YOU DON'T HAVE A SNOWBALL'S CHANCE IN HELL AGAINST ME.
CON-SIDERING YOUR AGE AND YOUR LACK OF EXPERIENCE...
...A MATCH LIKE THIS IS MEANING-LESS.
GIVE UP? DON'T MAKE M LAUGH.
YOU DIDN'T LAST FIVE SECONDS, REMEMBER?
mumble
WHA?!
WHY SHOULD I GIVE UP...
...AGAINST SOMEONE LIKE YOU?

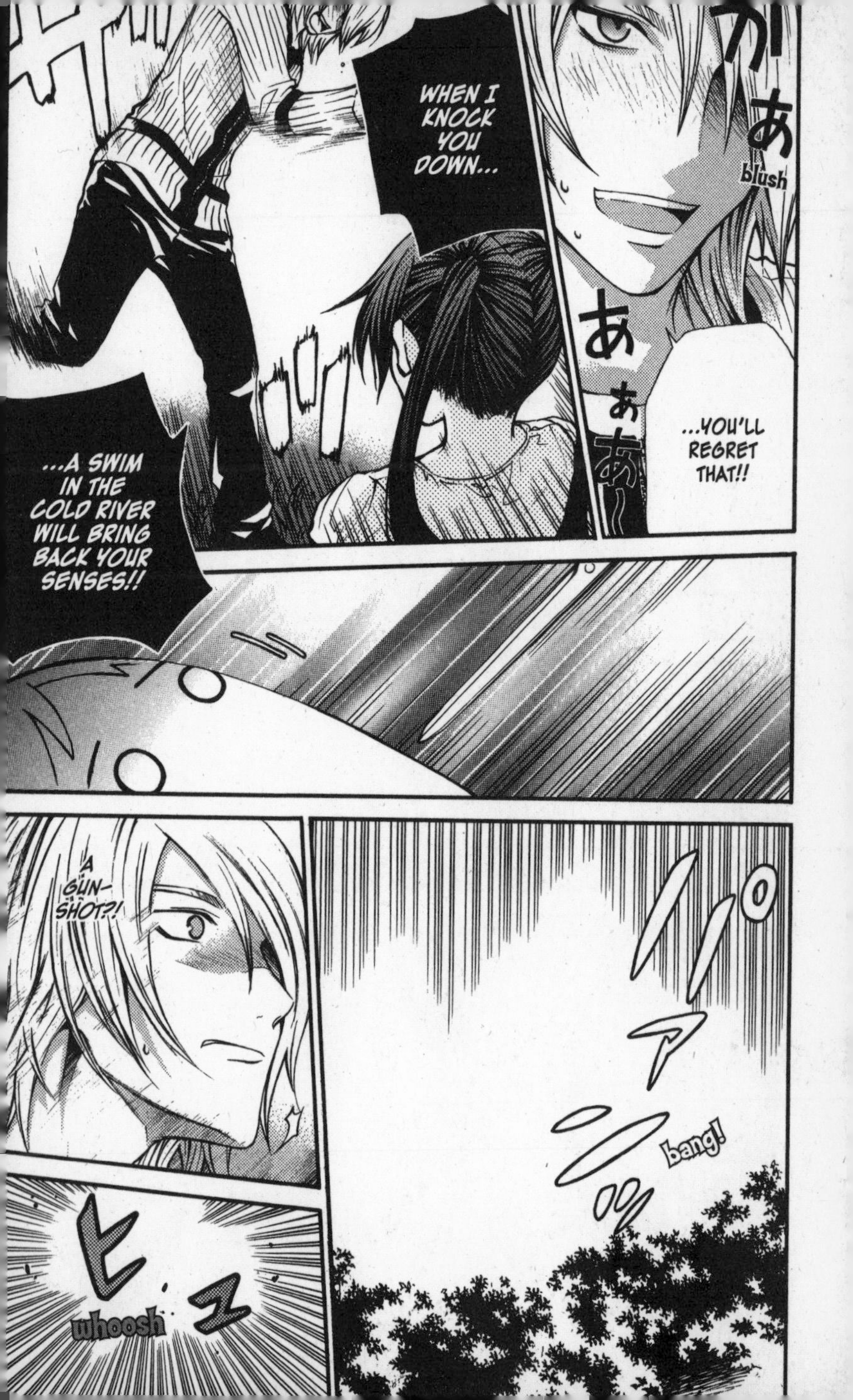
blush
...YOU'LL REGRET THAT!!
WHEN I KNOCK YOU DOWN...
...A SWIM IN THE COLD RIVER WILL BRING BACK YOUR SENSES!!
bang!
A GUN-SHOT?!
whoosh

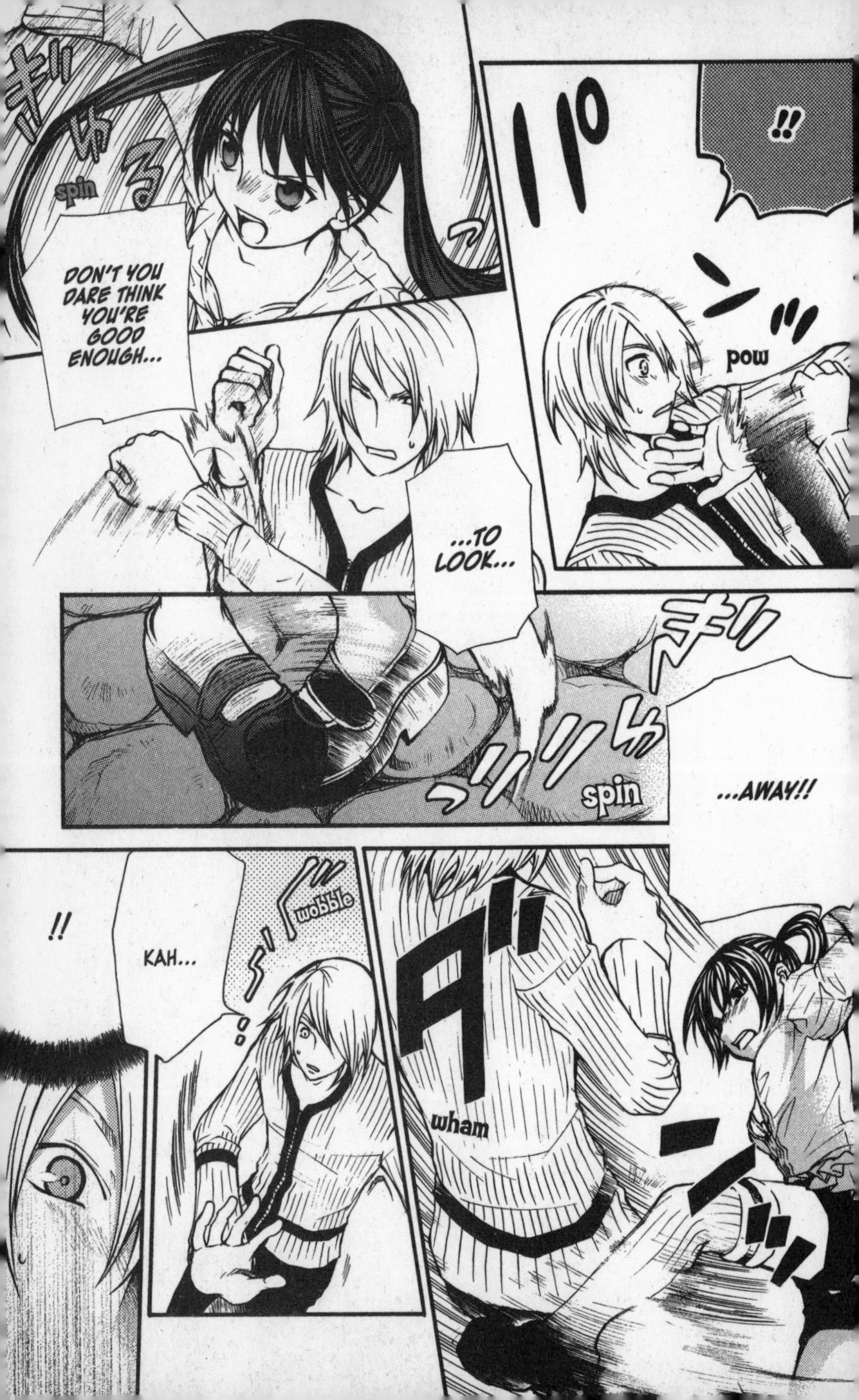
!!
pow
spin
DON'T YOU DARE THINK YOU'RE GOOD ENOUGH...
...TO LOOK...
spin
...AWAY!!
wham
wobble
KAH...
!!

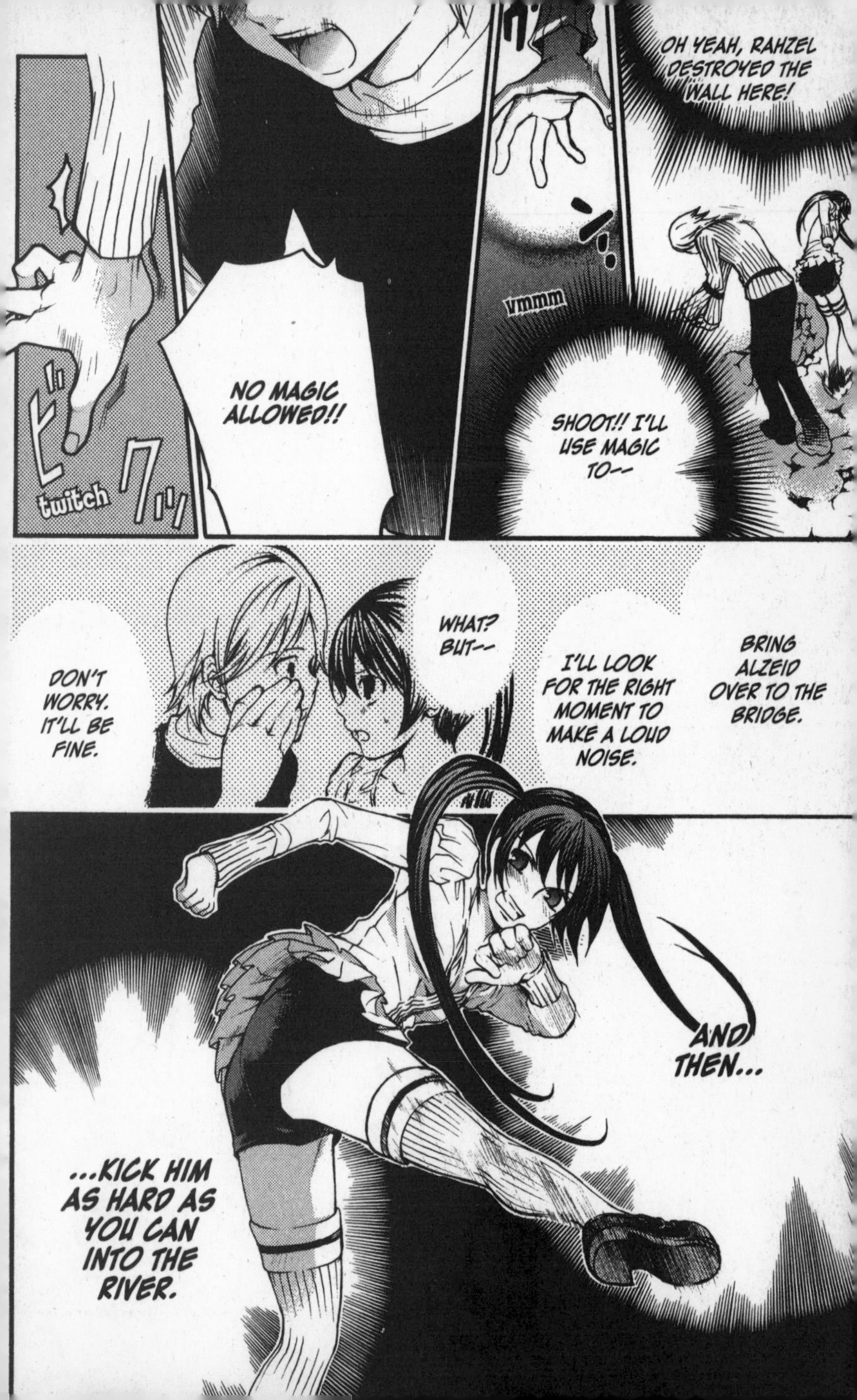
OH YEAH, RAHZEL DESTROYED THE WALL HERE!
vmmm
SHOOT!! I'LL USE MAGIC TO--
NO MAGIC ALLOWED!!
twitch
BRING ALZEID OVER TO THE BRIDGE.
I'LL LOOK FOR THE RIGHT MOMENT TO MAKE A LOUD NOISE.
WHAT? BUT--
DON'T WORRY. IT'LL BE FINE.
AND THEN...
...KICK HIM AS HARD AS YOU CAN INTO THE RIVER.

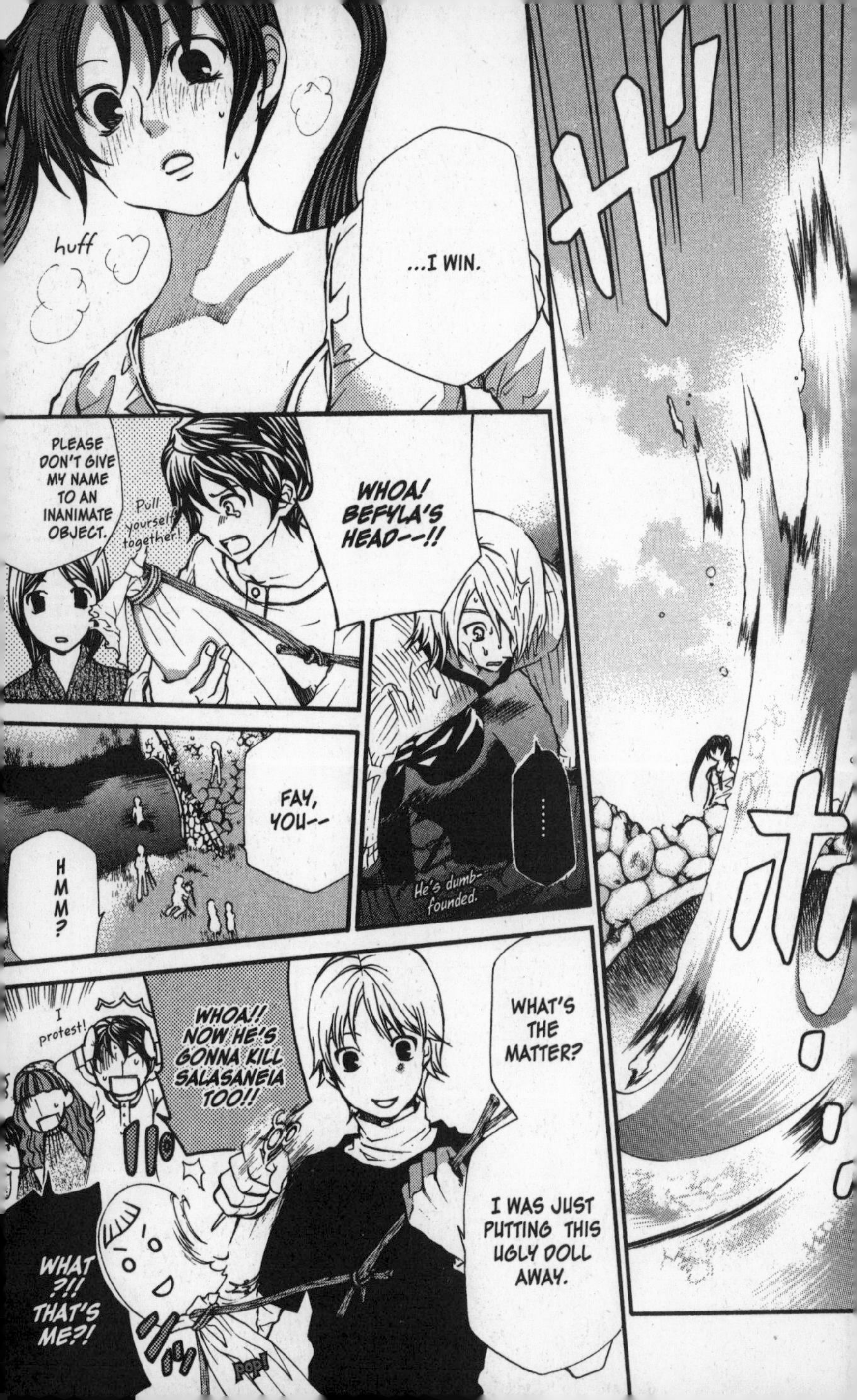
...I WIN.
huff
WHOA! BEFYLA'S HEAD--!!
PLEASE DON'T GIVE MY NAME TO AN INANIMATE OBJECT.
Pull yourself together!
......
He's dumb-founded.
FAY, YOU--
HMMM?
WHAT'S THE MATTER?
I WAS JUST PUTTING THIS UGLY DOLL AWAY.
WHOA!! NOW HE'S GONNA KILL SALASANEIA TOO!!
I protest!
WHAT?!! THAT'S ME?!
pop!

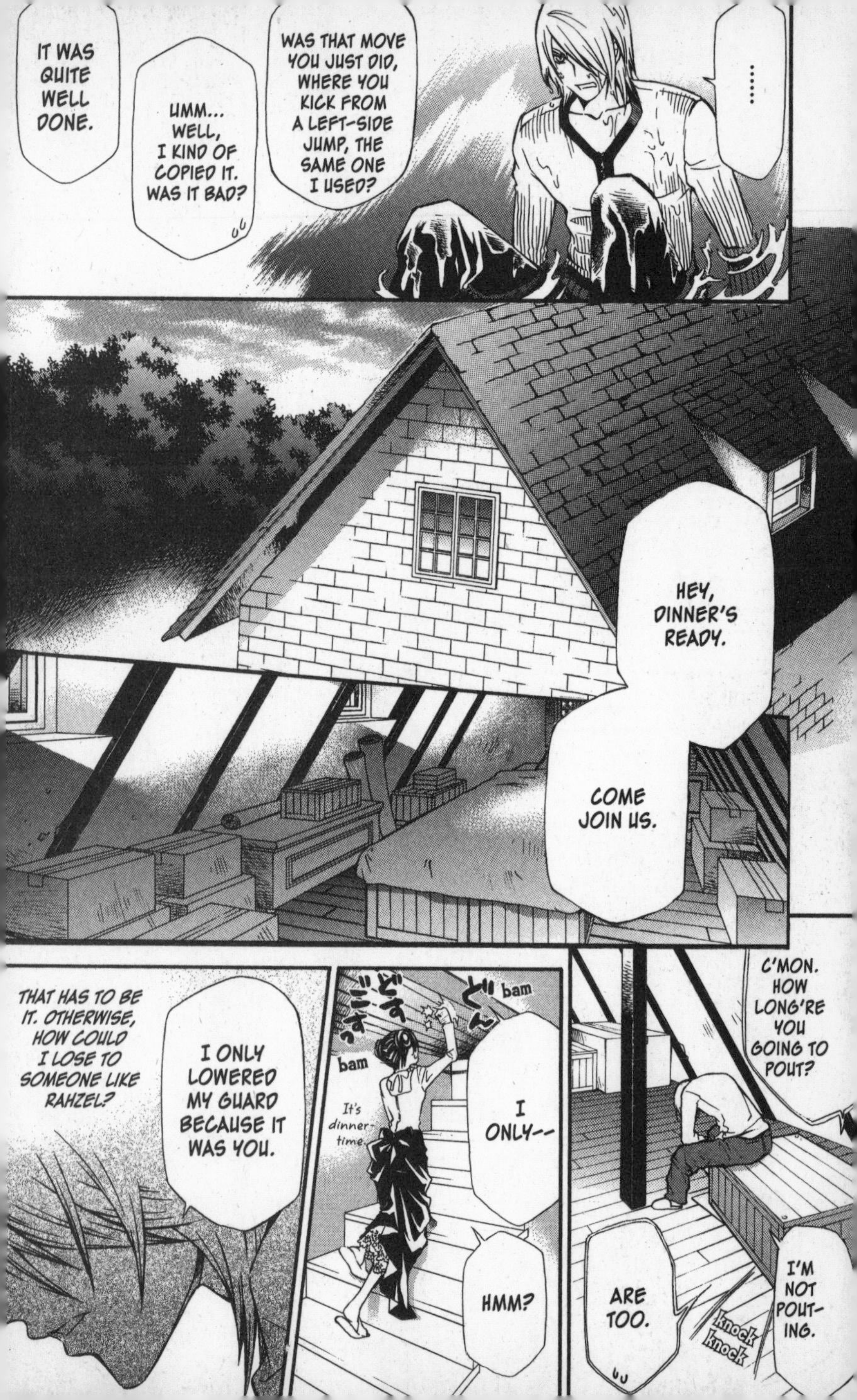
......
WAS THAT MOVE YOU JUST DID, WHERE YOU KICK FROM A LEFT-SIDE JUMP, THE SAME ONE I USED?
UMM... WELL, I KIND OF COPIED IT. WAS IT BAD?
IT WAS QUITE WELL DONE.
HEY, DINNER'S READY.
COME JOIN US.
C'MON. HOW LONG'RE YOU GOING TO POUT?
I'M NOT POUT-ING.
knock knock
ARE TOO.
bam
bam
It's dinner-time.
I ONLY--
HMM?
I ONLY LOWERED MY GUARD BECAUSE IT WAS YOU.
THAT HAS TO BE IT. OTHERWISE, HOW COULD I LOSE TO SOMEONE LIKE RAHZEL?

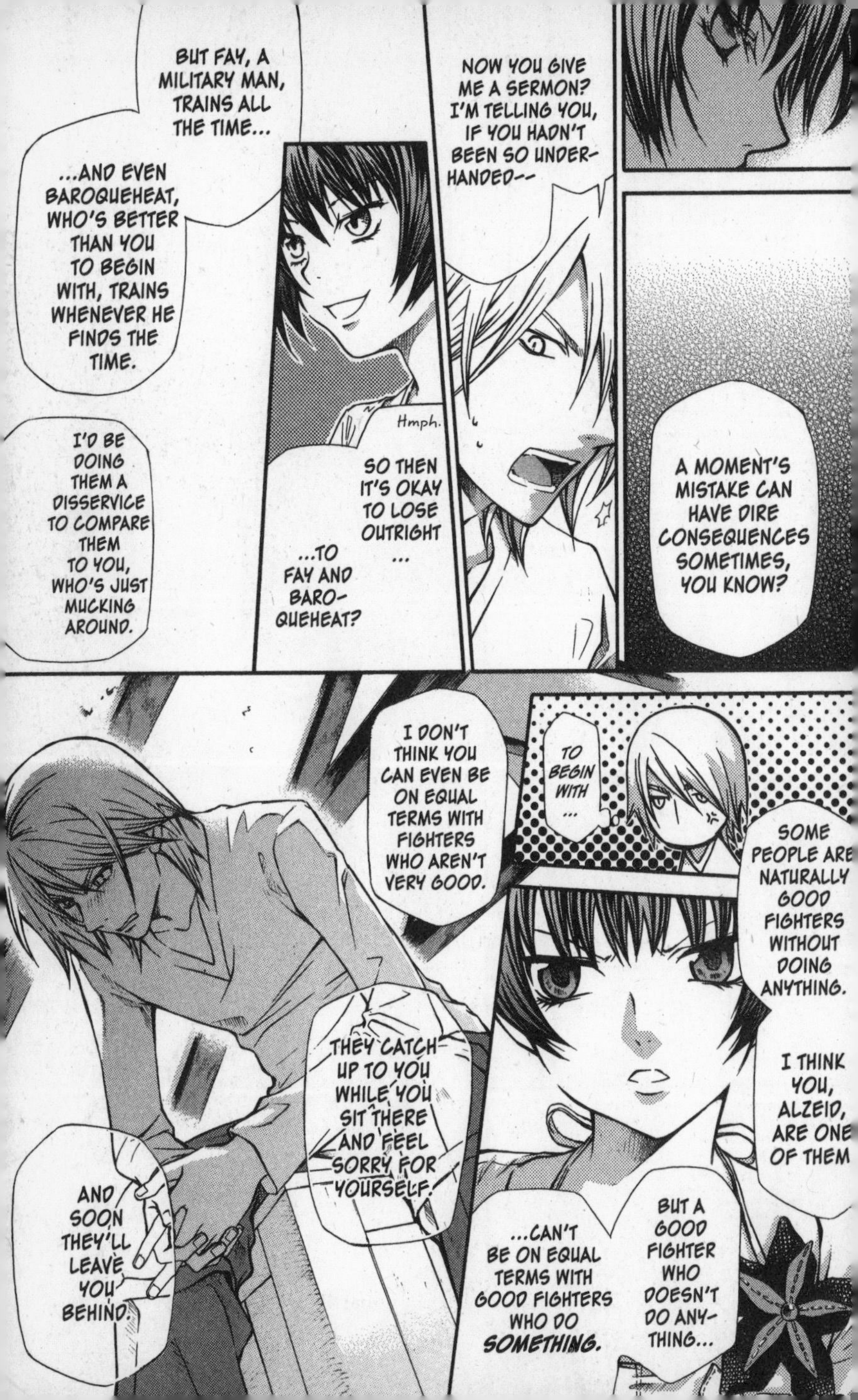
A MOMENT'S MISTAKE CAN HAVE DIRE CONSEQUENCES SOMETIMES, YOU KNOW?
NOW YOU GIVE ME A SERMON? I'M TELLING YOU, IF YOU HADN'T BEEN SO UNDER-HANDED--
BUT FAY, A MILITARY MAN, TRAINS ALL THE TIME...
...AND EVEN BAROQUEHEAT, WHO'S BETTER THAN YOU TO BEGIN WITH, TRAINS WHENEVER HE FINDS THE TIME.
Hmph.
SO THEN IT'S OKAY TO LOSE OUTRIGHT...
...TO FAY AND BARO-QUEHEAT?
I'D BE DOING THEM A DISSERVICE TO COMPARE THEM TO YOU, WHO'S JUST MUCKING AROUND.
SOME PEOPLE ARE NATURALLY GOOD FIGHTERS WITHOUT DOING ANYTHING.
I THINK YOU, ALZEID, ARE ONE OF THEM
BUT A GOOD FIGHTER WHO DOESN'T DO ANY-THING...
...CAN'T BE ON EQUAL TERMS WITH GOOD FIGHTERS WHO DO SOMETHING.
I DON'T THINK YOU CAN EVEN BE ON EQUAL TERMS WITH FIGHTERS WHO AREN'T VERY GOOD.
TO BEGIN WITH...
THEY CATCH UP TO YOU WHILE YOU SIT THERE AND FEEL SORRY FOR YOURSELF.
AND SOON THEY'LL LEAVE YOU BEHIND.

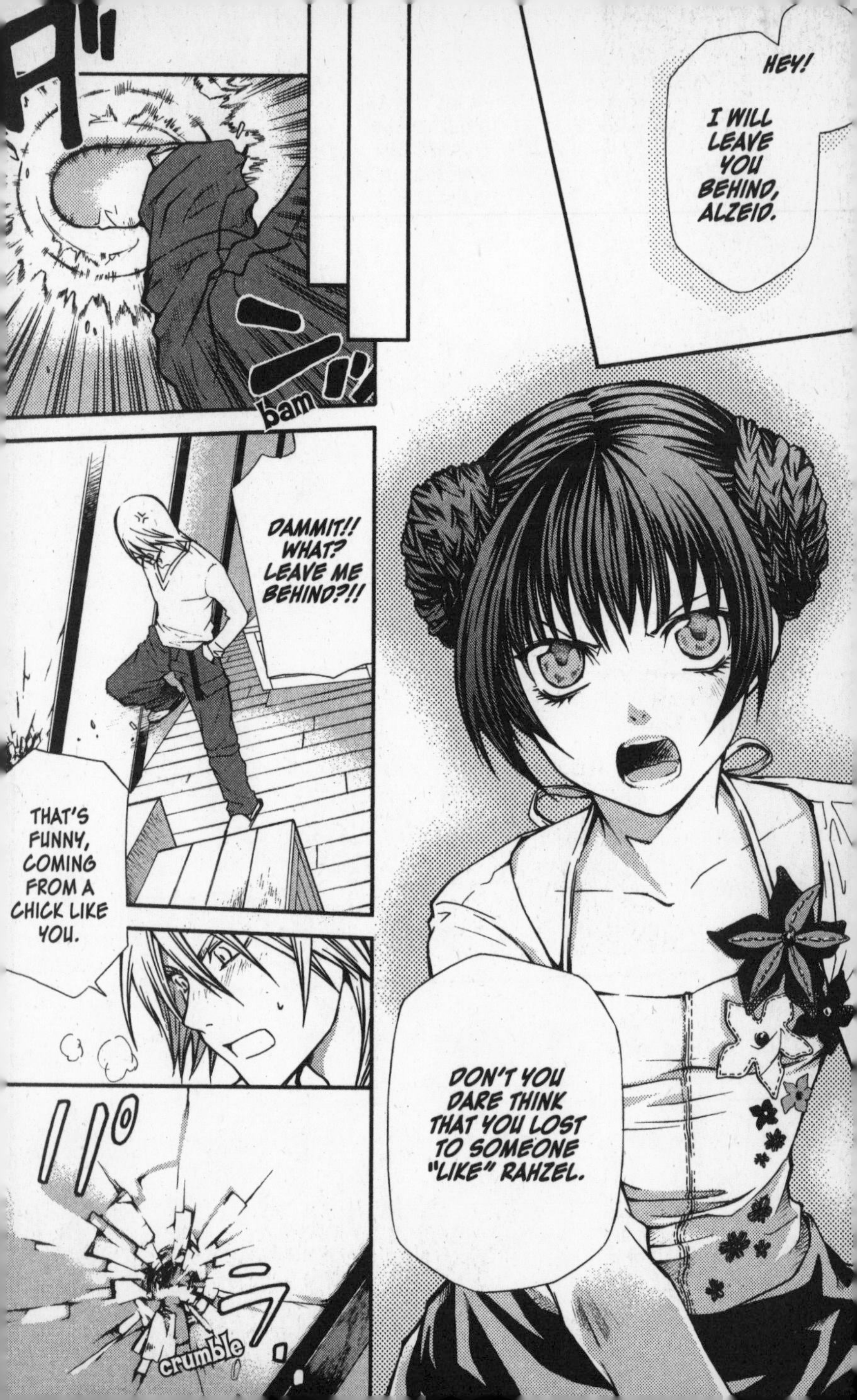
HEY!
I WILL LEAVE YOU BEHIND, ALZEID.
bam
DAMMIT!! WHAT? LEAVE ME BEHIND?!!
THAT'S FUNNY, COMING FROM A CHICK LIKE YOU.
crumble
DON'T YOU DARE THINK THAT YOU LOST TO SOMEONE "LIKE" RAHZEL.

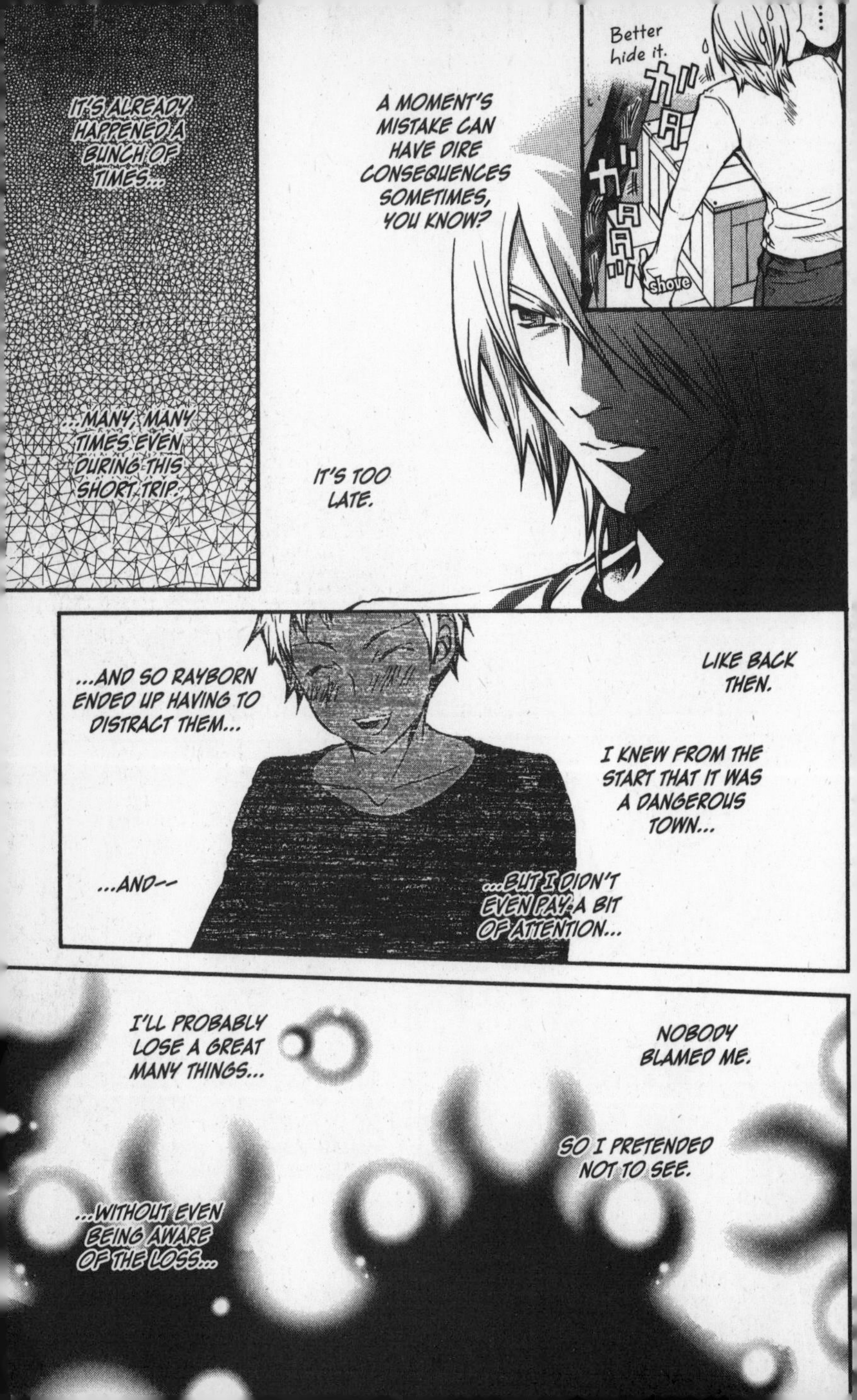
Better hide it.
shove
A MOMENT'S MISTAKE CAN HAVE DIRE CONSEQUENCES SOMETIMES, YOU KNOW?
IT'S TOO LATE.
IT'S ALREADY HAPPENED A BUNCH OF TIMES...
...MANY, MANY TIMES EVEN DURING THIS SHORT TRIP.
LIKE BACK THEN.
I KNEW FROM THE START THAT IT WAS A DANGEROUS TOWN...
...BUT I DIDN'T EVEN PAY A BIT OF ATTENTION...
...AND SO RAYBORN ENDED UP HAVING TO DISTRACT THEM...
...AND--
NOBODY BLAMED ME.
SO I PRETENDED NOT TO SEE.
I'LL PROBABLY LOSE A GREAT MANY THINGS...
...WITHOUT EVEN BEING AWARE OF THE LOSS...

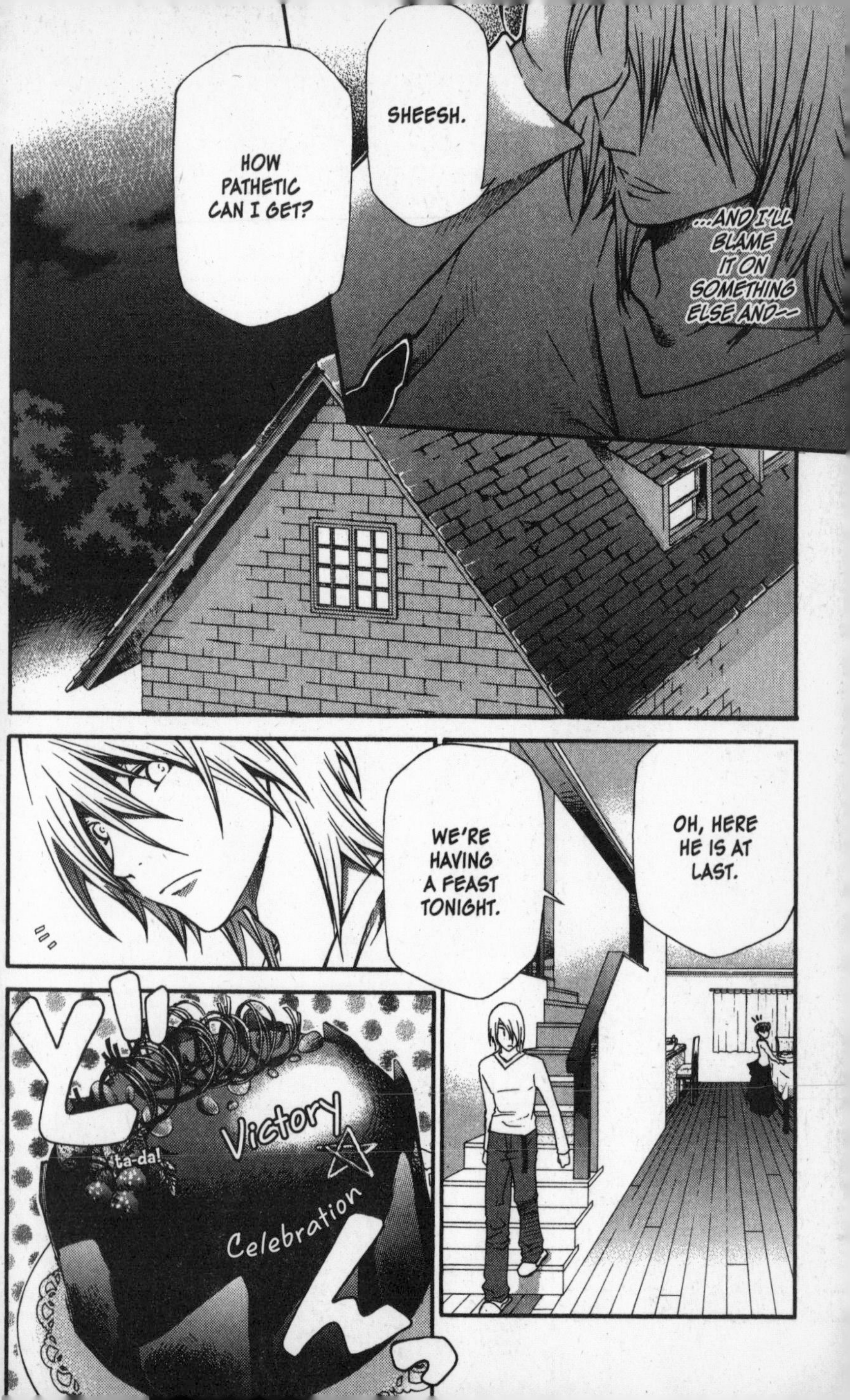
...AND I'LL BLAME IT ON SOMETHING ELSE AND--
SHEESH.
HOW PATHETIC CAN I GET?
OH, HERE HE IS AT LAST.
WE'RE HAVING A FEAST TONIGHT.
ta-da!
Victory
Celebration

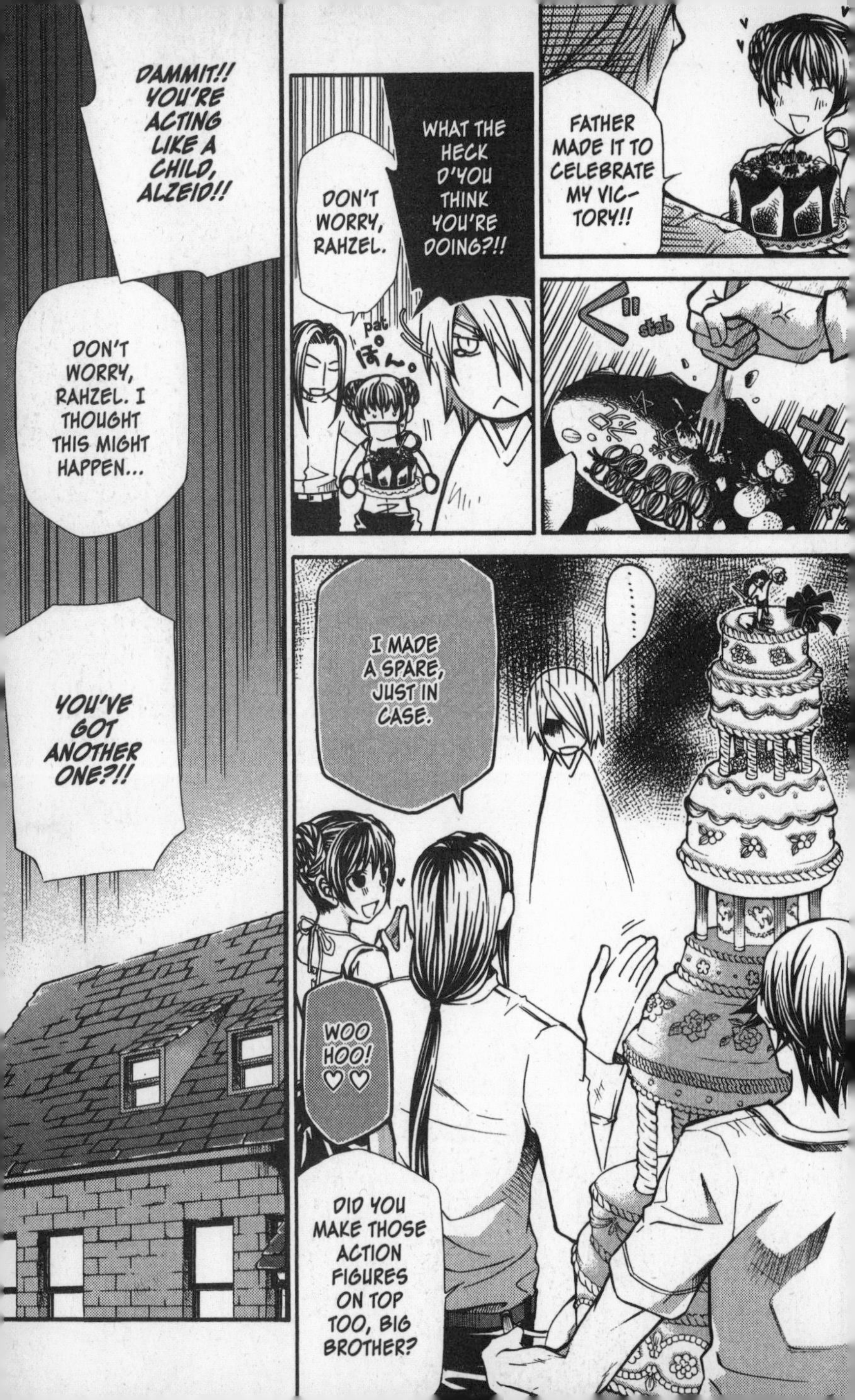
FATHER MADE IT TO CELEBRATE MY VIC-TORY!!
stab
WHAT THE HECK D'YOU THINK YOU'RE DOING?!!
DON'T WORRY, RAHZEL.
pat
DAMMIT!! YOU'RE ACTING LIKE A CHILD, ALZEID!!
DON'T WORRY, RAHZEL. I THOUGHT THIS MIGHT HAPPEN...
I MADE A SPARE, JUST IN CASE.
YOU'VE GOT ANOTHER ONE?!!
WOO HOO! ♡♡
DID YOU MAKE THOSE ACTION FIGURES ON TOP TOO, BIG BROTHER?

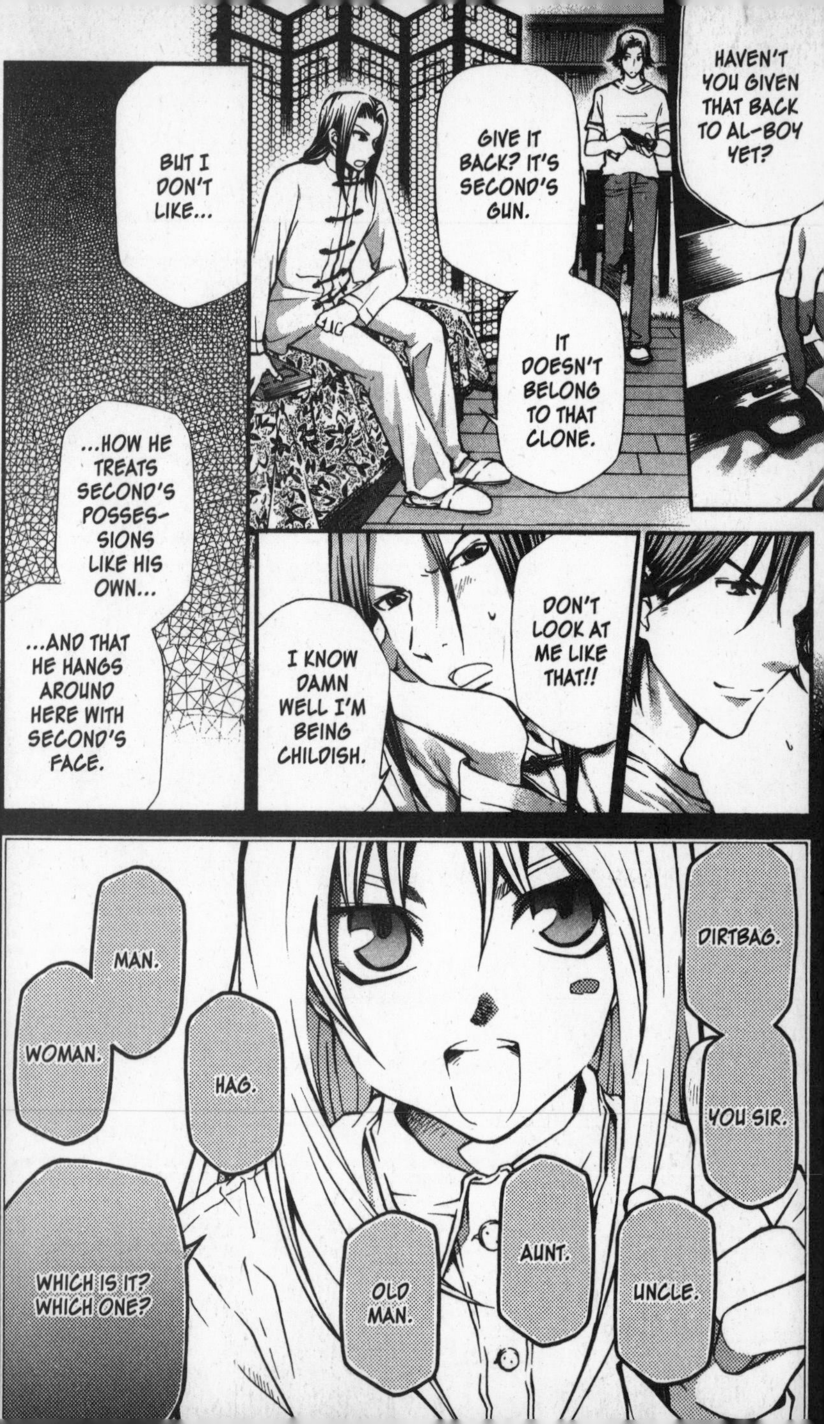
HAVEN'T YOU GIVEN THAT BACK TO AL-BOY YET?
GIVE IT BACK? IT'S SECOND'S GUN.
IT DOESN'T BELONG TO THAT CLONE.
BUT I DON'T LIKE...
...HOW HE TREATS SECOND'S POSSES-SIONS LIKE HIS OWN...
...AND THAT HE HANGS AROUND HERE WITH SECOND'S FACE.
DON'T LOOK AT ME LIKE THAT!!
I KNOW DAMN WELL I'M BEING CHILDISH.
DIRTBAG.
YOU SIR.
MAN.
WOMAN.
HAG.
UNCLE.
AUNT.
OLD MAN.
WHICH IS IT? WHICH ONE?

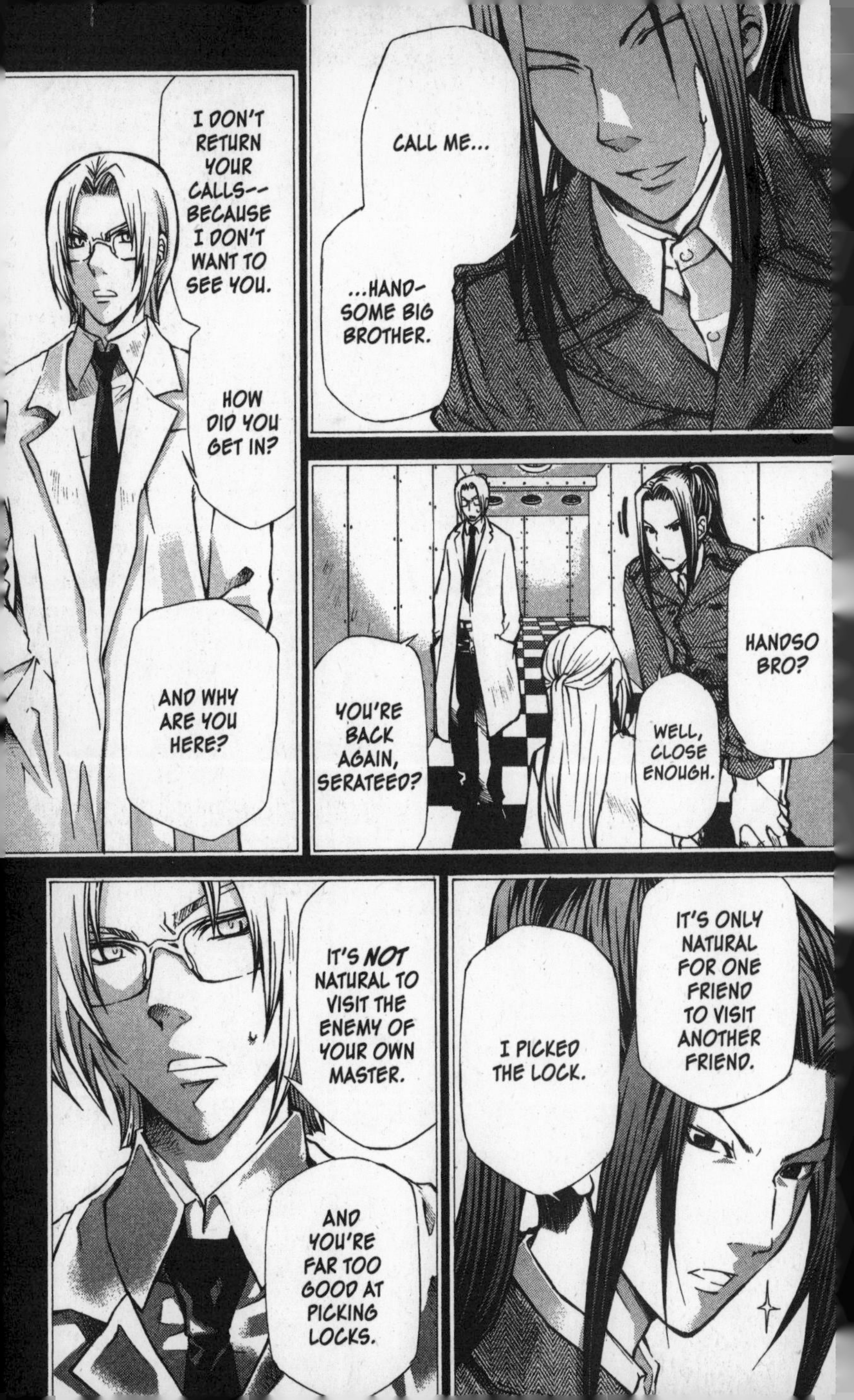

CALL ME...
...HAND-SOME BIG BROTHER.
HANDSO BRO?
WELL, CLOSE ENOUGH.
YOU'RE BACK AGAIN, SERATEED?
I DON'T RETURN YOUR CALLS-- BECAUSE I DON'T WANT TO SEE YOU.
HOW DID YOU GET IN?
AND WHY ARE YOU HERE?
IT'S ONLY NATURAL FOR ONE FRIEND TO VISIT ANOTHER FRIEND.
I PICKED THE LOCK.
IT'S *NOT* NATURAL TO VISIT THE ENEMY OF YOUR OWN MASTER.
AND YOU'RE FAR TOO GOOD AT PICKING LOCKS.

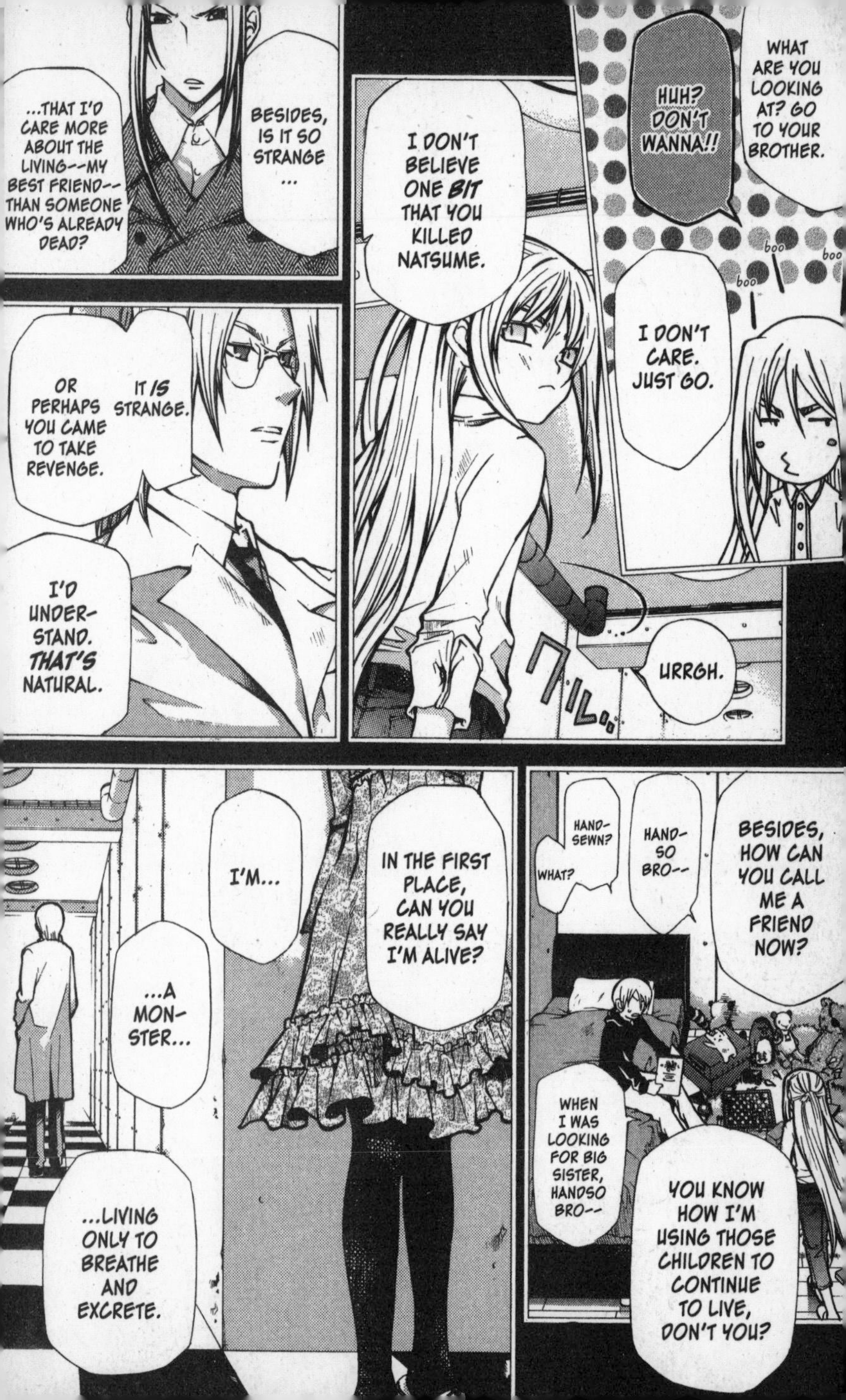
WHAT ARE YOU LOOKING AT? GO TO YOUR BROTHER.
HUH? DON'T WANNA!!
boo
boo
boo
I DON'T CARE. JUST GO.
URRGH.
I DON'T BELIEVE ONE *BIT* THAT YOU KILLED NATSUME.
BESIDES, IS IT SO STRANGE ...
...THAT I'D CARE MORE ABOUT THE LIVING--MY BEST FRIEND--THAN SOMEONE WHO'S ALREADY DEAD?
IT *IS* STRANGE.
OR PERHAPS YOU CAME TO TAKE REVENGE.
I'D UNDERSTAND. *THAT'S* NATURAL.
BESIDES, HOW CAN YOU CALL ME A FRIEND NOW?
HAND-SO BRO--
HAND-SEWN?
WHAT?
YOU KNOW HOW I'M USING THOSE CHILDREN TO CONTINUE TO LIVE, DON'T YOU?
WHEN I WAS LOOKING FOR BIG SISTER, HANDSO BRO--
IN THE FIRST PLACE, CAN YOU REALLY SAY I'M ALIVE?
I'M...
...A MON-STER...
...LIVING ONLY TO BREATHE AND EXCRETE.

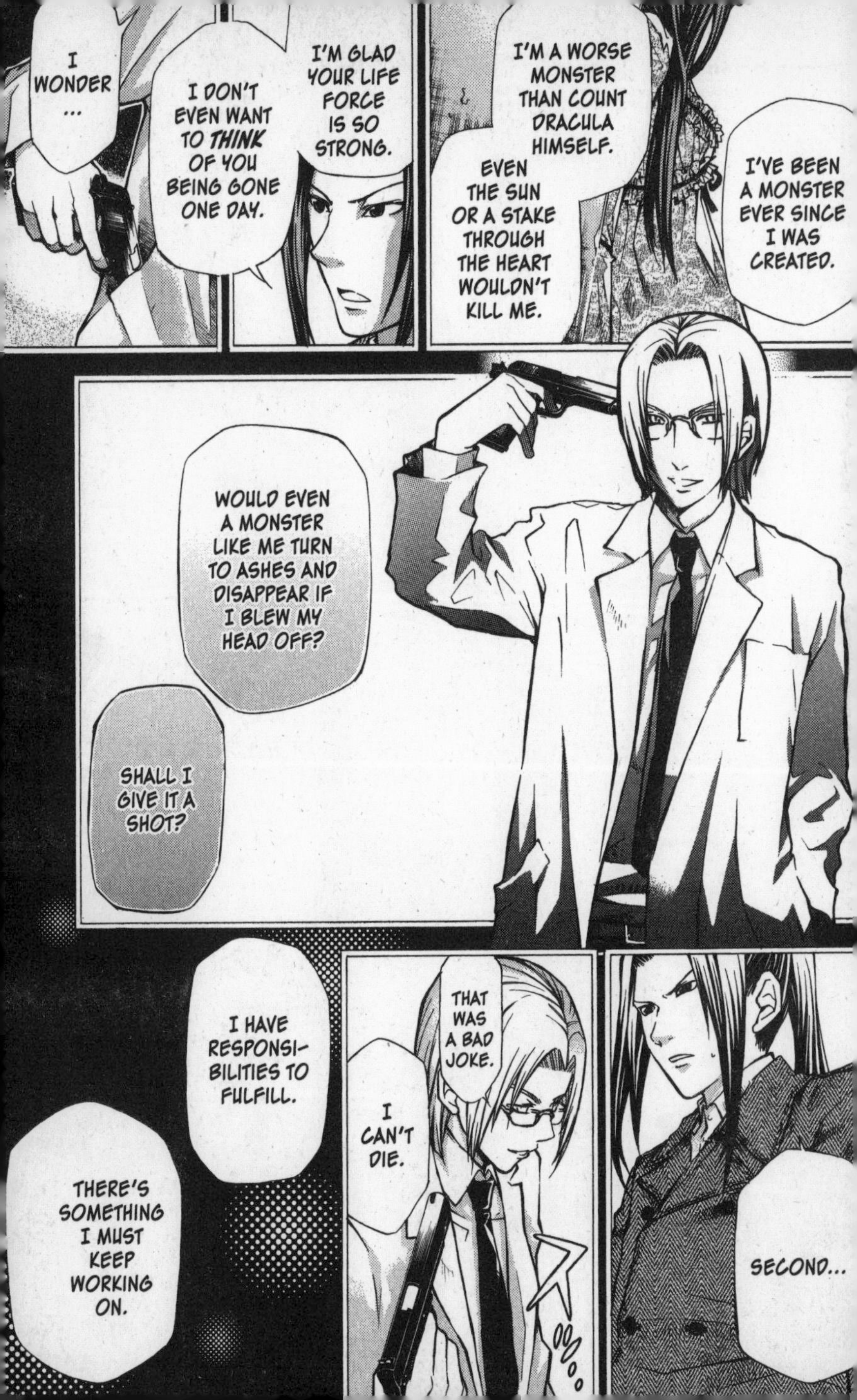
I'VE BEEN A MONSTER EVER SINCE I WAS CREATED.
I'M A WORSE MONSTER THAN COUNT DRACULA HIMSELF.
EVEN THE SUN OR A STAKE THROUGH THE HEART WOULDN'T KILL ME.
I'M GLAD YOUR LIFE FORCE IS SO STRONG.
I DON'T EVEN WANT TO *THINK* OF YOU BEING GONE ONE DAY.
I WONDER...
WOULD EVEN A MONSTER LIKE ME TURN TO ASHES AND DISAPPEAR IF I BLEW MY HEAD OFF?
SHALL I GIVE IT A SHOT?
SECOND...
THAT WAS A BAD JOKE.
I CAN'T DIE.
I HAVE RESPONSIBILITIES TO FULFILL.
THERE'S SOMETHING I MUST KEEP WORKING ON.

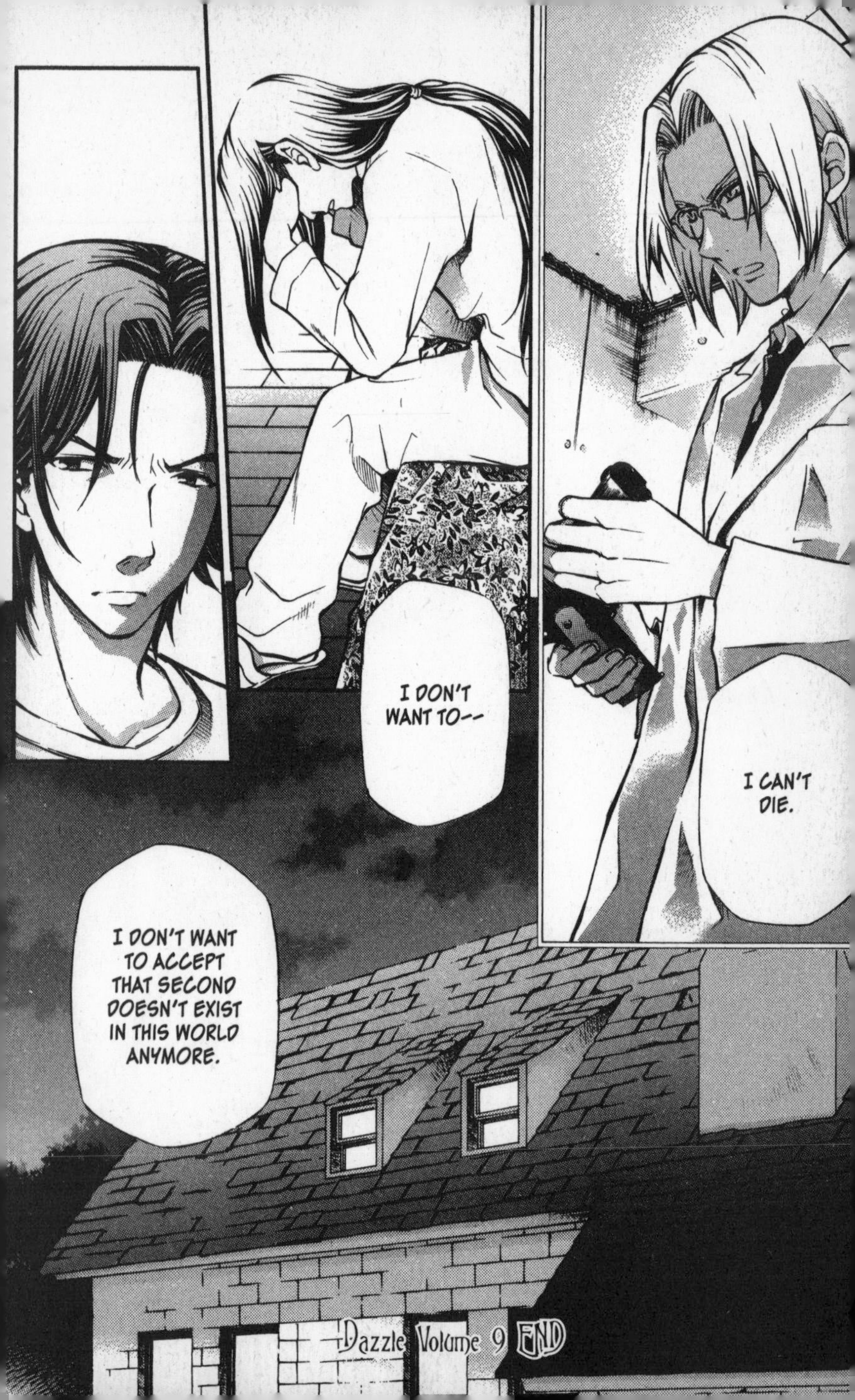
I CAN'T DIE.
I DON'T WANT TO--
I DON'T WANT TO ACCEPT THAT SECOND DOESN'T EXIST IN THIS WORLD ANYMORE.
Dazzle Volume 9 END

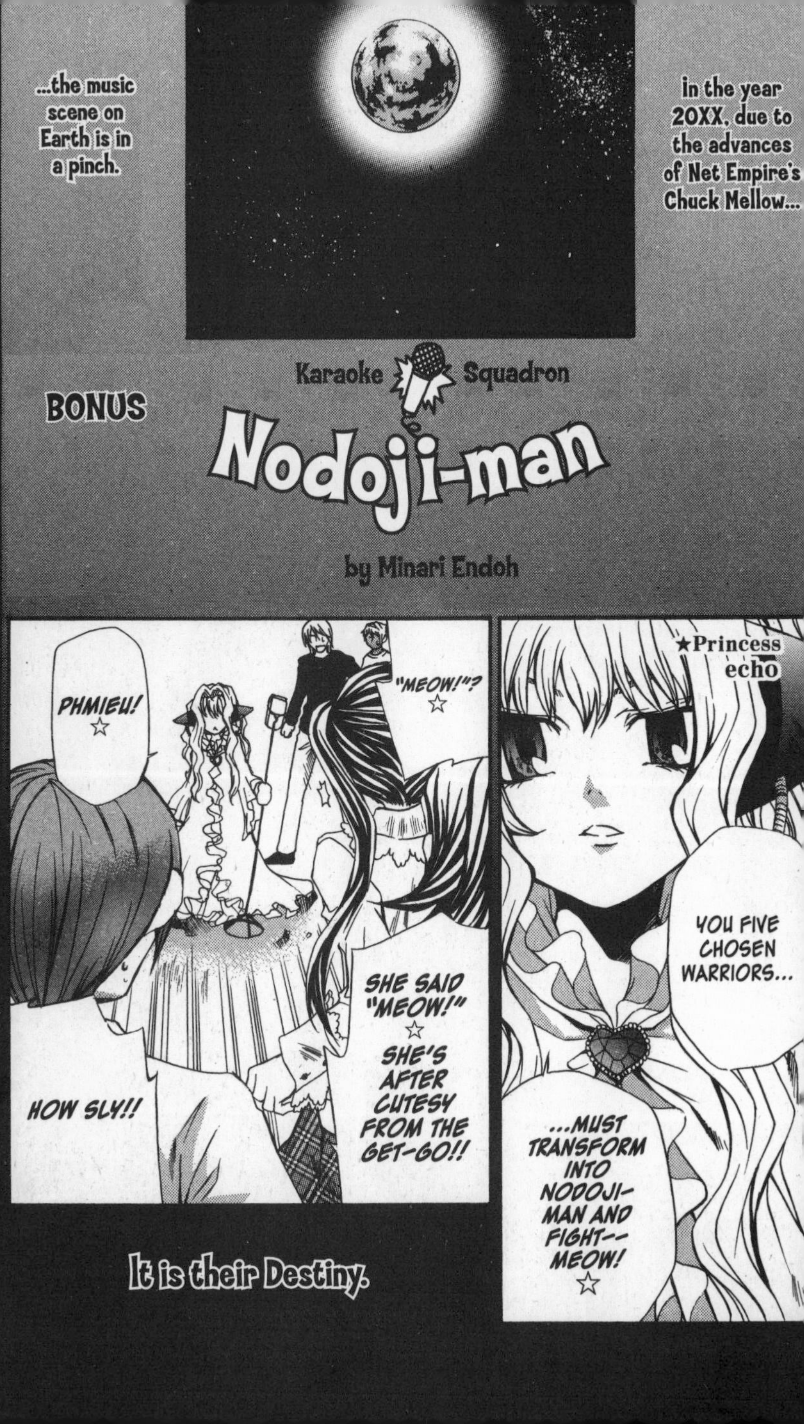
In the year 20XX, due to the advances of Net Empire's Chuck Mellow...
...the music scene on Earth is in a pinch.
BONUS
Karaoke Squadron
Nodoji-man
by Minari Endoh
★Princess echo
YOU FIVE CHOSEN WARRIORS...
...MUST TRANSFORM INTO NODOJI-MAN AND FIGHT--MEOW! ☆
"MEOW!"? ☆
PHMIEU! ☆
SHE SAID "MEOW!" ☆ SHE'S AFTER CUTESY FROM THE GET-GO!!
HOW SLY!!
It is their Destiny.

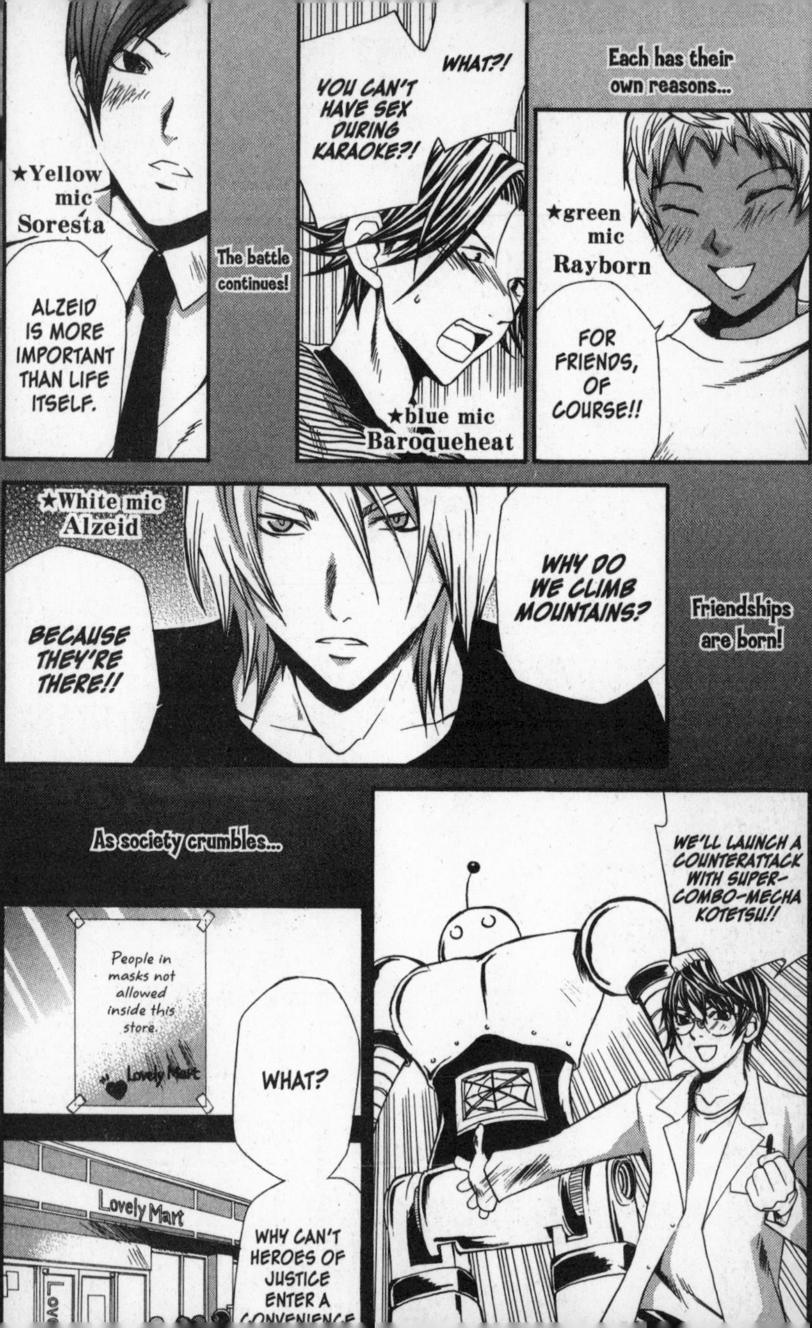
★Yellow mic Soresta
ALZEID IS MORE IMPORTANT THAN LIFE ITSELF.
The battle continues!
WHAT?!
YOU CAN'T HAVE SEX DURING KARAOKE?!
★blue mic Baroqueheat
Each has their own reasons...
★green mic Rayborn
FOR FRIENDS, OF COURSE!!
★White mic Alzeid
WHY DO WE CLIMB MOUNTAINS?
BECAUSE THEY'RE THERE!!
Friendships are born!
As society crumbles...
People in masks not allowed inside this store.
Lovely Mart
WHAT?
Lovely Mart
WHY CAN'T HEROES OF JUSTICE ENTER A CONVENIENCE
WE'LL LAUNCH A COUNTERATTACK WITH SUPER-COMBO-MECHA KOTETSU!!

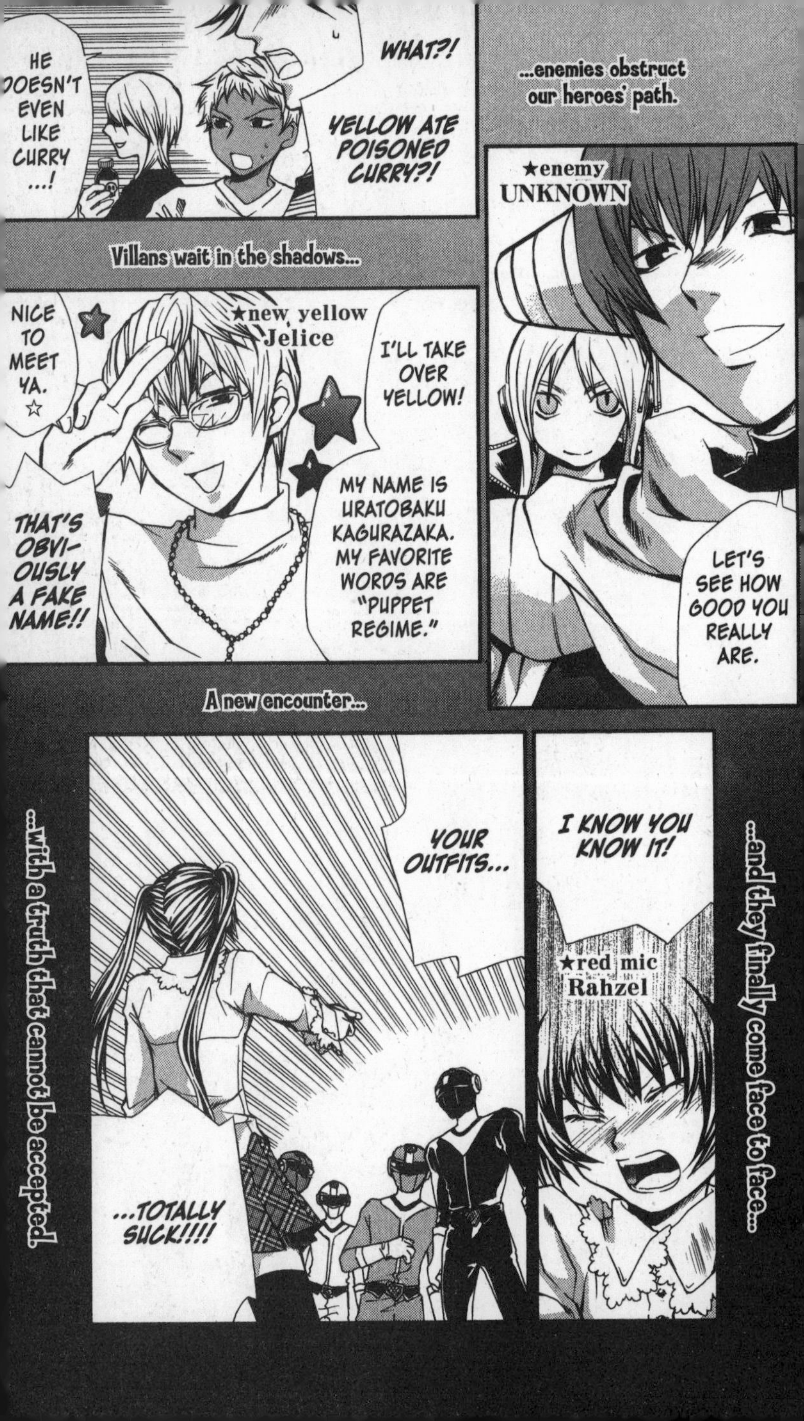
WHAT?!
YELLOW ATE POISONED CURRY?!
HE DOESN'T EVEN LIKE CURRY ...!
...enemies obstruct our heroes' path.
Villans wait in the shadows...
★enemy UNKNOWN
LET'S SEE HOW GOOD YOU REALLY ARE.
★new yellow Jelice
I'LL TAKE OVER YELLOW!
NICE TO MEET YA. ☆
MY NAME IS URATOBAKU KAGURAZAKA. MY FAVORITE WORDS ARE "PUPPET REGIME."
THAT'S OBVIOUSLY A FAKE NAME!!
A new encounter...
...and they finally come face to face...
I KNOW YOU KNOW IT!
★red mic Rahzel
YOUR OUTFITS...
...TOTALLY SUCK!!!!
...with a truth that cannot be accepted.

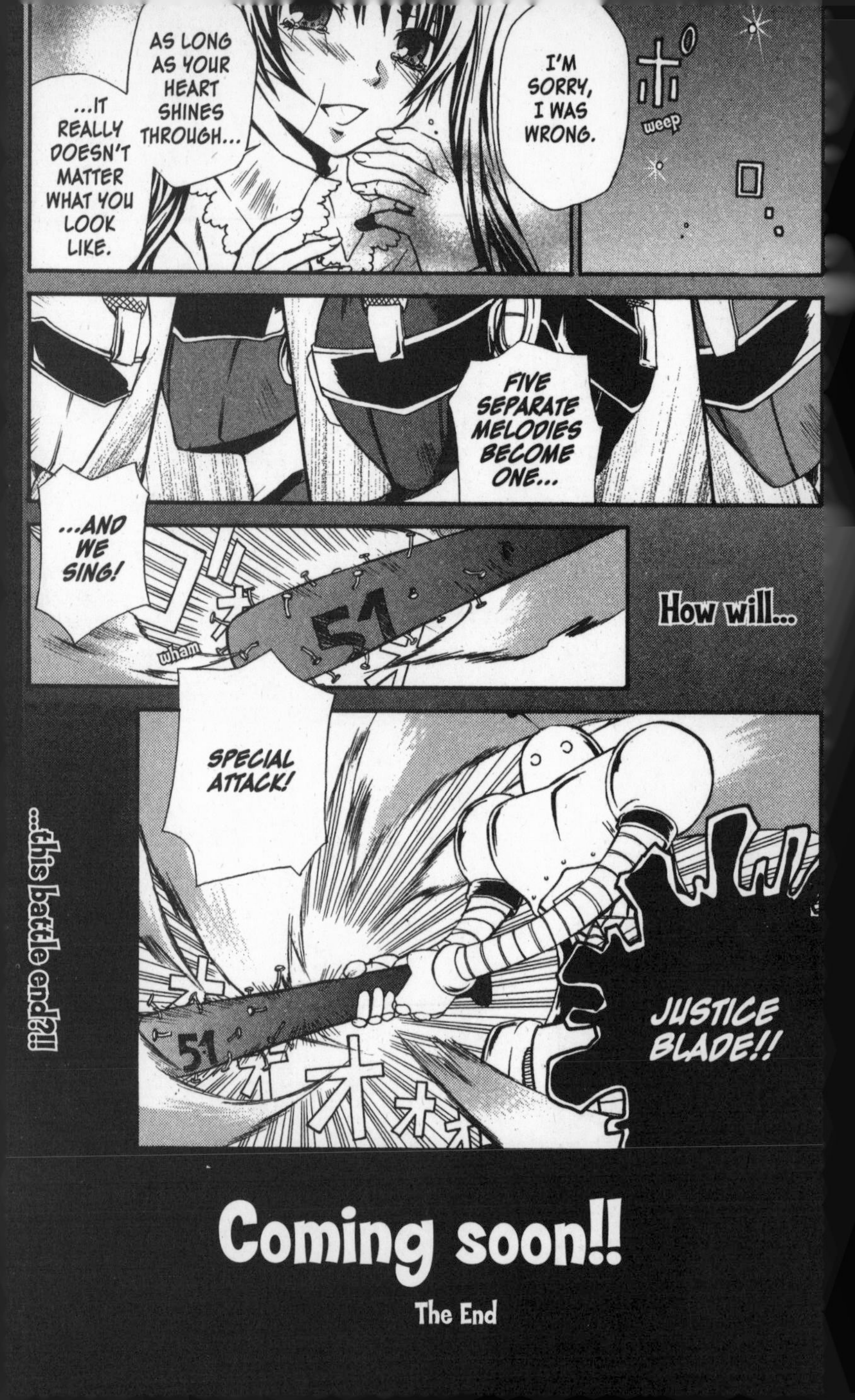
I'M SORRY, I WAS WRONG.
weep
AS LONG AS YOUR HEART SHINES THROUGH...
...IT REALLY DOESN'T MATTER WHAT YOU LOOK LIKE.
FIVE SEPARATE MELODIES BECOME ONE...
...AND WE SING!
wham
51
SPECIAL ATTACK!
JUSTICE BLADE!!
51

How will...

...this battle end?!!

Coming soon!!

The End

Dazzle Volume 9 Postscript

Sorry to keep you waiting for such a long time. I now bring you volume nine of Dazzle.

Chapter 62: Under the Deep Blue Sky
Alzeid-san's night before the parade of incompetence. Alzeid-san looks so good getting pummeled!

Chapter 63: A Fable for Someone
It's Alzeid-san's parade of incompetence. He doesn't hesitate to attack a small child from behind. Good going, Alzeid-san! It's also so cool how you get completely beaten up so easily!

Chapter 64: Fate Unknown
A little break from Alzeid-san's parade of incompetence. Alzeid-san doesn't appear in a single frame. He's so cool!

Chapter 65: In Time, Points Lead to Lines
Resuming Alzeid-san's parade of incompetence. One of my assistants said seriously, "I just can't get myself to like Alzeid. He's too childish." Alzeid-san, you're so rad!

Chapter 66: At Last, Daylight Slowly Breaks
The climax of Alzeid-san's parade of incompetence!! Big-talking, five-second-beat Alzeid-san is totally rad!

Chapter 67: In the Town Where It All Began
We're close to the end of Alzeid-san's parade of incompetence. Another totally childish outbreak ☆ from Alzeid-san. How completely cool!

Chapter 68: "I will leave you behind."
The night after Alzeid-san's parade of incompetence. Like singing songs around the campfire. It's like that. Alzeid-san, you're the man!!!

And so volume nine in its entirety was filled with Alzeid-san's parade of incompetence, but now I have a problem. How can I make Alzeid-san look good again?

I realized that there isn't a single episode in which Alzeid can reclaim his good name. That's right, all the way through to the very end, book after book after book. In the future, if you find Alzeid being nice in some situation, it's only because it was completely made up or the author wrote it without understanding how nice or cool he really is. By the way, we're nowhere near the ending at all. Dazzle will keep going for a long time to come.

In the next
Dazzle!

Rahzel and company's journey to Vellnene, the town with blue-eyed, black-haired residents where Alzeid hopes to gather clues about his father's killer, finally reaches its goal--but will he like the answers he finds? And why was Rahzel so reluctant to go there? The truth behind the night Rahzel was abandoned in the woods as a child is finally revealed--and at long last, Rahzel's father shows his face!

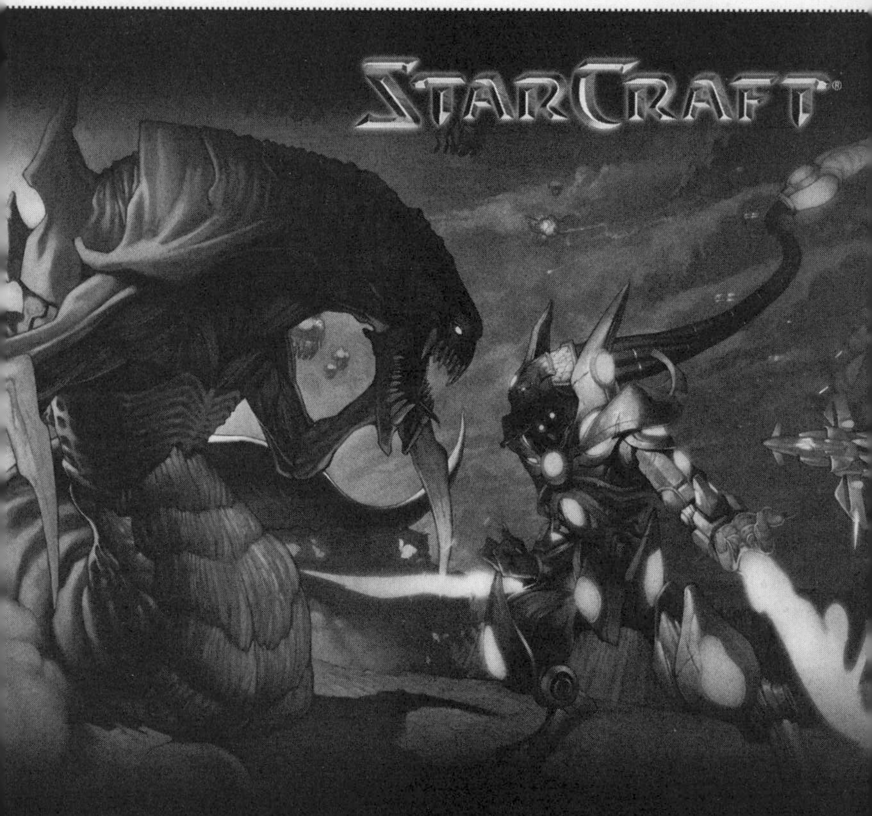
STARCRAFT

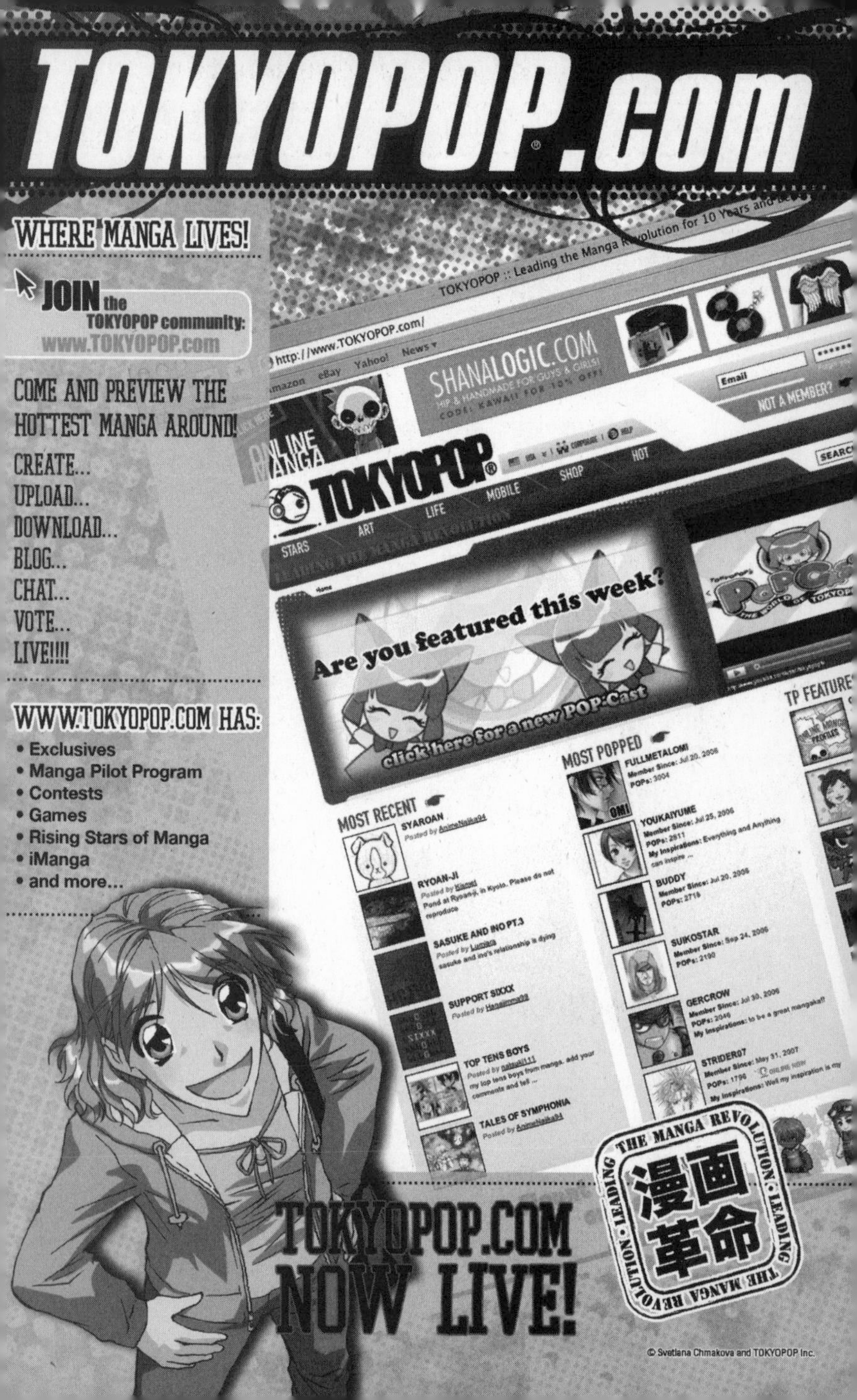

TOKYOPOP®.com
WHERE MANGA LIVES!
JOIN the TOKYOPOP community:
www.TOKYOPOP.com
COME AND PREVIEW THE HOTTEST MANGA AROUND!
CREATE...
UPLOAD...
DOWNLOAD...
BLOG...
CHAT...
VOTE...
LIVE!!!!
WWW.TOKYOPOP.COM HAS:
• Exclusives
• Manga Pilot Program
• Contests
• Games
• Rising Stars of Manga
• iManga
• and more...
TOKYOPOP :: Leading the Manga Revolution for 10 Years and Beyond
http://www.TOKYOPOP.com/
SHANALOGIC.COM
NOT A MEMBER?
TOKYOPOP®
STARS
ART
LIFE
MOBILE
SHOP
HOT
Are you featured this week?
click here for a new POP-Cast
MOST RECENT
MOST POPPED
TP FEATURES
TOKYOPOP.COM NOW LIVE!
THE MANGA REVOLUTION • LEADING THE MANGA REVOLUTION • LEADING
漫画革命
© Svetlana Chmakova and TOKYOPOP Inc.

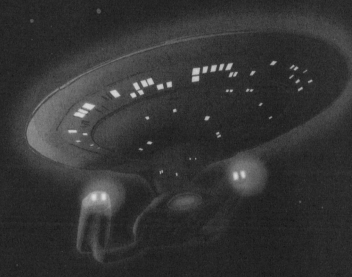